1,001 Sayings and Deeds of the Prophet Muhammad

The Companion to

Pain, Pleasure and Prejudice

Bernard Payeur

.

ISBN: 978-1-928023-03-6

Note for Librarians: A cataloguing record for this book is available from Library and Archives Canada at www.collectionscanada.gc.ca/amicus/index-e.html

Boreal Books
www.borealbooks.ca

To the memory of the poets al-Nadr, Abu Afak, Ka'b bin Al-Ashraf, Abu-Rafi and poetess Asma bint Marwan. May you not have died in vain.

Contents

Foreword

Any study beside that of the Quran is a distraction, except the Hadith and jurisprudence in the religion. Knowledge is what He narrated to us, and anything other than that is the whispering of the Satan.

Al-Qaeda's credo as stated in the December 2000 edition of the Taliban's English-language magazine The Islamic Emirate.

Islam is not so much a religion as a way of life with thousands of indelible rules which instruct every waking moment of a believer's existence.

First, there are God's revealed rules, those of the Koran which we have talked about in *Pain, Pleasure and Prejudice*, and then there are the hadiths (or Hadith, in English academic usage hadith is often both singular and plural), the sayings and example i.e. deeds of the Prophet Muhammad. If you are the Taliban or Al-Qaeda, the Koran and the hadiths define Islamic law as in "jurisprudence in the religion", and comprise all you need to know about the nature of your existence and how to lead a God-fearing life.

In learning about the hadiths, you will also get acquainted with the real Muhammad, the Prophet as his closest friends and his child-bride Aisha remember him.

Enjoy!

Bernard Payeur

Introduction

All hadiths in the database consulted are one paragraph. For readability, lengthy hadiths are broken into short paragraphs. Any text in a hadith contained within round brackets () is that of the translator unless in italics. Except for paragraph breaks and the correction of obvious typos, the hadiths are presented as is.

Hadith collections of the Sunni cannon referenced, and their translators: Sahih Al-Bukhari translated by M. Mohsin Khan, Sahih Muslim translated by Abdul Hamid Siddiqui, Sunan Abu-Dawud translated by Prof. Ahmad Hasan and Malik's Muwatta translated by Aisha Abdarahman at-Tarjumana and Yaqub Johnson

Hadiths are mostly hearsay evidence of what the Prophet Muhammad said and did, including his silent approval of actions taken in his presence – silence being very much a metaphor for God's Messenger not objecting to something done in his presence as in the following where laughter ensued:

> ... Umar then came forward, and when he had asked and had been granted permission he found the Prophet sitting sad and silent with his wives around him. He told that he decided to say something which would make the Prophet laugh, so he said, "Messenger of God, I wish you had seen the daughter of Kharija when she asked me for extra money and I got up and slapped her on the neck."
>
> God's messenger laughed and said, "They are around me as you see asking for extra money."
>
> Abu Bakr then got up, went to A'isha and slapped her on the neck, and Umar did the same to Hafsa ...
>
> *Sahih Muslim 9.3506*

A'isha was the daughter of Abu Bakr, and Hafsa the daughter of Umar. Abu Bakr would succeed the Prophet. His short rein as the first caliph would be followed by the caliphate of Umar.

Hadiths, which are often referred to as Traditions of the Prophet, are the second holiest scriptures in Islam after the Koran and are an integral part of Islamic law i.e. the Sharia. For example, the Koran in revelation 4:34 grants the husband the right to beat his wife, but it is a saying of the Prophet which pretty much guarantees the wife-beater immunity from prosecution.

Narrated Umar ibn al-Khattab:

The Prophet (peace be upon him) said: A man will not be asked as to why he beat his wife.

Abu Dawud 11.2142

Does it matter that the Prophet said she should not beaten about the head?

Narrated Abu Huraira:

The Prophet said, "If somebody fights (or beats somebody) then he should avoid the face."

Bukhari 46.734

In *Islam, A Short History (2002)*, Karen Armstrong, former nun and unabashed fan of the Prophet (her latest panegyric to God's Messenger is brazenly titled *Muhammad: A Prophet for Our Time, 2006*), explains why hadiths were made necessary and how they transformed Islam.

The Quran contains very little legislation, and what laws there were had been designed for a much simpler society. So some of the jurists began to collect reports about the Prophet and his companions to find out how they had behaved in a given situation ... Thus they believed they would gain true ilm, knowledge of what was right and how to behave. (p.49)

... the Prophet, the Perfect Man, became the person to imitate. By imitating the smallest details of his external life and by reproducing the way he ate, washed, loved, spoke and prayed, Muslims hoped to acquire his interior attitude of perfect surrender to God. (p. 60)

Most hadiths were collected approximately 200 years after the Prophet's passing by men who travelled the land asking people, who may have known of people, who knew of people, who were contemporaries of the Prophet and passed down to future generations what they remembered of what he said and did, or did not do. The task of collecting and classifying the hadiths was mostly completed by the end of the 9th century. A fatwa was issued declaring that all the knowledge about the nature of existence and whatever information humanity needed to know to conduct its affairs as God intended was in the Koran and the sanctioned collections of hadiths to which no further hadiths could be added.

The Pseudo-Science of Hadith Authentication

Sunni Islam considers the hadiths collected by six men – al-Bukhari, Imam Muslim, At-Tirmidi, Ibn Majah, Abu Dawood and An-Nisa'i – as the "six canonical collections." Al-Bukhari's (d. 870) collection of 7,275 hadiths is considered the most authoritative, and along with Imam Muslim's (d. 875) are considered to be authentic (sahih) by Sunnis. Shiites consider the recollections of the Companions of the Prophet suspect because they voted Abu Bakr, a good friend of the Prophet to whom he had given his nine old daughter Aisha in marriage, his successor when God's Messenger passed away, instead of Ali, the Prophet's cousin and son-in-law. Shiites have developed their own books of hadiths which are largely based on what members of the "House of the Prophet" reported; that would be the Prophet's daughter Fatima, Ali, and Ali's two sons, Hassan and Hussein.

Bukhari's hadiths are accepted as authentic without question because, in part, he is said to have collected over 600,000 and kept only approximately one percent as valid, therefore his scholarship in weeding out nonsense, erroneous recollections and outright lies is assumed to be beyond reproach. In collecting, more than a thousand years ago, recollections of what the Prophet said and did, or did not do, unproven assumptions were the rule, not the exception (by Western standards, assumptions are unproven by definition); assumptions that, along with the Koran, became the unalterable foundation of Islamic law.

In deciding that Bukhari's collection of hadiths was of unimpeachable quality, another assumption was made: that none of it contradicted the Koran. What to make of hadiths, such as the following, which appear to contradict Allah as to where the sun disappears at night?

Narrated Abu Dhar:

The Prophet asked me at sunset, "Do you know where the sun goes [at the time of sunset]?"

I replied, "Allah and His Apostle know better."

He said, "It goes till it prostrates itself underneath the Throne and takes the permission to rise again, and it is permitted and then [a time will come when] it will be about to prostrate itself but its prostration will not be accepted, and it will ask permission to go on its course but it will not be permitted, but it will be ordered to return whence it has come and so it will rise in the west. And that is the interpretation of the Statement of Allah: 'And the sun runs its fixed course for a term [decreed].That is The Decree of [Allah] The Exalted in Might, The All-Knowing.'"

Bukhari 54.421

The Koran is unequivocal, the sun disappears in a sea of mud on which a flat earth appears to float and re-emerges the next morning on the other side.

> 18:86 Then, when he (*Alexander the Great*) reached the setting-place of the sun, he found that it sets in a spring of black mud and found, by it, a people. We said: "O Dhul-Qarnayn, either you punish them or show them kindness."

Hadiths being hearsay evidence collected over two centuries after the Prophet's passing cannot be expected to have the clarity and easy to follow structure of verses from the Koran. The process by which the strength or weakness of a hadith is arrived at is considered the *Science of Hadith*. The process, which involves the weighing of hearsay evidence to establish a level of credibility, has little in common with the type of empirical proof required in the physical sciences. What Islam considers a scientific method (as opposed to a methodology) of ascertaining whether a hadith is genuine usually begins with ensuring that the hadith does not contradict the Koran, that would be like the Prophet refuting God (a reputable scholar of Islam, I am sure, could explain the apparent contradiction about where the sun sets).

With the possible exception of a Mutawatir hadith (see explanation which follows), one of the narrators, of a reputable chain of narrators, had to have heard or seen the Prophet in action. An example of a hadith received by way of Abu Al Nauman, who said he heard it from Said ibn Zayd, who said he heard it from Ali ibn Zayd, who said he heard it from Jabir ibn Abdullah, that the Prophet said: "Whoever has three daughters, cares and provides for them, and shows them mercy, will enter Paradise."

A Mutawatir hadith is a saying or story remembered by a sufficient number of people to be considered sahih. The rational being, that a large number of people reporting the same thing could not be "expected to agree upon a lie". An example is the story told by the Prophet about the coming of the Mahdi, the "prophesied redeemer of Islam"[Wiki]

> The Mahdi, a man named Muhammad b. `Abdullah and a descendant of the Prophet (may Allah bless him and grant him peace) through Fatimah [his daughter], who will be the Leader (Imam, Khalifah) of the Muslims, rule for seven years and fill the world with justice and equity after it had been filled with tyranny and oppression. He will also fight the Dajjal along with Jesus son of Mary ...

> The Concept of the Mahdi among the Ahl al-Sunnah (Sunnis) [has the support of] 69 later scholars who wrote in support of the concept, compared to 8 scholars who rejected the idea. The hadith prophesying the Dajjal (False Christ), a one-eyed man who will have miraculous powers and will be

followed by the Jews, and the return of Jesus Christ son of Mary (peace be upon them), who will descend in Damascus and pray behind the Mahdi, kill the Dajjal at the gate of Lod in Palestine, break the Cross, kill the Pig, marry and have children and live for forty years before dying a natural death, are Mutawatir in meaning.

Suhaib Hasan

The Mahdi in a hadith:

Narrated AbuSa'id al-Khudri:

The Prophet (peace be upon him) said: "The Mahdi will be of my stock, and will have a broad forehead a prominent nose. He will fill the earth will equity and justice as it was filled with oppression and tyranny, and he will rule for seven years.

Abu Dawud 36.4272

A authenticated hadith (sahih) or good (hasan) in Islam is a legal precedent if it does not contradict the Koran and can be traced, as mentioned earlier, to a witness (often referred to as Companions of the Prophet) of what the Prophet said or did, or did not do, via a chain of reliable transmitters. Even if the narrator of a hadith is unsure of where and when he heard it, it can still be considered authentic (ul fitr in the following hadiths is the festival which marks the end of Ramadan; ul Adha commemorates the end of the Hajj).

Narrated Abu Said Al-Khudri:

On 'Id ul Fitr or 'Id ul Adha Allah's Apostle (p.b.u.h) went out to the Musalla. After finishing the prayer, he delivered the sermon and ordered the people to give alms. He said, "O people! Give alms." Then he went towards the women and said. "O women! Give alms, for I have seen that the majority of the dwellers of Hell-Fire were you (women)."

The women asked, "O Allah's Apostle! What is the reason for it?"

"He replied, "O women! You curse frequently, and are ungrateful to your husbands. I have not seen anyone more deficient in intelligence and religion than you. O women, some of you can lead a cautious wise man astray."

Then he left. And when he reached his house, Zainab, the wife of Ibn Masud, came and asked permission to enter.

It was said, "O Allah's Apostle! It is Zainab."

He asked, "Which Zainab?"

The reply was that she was the wife of Ibn Mas'ub.

He said, "Yes, allow her to enter."

And she was admitted. Then she said, "O Prophet of Allah! Today you ordered people to give alms and I had an ornament and intended to give it as alms, but Ibn Masud said that he and his children deserved it more than anybody else."

The Prophet replied, "Ibn Masud had spoken the truth. Your husband and your children had more right to it than anybody else."

Bukhari 24.541

A weak (dhaeef) hadith is one where there is a break in the chain of transmitters and/or the integrity of the narrator(s) is suspect; or not enough people remember hearing about it. A weak hadith can still be considered a legal precedent depending on the circumstances and the school of Islamic law.

If the chain of narrators through the pseudo-science of hadith authentication is judged to be reliable then, what was reported by a Companion of the Prophet is considered beyond reproach; the scholarship ends with the first person to claim to have heard it from one of the Companions of the Prophet. It could not be any other way. To question what any of the Companions of the Prophet said they heard God's Messenger preach is to question the very validity of basing a legal system on immutable precedents derived from hearsay evidence about what someone said and did two hundred years earlier.

It is not always clear, to the layperson, what precedents can be found in many convoluted hadiths. An example:

Narrated Abu Humaid As-Sa'idi:

We took part in the holy battle of Tabuk in the company of the Prophet and when we arrived at the Wadi-al-Qura, there was a woman in her garden. The Prophet asked his companions to estimate the amount of the fruits in the garden, and Allah's Apostle estimated it at ten Awsuq (one Wasaq = 60 Sa's) and 1 Sa'= 3 kg. approximately).

The Prophet said to that lady, "Check what your garden will yield."

When we reached Tabuk, the Prophet said, "There will be a strong wind tonight and so no one should stand and whoever has a camel, should fasten it."

So we fastened our camels. A strong wind blew at night and a man stood up and he was blown away to a mountain called Taiy.

The King of Aila sent a white mule and a sheet for wearing to the Prophet as a present, and wrote to the Prophet that his people would stay in their place (and will pay Jizya taxation.)

When the Prophet reached Wadi-al-Qura he asked that woman how much her garden had yielded. She said, "Ten Awsuq," and that was what Allah's Apostle had estimated.

Then the Prophet said, "I want to reach Medina quickly, and whoever among you wants to accompany me, should hurry up."

The sub-narrator Ibn Bakkar said something which meant: When the Prophet (p.b.u.h) saw Medina he said, "This is Taba." And when he saw the mountain of Uhud, he said, "This mountain loves us and we love it. Shall I tell you of the best amongst the Ansar (*i.e. helpers, people of Medina who assisted the Muslims who fled Mecca*)?"

They replied in the affirmative.

He said, "The family of Bani-n-Najjar, and then the family of Bani Sa'ida or Bani Al-Harith bin Al-Khazraj. (The above-mentioned are the best) but there is goodness in all the families of Ansar."

Bukhari 24.559

Crime and Punishment

The Koran often defines the crime and the punishment, with the sayings of God's Messenger filling in the details. For example Allah said in revelation 17:33 "... Whoever is killed unjustly, We have given his heir the power [to demand satisfaction]; but let him not exceed the limit in slaying, for he will be the victor". Satisfaction does not have to be in the form of a murder for a murder if the family of the deceased is willing to accept monetary compensation for the loss of a loved one, which the Prophet set at a maximum of 100 camels.

And intentional murder shall be punished according to talion law (*Law of Retaliation*); where the murderess intention is not clear and the victim is killed using a club or a stone it will cost the perpetrator one hundred camels as blood money. Whoever demands more is a man from the time of ignorance (*the time before Islam*).

From a translation of the Prophet's last sermon by Islamic scholar and author Dr. Muhammad Hamidullah's [1908-2002]

Another case in point, it is the Prophet who established the threshold at which Allah's horrific punishment for stealing is to be applied.

Narrated 'Aisha:

The Prophet said, "The hand should be cut off for stealing something that is worth a quarter of a Dinar or more."

Bukhari 81.780

Narrated Abu Huraira:

Allah 's Apostle said, "Allah curses the thief who steals an egg (or a helmet) for which his hand is to be cut off, or steals a rope, for which his hand is to be cut off."

Bukhari 81.791

Narrated 'Abdullah bin 'Umar:

The Prophet cut off the hand of a thief for stealing a shield that was worth three Dirhams.

Bukhari 81.789

The most glaring and pitiful exception to the Koran setting the punishment and God's Messenger setting the threshold is the stoning of women, which, in a narration by Ali the fourth Caliph (Leader of the Believers) is a tradition established by his father-in-law,

Narrated Ash-Sha'bi, from 'Ali when the latter stoned a lady to death on a Friday:

'Ali said, "I have stoned her according to the tradition of Allah's Apostle."

Bukhari 82.803

The second Caliph Umar said that a revelation demanding the stoning of women guilty of illegal intercourse had been received but had been lost. If you believe Umar, then Allah's Messenger and Ali were just following orders.

Prosecutor and Judge

An example from the Prophet on the conduct of a trial:

Narrated Anas bin Malik:

A girl wearing ornaments, went out at Medina. Somebody struck her with a stone. She was brought to the Prophet while she was still alive. Allah's Apostle asked her, "Did such-and-such a person strike you?"

She raised her head, denying that.

He asked her a second time, saying, "Did so-and-so strike you?"

She raised her head, denying that.

He said for the third time, "Did so-and-so strike you?"

She lowered her head, agreeing.

Allah's Apostle then sent for the killer and killed him between two stones.

Bukhari 83.16

Narrated Anas bin Malik:

A Jew crushed the head of a girl between two stones, and the girl was asked, "Who has done that to you, so-and-so or so and so?" (Some names were mentioned for her) till the name of that Jew was mentioned (whereupon she agreed). The Jew was brought to the Prophet and the Prophet kept on questioning him till he confessed, whereupon his head was crushed with stones.

Bukhari 83.15

The Truth

One of the most quoted narrator as to why he memorized, then repeated what the Prophet said.

Narrated Abu Huraira:

People say that I have narrated many Hadiths (The Prophet's narrations). Had it not been for two verses in the Qur'an, I would not have narrated a single Hadith, and the verses are: "Verily those who conceal the clear sign and the guidance which We have sent down . . . (up to) Most Merciful." (2:159-160).

And no doubt our Muhajir (emigrant) brothers used to be busy in the market with their business (bargains) and our Ansari (people of Medina) brothers used to be busy with their property (agriculture). But I (Abu Huraira) used to stick to Allah's Apostle contented with what will fill my stomach and I used to attend that which they used not to attend and I used to memorize that which they used not to memorize.

Bukhari 3:118

Abu Huraira did not always have a good memory.

Narrated Abu Huraira:

I said to Allah's Apostle "I hear many narrations (Hadiths) from you but I forget them."

Allah's Apostle said, "Spread your Rida' (garment)."

I did accordingly and then he moved his hands as if filling them with something (and emptied them in my Rida') and then said, "Take and wrap this sheet over your body."

I did it and after that I never forgot anything.

Bukhari 3:119

Abu Huraira felt it was his duty as a believer to spread the truth and the truth is also very much what he and I are all about. The hadiths of the Sunni canon and the Shia collection are meant, in no particular order: to provide a rebuttal of empirical i.e. fact based history, an alternative scriptural history, a personal history, to fill in the blanks left by Allah, reinforce i.e. amplify what is written in the Koran, clarify God's intent, add to God's laws where necessary and, last but not least, provide a living example in the person of the Prophet, the embodiment of the perfect human being, as to how to worship God and to live as He intended.

You could not call yourself a Prophet if you did not make prophecies. Most of what God's Messenger had to say about the future have to do with the portents of the End Times and what will take place on Judgement Day with a scattering of predictions of a more personal nature, the majority surrounding his death. Like most prophecies that are said to have come to pass, a flexible interpretation by those who believe is a prerequisite to their validation. Example:

Narrated 'Aisha:

Some of the wives of the Prophet asked him, "Who amongst us will be the first to follow you (i.e. die after you)?"

He said, "Whoever has the longest hand."

So they started measuring their hands with a stick and Sauda's hand turned out to be the longest. (When Zainab bint Jahsh died first of all in the caliphate of 'Umar), we came to know that the long hand was a symbol of practicing charity, so she was the first to follow the Prophet and she used to love to practice charity. (Sauda died later in the caliphate of Muawiya).

Bukhari 24.501

Except for a few dozen hadiths, from Sahih Muslim mostly, it is mainly those of the greatest collector of them all, Bukhari, that you will find here. Like in the Koran, but to an even greater degree, there is a tremendous amount of duplication in the hadiths, with mostly minor variations. The 1,001 sayings and deeds of the Prophet are more than representative of what the Prophet said and did.

As you read the hadiths in *1,001 Sayings and Deeds of the Prophet Muhammad* keep in mind that it is a crime under Islamic law not to believe that whatever the Prophet said or did in authenticated hadiths, which are the only kind presented here, is the truth and nothing but the truth!

Allah said "kill them wherever you find them." An uncomfortable truth about the hadiths is the normalcy they bring to "killing them wherever you find them".

Narrated Jarir bin 'Abdullah:

Allah's Apostle has never refused to admit me since I embraced Islam, and whenever he saw me, he would smile.

(In another narration) Jarir bin 'Abdullah narrated: There was a house called Dhul-Khalasa (*a rival to the Prophet's Ka'ba in Mecca*) in the Pre-lslamic Period and it was also called Al-Ka'ba Al-Yamaniya or Al-Ka'ba Ash-Shamiya.

Allah's Apostle said to me, "Will you relieve me from Dhul-Khalasa?"

So I left for it with 150 cavalrymen from the tribe of Ahmas and then we destroyed it and killed whoever we found there. Then we came to the Prophet and informed him about it. He invoked good upon us and upon the tribe of Ahmas.

Bukhari 58.160

Narrated 'Abdur-Rahman bin 'Auf:

I got an agreement written between me and Umaiya bin Khalaf that Umaiya would look after my property (or family) in Mecca and I would look after his in Medina ...

On the day (of the battle) of Badr, when all the people went to sleep, I went up the hill to protect him. Bilal saw him (i.e. Umaiya) and went to a gathering of Ansar (*Muslims of Medina*) and said, "(Here is) Umaiya bin Khalaf! Woe to me if he escapes!"

So, a group of Ansar went out with Bilal to follow us ('Abdur-Rahman and Umaiya). Being afraid that they would catch us, I left Umaiya's son for them to keep them busy but the Ansar killed the son and insisted on following us.

Umaiya was a fat man, and when they approached us, I told him to kneel down, and he knelt, and I laid myself on him to protect him, but the Ansar killed him by passing their swords underneath me ...

Bukhari 38.498

The late Ayatollah Khomeini is quoted as saying "There is no humor in Islam. There is no fun in Islam. There can be no fun and joy in whatever is serious." What you are about to read, like Allah's revelations, is serious stuff. Any humour in a hadith is undoubtedly unintended and may only bring a smile to your lips and no one else.

Narrated Imran bin Husain:

I went to the Prophet and tied my she-camel at the gate. The people of Bani Tamim came to the Prophet who said "O Bani Tamim! Accept the good tidings."

They said twice, "You have given us the good tidings, now give us something"

Then some Yemenites came to him and he said, "Accept the good tidings, O people of Yemem, for Bani Tamim refused them."

They said, "We accept it, O Allah's Apostle! We have come to ask you about this matter (i.e. the start of creations)."

He said, "First of all, there was nothing but Allah, and (then He created His Throne). His throne was over the water, and He wrote everything in the Book (in the Heaven) and created the Heavens and the Earth."

Then a man shouted, "O Ibn Husain! Your she-camel has gone away!" So, I went away and could not see the she-camel because of the mirage. By Allah, I wished I had left that she-camel (but not that gathering).

Bukhari 54.414

A Palace in the Sky

Allah's not only differentiates between the Paradise worthiness of the believers by scattering them among the seven levels of His Paradise but also by the type of accommodations – from tents, apartments, single family homes to mansions. The Prophet's mansion will be a palace in the sky on an expanse of land where a river flows and on whose shores will be encampment of tents, very special tents.

Narrated Anas:

When the Prophet was made to ascend to the Heavens, he said (after his return), "I came upon a river the banks of which were made of tents of hollow pearls. I asked Gabriel. 'What is this (river)?' He replied, 'This is the Kauthar.'"

Bukhari 60.488

The Kauthar, the immense lake which feeds it, the encampments of tents made of pearl, the palace and the luxuries that come with it is a unique, some would say extravagant gift, from a grateful God to the best of Messengers.

Narrated Abu Bishr:

Said bin Jubair said that Ibn 'Abbas said about Al-Kauthar. "That is the good which Allah has bestowed upon His Apostle."

I said to Sa'id bin Jubair. "But the people claim that it is a river in Paradise."

Said said, "The river in Paradise is part of the good which Allah has bestowed on His Apostle."

Bukhari 60.490

God, in fashioning this exceptional gift for His beloved Apostle did not overlook His Disciple's love of the smell of musk.

Narrated Anas bin Malik:

The Prophet said: "While I was walking in Paradise (on the night of Mi'raj), I saw a river, on the two banks of which there were tents made of hollow pearls. I asked, 'What is this, O Gabriel?' He said, 'That is the Kauthar which Your Lord has given to you.' Behold! Its scent or its mud was sharp smelling musk!"

Bukhari 76.583

Guests of the Prophet may stay in tents, but they will be able to eat like rich people who can afford utensils.

Narrated Abu Ubaida:

I asked 'Aisha 'regarding the verse: "Verily we have granted you the Kauthar."

She replied, "The Kauthar is a river which has been given to your Prophet on the banks of which there are (tents of) hollow pearls and its utensils are as numberless as the stars."

Bukhari 60.489

The utensils mentioned in the previous hadith may actually have been vessels, as in sailing vessels.

Narrated Haritha bin Wahb:

I heard the Prophet mentioning the Lake-Fount (Al-Kauthar), saying, "(The width of the Lake-Fount) is equal to the distance between Medina and Sana' (capital of Yemen)."

Haritha said that he heard the Prophet saying that his Lake-Fount would be as large as the distance between Sana' and Medina.

Al-Mustaurid said to Haritha, "Didn't you hear him talking about the vessels?"

He said, "No."

Al-Mustaurid said, "The vessels are seen in it as (numberless as) the stars."

Bukhari 76.591

The distance between Medina and Sana is 1,122.9 Kilometers or 605.9 nautical miles. That would make Lake-Fount, assumed to be the source of the river Kauthar, a very big lake indeed.

Jugs by the millions, and another estimate of the width of Lake Fount as being as wide as the distance between Aila (modern day

Aqaba) and Sana which is, as the crow flies, 1,141 miles or 1,8361 kilometers.

Narrated Anas bin Malik:

Allah's Apostle said, "The width of my Lake-Fount is equal to the distance between Aila (a town in Sham) and Sana' (the capital of Yemen) and it has as many (numerous) jugs as the number of stars of the sky."

Bukhari 76.582

Not all of the Prophet's former companions will be welcomed at the Messenger's private retreat in the sky.

Narrated 'Abdullah:

The Prophet said, "I am your predecessor at the Lake-Fount (Kauthar) and some men amongst you will be brought to me, and when I will try to hand them some water, they will be pulled away from me by force whereupon I will say, 'O Lord, my companions!' Then the Almighty will say, 'You do not know what they did after you left, they introduced new things into the religion after you.'"

Bukhari 88.173

Narrated Sahl bin Sa'd:

I heard the Prophet saying, "I am your predecessor at the Lake-Fount (Kauthar), and whoever will come to it, will drink from it, and whoever will drink from it, will never become thirsty after that. There will come to me some people whom I know and they know me, and then a barrier will be set up between me and them."

Abu Sa'id Al-Khudri added that the Prophet further said: "I will say those people are from me. It will be said, 'You do not know what changes and new things they did after you.' Then I will say, 'Far removed (from mercy), far removed (from mercy), those who changed (the religion) after me!'"

Bukhari 88.174

There will be no need for signs warning apostates to stay away.

Narrated Asma:

The Prophet said, "I will be at my Lake-Fount (Kauthar) waiting for whoever will come to me. Then some people will be taken away from me whereupon I will say, 'My followers!' It will be said, 'You do not know they turned Apostates as renegades (deserted their religion).'"

Bukhari 88.172

Much of what we know about Paradise, Hell and Judgement Day are from dreams and lucid visions where God's Messenger is shown the reality of the afterlife, usually by angels or one angel in particular, Gabriel. Example of a straightforward lucid vision:

Narrated Anas bin Malik:

Once Allah's Apostle led us in prayer and then (after finishing it) ascended the pulpit and pointed with his hand towards the Qibla of the mosque and said, "While I was leading you in prayer, both Paradise and Hell were displayed in front of me in the direction of this wall. I had never seen a better thing (than Paradise) and a worse thing (than Hell) as I have seen today, I had never seen a better thing and a worse thing as I have seen today."

Bukhari 76.475

A long hadith where the Prophet is first shown his palace in the sky in a dream, but not before two angels of Allah take him for a stroll in a what you might consider a surreal landscape, but for the believers, it is nothing of the kind.

Narrated Samura bin Jundub:

Allah's Apostle very often used to ask his companions, "Did anyone of you see a dream?" So dreams would be narrated to him by those whom Allah wished to tell.

One morning the Prophet said, "Last night two persons came to me (in a dream) and woke me up and said to me, 'Proceed!' I set out with them and we came across a man lying down, and behold, another man was standing over his head, holding a big rock. Behold, he was throwing the rock at the man's head, injuring it. The rock rolled away and the thrower followed it and took it back. By the time he reached the man, his head returned to the normal state. The thrower then did the same as he had done before.

I said to my two companions, 'Subhan Allah! (*Glorious is God*) Who are these two persons?'

They said, 'Proceed!'

So we proceeded and came to a man lying flat on his back and another man standing over his head with an iron hook, and behold, he would put the hook in one side of the man's mouth and tear off that side of his face to the back (of the neck) and similarly tear his nose from front to back and his eye from front to back. Then he turned to the other side of the man's face and did just as he had done with the other side. He hardly completed this side when the other side returned to its normal state. Then he returned to it to repeat what he had done before.

I said to my two companions, 'Subhan Allah! Who are these two persons?'

They said to me, 'Proceed!'

So we proceeded and came across something like a Tannur (a kind of baking oven, a pit usually clay-lined for baking bread)."

I think the Prophet said, "In that oven there was much noise and voices."

The Prophet added, "We looked into it and found naked men and women, and behold, a flame of fire was reaching to them from underneath, and when it reached them, they cried loudly.

I asked them, 'Who are these?'

They said to me, 'Proceed!'

And so we proceeded and came across a river."

I think he said, ".... red like blood."

The Prophet added, "And behold, in the river there was a man swimming, and on the bank there was a man who had collected many stones. Behold. while the other man was swimming, he went near him. The former opened his mouth and the latter (on the bank) threw a stone into his mouth whereupon he went swimming again. He returned and every time the performance was repeated.

I asked my two companions, 'Who are these (two) persons?'

They replied, 'Proceed! Proceed!'

And we proceeded till we came to a man with a repulsive appearance, the most repulsive appearance, you ever saw a man having! Beside him there was a fire and he was kindling it and running around it.

I asked my companions, 'Who is this (man)?'

They said to me, 'Proceed! Proceed!'

So we proceeded till we reached a garden of deep green dense vegetation, having all sorts of spring colors. In the midst of the garden there was a very tall man and I could hardly see his head because of his great height, and around him there were children in such a large number as I have never seen.

I said to my companions, 'Who is this?'

They replied, 'Proceed! Proceed!'

So we proceeded till we came to a majestic huge garden, greater and better than I have ever seen! My two companions said to me, 'Go up and I went up'

The Prophet added, "So we ascended till we reached a city built of gold and silver bricks and we went to its gate and asked (the gatekeeper) to open the gate, and it was opened and we entered the city and found in it, men with one side of their bodies as handsome as the handsomest person you have ever seen, and the other side as ugly as the ugliest person you have ever seen.

My two companions ordered those men to throw themselves into the river. Behold, there was a river flowing across (the city), and its water was like milk in whiteness. Those men went and threw themselves in it and then returned to us after the ugliness (of their bodies) had disappeared and they became in the best shape."

The Prophet further added, "My two companions (angels) said to me, 'This place is the Eden Paradise, and that is your place.'

I raised up my sight, and behold, there I saw a palace like a white cloud!

My two companions said to me, 'That (palace) is your place.' I said to them, 'May Allah bless you both! Let me enter it.'

They replied, 'As for now, you will not enter it, but you shall enter it (one day)'

I said to them, 'I have seen many wonders tonight. What does all that mean which I have seen?'

They replied, 'We will inform you:

> As for the first man you came upon whose head was being injured with the rock, he is the symbol of the one who studies the Quran and then neither recites it nor acts on its orders, and sleeps, neglecting the enjoined prayers.

> As for the man you came upon whose sides of mouth, nostrils and eyes were torn off from front to back, he is the symbol of the man who goes out of his house in the morning and tells so many lies that it spreads all over the world.

> And those naked men and women whom you saw in a

construction resembling an oven, they are the adulterers and the adulteresses, and the man whom you saw swimming in the river and given a stone to swallow, is the eater of usury (Riba), and the bad looking man whom you saw near the fire kindling it and going round it, is Malik, the gatekeeper of Hell, and the tall man whom you saw in the garden, is Abraham and the children around him are those children who die with Al-Fitra (the Islamic Faith).'

The narrator added: "Some Muslims asked the Prophet, 'O Allah's Apostle! What about the children of pagans?'"

The Prophet replied, "And also the children of pagans."

The Prophet added, "My two companions added, 'The men you saw half handsome and half ugly were those persons who had mixed an act that was good with another that was bad, but Allah forgave them.'"

Bukhari 87.171

On another occasion, recounted in more than one hadith, the Prophet will accidently enter the palace of a companion and close collaborator of his, Umar. Umar bin Al-Khattab would succeed God's Messenger as the second caliph i.e. leader of the believers.

Narrated Abu Huraira:

We were sitting with Allah's Apostle, he said, "While I was sleeping, I saw myself in Paradise. Suddenly I saw a woman performing ablution beside a palace. I asked, 'For whom is this palace?' They (the angels) replied, 'It is for 'Umar bin Al-Khattab.' Then I remembered 'Umar's ghira (self-respect) and went back hurriedly."

On hearing that, 'Umar started weeping and said, "Let my father and mother be sacrificed for you. O Allah's Apostle! How dare I think of my ghira being offended by you?"

Bukhari 87.150

The wonder remains that adults who thrived on such unreal discussions could inspire generations through the ages to slaughter countless millions for doubting the veracity of the strange, fantastic stories told by God's alleged spokesperson and which permeate both the hadiths and the Koran.

Abdullah bin Salam

Abdullah bin Salam was a rabbi and a respected member of the Jewish community before he converted to Islam. He became a Muslim after a short meeting with the Prophet where God's Messenger answered three fatuous questions to the rabbi's satisfaction. It was fortuitous that the angel Gabriel, whom bin Salam then considered an enemy of the Jews, had just had a conversation with the Prophet about what was on bin Salam's mind.

Narrated Anas:

'Abdullah bin Salam heard the news of the arrival of Allah's Apostle (at Medina) while he was on a farm collecting its fruits. So he came to the Prophet and said, "I will ask you about three things which nobody knows unless he be a prophet. Firstly, what is the first portent of the Hour? What is the first meal of the people of Paradise? And what makes a baby look like its father or mother?"

The Prophet said, "Just now Gabriel has informed me about that."

'Abdullah said, "Gabriel?"

The Prophet said, "Yes."

'Abdullah said, "He, among the angels is the enemy of the Jews."

On that the Prophet recited this Holy Verse: "Whoever is an enemy to Gabriel (let him die in his fury!) for he has brought it (i.e. Qur'an) down to your heart by Allah's permission." (2:97)

Then he added, "As for the first portent of the Hour, it will be a fire that will collect the people from the East to West. And as for the first meal of the people of Paradise, it will be the caudite (i.e. extra) lobe of the fish liver. And if a man's discharge proceeded that of the woman, then the child resembles the father, and if the woman's discharge proceeded that of the man, then the child resembles the mother."

On hearing that, 'Abdullah said, "I testify that None has the right to be worshipped but Allah, and that you are the Apostle of Allah, O, Allah's Apostle; the Jews are liars, and if they should come to know that I have embraced Islam, they would accuse me of being a liar."

In the meantime some Jews came (to the Prophet) and he asked them, "What is 'Abdullah's status amongst you?"

They replied, "He is the best amongst us, and he is our chief and the son of our chief."

The Prophet said, "What would you think if 'Abdullah bin Salam embraced Islam?"

They replied, "May Allah protect him from this!"

Then 'Abdullah came out and said, "I testify that None has the right to be worshipped but Allah and that Muhammad is the Apostle of Allah."

The Jews then said, "Abdullah is the worst of us and the son of the worst of us," and disparaged him.

On that 'Abdullah said, "O Allah's Apostle! This is what I was afraid of!"

Bukhari 60.7

It the post-Jesus era, the Jews were moving away from the more brutal punishments specified in the Torah, such as the stoning of adulterers. The Prophet would have none of it, and with the help of bin Salem forced the Jews of Medina – over whom he had ultimate authority under the negotiated Constitution of Medina – to stick to the old ways, many of which became the news ways of the Koran.

Narrated 'Abdullah bin 'Umar:

The Jews came to Allah's Apostle and told him that a man and a woman from amongst them had committed illegal sexual intercourse.

Allah's Apostle said to them, "What do you find in the Torah (old Testament) about the legal punishment of Ar-Rajm (stoning)?"

They replied, "(But) we announce their crime and lash them."

Abdullah bin Salam said, "You are telling a lie; Torah contains the order of Rajm."

They brought and opened the Torah and one of them ~~solaced~~ [placed] his hand on the Verse of Rajm and read the verses preceding and following it.

Abdullah bin Salam said to him, "Lift your hand." When he lifted his hand, the Verse of Rajm was written there.

They said, "Muhammad has told the truth; the Torah has the Verse of Rajm.

The Prophet then gave the order that both of them should be stoned to death.

('Abdullah bin 'Umar said, "I saw the man leaning over the woman to shelter her from the stones.")

Bukhari 56.829.

Aisha

Much of Islam, as you will discover, was literally dreamt into existence. One of the very first, if not the very first communication from Allah made in this manner to the man who would become famous as the Prophet Muhammad, was to introduce him to his child bride when she was still a baby.

Aisha was as pretty as a picture. Considering Allah and His Messenger's aversion to lifelike reproductions of people and animals the following is quite extraordinary:

Narrated 'Aisha:

That the Prophet said to her, "You have been shown to me twice in my dream. I saw you pictured on a piece of silk and someone said (to me). 'This is your wife.' When I uncovered the picture, I saw that it was yours. I said, 'If this is from Allah, it will be done.'"

Bukhari 58.235

In another hadith it is Aisha in the flesh wrapped in silk and the disembodied voice has been identified as that of a man.

Narrated 'Aisha:

Allah's Apostle said (to me), "You were shown to me twice in (my) dream. Behold, a man was carrying you in a silken piece of cloth and said to me, 'She is your wife, so uncover her,' and behold, it was you."

I would then say (to myself), "If this is from Allah, then it must happen."

Bukhari 87.139

In still another hadith about the Prophet's dream (or dreams) of Aisha, God's Messenger not only repeats himself, as was his habit when he wanted to emphasize an important aspect of a communication he had recently received from Paradise, but it is he who tells, what is now an angel holding Aisha, to uncover her.

Narrated 'Aisha:

Allah's Apostle said to me, "You were shown to me twice (in my dream) before I married you. I saw an angel carrying you in a silken piece of cloth, and I said to him, 'Uncover (her),' and behold, it was you. I said (to myself), 'If this is from

Allah, then it must happen.' Then you were shown to me, the angel carrying you in a silken piece of cloth, and I said (to him), 'Uncover (her)', and behold, it was you. I said (to myself), 'If this is from Allah, then it must happen.'"

Bukhari 87.140

Aisha bint Abu Bakr is undoubtedly the second most famous woman in history, and that is only because Mary, the mother of Jesus, is the only female mentioned by name in the Koran. The early life of Abu Bakr's daughter has created the most important challenge to the designation of the Prophet Muhammad as being the embodiment of the perfect human being. Of all the gross indecencies associated with God's Messenger of which Allah ostensibly approved, and which apologists have the most difficulty in glossing over, is that of a fifty three year old man having sex with a nine year old girl.

It bears repeating many times over, as I do here, that Aisha was nine when she was invited to join a man who could have been her grandfather on the matrimonial mat.

Narrated Aisha:

The Prophet engaged me when I was a girl of six (years). We went to Medina and stayed at the home of Bani-al-Harith bin Khazraj. Then I got ill and my hair fell down.

Later on my hair grew (again) and my mother, Um Ruman, came to me while I was playing in a swing with some of my girlfriends. She called me, and I went to her, not knowing what she wanted to do to me.

She caught me by the hand and made me stand at the door of the house. I was breathless then, and when my breathing became all right, she took some water and rubbed my face and head with it.

Then she took me into the house. There in the house I saw some Ansari women (*women of Medina*) who said, "Best wishes and Allah's Blessing and a good luck."

Then she entrusted me to them and they prepared me (for the marriage).

Unexpectedly Allah's Apostle came to me in the forenoon and my mother handed me over to him, and at that time I was a girl of nine years of age.

Bukhari 58.234

Narrated 'Ursa:

The Prophet wrote the (marriage contract) with 'Aisha while she was six years old and consummated his marriage with her while she was nine years old and she remained with him for nine years (i.e. till his death).

Bukhari 62.88

Narrated 'Aisha:

That the Prophet married her when she was six years old and he consummated his marriage when she was nine years old, and then she remained with him for nine years (i.e., till his death).

Bukhari 62.64

Narrated Aisha:

When the Prophet married me, my mother came to me and made me enter the house (of the Prophet) and nothing surprised me but the coming of Allah's Apostle to me in the forenoon.

Bukhari 62.90

Narrated Hisham's father:

Khadija (*also spelled Khadijah, the Prophet's first wife*) died three years before the Prophet departed to Medina. He stayed there for two years or so and then he married 'Aisha when she was a girl of six years of age, and he consumed that marriage when she was nine years old.

Bukhari 58.236

Al-Tabari [838 - 923] author of the definitive history of Islam from Creation to 915 A.D., *The History of the Prophets and Kings*, quotes Aisha about the blessed day:

My mother came to me while I was being swung on a swing between two branches and got me down. My nurse took over and wiped my face with some water and started leading me. When I was at the door she stopped so I could catch my breath. I was brought in while Muhammad was sitting on a bed in our house. My mother made me sit on his lap. The other men and women got up and left. The Prophet consummated his marriage with me in my house when I was nine years old. Neither a camel nor a sheep was slaughtered on behalf of me.

Tabari IX:131

There was no wedding celebration, the meaning of "Neither a camel nor a sheep was slaughtered on behalf of me". What an unseemly celebration that would have been, a bearded past middle-age man marrying a nine year old child who still played with dolls, to be followed by a public exit by the bride and groom to consummate in private their union.

> 'A'isha (Allah be pleased with her) reported that Allah's Apostle (may peace be upon him) married her when she was seven (sic) years old, and she was taken to his house as a bride when she was nine, and her dolls were with her; and when he (the Holy Prophet) died she was eighteen years old.

Sahih Muslim 8.3311

> 'A'isha reported that she used to play with dolls in the presence of Allah's Messenger (may peace be upon him) and when her playmates came to her they left (the house) because they felt shy of Allah's Messenger (may peace be upon him), whereas Allah's Messenger (may peace be upon him) sent them to her.

Sahih Muslim 31.5981

In *The Prophet Muhammad, A Biography* Barnaby Rogerson's writes: "The ritual of marriage was simple; she shared a bowl of milk with Muhammad before they went to bed."

Scholars and clerics maintain that a grateful Abu Bakr offered his nine-year-old daughter, with whom the Prophet Muhammad had fallen in love, to cement his relationship with God's Messenger. Ayaan Hirsi Ali, in *The Caged Virgin*, writes that Aisha's father pleaded with his fifty-something friend to wait until his daughter reached adulthood before consuming the marriage.

> ... he fell in love with Aisha, his best friend's nine-year-old daughter. Her father said: "Please wait until she has reached adulthood." But Muhammad would not wait... In other words, Muhammad teaches us that it is fine to take away your best friend's child. By our Western standards Muhammad is a perverse man.

Ayaan Hirsi Ali. *The Caged Virgin*, p. 81

A hadith would appear to conform Hirsi Ali assertion that Aisha's father was not keen on marrying his daughter to God's Messenger at such a young age.

Narrated 'Ursa:

The Prophet asked Abu Bakr for 'Aisha's hand in marriage. Abu Bakr said "But I am your brother."

The Prophet said, "You are my brother in Allah's religion and His Book, but she (Aisha) is lawful for me to marry."

Bukhari 62.18

In his own mind, God's Messenger was not a pervert, for the child had given her consent.

Narrated Abu Huraira:

The Prophet said, "A matron should not be given in marriage except after consulting her; and a virgin should not be given in marriage except after her permission."

The people asked, "O Allah's Apostle! How can we know her permission?"

He said, "Her silence (indicates her permission)."

Bukhari 62.67

Aisha knew from experience that this was a specious justification for having your way with a child.

Narrated 'Aisha:

I said, "O Allah's Apostle! A virgin feels shy."

He said, "Her consent is (expressed by) her silence."

Bukhari 62.68

Shortly after taking power, the Ayatollah Khomeini lowered the age at which girls could be married off, from eighteen to nine to conform to Islamic law. In May 2006, the Iranian Parliament voted to overturn Khomeini's decree and made it compulsory for girls under the age of 15 and boys under 18 to have court approval to get married. The Guardian Council of the Constitution quashed the initiative, and reinstated Khomeini's ruling. What the legislature voted for was an innovation incompatible with the example of the Prophet and the principles of Islam.

Narrated Aisha:

Allah's Apostle said, "If somebody innovates something which is not in harmony with the principles of our religion, that thing is rejected."

Bukhari 49.861

No man has had more of an impact on an imperfect world than the person whom the believer consider the perfect human being whose every action is to be emulated as closely as possible.

Narrated 'Aisha:

The Prophet did something and allowed his people to do it, but some people refrained from doing it. When the Prophet learned of that, he delivered a sermon, and after having sent Praises to Allah, he said, "What is wrong with such people as refrain from doing a thing that I do? By Allah, I know

Allah better than they, and I am more afraid of Him than
they."

Bukhari 73.123

Today, what the perfect human being did to a child 1,400 years ago is
being repeated over and over in many parts of the believers' world
with disastrous consequences. Where Islam is making the greatest
advances is in Africa where we are now seeing an extraordinary
increase in a condition called vesicovaginal fistula or VVF where the
inflicted experience "the continuous involuntary discharge of urine
into the vaginal vault."

In Nigeria's Islamist north, for example, according to
ModernGhana, "thousands of underage child-wives are abandoned by
their pedophile husbands when these little girls develop VVF and
dribble urine - a complication of obstructed labour during underage
child birth." These child-mothers, and their female offsprings when
they, as children give birth to children and are also mutilated by
giving birth before their time are largely all doomed to a short
miserable existence and an ignominious death. This cannot be what
the perfect human being intended.

There is no doubt that the Prophet's lust gave way to what we
could consider genuine love for his child bride. It may have been
because she was playful, exciting and made him feel like a young man
again.

Narrated 'Aisha:

The Prophet and I used to take a bath from a single pot
called 'Faraq'.

Bukhari 5:250

Narrated Abu Salama:

'Aisha's brother and I went to 'Aisha and he asked her
about the bath of the Prophet. She brought a pot containing
about a Sa' of water and took a bath and poured it over her
head and at that time there was a screen between her and
us.

Bukhari: 5:251

He would elevate her above all the women in his household.

Narrated Anas:

The Prophet said, "The superiority of 'Aisha to other women
is like the superiority of Tharid to other kinds of food."

Bukhari 63.330

God's Messenger would deflect any criticism of his child bride. Aisha
was the only wife of the Prophet who, when she joined her husband

under the sheets, did not interrupt Allah's Revelations i.e. the Divine Inspirations, and that had to be significant.

Narrated Hisham's father:

The people used to send presents to the Prophet on the day of 'Aisha's turn.

'Aisha said, "My companions (i.e. the other wives of the Prophet) gathered in the house of Um Salama and said, "0 Um Salama! By Allah, the people choose to send presents on the day of 'Aisha's turn and we too, love the good (i.e. presents etc.) as 'Aisha does. You should tell Allah's Apostle to tell the people to send their presents to him wherever he may be, or wherever his turn may be."

Um Salama said that to the Prophet and he turned away from her, and when the Prophet returned to her (i.e. Um Salama), she repeated the same, and the Prophet again turned away, and when she told him the same for the third time, the Prophet said, "O Um Salama! Don't trouble me by harming 'Aisha, for by Allah, the Divine Inspiration never came to me while I was under the blanket of any woman amongst you except her."

Bukhari 57.119

Aisha knew that she was the apple of the Prophet's eye, and this probably emboldened her to say things to her husband that no other wife would have dared. For example, the more powerful and rich God's Messenger became, the more women threw themselves at him, including his aunt Khaula. What was a Prophet to do? God made it clear, that His Messenger could do pretty well whatever he wanted with the women who freely gave themselves to him, including postponing a wife's turn to accommodate an aspiring consort.

Narrated Hisham's father:

Khaula bint Hakim was one of those ladies who presented themselves to the Prophet for marriage. 'Aisha said, "Doesn't a lady feel ashamed for presenting herself to a man?"

But when the Verse: "(O Muhammad) You may postpone (the turn of) any of them (your wives) that you please," (33:51) was revealed, 'Aisha said, "O Allah's Apostle! I do not see, but, that your Lord hurries in pleasing you."

Bukhari 62.48

Aisha was not only jealous of her husband sleeping with other women, but his other wives as well; at least, that was what she admitted to after her husband's passing.

Narrated Muadha:

'Aisha said, "Allah's Apostle used to take the permission of that wife with whom he was supposed to stay overnight if he wanted to go to one other than her, after this Verse was revealed: 'You (O Muhammad) can postpone (the turn of) whom you will of them (your wives) and you may receive any (of them) whom you will; and there is no blame on you if you invite one whose turn you have set aside (temporarily).'" (33:51)

I asked Aisha, "What did you use to say (in this case)?"

She said, "I used to say to him, 'If I could deny you the permission (to go to your other wives) I would not allow your favor to be bestowed on any other person.'"

Bukhari 60.312

Aisha was not even afraid of being angry at her husband and showing it.

Narrated Aisha:

That Allah's Apostle said to her, "I [know if] you are pleased with me or angry with me."

I said, "Whence do you know that?"

He said, "When you are pleased with me, you say, 'No, by the Lord of Muhammad,' but when you are angry with me, then you say, 'No, by the Lord of Abraham.'"

Thereupon I said, "Yes (you are right), but by Allah, O Allah's Apostle, I leave nothing but your name."

Bukhari 62.155

The one thing that her husband would not let her get away with:

Narrated Anas:

Aisha had a thick curtain (having pictures on it) and she screened the side of her house with it. The Prophet said to her, "Remove it from my sight, for its pictures are still coming to my mind in my prayers."

Bukhari 72.842

Narrated 'Aisha:

Allah's Apostle returned from a journey when I had placed a curtain of mine having pictures over (the door of) a chamber of mine. When Allah's Apostle saw it, he tore it and said, "The people who will receive the severest punishment on the

Day of Resurrection will be those who try to make the like of Allah's creations."

So we turned it (i.e., the curtain) into one or two cushions.

Bukhari 72.838

It may not have made any difference!

Narrated 'Aisha:

I stuffed for the Prophet a pillow decorated with pictures (of animals) which looked like a Namruqa (i.e. a small cushion). He came and stood among the people with excitement apparent on his face. I said, "O Allah's Apostle! What is wrong?"

He said, "What is this pillow?"

I said, "I have prepared this pillow for you, so that you may recline on it."

He said, "Don't you know that angels do not enter a house wherein there are pictures; and whoever makes a picture will be punished on the Day of Resurrection and will be asked to give life to (what he has created)?"

Bukhari 54.447

The Prophet had a well-groomed, nice smelling, shiny head of hair thanks, in part, to Aisha.

Narrated 'Aisha:

I used to perfume Allah's Apostle with the best scent available till I saw the shine of the scent on his head and shine beard.

Bukhari 72.806

Narrated 'Aisha:

While in menses, I used to comb the hair of Allah's Apostle.

Bukhari 6.294

One of the first revelations remembered by the Prophet's child bride.

Narrated Yusuf bin Mahik:

I was in the house of 'Aisha, the mother of the Believers. She said, "This revelation: 'Nay, but the Hour is their appointed time (for their full recompense); and the Hour will be more previous and most bitter.' (54:46) was revealed to Muhammad at Mecca while I was a playful little girl."

Bukhari 60.399

Aisha seems to have enjoyed her eight years with God's Messenger, which makes her death bed admission that more puzzling. Did she regret her lost childhood and the type of life she might have had, had she married an ordinary man closer to her own age.

Narrated Ibn Abu Mulaika:

Ibn 'Abbas asked permission to visit Aisha before her death, and at that time she was in a state of agony. She then said. "I am afraid that he will praise me too much."

And then it was said to her, "He is the cousin of Allah's Apostle and one of the prominent Muslims."

Then she said, "Allow him to enter."

(When he entered) he said, "How are you?"

She replied, "I am alright if I fear (Allah)."

Ibn Abbas said, "Allah willing, you are alright as you are the wife of Allah's Apostle and he did not marry any virgin except you and proof of your innocence was revealed from the Heaven."

Later on Ibn Az-Zubair entered after him and 'Aisha said to him, "Ibn 'Abbas came to me and praised me greatly, but I wish that I was a thing forgotten and out of sight."

Bukhari 60.277

It is to Aisha, as you will come to appreciate as your reading takes you further into the her husband's mind, that we owe the plentiful spontaneous forthright narrations volunteered by a bold young girl who said what needed to be said.

The Necklace

The Necklace is my name for a hadith by Bukhari in which the Prophet's child bride tells, in her own words, why she spent the night alone in the desert before being found by a young man who brought her back to her husband the next day, and what happened next. Much is revealed about the relationship between a young girl married to an older man with an omnipotent concerned God as a friend and ally. Read it more than once to get the full impact of what Aisha has to say.

Narrated Aisha:

Whenever Allah's Apostle intended to go on a journey, he would draw lots amongst his wives and would take with him the one upon whom the lot fell. During a Ghazwa (military expedition) of his, he drew lots amongst us and the lot fell upon me, and I proceeded with him after Allah had decreed the use of the veil by women. I was carried in a Howdah (on the camel) and dismounted while still in it.

When Allah's Apostle was through with his Ghazwa and returned home, and we approached the city of Medina, Allah's Apostle ordered us to proceed at night.

When the order of setting off was given, I walked till I was past the army to answer the call of nature. After finishing I returned (to the camp) to depart (with the others) and suddenly realized that my necklace over my chest was missing. So, I returned to look for it and was delayed because of that.

The people who used to carry me on the camel, came to my Howdah and put it on the back of the camel, thinking that I was in it, as, at that time, women were light in weight, and thin and lean, and did not use to eat much. So, those people did not feel the difference in the heaviness of the Howdah while lifting it, and they put it over the camel. At that time I was a young lady.

They set the camel moving and proceeded on. I found my necklace after the army had gone, and came to their camp to find nobody. So, I went to the place where I used to stay, thinking that they would discover my absence and come back in my search.

While in that state, I felt sleepy and slept.

Safwan bin Mu'attal As-Sulami Adh-Dhakwani was behind the army and reached my abode in the morning. When he saw a sleeping person, he came to me, and he used to see me before veiling. So, I got up when I heard him saying, "Inna lil-lah-wa inn a ilaihi rajiun (We are for Allah, and we will return to Him)."

He made his camel knell down. He got down from his camel, and put his leg on the front legs of the camel and then I rode and sat over it.

Safwan set out walking, leading the camel by the rope till we reached the army who had halted to take rest at midday. Then whoever was meant for destruction, fell into destruction, (some people accused me falsely) and the leader of the false accusers was 'Abdullah bin Ubai bin Salul.

After that we returned to Medina, and I became ill for one month while the people were spreading the forged statements of the false accusers. I was feeling during my ailment as if I were not receiving the usual kindness from the Prophet which I used to receive from him when I got sick. But he would come, greet and say, 'How is that (girl)?'

I did not know anything of what was going on till I recovered from my ailment and went out with Um Mistah to the Manasi where we used to answer the call of nature, and we used not to go to answer the call of nature except from night to night and that was before we had lavatories near to our houses. And this habit of ours was similar to the habit of the old 'Arabs in the open country (or away from houses).

So. I and Um Mistah bint Ruhm went out walking. Um Mistah stumbled because of her long dress and on that she said, 'Let Mistah (cousin of Abu Bakr) be ruined.' I said, 'You are saying a bad word. Why are you abusing a man who took part in (the battle of) Badr?'

She said, 'O Hanata (you there) didn't you hear what they said?' Then she told me the rumors of the false accusers.

My sickness was aggravated, and when I returned home, Allah's Apostle came to me, and after greeting he said, 'How is that (girl)?' I requested him to allow me to go to my parents. I wanted then to be sure of the news through them.

Allah's Apostle allowed me, and I went to my parents and asked my mother, 'What are the people talking about?' She said, 'O my daughter! Don't worry much about this matter. By Allah, never is there a charming woman loved by her husband who has other wives, but the women would forge false news about her.'

I said, 'Glorified be Allah! Are the people really taking of this matter?' That night I kept on weeping and could not sleep till morning.

In the morning Allah's Apostle called Ali bin Abu Talib and Usama bin Zaid when he saw the Divine Inspiration delayed, to consul them about divorcing his wife (i.e. 'Aisha). Usama bin Zaid said what he knew of the good reputation of his wives and added, 'O Allah's Apostle! Keep you wife, for, by Allah, we know nothing about her but good.'

'Ali bin Abu Talib said, 'O Allah's Apostle! Allah has no imposed restrictions on you, and there are many women other than she, yet you may ask the woman-servant who will tell you the truth.'

On that Allah's Apostle called Buraira and said, 'O Burair. Did you ever see anything which roused your suspicions about her?'

Buraira said, 'No, by Allah Who has sent you with the

Truth, I have never seen in her anything faulty except that she is a girl of immature age, who sometimes sleeps and leaves the dough for the goats to eat.'

On that day Allah's Apostle ascended the pulpit and requested that somebody support him in punishing 'Abdullah bin Ubai bin Salul. Allah's Apostle said, 'Who will support me to punish that person ('Abdullah bin Ubai bin Salul) who has hurt me by slandering the reputation of my family? By Allah, I know nothing about my family but good, and they have accused a person about whom I know nothing except good, and he never entered my house except in my company.'

Sad bin Mu'adh got up and said, 'O Allah's Apostle! by Allah, I will relieve you from him. If that man is from the tribe of the Aus, then we will chop his head off, and if he is from our brothers, the Khazraj, then order us, and we will fulfill your order.'

On that Sad bin 'Ubada, the chief of the Khazraj and before this incident, he had been a pious man, got up, motivated by his zeal for his tribe and said, 'By Allah, you have told a lie; you cannot kill him, and you will never be able to kill him.'

On that Usaid bin Al-Hadir got up and said (to Sad bin 'Ubada), 'By Allah! you are a liar. By Allah, we will kill him; and you are a hypocrite, defending the hypocrites.'

On this the two tribes of Aus and Khazraj got excited and were about to fight each other, while Allah's Apostle was standing on the pulpit. He got down and quietened them till they became silent and he kept quiet.

On that day I kept on weeping so much so that neither did my tears stop, nor could I sleep. In the morning my parents were with me and I had wept for two nights and a day, till I thought my liver would burst from weeping.

While they were sitting with me and I was weeping, an Ansari woman asked my permission to enter, and I allowed her to come in. She sat down and started weeping with me. While we were in this state, Allah's Apostle came and sat down and he had never sat with me since the day they forged the accusation.

No revelation regarding my case came to him for a month. He recited Tashah-hud (i.e. None has the right to be worshipped but Allah and Muhammad is His Apostle) and then said, 'O 'Aisha! I have been informed such-and-such about you; if you are innocent, then Allah will soon reveal your innocence, and if you have committed a sin, then repent to Allah and ask Him to forgive you, for when a person confesses his sin and asks Allah for forgiveness, Allah accepts his repentance.'

When Allah's Apostle finished his speech my tears ceased completely and there remained not even a single drop of it.

I requested my father to reply to Allah's Apostle on my behalf. My father said, 'By Allah, I do not know what to say to Allah's Apostle.' I said to my mother, 'Talk to Allah's Apostle on my behalf.' She said, 'By Allah, I do not know what to say to Allah's Apostle.'

I was a young girl and did not have much knowledge of the Quran. I said. 'I know, by Allah, that you have listened to what people are saying and that has been planted in your minds and you have taken it as a truth. Now, if I told you that I am innocent and Allah knows that I am innocent, you would not believe me and if I confessed to you falsely that I am guilty, and Allah knows that I am innocent you would believe me. By Allah, I don't compare my situation with you except to the situation of Joseph's father (i.e. Jacob) who said, 'So (for me) patience is most fitting against that which you assert and it is Allah (Alone) whose help can be sought.' Then I turned to the other side of my bed hoping that Allah would prove my innocence.

By Allah I never thought that Allah would reveal Divine Inspiration in my case, as I considered myself too inferior to be talked of in the Holy Qur'an. I had hoped that Allah's Apostle might have a dream in which Allah would prove my innocence.

By Allah, Allah's Apostle had not got up and nobody had left the house before the Divine Inspiration came to Allah's Apostle. So, there overtook him the same state which used to overtake him, (when he used to have, on being inspired divinely). He was sweating so much so that the drops of the sweat were dropping like pearls though it was a (cold) wintry day.

When that state of Allah's Apostle was over, he was smiling and the first word he said, 'Aisha! Thank Allah, for Allah has declared your innocence.'

My mother told me to go to Allah's Apostle .

I replied, 'By Allah I will not go to him and will not thank but Allah.'

So Allah revealed: "Verily! They who spread the slander are a gang among you . . ." (24:11)

When Allah gave the declaration of my Innocence, Abu Bakr, who used to provide for Mistah bin Uthatha for he was his relative, said, 'By Allah, I will never provide Mistah with anything because of what he said about Aisha.' But Allah later revealed: "And let not those who are good and wealthy among you swear not to help their kinsmen, those in need and those who left their homes in Allah's Cause. Let them forgive and overlook. Do you not wish that Allah should forgive you? Verily! Allah is Oft-forgiving, Most Merciful." (24:22)

After that Abu Bakr said, 'Yes ! By Allah! I like that Allah should forgive me,' and resumed helping Mistah whom he used to help before.

Allah's Apostle also asked Zainab bint Jahsh (*another wife of the Prophet*) about me saying, 'What do you know and what did you see?'

She replied, 'O Allah's Apostle! I refrain to claim hearing or seeing what I have not heard or seen. By Allah, I know nothing except goodness about Aisha.'

Aisha further added "Zainab was competing with me (in her beauty and the Prophet's love), yet Allah protected her (from being malicious), for she had piety."

Bukhari 48.829

In another story about a loss necklace, Aisha is hit by her father for her carelessness.

Narrated 'Aisha:

We set out with Allahs Apostle on one of his journeys till we reached Al-Baida' or Dhatul-Jaish, a necklace of mine was broken (and lost). Allah's Apostle stayed there to search for it, and so did the people along with him. There was no water at that place, so the people went to Abu- Bakr As-Siddiq and said, "Don't you see what 'Aisha has done? She has made Allah's Apostle and the people stay where there is no water and they have no water with them."

Abu Bakr came while Allah's Apostle was sleeping with his head on my thigh, He said, to me: "You have detained Allah's Apostle and the people where there is no water and they have no water with them." So he admonished me and said what Allah wished him to say and hit me on my flank with his hand.

Nothing prevented me from moving (because of pain) but the position of Allah's Apostle on my thigh. Allah's Apostle got up when dawn broke and there was no water. So Allah revealed the Divine Verses of Tayammum (4:43). So they all performed Tayammum (*ablution with sand*).

Usaid bin Hudair said, "O the family of Abu Bakr! This is not the first blessing of yours." Then the camel on which I was riding was caused to move from its place and the necklace was found beneath it.

Bukhari 7.330

What Aisha Saw

The following hadith is from *The Book of Prayers* (Kitab Al-Salat)' of Sahih Muslim; it begins with a typical introduction with the narrator identifying himself, and if it is hearsay, as most are, who he heard it from, followed by some atypical comments from his audience:

Muhammad b. Qais said (to the people): Should I not narrate to you (a hadith of the Holy Prophet) on my authority and on the authority of my mother? We thought that he meant the mother who had given him birth. He (Muhammad b. Qais) then reported that it was 'A'isha who had narrated this: Should I not narrate to you about myself and about the Messenger of Allah (may peace be upon him)? We said: Yes.

From Aisha we learn that it all started when she joined her husband for an intimate moment, after which, thinking she is asleep God's Messenger leaves her side.

She said: When it was my turn for Allah's Messenger (may peace be upon him) to spend the night with me, he turned his side, put on his mantle and took off his shoes and placed them near his feet, and spread the corner of his shawl on his bed and then lay down till he thought that I had gone to sleep. He took hold of his mantle slowly and put on the shoes slowly, and opened the door and went out and then closed it lightly.

Aisha is not asleep and decides to follow the Prophet outside where she observes God's Messenger doing hand gestures, after which they both return to the house, Aisha rushing ahead of her husband and hopping into bed hoping he is none the wiser.

I covered my head, put on my veil and tightened my waist wrapper, and then went out following his steps till he reached Baqi'. He stood there and he stood for a long time. He then lifted his hands three times, and then returned and

> I also returned. He hastened his steps and I also hastened my steps. He ran and I too ran. He came (to the house) and I also came (to the house). I, however, preceded him and I entered (the house), and as I lay down in the bed, he (the Holy Prophet) entered the (house), and said:

The Prophet is no fool, he notices she is out of breath and asks the obvious question; and she better tell him the truth because if she does not, Allah will tell on her.

> Why is it, O 'A'isha, that you are out of breath? I said: There is nothing. He said: Tell me or the Subtle and the Aware would inform me.

Aisha tells whatever she tells God s Messenger, swearing it is the truth, and this is when her husband strikes her.

> I said: Messenger of Allah, may my father and mother be ransom for you, and then I told him (the whole story). He said: Was it the darkness (of your shadow) that I saw in front of me? I said: Yes. He struck me on the chest which caused me pain, and then said: Did you think that Allah and His Apostle would deal unjustly with you? She said: Whatsoever the people conceal, Allah will know it.

At this point, the Prophet feels compel to explain to an obviously skeptical young woman why she did not observe him and the angel Gabriel in animated conversation; one of the reason being that she was not appropriately dressed.

> He said: Gabriel came to me when you saw me. He called me and he concealed it from you. I responded to his call, but I too concealed it from you (for he did not come to you), as you were not fully dressed. I thought that you had gone to sleep, and I did not like to awaken you, fearing that you may be frightened.

The hadith ends with the Prophet, on Gabriel's order, instructing his wife to go to a graveyard, where he will join her later, and pray for the dead as penance for having spied on her husband.

> He (Gabriel) said: Your Lord has commanded you to go to the inhabitants of Baqi' (to those lying in the graves) and beg pardon for them. I said: Messenger of Allah, how should I pray for them (How should I beg forgiveness for them)? He said: Say, Peace be upon the inhabitants of this city (graveyard) from among the Believers and the Muslims, and may Allah have mercy on those who have gone ahead of us, and those who come later on, and we shall, God willing, join you.

Sahih Muslim 4.2127

A Taste of Honey

A small percentage of the Koran is devoted to ensuring that God's Messenger has a varied and abundant sex life and controlling the Prophet's ever expanding household of wives, concubines and slave-girls. But that small amount of holy text devoted to the domestic and libido issues of just one man adds an inordinate amount of weirdness to a Book that is said to have been carved in a tablet in Paradise at the beginning of eternity and is meant to guide humanity to God, until He brings an end to His Creation. And even then it will still be around for as long as eternity endures.

A sample of this weirdness has to do with honey. In the Koran, Allah, Who is not amused as His tirade against the teenager and her slightly older accomplice will attest, does not tell us whose idea it was to use the Prophet's love of honey to have some fun at His Messenger's expense. For that we have to look to the hadiths. In the first two narrations we are told that the prank was concocted by the Prophet's two youngest wives, Aisha and Hafsa.

Narrated 'Ubaid bin 'Umar:

I heard 'Aisha saying, "The Prophet used to stay for a long while with Zanab bint Jahsh and drink honey at her house. So Hafsa and I decided that if the Prophet came to anyone of us, she should say [to] him, 'I detect the smell of Maghafir (a nasty smelling gum) in you. Have you eaten Maghafir?'"

So the Prophet visited one of them and she said to him similarly.

The Prophet said, "Never mind, I have taken some honey at the house of Zainab bint Jahsh, but I shall never drink of it anymore. So there was revealed: 'O Prophet! Why do you ban (for you) that which Allah has made lawful for you . . . If you two (wives of Prophet) turn in repentance to Allah,' (66:1-4) addressing Aisha and Hafsa. 'When the Prophet disclosed a matter in confidence to some of his wives.' (66:3) namely his saying: But I have taken some honey."

Bukhari 63.192

Ibn 'Abbas, a companion of the Prophet, only learned about who were the wives with whom Allah was so upset during a conversation he had with the Prophet's successor, Abu Bakr, while the former was answering the call of nature.

Narrated 'Abdullah bin 'Abbas:

I had been eager to ask 'Umar about the two ladies from among the wives of the Prophet regarding whom Allah said (in the Qur'an saying): If you two (wives of the Prophet namely Aisha and Hafsa) turn in repentance to Allah your hearts are indeed so inclined (to oppose what the Prophet likes) (66:4), till performed the Hajj along with 'Umar (and on our way back from Hajj) he went aside (to answer the call of nature) and I also went aside along with him carrying a tumbler of water. When he had answered the call of nature and returned. I poured water on his hands from the tumbler and he performed ablution.

I said, "O Chief of the believers! Who were the two ladies from among the wives of the Prophet to whom Allah said: 'If you two return in repentance (66:4)?'"

He said, "I am astonished at your question, O Ibn 'Abbas. They were Aisha and Hafsa."

Bukhari 43.648

In a longer narration about fun and games in the Prophet's house (perhaps it is about a separate incident), Allah's Messenger has a taste of honey at Hafsa's house, not Zanab's, and Aisha is the sole instigator.

Narrated 'Aisha:

Allah's Apostle was fond of honey and sweet edible things and (it was his habit) that after finishing the 'Asr prayer he would visit his wives and stay with one of them at that time. Once he went to Hafsa, the daughter of 'Umar and stayed with her more than usual. I got jealous and asked the reason for that. I was told that a lady of her folk had given her a skin filled with honey as a present, and that she made a syrup from it and gave it to the Prophet to drink (and that was the reason for the delay).

I said, "By Allah we will play a trick on him (to prevent him from doing so)."

So I said to Sada bint Zam'a "The Prophet will approach you, and when he comes near you, say: 'Have you taken Maghafir (a bad-smelling gum]?'

He will say, 'No.'

Then say to him: 'Then what is this bad smell which I smell from you?'

He will say to you, 'Hafsa made me drink honey syrup.'

Then say: 'Perhaps the bees of that honey had sucked the juice of the tree of Al-'Urfut.'

I shall also say the same. O you, Safiyya, say the same."

Later Sada said, "By Allah, as soon as he (the Prophet) stood at the door, I was about to say to him what you had ordered me to say because I was afraid of you."

So when the Prophet came near Sada, she said to him, "O Allah's Apostle! Have you taken Maghafir?"

He said, "No."

She said. "Then what is this bad smell which I detect on you?"

He said, "Hafsa made me drink honey syrup."

She said, "Perhaps its bees had sucked the juice of Al-'Urfut tree."

When he came to me, I also said the same, and when he went to Safiyya, she also said the same. And when the Prophet again went to Hafsa, she said, "O Allah's Apostle! Shall I give you more of that drink?"

He said, "I am not in need of it."

Sada said, "By Allah, we deprived him (of it)."

I said to her, "Keep quiet."'

Bukhari 63.193

At one point, the Prophet, tiring of his wives shenanigans threatened to divorce them all. It may have all been a charade to get them to behave.

Narrated 'Aisha:

When Allah's Apostle was ordered to give option to his wives, he started with me, saying, "I am going to mention to you something, but you shall not hasten (to give your reply) unless you consult your parents."

The Prophet knew that my parents would not order me to leave him.

Then he said, "Allah says: 'O Prophet (Muhammad)! Say to your wives: If you desire the life of this world and its glitter ... a great reward." (33:28-29)

I said, "Then why I consult my parents? Verily, I seek Allah, His Apostle and the Home of the Hereafter."

Then all the other wives of the Prophet did the same as I did.

Bukhari 60.309

Angels

Angels are everywhere in the Koran and in the hadiths. You cannot call yourself a Muslim if you do not believe in angels and everything Allah and His Messenger revealed about them. Some of what you will read here, and elsewhere about Allah's indispensable winged wonders may produce a sense of déja vu. If that should happen, chances are it will be a different narrator; a different companion recalling what God's Messenger said and did – more or less.

Allah is not a god who gets bored easily. Every day a billion or more believers pray five (Sunnis) and three (Shias) times a day and every day, Allah has the same conversion with his angels.

Narrated Abu Huraira:

Allah's Apostle said, "Allah has some angels who look for those who celebrate the Praises of Allah on the roads and paths. And when they find some people celebrating the Praises of Allah, they call each other, saying, 'Come to the object of your pursuit.'"

He added, "Then the angels encircle them with their wings up to the sky of the world."

He added. "(after those people celebrated the Praises of Allah, and the angels go back), their Lord, asks them (those angels) - though He knows better than them - 'What do My slaves say?'

The angels reply, 'They say: Subhan Allah, Allahu Akbar, and Alham-du-lillah (*Glorious is God, Allah is greater, Praise to God*)'.

Allah then says 'Did they see Me?'

The angels reply, 'No! By Allah, they didn't see You.'

Allah says, 'How it would have been if they saw Me?'

The angels reply, 'If they saw You, they would worship You more devoutly and celebrate Your Glory more deeply, and declare Your freedom from any resemblance to anything more often.'

Allah says (to the angels), 'What do they ask Me for?'

The angels reply, 'They ask You for Paradise.'

Allah says (to the angels), 'Did they see it?'

The angels say, 'No! By Allah, O Lord! They did not see it.'

Allah says, 'How it would have been if they saw it?'

The angels say, 'If they saw it, they would have greater covetousness for it and would seek It with greater zeal and would have greater desire for it.'

Allah says, 'From what do they seek refuge?'

The angels reply, 'They seek refuge from the (Hell) Fire.'

Allah says, 'Did they see it?'

The angels say, 'No By Allah, O Lord! They did not see it.'

Allah says, 'How it would have been if they saw it?'

The angels say, 'If they saw it they would flee from it with the extreme fleeing and would have extreme fear from it.'

Then Allah says, 'I make you witnesses that I have forgiven them.'"

Allah's Apostle added, "One of the angels would say, 'There was so-and-so amongst them, and he was not one of them, but he had just come for some need.' Allah would say, 'These are those people whose companions will not be reduced to misery.'"

Bukhari 75.417

Angels don't like those who don't spend to further Allah's plans for world domination.

Narrated Abu Huraira:

The Prophet said, "Every day two angels come down from Heaven and one of them says, 'O Allah! Compensate every person who spends in Your Cause,' and the other (angel) says, 'O Allah! Destroy every miser.'"

Bukhari 24.522

A lot of praying going on, of which Allah will be kept diligently informed by his angels.

Narrated Abu Huraira:

Allah's Apostle said, "(A group of) angels stay with you at night and (another group of) angels by daytime, and both groups gather at the time of the 'Asr and Fajr prayers. Then those angels who have stayed with you overnight, ascend (to Heaven) and Allah asks them (about you) - and He knows everything about you. 'In what state did you leave My slaves?' The angels reply, 'When we left them, they were praying, and when we reached them they were praying.'"

Bukhari 93.525

Try to avoid farting while praying if you want Allah to accept your prayer and the angels to keep interceding with Allah on your behalf.

Narrated Abu Huraira:

The Prophet said, "Allah does not accept prayer of anyone of you if he does hadath (passes wind) till he performs the ablution (anew)."

Bukhari 86.86

Narrated Abu Huraira:

Allah's Apostle said, "The angels keep on asking Allah's forgiveness for anyone of you, as long as he is at his Musalla (praying place) and he does not pass wind (Hadath). They say, 'O Allah! Forgive him, O Allah! be Merciful to him.'"

Bukhari 8.436

Say "Amin" at just the right time, and it will be as if you died in Allah's Cause.

Narrated Abu Huraira:

The Prophet said, "When the Imam says 'Amin', then you should all say 'Amin', for the angels say 'Amin' at that time, and he whose 'Amin' coincides with the 'Amin' of the angels, all his past sins will be forgiven."

Bukhari 75.411

It is an angel who informs Allah of a fetus' progress, and takes down Allah instructions as to what the future holds for the growing embryo.

Narrated Anas bin Malik:

The Prophet said, "Allah puts an angel in charge of the uterus and the angel says, 'O Lord, (it is) semen! O Lord, (it is now) a clot (*a glub of blood*)! O Lord, (it is now) a piece of flesh.' And then, if Allah wishes to complete its creation, the angel asks, 'O Lord, (will it be) a male or a female? A wretched (an evil doer) or a blessed (doer of good)? How much will his provisions be? What will his age be?' So all that is written while the creature is still in the mother's womb."

Bukhari 77.594

In another hadith, the Prophet is clearer as to what timeframe we are talking about here. The following saying of the Prophet may be important for those who would like to see Islam allow early term abortions. If Allah's Messenger says Allah breathes a soul into an embryo 120 days after conception, why not allow abortions until this takes place.

Narrated 'Abdullah:

Allah's Apostle, the truthful and truly-inspired, said, "Each one of you collected in the womb of his mother for forty days, and then turns into a clot for an equal period (of forty days) and turns into a piece of flesh for a similar period (of forty days) and then Allah sends an angel and orders him to write four things, i.e., his provision, his age, and whether he will be of the wretched or the blessed (in the Hereafter). Then the soul is breathed into him. And by Allah, a person among you (or a man) may do deeds of the people of the Fire till there is only a cubit or an arm-breadth distance between him and the Fire, but then that writing (which Allah has ordered the angel to write) precedes, and he does the deeds of the people of Paradise and enters it; and a man may do the deeds of the people of Paradise till there is only a cubit or two between him and Paradise, and then that writing precedes and he does the deeds of the people of the Fire and enters it."

Bukhari 77.593

Allah taught His angels how to write your good and bad deeds; therefore, I think it is safe to assume that in the following hadith, it is His angels who do most of the scribbling, not Allah personally.

Narrated Ibn 'Abbas:

The Prophet narrating about his Lord said, "Allah ordered (the appointed angels over you) that the good and the bad deeds be written, and He then showed (the way) how (to write). If somebody intends to do a good deed and he does not do it, then Allah will write for him a full good deed (in his account with Him); and if he intends to do a good deed and actually did it, then Allah will write for him (in his account) with Him (its reward equal) from ten to seven hundred times to many more times: and if somebody intended to do a bad deed and he does not do it, then Allah will write a full good deed (in his account) with Him, and if he intended to do it (a bad deed) and actually did it, then Allah will write one bad deed (in his account)."

Bukhari 76.498

Perhaps the most important thing some angels ever did was showing the Prophet around Paradise and Hell. God's Messenger's vivid reports about what he saw during these guided tours would not have been possible without the assistance of these selfless fearless guides. One hadith among more than a hundred about these informative out-of-this-world excursions:

Narrated Jabir:

The Prophet, said, "I entered Paradise and saw a palace and asked whose palace is this? They (the Angels) said, "This palace belongs to 'Umar bin Al-Khattab.' I intended to enter it, and nothing stopped me except my knowledge about your sense of Ghira (self-respect (O Umar).'"

Umar said, "O Allah's Apostle! Let my father and mother be sacrificed for you! O Allah's Prophet! How dare I think of my Ghira (self-respect) being offended by you?"

Bukhari 62.153

Angels have been known to quarrel among themselves.

Narrated Abu Said Al-Khudri:

The Prophet said, "Amongst the men of Bani (*tribe of*) Israel there was a man who had murdered ninety-nine persons. Then he set out asking (whether his repentance could be accepted or not). He came upon a monk and asked him if his repentance could be accepted. The monk replied in the negative and so the man killed him. He kept on asking till a man advised to go to such and such village. (So he left for it) but death overtook him on the way. While dying, he turned his chest towards that village (where he had hoped his repentance would be accepted), and so the angels of mercy and the angels of punishment quarreled amongst themselves regarding him. Allah ordered the village (towards which he was going) to come closer to him, and ordered the village (whence he had come), to go far away, and then He ordered the angels to measure the distances between his body and the two villages. So he was found to be one span closer to the village (he was going to). So he was forgiven."

Bukhari 56.676

Angels who joined the Prophet at the battle of Badr were also the best of the bunch, as their commander reminded God's Messenger.

Narrated Rifaa (who was one of the Badr warriors):

Gabriel came to the Prophet and said, "How do you look upon the warriors of Badr among yourselves?"

The Prophet said, "As the best of the Muslims" or said a similar statement.

On that, Gabriel said, "And so are the Angels who participated in the Badr (battle)."

Bukhari 59.327

Who watches you not having sex:

Narrated Abu Huraira:

The Prophet said, "If a man invites his wife to sleep with him and she refuses to come to him, then the angels send their curses on her till morning."

Bukhari 62.121

Narrated Abu Huraira:

The Prophet said, "If a woman spends the night deserting her husband's bed (does not sleep with him), then the angels send their curses on her till she comes back (to her husband)."

Bukhari 61.122

If you want angels to show up at your place, get rid of any pictures including cushions with pictures.

Narrated 'Aisha:

I purchased a cushion with pictures on it. The Prophet (came and) stood at the door but did not enter. I said (to him), "I repent to Allah for what (the guilt) I have done."

He said, "What is this cushion?"

I said, "It is for you to sit on and recline on."

He said, "The makers of these pictures will be punished on the Day of Resurrection and it will be said to them, 'Make alive what you have created.' Moreover, the angels do not enter a house where there are pictures."

Bukhari 72.840

Apostates

Narrated 'Abdullah:

Allah's Apostle said, "The blood of a Muslim who confesses that none has the right to be worshipped but Allah and that I am His Apostle, cannot be shed except in three cases: In Qisas (the right of the family of a murder victim to demand the murderer be put to death) for murder, a married person who commits illegal sexual intercourse and the one who reverts from Islam (apostate) and leaves the Muslims."

Bukhari 83.17

Kill those who unconvert (sic) after converting to Islam and those who were born into the perfect religion and now would leave it for one less perfect or no religion at all. Is it any wonder Islam has been on a continuous growth curve since its founding?

Kill the apostates, and get a reward!

Narrated 'Ali:

Whenever I tell you a narration from Allah's Apostle, by Allah, I would rather fall down from the sky than ascribe a false statement to him, but if I tell you something between me and you (not a Hadith) then it was indeed a trick (i.e., I may say things just to cheat my enemy).

No doubt I heard Allah's Apostle saying, "During the last days there will appear some young foolish people who will say the best words but their faith will not go beyond their throats (i.e. they will have no faith) and will go out from (leave) their religion as an arrow goes out of the game. So, wherever you find them, kill them, for whoever kills them shall have reward on the Day of Resurrection."

Bukhari 84.64

Ali, the Prophet's son-in-law and the fourth Caliph (Leader of the Believers), second only to his father-in-law in esteem among the Shiites, used to burned apostates.

Narrated Ikrima:

Ali burnt some people and this news reached Ibn 'Abbas, who said, "Had I been in his place I would not have burnt them, as the Prophet said, 'Don't punish (anybody) with

Allah's Punishment.' No doubt, I would have killed them, for the Prophet said, 'If somebody (a Muslim) discards his religion, kill him.'"

Bukhari 52.260

Narrated Abu Huraira:

Allah's Apostle sent us in a mission (i.e. an army-unit) and said, "If you find so-and-so and so-and-so, burn both of them with fire."

When we intended to depart, Allah's Apostle said, "I have ordered you to burn so-and-so and so-and-so, and it is none but Allah Who punishes with fire, so, if you find them, kill them."

Bukhari 52.259

The casual killing of an apostate:

Narrated Abu Burda:

Abu Musa said, "I came to the Prophet along with two men (from the tribe) of Ash'ariyin, one on my right and the other on my left, while Allah's Apostle was brushing his teeth (with a Siwak), and both men asked him for some employment. The Prophet said, 'O Abu Musa (O 'Abdullah bin Qais!).' I said, 'By Him Who sent you with the Truth, these two men did not tell me what was in their hearts and I did not feel (realize) that they were seeking employment.' As if I were looking now at his Siwak being drawn to a corner under his lips, and he said, 'We never (or, we do not) appoint for our affairs anyone who seeks to be employed. But O Abu Musa! (or 'Abdullah bin Qais!) go to Yemen.'"

The Prophet then sent Mu'adh bin Jabal (*another companion of the Prophet and one of the most revered scholars of Islam*) after him and when Mu'adh reached him, he spread out a cushion for him and requested him to get down (and sit on the cushion). Behold: There was a fettered man beside Abu Muisa.

Mu'adh asked, "Who is this (man)?"

Abu Muisa said, "He was a Jew and became a Muslim and then reverted back to Judaism."

Then Abu Muisa requested Mu'adh to sit down but Mu'adh said, "I will not sit down till he has been killed. This is the judgment of Allah and His Apostle (for such cases) and repeated it thrice.

Then Abu Musa ordered that the man be killed, and he was killed.

Abu Musa added, "Then we discussed the night prayers and one of us said, 'I pray and sleep, and I hope that Allah will reward me for my sleep as well as for my prayers.'"

Bukhari 84.58

The first person the Prophet ordered killed after the conquest of Mecca was an apostate.

Narrated Anas bin Malik:

Allah's Apostle entered Mecca in the year of its Conquest wearing an Arabian helmet on his head and when the Prophet took it off, a person came and said, "Ibn Khatal is holding the covering of the Ka'ba (taking refuge in the Ka'ba)."

The Prophet said, "Kill him."

Bukhari 29.72

Khatal had been one of the Prophet's Zakat (charity) collectors. He later abandoned Islam and returned to Mecca. He was one of six men and four women God's Messenger ordered assassinated upon taking Mecca. The Prophet, in a rambling hadith which touches on both the sacred and the mundane, justified the assassinations. This was after promising the Meccans that he would not harm anyone if the city surrendered without a fight. Allah, it would seem, had consented to suspend His interdiction, if only temporally and only for His Messenger, against killing anyone in the sanctuary that was His City.

Narrated Abu Huraira:

In the year of the Conquest of Mecca, the tribe of Khuza'a killed a man from the tribe of Bani Laith in revenge for a killed person, belonging to them.

They informed the Prophet about it. So he rode his Rahila (she-camel for riding) and addressed the people saying, "Allah held back the killing from Mecca. (The sub-narrator is in doubt whether the Prophet said 'elephant or killing' as the Arabic words standing for these words have great similarity in shape), but He (Allah) let His Apostle and the believers overpower the infidels of Mecca. Beware! (Mecca is a sanctuary) Verily! Fighting in Mecca was not permitted for anyone before me nor will it be permitted for anyone after me. It (war) in it was made legal for me for few hours or so on that day. No doubt it is at this moment a sanctuary, it is not allowed to uproot its thorny shrubs or to uproot its trees or to pick up its Luqatt (fallen things) except by a person who will look for its owner (announce it publicly). And if somebody is killed, then his closest relative has the right to choose one of the two, the blood money (Diyya) or retaliation having the killer killed."

In the meantime a man from Yemen came and said, "O Allah's Apostle! Get that written for me."

The Prophet ordered his companions to write that for him.

Then a man from Quraish said, "Except Al-Iqhkhir (a type of grass that has good smell) O Allah's Apostle, as we use it in our houses and graves."

The Prophet said, "Except Al-Iqhkhir. Al-Idhkhir is allowed to be plucked."

Bukhari 3.112

Truth had triumph over disbelief, and disbelief had to die; both literally and figuratively.

Narrated 'Abdullah bin Masud:

The Prophet entered Mecca and (at that time) there were three hundred-and-sixty idols around the Ka'ba. He started stabbing the idols with a stick he had in his hand and reciting: "Truth (Islam) has come and Falsehood (disbelief) has vanished."

Bukhari 43.658

The Unwelcoming Grave of an Apostate

The fantastic story of a Christian who became a Muslim, who became a Christian and then died, and whose body was repeatedly rejected by his grave is not explicitly attributed to the Prophet, but Bukhari thought it important enough to include in his collection.

Narrated Anas:

There was a Christian who embraced Islam and read Surat-al-Baqara and Al-Imran, and he used to write (the revelations) for the Prophet. Later on he returned to Christianity again and he used to say: "Muhammad knows nothing but what I have written for him."

Then Allah caused him to die, and the people buried him, but in the morning they saw that the earth had thrown his body out.

They said, "This is the act of Muhammad and his companions. They dug the grave of our companion and took his body out of it because he had run away from them."

They again dug the grave deeply for him, but in the morning they again saw that the earth had thrown his body out.

They [again] said, "This is an act of Muhammad and his companions. They dug the grave of our companion and threw his body outside it, for he had run away from them."

They dug the grave for him as deep as they could, but in the morning they again saw that the earth had thrown his body out. So they believed that what had befallen him was not done by human beings and had to leave him thrown (on the ground).

Bukhari 56.814

Babies

Every child is born a Muslim with no defects.

Narrated Abu Huraira:

The Prophet said, "Every child is born with a true faith of Islam (i.e. to worship none but Allah Alone) and his parents convert him to Judaism or Christianity or Magianism, as an animal delivers a perfect baby animal. Do you find it mutilated?"

Bukhari 23.467

It is not the slap of the doctor or the midwife which makes a baby cry after exiting the birth canal.

Narrated Said bin Al-Musaiyab:

Abu Huraira said, "I heard Allah's Apostle saying, 'There is none born among the off-spring of Adam, but Satan touches it. A child therefore, cries loudly at the time of birth because of the touch of Satan, except Mary and her child.'"

Bukhari 55.641

The sex of an individual is decided when the gestation process is well advanced.

Narrated Anas bin Malik:

The Prophet said, "Allah has appointed an angel in the womb, and the angel says, 'O Lord! A drop of discharge (i.e. of semen), O Lord! a clot, O Lord! a piece of flesh.' And then, if Allah wishes to complete the child's creation, the angel will say. 'O Lord! A male or a female? O Lord! wretched or blessed (in religion)? What will his livelihood be? What will his age be?' The angel writes all this while the child is in the womb of its mother."

Bukhari 55.550

Islamic scholars often point to the words "He created man from a clot" in the following hadith as proof that Allah knew more about conception then was known at the time of the Prophet (although not unknown to the Greeks of antiquity). God's Messenger, in the following hadith, explains what Allah meant by clot, and it is not a zygote by any stretch of the imagination, it is something completely alien to what we know about the gestation process.

Narrated 'Abdullah bin Mus'ud:

Allah's Apostle, the true and truly inspired said, "(The matter of the Creation of) a human being is put together in the womb of the mother in forty days, and then he becomes a clot of thick blood for a similar period, and then a piece of flesh for a similar period. Then Allah sends an angel who is ordered to write four things. He is ordered to write down his (i.e. the new creature's) deeds, his livelihood, his (date of) death, and whether he will be blessed or wretched (in religion). Then the soul is breathed into him. So, a man amongst you may do (good deeds till there is only a cubit between him and Paradise and then what has been written for him decides his behavior and he starts doing (evil) deeds characteristic of the people of the (Hell) Fire. And similarly a man amongst you may do (evil) deeds till there is only a cubit between him and the (Hell) Fire, and then what has been written for him decides his behavior, and he starts doing deeds characteristic of the people of Paradise."

Bukhari 54.430

The mother's sperm, if she ejaculates before her husband, is what causes a child to resemble its mother instead of the father.

Narrated Um Salama:

Um-Sulaim came to Allah's Apostle and said, "Verily, Allah is not shy of (telling you) the truth. Is it necessary for a woman to take a bath after she has a wet dream (nocturnal sexual discharge?)"

The Prophet replied, "Yes, if she notices a discharge."

Um Salama, then covered her face and asked, "O Allah's Apostle! Does a woman get a discharge?"

He replied, "Yes, let your right hand be in dust (an Arabic expression you say to a person when you contradict his statement meaning 'you will not achieve goodness'), and that is why the son resembles his mother."

Bukhari 3:132

Umm Salama, wife number six, was thirty when she accepted an offer of marriage from God's Messenger after her husband died from wounds sustained in battle. The Prophet's answer about a woman's ejaculate brought a smile to a mature woman who may have known better.

Narrated Abu Salama:

Um Salama said, "O Allah's Apostle! Allah does not refrain from saying the truth! Is it obligatory for a woman to take a bath after she gets nocturnal discharge?"

He said, "Yes, if she notices the water (i.e. discharge)."

Um Salama wife smiled and said, "Does a woman get discharge?"

Allah's Apostle said. "Then why does a child resemble (its mother)?"

Bukhari 55.545

Wild snakes can trigger a spontaneous abortion, but perhaps not the domesticated ones.

Narrated Ibn Umar:

That he heard the Prophet delivering a sermon on the pulpit saying, "Kill snakes and kill Dhu-at-Tufyatain (i.e. a snake with two white lines on its back) and ALBATROSS (i.e. a snake with short or mutilated tail) for they destroy the sight of one's eyes and bring about abortion."

('Abdullah bin 'Umar further added): Once while I was chasing a snake in order, to kill it, Abu Lubaba called me saying: "Don't kill it," I said. "Allah's Apostle ordered us to kill snakes." He said, "But later on he prohibited the killing of snakes living in the houses." (Az-Zubri said. "Such snakes are called Al-Awamir.")

Bukhari 54.518

The price of an aborted fetus:

Narrated Abu Huraira:

Two women from the tribe of Hudhail (fought with each other) and one of them threw (a stone at) the other, causing her to have a miscarriage and Allah's Apostle gave his verdict that the killer (of the fetus) should give a male or female slave (as a Diya i.e. blood-money).

Bukhari 83.41

Bible Stories

Bibles Stories should be read in conjunction with *Shared Prophets, Boreal Books (2012)*, or *The Old Testament vs. the Koran Parts 1 and II* and *The New Testament vs. the Koran* of *Pain, Pleasure and Prejudice, Boreal Books (2012)*.

All the Prophet's recollections of past events could be considered apocryphal tales (stories of doubtful authenticity), with his remembrances of stuff the Bible mostly left out the most deserving of scepticism, much of it the results of visions into the pass and from ethereal conversations he had with the angel Gabriel.

Narrated Ibn Abbas:

The Prophet once came to us and said, "All the nations were displayed in front of me, and I saw a large multitude of people covering the horizon. Somebody said, 'This is Moses and his followers.'"

Bukhari 55.622

Abraham

Abraham was a skyscraper of a man.

Narrated Samura:

Allah's Apostle said, "Two persons came to me at night (in [a]dream) (and took me along with them). We passed by a tall man who was so tall that I was not able to see his head and that person was Abraham."

Bukhari 55.573

On two separate occasions, in the Koran, Abraham's people attempt to burn him to a crisp, and both times the Patriarch of Muslims and Jews walks out of the fire without even a hair being singed. The second time, Abraham has had enough and asks Allah to give him a new people to lead. We don't know if Allah acquiesced to the Patriarch's request, what we do know from the hadiths is that God's Messenger took revenge on the specie of lizard that supplied the fire with which Abraham's kin tried to incinerate him.

Narrated Um Sharik:

Allah's Apostle ordered that the salamander should be killed and said, "It (i.e. the salamander) blew (the fire) on Abraham."

Bukhari 55.579

Sarah

There is no reliable record of written Hebrew before the tenth century B.C. the principal language of the Hebrew Bible. That is well after the resettlement of the Israelis in Canaan after their escape from Egypt ... this means that the supposedly historical stories of at least the first books of the Bible were preserved originally not as written text but as oral tradition, beginning with the wonderings of Abraham and ending with the resettlement of Canaan under Joshua. What we are reading are oral tales, collected and edited for the first (but not the last time) in the tenth century during and after the kingship of David.

Thomas Cahill, The Gifts of the Jew, Anchor Books, 1998

The oral histories of the Jewish people, modified and adapted to fit Allah's narrative are the scriptural history of the Koran. Adding to that scriptural history is the Prophet's own recollections of stories from the Bible. Like his Mentor, God's Messenger reveals previously unknown details which are meant to correct errors in or add to the Biblical accounts. The story of Abraham's visit to the land ruled by Abimelek – an anonymous king or tyrant in the Prophet's account – where Abraham pretends that Sarah is his sister, prompting the king to take her as his wife, is one of those Prophet-enhanced narratives.

The "Apostle" in Sarah's declaration of "O Allah! If I have believed in You and Your Apostle" in God's Messenger's account, which follows, can only be Muhammad. This is not that unusual.

Narrated Abu Huraira:

The Prophet said, "The Prophet Abraham emigrated with Sarah and entered a village where there was a king or a tyrant. (The king) was told that Abraham had entered (the village) accompanied by a woman who was one of the most charming women. So, the king sent for Abraham and asked, 'O Abraham! Who is this lady accompanying you?'

Abraham replied, 'She is my sister (i.e. in religion).'

Then Abraham returned to her and said, 'Do not contradict my statement, for I have informed them that you are my sister. By Allah, there are no true believers on this land except you and I.' Then Abraham sent her to the king.

When the king got to her, she got up and performed ablution, prayed and said, 'O Allah! If I have believed in You and Your Apostle, and have saved my private parts from everybody except my husband, then please do not let this pagan overpower me.'

On that the king fell in a mood of agitation and started moving his legs. Seeing the condition of the king, Sarah said, 'O Allah! If he should die, the people will say that I have killed him.'

The king regained his power, and proceeded towards her but she got up again and performed ablution, prayed and said, 'O Allah! If I have believed in You and Your Apostle and have kept my private parts safe from all except my husband, then please do not let this pagan overpower me.' The king again fell in a mood of agitation and started moving his legs.

On seeing that state of the king, Sarah said, 'O Allah! If he should die, the people will say that I have killed him.'

The king got either two or three attacks, and after recovering from the last attack he said, 'By Allah! You have sent a Satan to me. Take her to Abraham and give her Ajar.'

So she came back to Abraham and said, 'Allah humiliated the pagan and gave us a slave-girl for service.'"

Bukhari 34.420

In a second-hand narration of what the Prophet said, it's not wobbly legs but a paralyzed hand which stops the king/tyrant from having his way with Sarah, and the slave he gives her for inconveniencing her is no other than Hagar the mother of the Arabs.

Narrated Abu Huraira:

Abraham did not tell a lie except on three occasion. Twice for the Sake of Allah when he said, "I am sick," and he said, "(I have not done this but) the big idol has done it (*Koran 21:63*)." The (third was) that while Abraham and Sarah (his wife) were going (on a journey) they passed by (the territory of) a tyrant. Someone said to the tyrant, "This man (i.e. Abraham) is accompanied by a very charming lady."

So, he sent for Abraham and asked him about Sarah saying, "Who is this lady?"

Abraham said, "She is my sister."

Abraham went to Sarah and said, "O Sarah! There are no believers on the surface of the earth except you and I. This man asked me about you and I have told him that you are my sister, so don't contradict my statement."

The tyrant then called Sarah and when she went to him, he tried to take hold of her with his hand, but (his hand got stiff and) he was confounded. He asked Sarah. "Pray to Allah for me, and I shall not harm you." So Sarah asked Allah to cure him and he got cured. He tried to take hold of her for the second time, but (his hand got as stiff as or stiffer than before and) was more confounded. He again requested Sarah, "Pray to Allah for me, and I will not harm you."

Sarah asked Allah again and he became alright. He then called one of his guards (who had brought her) and said, "You have not brought me a human being but have brought me a devil."

The tyrant then gave Hajar as a girl-servant to Sarah. Sarah came back (to Abraham) while he was praying. Abraham, gesturing with his hand, asked, "What has happened?"

She replied, "Allah has spoiled the evil plot of the infidel (or immoral person) and gave me Hajar for service."

(Abu Huraira then addressed his listeners saying, "That (Hajar) was your mother, O Bani Ma-is-Sama (i.e. the Arabs, the descendants of Ishmael, Hajar's son)."

Bukhari 55.578

The Prophet in another, shorter narration makes it clear it was a leg issue that impeded the king/tyrant.

Narrated Abu Huraira:

Allah's Apostle said, "(The Prophet) Abraham migrated with his wife Sarah till he reached a town where there was a king or a tyrant who sent a message, to Abraham, ordering him to send Sarah to him. So when Abraham had sent Sarah, the tyrant got up, intending to do evil with her, but she got up and performed ablution and prayed and said, 'O Allah! If I have believed in You and in Your Apostle, then do not empower this oppressor over me.' So he (the king) had an epileptic fit and started moving his legs violently."

Bukhari 85.82

Hagar

Muslims believe that after Abraham's wife Sarah became pregnant, he was told by Allah to take Hagar and their son Ishmael (Muslims consider Hagar a legitimate wife of Abraham and Ishmael, not Isaac, the Patriarchs' first born son) from their home in Palestine to the desert wilderness of Arabia and leave them there. When their water ran out, Hagar ran frantically between the hills of Safa and Marwa until she collapsed next to her son who struck his foot on the ground causing a spring to gush forth, the famous well of Zam Zam. God's Messenger explained why this spring today is not a stream. It's all Hagar's fault, and he hopes Allah will forgive the mother of the Arabs for what she did.

Narrated Ibn 'Abbas:

The Prophet said, "May Allah be merciful to the mother of Ishmael! If she had left the water of Zam-Zam (fountain) as it was, (without constructing a basin for keeping the water), (or said, "If she had not taken handfuls of its water"), it would have been a flowing stream.

Jurhum (an Arab tribe) came and asked her, 'May we settle at your dwelling?' She said, 'Yes, but you have no right to possess the water.'

They agreed."

Bukhari 40.556

Adam

Poor omnipotent Allah, the abuse He suffers to this day started with the son, or more accurately the sons of Adam.

Narrated Abu Huraira:

Allah's Apostle said, "Allah said, 'The son of Adam hurts me for he abuses Time though I am Time: in My Hands are all things, and I cause the revolution of day and night.'"

Bukhari 60.351

How the son(s) of Adam lie about and abuse Allah:

Narrated Ibn Abbas:

The Prophet said, "Allah said, 'The son of Adam tells a lie against me though he has no right to do so, and he abuses Me though he has no right to do so. As for his telling a lie against Me, it is that he claims that I cannot recreate him as I created him before; and as for his abusing Me, it is his statement that I have offspring. No! Glorified be Me! I am far from taking a wife or offspring. "

Bukhari 60.9

The son(s) of Adam are one avaricious bunch indeed!

Narrated Sahl bin Sa'd:

I heard Ibn Az-Zubair who was on the pulpit at Mecca, delivering a sermon, saying, "O men! The Prophet used to say, 'If the son of Adam were given a valley full of gold, he would love to have a second one; and if he were given the second one, he would love to have a third, for nothing fills the belly of Adam's son except dust. And Allah forgives he who repents to Him.'"

Ubai said, "We considered this as a saying from the Qur'an till the Sura (beginning with) 'The mutual rivalry for piling up of worldly things diverts you..' (102:1) was revealed."

Bukhari 76.446

How Allah makes the son(s) of Adam, whose destiny He has pre-ordained, spend some of their wealth.

Narrated Abu Huraira:

The Prophet said (that Allah said), "Vowing does not bring to the son of Adam anything I have not already written in his fate, but vowing is imposed on him by way of fore ordainment. Through vowing I make a miser spend of his wealth."

Bukhari 77.606

Like in the Old Testament, adultery is more than just doing it. In the hadiths it is your private parts, which the Prophet may have literally believed had a mind of their own, that ultimately decide whether you actually do it.

Narrated Ibn 'Abbas:

I did not see anything so resembling minor sins as what Abu Huraira said from the Prophet, who said, "Allah has written for the son of Adam his inevitable share of adultery whether he is aware of it or not: The adultery of the eye is the looking (at something which is sinful to look at), and the adultery of the tongue is to utter (what it is unlawful to utter), and the inner self wishes and longs for (adultery) and the private parts turn that into reality or refrain from submitting to the temptation."

Bukhari 77.609

What Allah has ordained for the daughters of Adam:

Narrated Al-Qasim:

'Aisha said, "We set out with the sole intention of

performing Hajj and when we reached Sarif, (a place six miles from Mecca) I got my menses. Allah's Apostle came to me while I was weeping. He said 'What is the matter with you? Have you got your menses?' I replied, 'Yes.' He said, 'This is a thing which Allah has ordained for the daughters of Adam. So do what all the pilgrims do with the exception of the Taw-af (Circumambulation) round the Ka'ba.'"

'Aisha added, "Allah's Apostle sacrificed cows on behalf of his wives."

Bukhari 6.293

Cain

It was of course Cain who started what became a tradition of unjustified homicides i.e. murders not sanctioned by Allah.

Narrated Abdullah:

Allah's Apostle said, "Whenever a person is murdered unjustly, there is a share from the burden of the crime on the first son of Adam for he was the first to start the tradition of murdering."

Bukhari 55.552

David

How David got anything done is a mystery!

Narrated Abdullah bin Amr:

Allah's Apostle said to me, "The most beloved fasting to Allah was the fasting of (the Prophet) David who used to fast on alternate days. And the most beloved prayer to Allah was the prayer of David who used to sleep for (the first) half of the night and pray for 1/3 of it and (again) sleep for a sixth of it."

Bukhari 55.631

It must have been difficult for King David due to his weaken state brought on by fasting half the time, his lack of sleep, his time spent at prayer, to work enough hours as a manual labourer to earn enough to feed himself, his seven wives and twenty-one children.

Narrated Abu Huraira:

The Prophet said, "The reciting of the Zabur (i.e. Psalms) was made easy for David. He used to order that his riding animals be saddled, and would finish reciting the Zabur before they were saddled. And he would never eat except from the earnings of his manual work."

Bukhari 55.628

Eve's Burden

If it wasn't for the Jews we would have no need of refrigerators to keep meat from spoiling, and it is Eve's fault if women are cruelly stoned to death for adultery.

Narrated Abu Huraira:

The Prophet said, "Were it not for Bani (children of) Israel, meat would not decay; and were it not for Eve, no woman would ever betray her husband."

Bukhari 55.611

Jesus

Jesus was the next to last Prophet of Allah, Muhammad being the last. If all Prophets are paternal brothers, meaning they share the same father, then who is the daddy of them all?

Narrated Abu Huraira:

I heard Allah's Apostle saying, "I am the nearest of all the people to the son of Mary, and all the prophets are paternal brothers, and there has been no prophet between me and him (i.e. Jesus)."

Bukhari 55.651

Jesus was a hard Prophet to fool.

Narrated Abu Huraira:

The Prophet said, "Jesus, seeing a man stealing, asked him, 'Did you steal?' He said, 'No, by Allah, except Whom there is None who has the right to be worshipped' Jesus said, 'I believe in Allah and suspect my eyes.'"

Bukhari 55.653

Almost like in the Bible, Jesus, during the End Times, will lead the forces of good, in this instance the Muslims, against those of evil, and you can guess who those will be.

Narrated Abu Huraira:

Allah's Apostle said, "By Him in Whose Hands my soul is, surely (Jesus,) the son of Mary will soon descend amongst you and will judge mankind justly (as a Just Ruler); he will break the Cross and kill the pigs and there will be no Jizya (i.e. taxation taken from non-Muslims). Money will be in abundance so that nobody will accept it, and a single prostration to Allah (in prayer) will be better than the whole world and whatever is in it."

Abu Huraira added "If you wish, you can recite (this verse of the Holy Book): 'And there is none Of the people of the Scriptures (Jews and Christians) But must believe in him (i.e. Jesus as an Apostle of Allah and a human being) Before his death. And on the Day of Judgment He will be a witness Against them.' (4:159) "

Bukhari 55.657

Jesus told his brethren to love their fellow Jews as they loved themselves. Over time this message has changed to be all-inclusive. It may be too much to hope that a comparable message of the Prophet will ever experience the same transformation into a message of universal love for one another.

Narrated Anas:

The Prophet said, "None of you will have faith till he wishes for his (Muslim) brother what he likes for himself."

Bukhari 2.12

Job

Narrated Abu Huraira:

The Prophet said, "While Job was naked, taking a bath, a swarm of gold locusts fell on him and he started collecting them in his garment. His Lord called him, 'O Job! Have I not made you rich enough to need what you see? He said, 'Yes, O Lord! But I cannot dispense with your Blessing.'"

Bukhari 55.604

Joshua

In the Bible, God is angry at the Israelites because after He has stopped the sun at Jericho so that they may complete the extermination of every man, woman and child in the city, one of them has disobeyed Joshua's order that everything found in Jericho must be destroyed except "for all the silver and gold, and the articles of bronze and iron, [which] are dedicated to the Lord and must go into the Lord's treasury."

In the Bible, the culprit, at Joshua's insistence, confesses and he and his family are put to death, and God is appeased.

The Koran is in agreement that a prophet, assumed to be Joshua, stopped the sun in its tracks and was victorious and that someone stole what God expected to be destroyed i.e. burnt. In the Koran, no one is put the death, and the theft causes Allah to have a change of heart about plunder, that it rightfully belongs to the believers for it can only make them stronger, and that is good thing.

Narrated Abu Huraira:

The Prophet said, "A prophet amongst the prophets carried out a holy military expedition, so he said to his followers, 'Anyone who has married a woman and wants to consummate the marriage, and has not done so yet, should not accompany me; nor should a man who has built a house but has not completed its roof; nor a man who has sheep or she-camels and is waiting for the birth of their young ones.'

So, the prophet carried out the expedition and when he reached that town at the time or nearly at the time of the 'Asr prayer, he said to the sun, 'O sun! You are under Allah's Order and I am under Allah's Order O Allah! Stop it (i.e. the sun) from setting.'

It was stopped till Allah made him victorious. Then he collected the booty and the fire came to burn it, but it did not burn it. He said (to his men), 'Some of you have stolen something from the booty. So one man from every tribe should give me a pledge of allegiance by shaking hands with me.' (They did so and) the hand of a man got stuck over the hand of their prophet.

Then that prophet said (to the man), 'The theft has been committed by your people. So all the persons of your tribe should give me the pledge of allegiance by shaking hands with me.' The hands of two or three men got stuck over the hand of their prophet and he said, 'You have committed the theft.'

Then they brought a head of gold like the head of a cow and put it there, and the fire came and consumed the booty. The Prophet added: Then Allah saw our weakness and disability, so he made booty legal for us."

Bukhari 53.353

Moses

Of all the prophets from the Old Testament, Moses was Muhammad favourite. God's Messenger saw himself very much as the Arab's Moses to the extent that he claimed him for the believers.

Narrated Ibn 'Abbas:

The Prophet came to Medina and saw the Jews fasting on the day of Ashura. He asked them about that. They replied, "This is a good day, the day on which Allah rescued Bani Israel from their enemy. So, Moses fasted this day."

The Prophet said, "We have more claim over Moses than you." So, the Prophet fasted on that day and ordered (the Muslims) to fast (on that day).

Bukhari 31.222

Moses had curly hair, a brown complexion and rode a red camel.

Narrated Mujahid:

That when the people mentioned before Ibn 'Abbas that the Dajjal (*false messiah*) would have the word Kafir, (i.e. unbeliever) or the letters Kafir (the root of the Arabic verb 'disbelieve') written on his forehead.

I heard Ibn 'Abbas saying, "I did not hear this, but the Prophet said, 'If you want to see Abraham, then look at your companion (i.e. the Prophet) but Moses was a curly-haired, brown man (who used to ride) a red camel, the reins of which was made of fires of date-palms. As if I were now looking down a valley."

Bukhari 55.574

Moses was ostensibly a shy leader of men. The children of Israel suspected that this shyness, which was characterised by a reluctance to be seen naked, was that their leader had some kind of physical defect. This was until Allah found a way so bizarre to prove them wrong, that it should have made it into the Torah.

Narrated Abu Huraira:

Allah's Apostle said, "(The Prophet) Moses was a shy person and used to cover his body completely because of his extensive shyness. One of the children of Israel hurt him by saying, 'He covers his body in this way only because of some defect in his skin, either leprosy or scrotal hernia, or he has some other defect.'

Allah wished to clear Moses of what they said about him, so one day while Moses was in seclusion, he took off his clothes and put them on a stone and started taking a bath. When he had finished the bath, he moved towards his clothes so as to take them, but the stone took his clothes and fled; Moses picked up his stick and ran after the stone saying, 'O stone! Give me my garment!' Till he reached a group of Bani (Children of) Israel who saw him naked then, and found him the best of what Allah had created, and Allah cleared him of what they had accused him of.

The stone stopped there and Moses took and put his garment on and started hitting the stone with his stick. By Allah, the stone still has some traces of the hitting, three, four or five marks. This was what Allah refers to in His Saying: 'O you who believe! Be you not like those Who annoyed Moses, But Allah proved his innocence of that which they alleged, And he was honorable In Allah's Sight.' (33:69)"

Bukhari 55.616

Often when the Prophet was annoyed at his followers questioning the way he did things, such as his distribution of the booty, he would remind himself of what they did to Moses and take comfort in that.

Narrated Abdullah:

Once the Prophet distributed something (among his followers. A man said, "This distribution has not been done (with justice) seeking Allah's Countenance."

I went to the Prophet and told him (of that).

He became so angry that I saw the signs of anger on his face. Then he said, "May Allah bestow His Mercy on Moses, for he was harmed more (in a worse manner) than this; yet he endured patiently."

Bukhari 55.617

Where you will find Moses on Judgement Day.

Narrated Abu Huraira:

Two persons, a Muslim and a Jew, quarreled. The Muslim said, "By Him Who gave Muhammad superiority over all the people!"

The Jew said, "By Him Who gave Moses superiority over all the people!" At that the Muslim raised his hand and slapped the Jew on the face.

The Jew went to the Prophet and informed him of what had happened between him and the Muslim. The Prophet sent for the Muslim and asked him about it. The Muslim informed him of the event.

The Prophet said, "Do not give me superiority over Moses, for on the Day of Resurrection all the people will fall unconscious and I will be one of them, but I will be the first to gain consciousness, and will see Moses standing and holding the side of the Throne (of Allah). I will not know whether (Moses) has also fallen unconscious and got up before me, or Allah has exempted him from that stroke."

Bukhari 41.594

Where Moses is buried:

Narrated Abu Huraira:

The Angel of Death was sent to Moses when he came to Moses, Moses slapped him on the eye. The angel returned to his Lord and said, "You have sent me to a slave who does not want to die."

Allah said, "Return to him and tell him to put his hand on the back of an ox and for every hair that will come under it, he will be granted one year of life."

Moses said, "O Lord! What will happen after that?"

Allah replied, "Then death."

Moses said, "Let it come now."

Moses then requested Allah to let him die close to the Sacred Land so much so that he would be at a distance of a stone's throw from it.

Abu Huraira added, "Allah's Apostle said, 'If I were there, I would show you his grave below the red sand hill on the side of the road.'"

Bukhari 55.619

Moses and Adam Together

The Prophet did not shy away from telling the same story over and over, with slight variations in each retelling. The same narrator is a good indication that the same story was told on different occasions. On at least three occasions Abu Huraira must have heard God's Messenger tell the same tale of how Adam and Moses settled a disagreement as to whom is most responsible for mankind's miserable existence.

Narrated Abu Huraira:

Allah's Apostle said, "Adam and Moses argued with each other. Moses said to Adam. 'You are Adam whose mistake expelled you from Paradise.' Adam said to him, 'You are Moses whom Allah selected as His Messenger and as the one to whom He spoke directly; yet you blame me for a thing which had already been written in my fate before my creation?'"

Allah's Apostle said twice, "So, Adam overpowered Moses."

Bukhari 55.621

Narrated Abu Huraira:

The Prophet said, "Moses argued with Adam and said to him (Adam), 'You are the one who got the people out of Paradise by your sin, and thus made them miserable.' Adam replied, 'O Moses! You are the one whom Allah selected for His Message and for His direct talk. Yet you blame me for a thing which Allah had ordained for me before He created me.'"

Allah's Apostle further said, "So Adam overcame Moses by this Argument."

Bukhari 60.262

Narrated Abu Huraira:

The Prophet said, "Adam and Moses argued with each other. Moses said to Adam. 'O Adam! You are our father who disappointed us and turned us out of Paradise.' Then Adam said to him, 'O Moses! Allah favored you with His talk (talked to you directly) and He wrote (the Torah) for you with His Own Hand. Do you blame me for action which Allah had written in my fate forty years before my creation?' So Adam confuted Moses, Adam confuted Moses."

The Prophet added, repeating the Statement three times.

Bukhari 77.611

Noah

Muhammad will vouch for Noah on Judgement Day.

Narrated Abu Said Al-Khudri:

Allah's Apostle said, "Noah will be brought (before Allah) on the Day of Resurrection, and will be asked, 'Did you convey the message of Allah?'

He will reply, 'Yes, O Lord.'

And then Noah's nation will be asked, 'Did he (Noah) convey Allah's message to you?'

They will reply, 'No warner came to us.'

Then Noah will be asked, 'Who are your witnesses?'

He will reply. '(My witnesses are) Muhammad and his followers.' Thereupon you (Muslims) will be brought and you will bear witness."

Then the Prophet recited: "And thus We have made of you (Muslims) a just and the best nation, that you might be witness over the nations, and the Apostle a witness over you." (2:143)

Bukhari 92.448

Noah, like every other Prophet before and after him, including the Prophet Muhammad, warned his people about the one-eyed false messiah.

Narrated Ibn Umar:

Once Allah's Apostle stood amongst the people, glorified and praised Allah as He deserved and then mentioned the Dajjal saying, "l warn you against him (i.e. the Dajjal) and there was no prophet but warned his nation against him. No doubt, Noah warned his nation against him but I tell you about him something of which no prophet told his nation before me. You should know that he is one-eyed, and Allah is not one-eyed."

Bukhari 55.553

Solomon

In the Bible, Solomon rules between two women who both claim to be the mother of a child. In the Bible one of the women accidently smothered her infant son. In the Prophet's account, the child was taken by a wolf. Before the women go see Solomon, they first drop in on David who rules the child belongs to the wrong women, necessitating an appeal to Solomon who gets it right.

Narrated Abu Huraira:

Allah's Apostle said, "My example and the example of the people is like that of a person who lit a fire and let the moths, butterflies and these insects fall in it."

He also said, "There were two women, each of whom had a child with her. A wolf came and took away the child of one of them, whereupon the other said, 'It has taken your child.'

The first said, 'But it has taken your child.'

So they both carried the case before David who judged that the living child be given to the elder lady. So both of them went to Solomon and David informed him (of the case).

He said, 'Bring me a knife so as to cut the child into two pieces and distribute it between them.'

The younger lady said, 'May Allah be merciful to you! Don't do that, for it is her (i.e. the other lady's) child.' So he gave the child to the younger lady."

Bukhari 55.637

The night Solomon had sex with perhaps one hundred women:

Narrated Abu Huraira:

Allah's Apostle said, "Once Solomon, son of David said, '(By Allah) tonight I will have sexual intercourse with one hundred (or ninety-nine) women each of whom will give birth to a knight who will fight in Allah's Cause.' On that a (i.e. if Allah wills) but he did not say, 'Allah willing.' Therefore only one of those women conceived and gave birth to a half-man. By Him in Whose Hands Muhammad's life is, if he had said, "Allah willing', (he would have begotten sons) all of whom would have been knights striving in Allah's Cause."

Bukhari 52.74

More hadiths about biblical figures who made it into the Koran can be found in the section *Judgement Day*.

Booty and the Believers

Booty and the Believers should be read in conjunction with *Allah's War on the Unbelievers, Boreal Books (2012)* or *Pain, Pleasure and Prejudice - Civil War, Boreal Books (2012)*.

At forty-something the merchant Abū al-Qāsim Muhammad ibn Abd Allāh ibn Abd al-Mualib ibn Hāshim suffered what we might call a midlife crisis; a midlife crisis that may have been acerbated by a severe sunstroke suffered while helping with renovations of the Ka'ba, and from which he almost died. A hadith to that effect:

Narrated Jabir bin 'Abdullah:

When the Ka'ba was rebuilt, the Prophet and 'Abbas went to carry stones. 'Abbas said to the Prophet "(Take off and) put your waist sheet over your neck so that the stones may not hurt you." (But as soon as he took off his waist sheet) he fell unconscious on the ground with both his eyes towards the sky. When he came to his senses, he said, "My waist sheet! My waist sheet!" Then he tied his waist sheet (round his waist).

Bukhari 58.170

It was after one of these life-threatening traumas that the man who would achieve immortal fame as the Prophet Muhammad received his first visit from the angel Gabriel in a cave overlooking Mecca, where he had gone to spend the night to pray and meditate.

The celebrated angel informed him that he had been chosen as God's Messenger to deliver the Almighty's final message for mankind as to how He should be worshipped and how humanity must behave less His Anger destroy them all. It was all in a book God had authored which He called the Koran, the most accepting meaning being "to recite". To memorize, recite and inform his kin of what the angel conveyed to him about the contents of that Book was what God expected His latest spokesperson to do, as the original and only copy of this Koran, He kept near Him at all times in Paradise for safekeeping.

Muhammad's kin was the powerful tribe, the Quraysh, whose head inherited the leadership of the "tribal council" which had ruled Mecca from time immemorial. The tribal leaders, when Muhammad told them that he had been appointed God's Messenger, saw his newfound prophethood as a scheme to rule over them (revelation 38:6), and would no longer have anything to do with him.

Having failed to convince the rich and powerful of Mecca of his pre-eminence among men, God's latest spokesperson turned to the poor of Mecca. His message was simple: listened to him and do as you are told, and when you die you will have, in the afterlife, what the rich and powerful have in the here-and-now i.e. mansions, riches and women (or facsimiles e.g. houris), while the rich will be held to account, and the women they could not afford sent to Hell for not being more grateful to those who could.

Narrated Usama:

The Prophet said, "I stood at the gate of Paradise and saw that the majority of the people who entered it were the poor, while the wealthy were stopped at the gate (for the accounts). But the companions of the Fire were ordered to be taken to the Fire. Then I stood at the gate of the Fire and saw that the majority of those who entered it were women."

Bukhari 62.124

Allah promised the poor harems of houris, sexual beings designed by Him to satisfy a man's most intimate, most extravagant carnal desires. Fabricated whores, who will be wedded to the believers to avoid them committing illegal intercourse even in Paradise, may have been made necessary by the paucity of real women Allah will admit into His hedonistic sanctuary in the sky.

Imran b. Husain reported that Allah's Messenger said: Amongst the inmates of Paradise the women would form a minority.

Sahih Muslim 36.6600

This pitch had limited success. We don't know exactly when the Prophet hit upon the idea, or God told him to modify the message and tell the poor and the powerless who converted that they could have the property of the unbelievers legally if they were willing to fight and even kill them for it. It's in the Koran, but also in the hadiths.

Narrated Jabir bin 'Abdullah:

The Prophet said, "I have been given five things which were not given to anyone else before me.

1. Allah made me victorious by awe, (by His frightening my enemies) for a distance of one month's journey.

2. The earth has been made for me (and for my followers) a place for praying and a thing to perform Tayammum (dry ablution i.e. washing oneself before prayer using sand or dust if no water available), therefore anyone of my followers

can pray wherever the time of a prayer is due.

3. The booty has been made Halal (lawful) for me (and my followers) yet it was not lawful for anyone else before me.

4. I have been given the right of intercession (on the Day of Resurrection).

5. Every Prophet used to be sent to his nation only but I have been sent to all mankind."

Bukhari 7.331

In another hadith quoted in its entirety elsewhere, booty was made legal for the Muslims because of their weakness.

Narrated Abu Huraira:

... The Prophet added: "Then Allah saw our weakness and disability, so he made booty legal for us."

Bukhari 53.353

As a bonus, if a believer died trying to kill an unbeliever and abscond with his property, he was guaranteed immediate access to Paradise no questions asked.

Narrated Abu Huraira:

Allah's Apostle said, "Allah guarantees to the person who carries out Jihad for His Cause and nothing compelled him to go out but the Jihad in His Cause, and belief in His Words, that He will either admit him into Paradise or return him with his reward or the booty he has earned to his residence from where he went out."

Bukhari 93.549

God's Messenger even promised the natural-born and professional killers tempted by a new religion that legalized the killing and absconding with the property (including their wives and children) of people who did not believe in *The God*, to the exclusion of all others, that their previous murders would be forgiven and Paradise would be theirs, no questions asked, if they converted and died while killing on Allah's behalf.

Narrated Abu Huraira:

Allah's Apostle said, "Allah welcomes two men with a smile; one of whom kills the other and both of them enter Paradise. One fights in Allah's Cause and gets killed. Later on Allah forgives the killer who also get martyred (in Allah's Cause)."

Bukhari 52.80

The new message, like the one delivered a few thousand years earlier by Noah, had the desired effect (read *Pain, Pleasure and Prejudice* or *Shared Prophets - Criminals on the Ark*) and would give rise to the holy warriors who would become the prime mover of Allah's Message. A hadith about some of the people the Prophet's new religion attracted and which God's Messenger defended as being more worthy than the people they robbed (and killed):

Narrated Abu Bakra:

Al-Aqra' bin Habis said to the Prophet "Nobody gave you the pledge of allegiance but the robbers of the pilgrims (i.e. those who used to rob the pilgrims) from the tribes of Aslam, Ghifar, Muzaina." (Ibn Abi Ya'qub is in doubt whether Al-Aqra' added. 'And Juhaina.')

The Prophet said, "Don't you think that the tribes of Aslam, Ghifar, Muzaina (and also perhaps) Juhaina are better than the tribes of Bani Tamim, Bani Amir, Asad, and Ghatafan?"

Somebody said, "They were unsuccessful and losers!"

The Prophet said, "Yes, by Him in Whose Hands my life is, they (i.e. the former) are better than they (i.e. the latter)."

Abu Huraira said, "(The Prophet said), '(The people of) Bani Aslam, Ghifar and some people of Muzaina (or some people of Juhaina or Muzaina) are better in Allah's Sight (or on the Day of Resurrection) than the tribes of Asad, Tamim, Hawazin and Ghatafan.'"

Bukhari 56.719

The allocation of the booty was a straightforward if sometime gruesome affair. God's Messenger would ask or ascertain who killed whom and was therefore entitled to the murdered man's property, which would normally have included his wife and children.

Narrated Abu Qatada:

We set out in the company of Allah's Apostle on the day (of the battle) of Hunain. When we faced the enemy, the Muslims retreated and I saw a pagan throwing himself over a Muslim. I turned around and came upon him from behind and hit him on the shoulder with the sword He (i.e. the pagan) came towards me and seized me so violently that I felt as if it were death itself, but death overtook him and he released me.

I followed 'Umar bin Al Khattab and asked (him), "What is wrong with the people (fleeing)?"

He replied, "This is the Will of Allah."

After the people returned, the Prophet sat and said, "Anyone who has killed an enemy and has a proof of that, will possess his spoils."

I got up and said, "Who will be a witness for me?" and then sat down.

The Prophet again said, "Anyone who has killed an enemy and has proof of that, will possess his spoils."

I (again) got up and said, "Who will be a witness for me?" and sat down.

Then the Prophet said the same for the third time.

I again got up, and Allah's Apostle said, "O Abu Qatada! What is your story?" Then I narrated the whole story to him.

A man (got up and) said, "O Allah's Apostle! He is speaking the truth, and the spoils of the killed man are with me. So please compensate him on my behalf."

On that Abu Bakr As-Siddiq said, "No, by Allah, he (i.e. Allah's Apostle) will not agree to give you the spoils gained by one of Allah's Lions who fights on the behalf of Allah and His Apostle."

The Prophet said, "Abu Bakr has spoken the truth."

So, Allah's Apostle gave the spoils to me. I sold that armor (i.e. the spoils) and with its price I bought a garden at Bani Salima, and this was my first property which I gained after my conversion to Islam.

Bukhari 53.370

When it came to the booty, God's Messenger knew no shame.

Narrated 'Abdur-Rahman bin 'Auf:

While I was standing in the row on the day (of the battle) of Badr, I looked to my right and my left and saw two young Ansari boys, and I wished I had been stronger than they. One of them called my attention saying, "O Uncle! Do you know Abu Jahl?"

I said, "Yes, What do you want from him, O my nephew?"

He said, "I have been informed that he abuses Allah's Apostle. By Him in Whose Hands my life is, if I should see him, then my body will not leave his body till either of us meet his fate."

I was astonished at that talk. Then the other boy called my attention saying the same as the other had said.

After a while I saw Abu Jahl walking amongst the people. I said (to the boys), "Look! This is the man you asked me about." So, both of them attacked him with their swords and struck him to death and returned to Allah's Apostle to inform him of that.

Allah's Apostle asked, "Which of you has killed him?"

Each of them said, "I Have killed him."

Allah's Apostle asked, "Have you cleaned your swords?"

They said, "No."

He then looked at their swords and said, "No doubt, you both have killed him and the spoils of the deceased will be given to Muadh bin Amr bin Al-Jamuh."

The two boys were Muadh bin 'Afra and Muadh bin Amr bin Al-Jamuh.

Bukhari 53.369

The Prophet Muhammad, as God's Messenger, was not only entitled to one fifth of the booty obtained the hard way, but all the booty that was obtained without a fight, the Fai'.

Narrated Umar:

The properties of Banu Nadir were among the booty that Allah gave to His Apostle such booty were not obtained by any expedition on the part of Muslims, neither with cavalry, nor with camelry (sic). So those properties were for Allah's Apostle only, and he used to provide thereof the yearly expenditure for his wives, and dedicate the rest of its revenues for purchasing arms and horses as war material to be used in Allah's Cause.

Bukhari 60.407

The exile and dispossession of the Jews of Medina, the first such bloodless victory, made the Prophet an extremely wealthy man causing some holy warriors to grumble (on more than one occasion) about the fairness of it all, even if was the Prophet's private plunder to do with as he pleased, prompting Allah to send the following revelation:

59:6 Whatever spoils Allah has bestows on His Messenger from them, you did not send against them any horses or other mounts; but Allah confers on His Messengers authority over whoever he pleases. Allah has power over everything.

In an observation of the Prophet, it is obvious that he was not always trusted to be fair in the dispositicn of the booty obtained through blood, sweat and slaughter.

Narrated Jabir bin Abdullah:

While Allah's Apostle was distributing the booty at Al-Ja'rana, somebody said to him "Be just (in your distribution)."

The Prophet replied, "Verily I would be miserable if I did not act justly."

Bukhari 53.366

They did not understand that Islam was in its infancy and vulnerable, and some of the booty was needed to keep vacillating believers believing and recent converts confident in the profitability of their choice, if the new religion was to survive.

Narrated 'Amr bin Taghlib:

Allah's Apostle gave (gifts) to some people to the exclusion of some others. The latter seemed to be displeased by that.

The Prophet said, "I give to some people, lest they should deviate from True Faith or lose patience, while I refer other people to the goodness and contentment which Allah has put in their hearts, and 'Amr bin Taghlib is amongst them."

Amr bin Taghlib said, "The statement of Allah's Apostle is dearer to me than red camels."

Bukhari 53.373

Narrated Anas:

The Prophet said, "I give to Quraish people in order to let them adhere to Islam, for they are near to their life of Ignorance (i.e. they have newly embraced Islam and it is still not strong in their hearts)."

Bukhari 53.374

God's Messenger would not always justify his distribution, and later nobody would raise a question as to the Prophet's fairness in handing out the property of those killed by his followers; not only because this tested the patience of the Messenger, but the war on the unbelievers was producing booty at an unprecedented rate.

Narrated 'Abdullah:

On the day (of the battle) of Hunain, Allah's Apostle favored some people in the distribution of the booty (to the exclusion of others); he gave Al-Aqra' bin Habis one-hundred camels and he gave 'Uyaina the same amount, and also gave to some of the eminent Arabs, giving them preference in this regard. Then a person came and said, "By Allah, in this distribution justice has not been observed, nor has Allah's Pleasure been aimed at."

I said (to him), "By Allah, I will inform the Prophet (of what you have said)," I went and informed him, and he said, "If Allah and His Apostle did not act justly, who else would act justly. May Allah be merciful to Moses, for he was harmed with more than this, yet he kept patient."

Bukhari 53.378

A rider was entitled to two additional share of the booty because of his horse.

Narrated Ibn 'Umar:

On the day of Khaibar, Allah's Apostle divided (the war booty of Khaibar) with the ratio of two shares for the horse and one-share for the foot soldier. (The sub-narrator, Nafi' explained this, saying, "If a man had a horse, he was given three shares and if he had no horse, then he was given one share.")

Bukhari 59.537

Take more than your fair share of the booty at your risk and peril.

Narrated Abu Huraira:

We went out in the company of Allah's Apostle on the day of (the battle of) Khaibar, and we did not get any gold or silver as war booty, but we got property in the form of things and clothes. Then a man called Rifa'a bin Zaid, from the tribe of Bani Ad-Dubaib, presented a slave named Mid'am to Allah's Apostle.

Allah's Apostle headed towards the valley of Al-Qura, and when he was in the valley of Al-Qura an arrow was thrown by an unidentified person, struck and killed Mid'am who was making a she-camel of Allah's Apostle kneel down.

The people said, "Congratulations to him (the slave) for gaining Paradise."

Allah's Apostle said, "No! By Him in Whose Hand my soul is, for the sheet which he stole from the war booty before its distribution on the day of Khaibar, is now burning over him."

When the people heard that, a man brought one or two Shiraks (leather straps of shoes) to the Prophet. The Prophet said, "A Shirak of fire, or two Shiraks of fire."

Bukhari 78.698

The lure of the female booty at the battle of Uhud was responsible for one of the few Muslim defeats.

Narrated Al-Bara bin Azib:

The Prophet appointed 'Abdullah bin Jubair as the commander of the infantry men (archers) who were fifty on the day (of the battle) of Uhud. He instructed them, "Stick to your place, and don't leave it even if you see birds snatching us, till I send for you; and if you see that we have defeated the infidels and made them flee, even then you should not leave your place till I send for you."

Then the infidels were defeated. By Allah, I saw the women fleeing lifting up their clothes revealing their leg-bangles and their legs. So, the companions of 'Abdullah bin Jubair said, "The booty! O people, the booty! Your companions have become victorious, what are you waiting for now?"

'Abdullah bin Jubair said, "Have you forgotten what Allah's Apostle said to you?"

They replied, "By Allah! We will go to the people (*i.e. the enemy*) and collect our share from the war booty." But when they went to them, they were forced to turn back defeated.

Bukhari 52.276

At the battle of Hunayn the Prophet was successful in rallying his booty-obsessed troops and turn the tide.

Narrated Abu Ishaq:

Somebody asked Al-Bar-a bin 'Azib, "Did you flee deserting Allah's Apostle during the battle of Hunain?"

Al-Bara replied, "But Allah's Apostle did not flee. The people of the Tribe of Hawazin were good archers. When we met them, we attacked them, and they fled. When the Muslims started collecting the war booty, the pagans faced us with arrows, but Allah's Apostle did not flee. No doubt, I saw him on his white mule and Abu Sufyan was holding its reins and the Prophet was saying, 'I am the Prophet in truth: I am the son of 'Abdul Muttalib.'"

Bukhari 52.116

Kill an alleged spy and you get his belonging without impacting on your regular share of the war booty.

Narrated Salama bin Al-Akwa:

An infidel spy came to the Prophet while he was on a journey. The spy sat with the companions of the Prophet and started talking and then went away. The Prophet said (to his companions), "Chase and kill him." So, I killed him. The Prophet then gave him the belongings of the killed spy (in addition to his share of the war booty).

Bukhari 52.286

A generous Prophet gave a share of the booty to a son-in-law who had not participated in the battle of Badr not willing to leave his ill wife's side.

Narrated Ibn 'Umar:

'Uthman did not join the Badr battle because he was married to one of the daughters of Allah's Apostle and she was ill. So, the Prophet said to him. "You will get a reward and a share (from the war booty) similar to the reward and the share of one who has taken part in the Badr battle."

Bukhari 53.359

Foodstuff obtained as war booty, for obvious reason, was often consumed on the spot.

Narrated Ibn Umar:

In our holy battles, we used to get honey and grapes, as war booty which we would eat and would not store.

Bukhari 53.382

Booty was not exempt from the obligatory twenty percent charitable donation levy, the Zakat, with the Khumus being the Zakat on booty earmarked for Allah's Cause i.e. His war on unbelievers. However, until the Prophet's tax collector showed up to collect God's share of the booty, you could still have sex with it.

Narrated Buraida:

The Prophet sent 'Ali to Khalid to bring the Khumus (of the booty) and I hated Ali, and 'Ali had taken a bath (after a sexual act with a slave-girl from the Khumus).

I said to Khalid, "Don't you see this (i.e. Ali)?"

When we reached the Prophet I mentioned that to him.

He said, "O Buraida! Do you hate Ali?"

I said, "Yes."

He said, "Do you hate him, for he deserves more than that from the Khumus."

Bukhari 59.637

Dead pagans down the well and booty for the victors. What a God!

Narrated Ibn Shihab:

These were the battles of Allah's Apostle (which he fought), and while mentioning (the Badr battle) he said, "While the corpses of the pagans were being thrown into the well, Allah's Apostle said (to them), 'Have you found what your Lord promised true?'"

'Abdullah said, "Some of the Prophet's companions said, 'O Allah's Apostle! You are addressing dead people.' Allah's Apostle replied, 'You do not hear what I am saying, better than they.' The total number of Muslim fighters from Quraish who fought in the battle of Badr and were given their share of the booty, were 81 men."

Az-Zubair said, "When their shares were distributed, their number was 101 men. But Allah knows it better."

Bukhari 59.360

It is a given that you can have non-consensual sex with your female booty. What about coitus interruptus?

Narrated Abu Said Al-Khudri:

That while he was sitting with the Prophet a man from the Ansar came and said, "O Allah's Apostle! We get slave girls [*as booty*] from the war captives and we love property; what do you think about coitus interruptus?"

Allah's Apostle said, "Do you do that? It is better for you not to do it, for there is no soul which Allah has ordained to come into existence but will be created."

Bukhari 77.600

As reported by the BBC, such views have encouraged "more conservative Islamic leaders ~~have~~ [to] openly campaigned against the use of condoms or other birth control methods, thus making population planning in many countries ineffective." While a majority of Islamic Schools of Law allow contraceptives within a marriage setting, all are against men having a vasectomy or women a tubal ligation for this would be interfering with Allah's right to schedule a pregnancy at some point in the future.

Breast Milk

Some of the more bizarre observations about women have to be the Prophet's remarks about the extraordinary properties of breast milk.

God's Messenger believed that a woman who suckled an unrelated adult male transformed him into a close relation who could spend time with her alone for any desire for her had been extinguished by the breast milk and she was now also unlawful for him to marry.

> The Ulema'A'isha (Allah be pleased with her) reported that Salim, the freed slave of Abu Hadhaifa, lived with him and his family in their house. She (i. e. the daughter of Suhail came to Allah's Apostle (may peace be upon him) and said: Salim has attained (puberty) as men attain, and he understands what they understand, and he enters our house freely, I, however, perceive that something (rankles) in the heart of Abu Hudhaifa, whereupon Allah's Apostle (may peace be upon him) said to her: Suckle him and you would become unlawful for him, and (the rankling) which Abu Hudhaifa feels in his heart will disappear. She returned and said: So I suckled him, and what (was there) in the heart of Abu Hudhaifa disappeared.

Sahih Muslim 8:3425

If a female was suckled by the wife of a man, any man it would seem, it made that man her relation and that man's brothers her uncles, for the breast milk she got was the "brother's milk" even if it was his wife's milk on which she nursed.

Narrated Aisha:

Aflah asked the permission to visit me but I did not allow him. He said, "Do you veil yourself before me although I am your uncle?"

'Aisha said, "How is that?"

Aflah replied, "You were suckled by my brother's wife with my brother's milk."

I asked Allah's Apostle about it, and he said, "Aflah is right, so permit him to visit you."

Bukhari 48.812

It's complicated I know, so here is a variation which may make it easier to understand.

Narrated 'Aisha:

That while Allah's Apostle was with her, she heard a voice of a man asking permission to enter the house of Hafsa.

'Aisha added: I said, "O Allah's Apostle! This man is asking permission to enter your house."

The Prophet said, "I think he is so-and-so," naming the foster-uncle of Hafsa.

'Aisha said, "If so-and-so," naming her foster uncle, "were living, could he enter upon me?"

The Prophet said, "Yes, for foster suckling relations make all those things unlawful which are unlawful through corresponding birth (blood) relations."

Bukhari 62.36

Having been made unlawful to marry i.e. Muhrim by sulking milk meant for an infant, did not mean could now just drop in on the woman's whose breast or breasts you had cupped and supped on dressed and perfumed anyway you like.

Narrated Ibn 'Umar:

A person asked Allah's Apostle, "What should a Muhrim wear?"

He replied, "He should not wear shirts, trousers, a burnus (a hooded cloak), or clothes which are stained with saffron or Wars (a kind of perfume). Whoever does not find a sandal to wear can wear Khuffs, but these should be cut short so as not to cover the ankles

Bukhari 8.362

The witty and bold Aisha was not afraid to use sarcasm, which her husband may not have appreciated, to let him know when she thought he was spouting nonsense.

Narrated 'Aisha:

My foster uncle came and asked permission (to enter) but I refused to admit him till I asked Allah's Apostle about that. He said, "He is your uncle, so allow him to come in."

I said, "O Allah's Apostle! I have been suckled by a woman and not by a man."

Allah's Apostle said, "He is your uncle, so let him enter upon you."

Bukhari 62.166

A foster brother could spend time alone with the daughter of the parents who raised him if he had been suckled while in their care before the age of two:

Narrated Aisha:

Once the Prophet came to me while a man was in my house. He said, "O 'Aisha! Who is this (man)?"

I replied, "My foster brothers"

He said, "O 'Aisha! Be sure about your foster brothers, as fostership (sic) is only valid if it takes place in the suckling period (before two years of age)."

Bukhari 48.815

Breast milk could sour a marriage:

Narrated Abdullah bin Abu Mulaika from 'Uqba bin Al-Harith:

Uqba married the daughter of Abu Ihab bin Aziz, and then a woman came and said, "I suckled 'Uqba and his wife."

'Uqba said to her, "I do not know that you have suckled me, and you did not inform me." He then sent someone to the house of Abu Ihab to enquire about that but they did not know that she had suckled their daughter.

Then 'Uqba went to the Prophet in Medina and asked him about it.

The Prophet said to him, "How (can you keep your wife) after it has been said (that both of you were suckled by the same woman)?" So, he divorced her and she was married to another (husband).

Bukhari 48.808

The woman who soured Uqba's marriage was a" black lady".

Narrated 'Uqba bin Al-Harith:

I married a woman and then a black lady came to us and said, "I have suckled you both (you and your wife)."

So I came to the Prophet and said, "I married so-and-so and then a black lady came to us and said to me, 'I have suckled both of you.' But I think she is a liar."

The Prophet turned his face away from me and I moved to face his face, and said, "She is a liar."

The Prophet said, "How (can you keep her as your wife) when that lady has said that she has suckled both of you? So abandon (i.e., divorce) her (your wife)."

Bukhari 62.41

There is no mention in the hadiths of Bukhari as to whether this had any effect on the complexion of Uqba's or that of his soon-to-be-divorced wife's skin, as could have been expected considering the powers the Prophet attributed to breast milk.

Call of Nature

Nothing, absolutely nothing escaped the Prophet's attention, not even the number of stones needed to wipe oneself in the desert home of Islam. Why anyone could possibly think that the following hadiths are revealed truths (except perhaps for the common sense recommendation about not wiping yourself with dung) and a lasting example for mankind is quite extraordinary, to say the least.

Narrated Abu Huraira:

I followed the Prophet while he was going out to answer the call of nature. He used not to look this way or that. So, when I approached near him he said to me, "Fetch for me some stones for cleaning the privates parts (or said something similar), and do not bring a bone or a piece of dung."

So I brought the stones in the corner of my garment and placed them by his side and I then went away from him. When he finished (from answering the call of nature) he used them.

Bukhari 4:157

Narrated 'Abdullah:

The Prophet went out to answer the call of nature and asked me to bring three stones. I found two stones and searched for the third but could not find it. So took a dried piece of dung and brought it to him. He took the two stones and threw away the dung and said, "This is a filthy thing."

Bukhari 4:158

Narrated Abu Huraira:

The Prophet said, "Whoever performs ablution should clean his nose with water by putting the water in it and then blowing it out, and whoever cleans his private parts with stones should do it with odd number of stones."

Bukhari 4:162

You would also think that toilet paper, for believers like those found in Saudi Arabia, would have replaced stones. But you would be wrong. Stones may no longer be in fashion, but neither is toilet paper.

That wonderful convenience did not exist at the time of the Prophet therefore to use it is to deviate from his example.

God's Messenger also warned his followers that to innovate in anything after his passing was a one way ticket to Hell for the innovator ("Every innovation is a misguidance and every misguidance goes to Hell Fire") and it is assumed, the user of the damned innovation. For Islamists, those who would see a return to the good old days, no stones no problem, that is what your left hand is for, and water, if it is available.

Narrated Anas bin Malik:

Whenever Allah's Apostle went to answer the call of nature, I along with another boy used to accompany him with a tumbler full of water. (Hisham commented, "So that he might wash his private parts with it.")

Bukhari 4:152

If a man needs to hold his penis while urinating, he should do so with his left hand.

Narrated Abu Qatada:

Allah's Apostle said, "Whenever anyone of you drinks water, he should not breathe in the drinking utensil, and whenever anyone of you goes to a lavatory, he should neither touch his penis nor clean his private parts with his right hand."

Bukhari 4:155

Before answering the call of nature, God's Messenger offered a prayer, possibly to ward off evil spirits in the vicinity.

Narrated Anas:

Whenever the Prophet went to answer the call of nature, he used to say, "Allah-umma inni a'udhu bika minal khubuthi wal khaba'ith (*O Allah, I seek Refuge with You from all offensive and wicked things (evil deeds and evil spirits)*)."

Bukhari 4:144

You did your business squatting sideways to the Ka'ba, unless there was a partition between you and It.

Narrated Abu Aiyub Al-Ansari:

Allah's Apostle said, "If anyone of you goes to an open space for answering the call of nature he should neither face nor turn his back towards the Qibla; he should either face the east or the west."

Bukhari 4:146

The same for Jerusalem:

Narrated 'Abdullah bin 'Umar:

People say, "Whenever you sit for answering the call of nature, you should not face the Qibla or Bait-ulMaqdis (Jerusalem)."

I told them, "Once I went up the roof of our house and I saw Allah's Apostle answering the call of nature while sitting on two bricks facing Bait-ul-Maqdis (Jerusalem) but there was a screen covering him."

Bukhari 4:147

Sometimes you have to improvise, and ask Allah for forgiveness.

Narrated Abu Aiyub Al-Ansari:

The Prophet said, "While defecating, neither face nor turn your back to the Qibla but face either east or west."

Abu Aiyub added. "When we arrived in Sham we came across some lavatories facing the Qibla; therefore we turned ourselves while using them and asked for Allah's forgiveness."

Bukhari 8.388

Dead Poets

Allah said: "kill them wherever you find them"! Nowhere was this more true than for the unfortunate poets who lampooned the Prophet, or whom people thought better versifiers than God's Messenger. In their murder the Prophet took a personal interest.

The first poet to be killed was al-Nadr. The Meccans had praised his verses as superior to those of the Prophet and this had enraged the perfect human being. When God's Messenger spotted al-Nadr among the prisoners captured at Badr he had him beheaded on the spot. The next to die was the oldest poet, if not the oldest man of Medina, the centenarian Abu Afak.

> He waited for an opportunity until a hot night came, and Abu Afak slept in an open place. Salim b. 'Umayr knew it, so he placed the sword on his liver and pressed it till it reached his bed. The enemy of Allah screamed and the people, who were his followers rushed him, took him to his house and interred him.

> *Ibn S'ad, a companion of the Prophet*

The poetess Asma bint Marwan condemned in verse the murder of the old wordsmith. In the tradition of every despot through the ages she then became the target of the assassin's blade. With an infant suckling at her breast, which her killer pushed aside, she too was stabbed to death while sleeping. After every murder, the assassin would normally go to the Mosque to inform God's Messenger, and be praised for what he had done at the Prophet's insistence.

> Umayr Ibn Adi came to her in the night and entered her house. Her children were sleeping around her. There was one whom she was suckling. He searched her with his hand because he was blind, and separated the child from her. He thrust his sword in her chest till it pierced up to her back. Then he offered the morning prayers with the Prophet at Medina. The apostle of Allah said to him: "Have you slain the daughter of Marwan?"

> When Umayr replied that the job had been carried out with success, Muhammad said, "You have helped God and His apostle, O 'Umayr!'"

> When Umayr asked if he would have to bear any evil consequences, the apostle said, "Two goats won't butt their

heads about her." Muhammad then praised Umayr in front of all gathered for prayer for his act of murder, and Umayr went back to his people.

Ibn S'ad

The now powerful Prophet dared the men of her tribe to seek revenge for her murder, as was the custom. Knowing that there was nothing God's latest Messenger was not capable of, instead, they avoided their own destruction by becoming Muslims.

The next poet murdered on the Prophet's instructions was Abu-Rafi.

Narrated Al-Bara bin Azib:

Allah's Apostle sent a group of Ansari men to kill Abu-Rafi. One of them set out and entered their (i.e. the enemies) fort. That man said, "I hid myself in a stable for their animals. They closed the fort gate. Later they lost a donkey of theirs, so they went out in its search. I, too, went out along with them, pretending to look for it. They found the donkey and entered their fort. And I, too, entered along with them.

They closed the gate of the fort at night, and kept its keys in a small window where I could see them. When those people slept, I took the keys and opened the gate of the fort and came upon Abu Rafi and said, 'O Abu Rafi.'

When he replied me, I proceeded towards the voice and hit him. He shouted and I came out to come back, pretending to be a helper.

I said, 'O Abu Rafi', changing the tone of my voice.

He asked me, 'What do you want; woe to your mother?'

I asked him, 'What has happened to you?'

He said, 'I don't know who came to me and hit me.' Then I drove my sword into his belly and pushed it forcibly till it touched the bone. Then I came out, filled with puzzlement and went towards a ladder of theirs in order to get down but I fell down and sprained my foot. I came to my companions and said, 'I will not leave till I hear the wailing of the women.'

So, I did not leave till I heard the women bewailing Abu Rafi, the merchant of Hijaz. Then I got up, feeling no ailment, (and we proceeded) till we came upon the Prophet and informed him."

Bukhari 52.264

The murder of the poet Ka'b bin Al-Ashraf:

Narrated Jabir bin 'Abdullah:

Allah's Apostle said, "Who would kill Ka'b bin Al-Ashraf (Ka'b, a poet, who wrote poems lampooning of Allan's Messenger) as he has harmed Allah and His Apostle?"

Muhammad bin Maslama (got up and) said, "I will kill him."

So, Muhammad bin Maslama went to Ka'b and said, "I want a loan of one or two Wasqs of food grains."

Ka'b said, "Mortgage your women to me."

Muhammad bin Maslama said, "How can we mortgage our women, and you are the most handsome among the Arabs?"

He said, "Then mortgage your sons to me."

Muhammad said, "How can we mortgage our sons, as the people will abuse them for being mortgaged for one or two Wasqs of food grains? It is shameful for us. But we will mortgage our arms to you."

So, Muhammad bin Maslama promised him that he would come to him next time. They (Muhammad bin Maslama and his companions) came to him as promised and murdered him. Then they went to the Prophet and told him about it.

Bukhari 45.687

The irony is that the man who wanted to be known for his poetry would end up hating the genre and its practitioners.

Narrated Ubai bin Ka'b:

Allah's Apostle said, "Some poetry contains wisdom."

Bukhari 73.166

Narrated Ibn 'Umar:

The Prophet said, "It is better for a man to fill the inside of his body with pus than to fill it with poetry."

Bukhari 73.175

Perhaps it was because, even with the help of the God who taught Shakespeare, he could not be as eloquent as the poet who lamented the loss of his kin with whom he ate, drank and enjoyed the performances of female singers. His kin died at the battle of Badr or were killed on orders of God's Messenger after the battle and thrown down a well.

Narrate Aisha:

Abu Bakr married a woman from the tribe of Bani Kalb, called Um Bakr. When Abu Bakr migrated to Medina, he divorced her and she was married by her cousin, the poet who said the following poem lamenting the infidels of Quraish:

> What is there kept in the well, The well of Badr, (The owners of) the trays of Roasted camel humps?

> What is there kept in the well, The well of Badr, (The owners of) lady singers and friends of the honorable companions; who used to drink (wine) together,

> Um Bakr greets us with the greeting of peace, But can I find peace after my people have gone?

> The Apostle tells us that We shall live again, But what sort of life will owls and skulls live?

Bukhari 58.258

The Prophet's pitiless attitude towards apostates in particular, unbelievers in general and anyone who doubted his words may have had a lot to do with an early attempt to kill him by suffocating him with the stomach of a dead camel.

Narrated 'Abdullah bin Mas'ud:

Once the Prophet was offering prayers at the Ka'ba. Abu Jahl was sitting with some of his companions. One of them said to the others, "Who amongst you will bring the abdominal contents (intestines, etc.) of a camel of Bani so and so and put it on the back of Muhammad, when he prostrates?"

The most unfortunate of them got up and brought it. He waited till the Prophet prostrated and then placed it on his back between his shoulders.

I was watching but could not do anything. I wish I had some people with me to hold out against them.

They started laughing and falling on one another.

Allah's Apostle was in prostration and he did not lift his head up till Fatima (Prophet's daughter) came and threw that (camel's abdominal contents) away from his back.

He raised his head and said thrice, "O Allah! Punish Quraish."

So it was hard for Abu Jahl and his companions when the Prophet invoked Allah against them as they had a conviction that the prayers and invocations were accepted in this city (Mecca).

The Prophet said, "O Allah! Punish Abu Jahl, 'Utba bin Rabi'a, Shaiba bin Rabi'a, Al-Walid bin 'Utba, Umaiya bin Khalaf, and 'Uqba bin Al Mu'it (and he mentioned the seventh whose name I cannot recall). By Allah in Whose Hands my life is, I saw the dead bodies of those persons who were counted by Allah's Apostle in the Qalib (one of the wells) of Badr.

Bukhari 4:241

Death of the Prophet

Omen!

Narrated 'Aisha:

Once Fatima (*a daughter of God's Messenger*) came walking and her gait resembled the gait of the Prophet. The Prophet said, "Welcome, O my daughter!" Then he made her sit on his right or on his left side, and then he told her a secret and she started weeping.

I asked her, "Why are you weeping?"

He again told her a secret and she started laughing.

I said, "I never saw happiness so near to sadness as I saw today."

I asked her what the Prophet had told her.

She said, "I would never disclose the secret of Allah's Apostle."

When the Prophet died, I asked her about it.

She replied. "The Prophet said. 'Every year Gabriel used to revise the Qur'an with me once only, but this year he has done so twice. I think this portends my death, and you will be the first of my family to follow me.' So I started weeping. Then he said. 'Don't you like to be the mistress of all the ladies of Paradise or the mistress of all the lady believers?' So I laughed for that."

Bukhari 56.819

It was the Prophet who decided it was time to die.

Narrated 'Aisha:

When Allah's Apostle was in good health, he used to say, "No prophet's soul is ever captured unless he is shown his place in Paradise and given the option (to die or survive)." So when the death of the Prophet approached and his head was on my thigh, he became unconscious for a while and then he came to his senses and fixed his eyes on the ceiling and said, "O Allah (with) the highest companions."

I said, "Hence he is not going to choose us." And I came to know that it was the application of the narration which he (the Prophet) used to narrate to us. And that was the last statement of the Prophet (before his death) i.e., "O Allah! With the highest companions."

Bukhari 76.516

4:69 Those who obey Allah and the Messenger will be in the company of those whom God favoured of the Prophets, the saints, the martyrs and the righteous people. What excellent companions they are!

God's Messenger spent his last days on earth in the house of his favourite wife and confidant, Aisha.

Narrated 'Aisha:

When the ailment of the Prophet became aggravated and his disease became severe, he asked his wives to permit him to be nursed (treated) in my house. So they gave him the permission. Then the Prophet came (to my house) with the support of two men, and his legs were dragging on the ground, between 'Abbas, and another man.

'Ubaid-Ullah (the sub narrator) said, "I informed 'Abdullah bin 'Abbas of what 'Aisha said. Ibn 'Abbas said: 'Do you know who was the other man?' I replied in the negative. Ibn 'Abbas said, 'He was 'Ali (bin Abi Talib)."

'Aisha further said, "When the Prophet came to my house and his sickness became aggravated he ordered us to pour seven skins full of water on him, so that he might give some advice to the people. So he was seated in a Mikhdab (brass tub) belonging to Hafsa, the wife of the Prophet. Then, all of us started pouring water on him from the water skins till he beckoned to us to stop and that we have done (what he wanted us to do). After that he went out to the people."

Bukhari 4:197

The Prophet disliked taking medicine.

Narrated 'Aisha:

We poured medicine in one side of the Prophet's mouth during his illness and he started pointing to us, meaning to say, "Don't pour medicine in my mouth."

We said, "(He says so) because a patient dislikes medicines."

When he improved and felt a little better, he said, "Didn't I forbid you to pour medicine in my mouth?"

We said, "(We thought it was because of) the dislike, patients have for medicines."

He said, "Let everyone present in the house be given medicine by pouring it in his mouth while I am looking at him, except 'Abbas as he has not witnessed you (doing the same to me)."

Bukhari 59.735

During his last days the Prophet asked Abu Bakr, who would succeed him as leader of the believers, to lead his flock in prayer:

Narrated Al-Aswad:

"We were with 'Aisha discussing the regularity of offering the prayer and dignifying it. She said, 'When Allah's Apostle fell sick with the fatal illness and when the time of prayer became due and Adhan was pronounced, he said, 'Tell Abu Bakr to lead the people in prayer.' He was told that Abu Bakr was a soft-hearted man and would not be able to lead the prayer in his place. The Prophet gave the same order again but he was given the same reply. He gave the order for the third time and said, 'You (women) are the companions of Joseph. Tell Abu Bakr to lead the prayer.' So Abu Bakr came out to lead the prayer. In the meantime the condition of the Prophet improved a bit and he came out with the help of two men one on each side. As if I was observing his legs dragging on the ground owing to the disease. Abu Bakr wanted to retreat but the Prophet beckoned him to remain at his place and the Prophet was brought till he sat beside Abu Bakr.'"

Al-A'mash was asked, "Was the Prophet praying and Abu Bakr following him, and were the people following Abu Bakr in that prayer?"

Al-A'mash replied in the affirmative with a nod of his head.

Abu Muawiya said, "The Prophet was sitting on the left side of Abu Bakr who was praying while standing."

Bukhari 11.633

As his condition deteriorated the Prophet could only watch the believers at prayer.

Narrated Anas:

The Prophet did not come out for three days. The people stood for the prayer and Abu Bakr went ahead to lead the prayer. (In the meantime) the Prophet caught hold of the curtain and lifted it. When the face of the Prophet appeared we had never seen a scene more pleasing than the face of the Prophet as it appeared then. The Prophet beckoned to Abu Bakr to lead the people in the prayer and then let the curtain fall. We did not see him (again) till he died.

Bukhari 11.649

The last two chapters of the Koran, 113 and 114, are known as the Muawidhatan (also spelled Mu'awwidhatayn) the *Verses of Refuge*. When he feared his time had come, God's Messenger repeated over and over these two short surahs.

Narrated Aisha:

Whenever Allah's Apostle became ill, he used to recite the Muawidhatan and blow his breath over himself (after their recitation) and rubbed his hands over his body. So when he was afflicted with his fatal illness. I started reciting the Muawidhatan and blowing my breath over him as he used to blow and made the hand of the Prophet pass over his body.

Bukhari 59.723

In the Prophet's time, witches were thought to blow into knots to cast spells; another superstition from the Dark Ages which found its way into the Koran and from which God's Messenger sought protection while he slept. Surah 113, in particular, as a choice for a last appeal to a higher power before the darkness closes in is also revealing in that there is an admission that Allah is the source of all evil.

THE DAYBREAK

113 Al-Falaq

In the Name of Allah,
the Compassionate, the Merciful

1. Say: "I seek refuge with the Lord of the Daybreak,

2. "From the evil of what He has created,

3. "And the evil of the darkness when it gathers,

4. "And the evil of those who blow into knotted reeds (witches or sorceresses),

5. "And from the evil of the envious when he envies."

The Prophet's last orders:

Narrated Said bin Jubair:

That he heard Ibn 'Abbas saying, "Thursday! And you know not what Thursday is?"

After that Ibn 'Abbas wept till the stones on the ground were soaked with his tears. On that I asked Ibn 'Abbas, "What is (about) Thursday?"

He said, "When the condition (i.e. health) of Allah's Apostle deteriorated, he said, 'Bring me a bone of scapula, so that I may write something for you after which you will never go astray.' The people differed in their opinions although it was improper to differ in front of a prophet, They said, 'What is wrong with him? Do you think he is delirious? Ask him (to understand).'

The Prophet replied, 'Leave me as I am in a better state than what you are asking me to do.' Then the Prophet ordered them to do three things saying, 'Turn out all the pagans from the Arabian Peninsula, show respect to all foreign delegates by giving them gifts as I used to do.'"

The sub-narrator added, "The third order was something beneficial which either Ibn 'Abbas did not mention or he mentioned but I forgot."

Bukhari 53.393

A bad attempt at cheering up a dying man:

Narrated 'Aisha:

When the Prophet became ill, some of his wives talked about a church which they had seen in Ethiopia and it was called Mariya. Um Salma and Um Habiba had been to Ethiopia, and both of them narrated its (the Church's) beauty and the pictures it contained.

The Prophet raised his head and said, "Those are the people who, whenever a pious man dies amongst them, make a place of worship at his grave and then they make those pictures in it. Those are the worst creatures in the Sight of Allah."

Bukhari 23.425

The diet of those who attended God's Messenger during his last days consisted of dates and water.

Narrated Abu Huraira:

The family of Muhammad did not eat their fill for three successive days till he died.

Bukhari 65.287

Narrated 'Aisha:

The Prophet died when we had satisfied our hunger with the two black things, i.e. dates and water.

Bukhari 65.295

When the Prophet died, Aisha's cupboards were bare.

Narrated 'Aisha:

When the Prophet died, nothing which can be eaten by a living creature was left on my shelf except some barley grain. I ate of it for a period and when I measured it, it finished.

Bukhari 76.458

The Prophet's last meal:

Narrated Qatada:

We were in the company of Anas whose baker was with him. Anas said, "The Prophet did not eat thin bread, or a roasted sheep till he met Allah (died)."

Bukhari 65.297

Before he died the Prophet wanted to write down his last instructions but bickering among those around him prevented him from doing so.

Narrated Ubaidullah bin 'Abdullah:

Ibn Abbas said, "When Allah's Apostle was on his deathbed and there were some men in the house, he said, 'Come near, I will write for you something after which you will not go astray.'

Some of them (i.e. his companions) said, 'Allah's Apostle is seriously ill and you have the (Holy) Quran. Allah's Book is sufficient for us.'

So the people in the house differed and started disputing. Some of them said, 'Give him writing material so that he may write for you something after which you will not go astray.' while the others said the other way round.

So when their talk and differences increased, Allah's Apostle said, 'Get up.'"

Ibn Abbas used to say, "No doubt, it was very unfortunate (a great disaster) that Allah's Apostle was prevented from writing for them that writing because of their differences and noise."

Bukhari 59.717

Perhaps he wanted to make out a will which the Koran had made mandatory for adult males. The fact that God's Messenger ignored this Devine Ordinance surprised some people.

Narrated Talha bin Musarrif:

I asked 'Abdullah bin Abu Aufa "Did the Prophet make a will?"

He replied, "No,"

I asked him, "How is it then that the making of a will has been enjoined on people, (or that they are ordered to make a will)?"

He replied, "The Prophet bequeathed Allah's Book (i.e. quran)."

Bukhari 51.3

What the Prophet was wearing when he passed away:

Narrated Abu Burda:

Aisha brought out to us a Kisa and an Izar and said, "The Prophet died while wearing these two." (Kisa, a square black piece of woolen cloth. Izar, a sheet cloth garment covering the lower half of the body).

Bukhari 72.707

The passing of God's Messenger:

Narrated Aisha:

It was one of the favors of Allah towards me that Allah's Apostle expired in my house on the day of my turn while he was leaning against my chest and Allah made my saliva mix with his saliva at his death.

'Abdur-Rahman entered upon me with a Siwak in his hand and I was supporting (the back of) Allah's Apostle (against my chest). I saw the Prophet looking at it (i.e. Siwak) and I knew that he loved the Siwak, so I said (to him), "Shall I take it for you?"

He nodded in agreement. So I took it and it was too stiff for him to use, so I said, "Shall I soften it for you?"

He nodded his approval. So I softened it and he cleaned his teeth with it.

In front of him there was a jug or a tin containing water. He started dipping his hand in the water and rubbing his face with it, he said, "None has the right to be worshipped except Allah. Death has its agonies."

He then lifted his hands (towards the sky) and started saying, "With the highest companion," till he expired and his hand dropped down.

Bukhari 59.730

Narrated 'Aisha:

I heard the Prophet and listened to him before his death while he was lying supported on his back, and he was saying, "O Allah! Forgive me, and bestow Your Mercy on me, and let me meet the (highest) companions (of the Hereafter)."

Bukhari 59.715

The Prophet's last words are curious considering his role on Judgement Day which would appear to negate the need to ask for forgiveness.

Narrated Anas:

The Prophet said, "On the Day of Resurrection the Believers will assemble and say, 'Let us ask somebody to intercede for us with our Lord.' So they will go to Adam and say, 'You are the father of all the people, and Allah created you with His Own Hands, and ordered the angels to prostrate to you, and taught you the names of all things; so please intercede for us with your Lord, so that He may relieve us from this place of ours.'

Adam will say, 'I am not fit for this (i.e. intercession for you).' Then Adam will remember his sin and feel ashamed thereof. He will say, 'Go to Noah, for he was the first Apostle, Allah sent to the inhabitants of the earth.'

They will go to him and Noah will say, 'I am not fit for this undertaking.' He will remember his appeal to his Lord to do what he had no knowledge of, then he will feel ashamed thereof and will say, 'Go to the Khalil-r-Rahman (*Abraham*).'

They will go to him and he will say, 'I am not fit for this undertaking. Go to Moses, the slave to whom Allah spoke (directly) and gave him the Torah.'

So they will go to him and he will say, 'I am not fit for this undertaking.' and he will mention (his) killing a person who was not a killer, and so he will feel ashamed thereof before his Lord, and he will say, 'Go to Jesus, Allah's Slave, His Apostle and Allah's Word and a Spirit coming from Him.'

Jesus will say, 'I am not fit for this undertaking, go to Muhammad the Slave of Allah whose past and future sins were forgiven by Allah.'

So they will come to me and I will proceed till I will ask my Lord's Permission and I will be given permission. When I see my Lord, I will fall down in Prostration and He will let me remain in that state as long as He wishes and then I will be addressed. '(Muhammad!) Raise your head. Ask, and your request will be granted; say, and your saying will be listened to; intercede, and your intercession will be accepted.'

I will raise my head and praise Allah with a saying (*invocation*) He will teach me, and then I will intercede. He will fix a limit for me (to intercede for) whom I will admit into Paradise.

Then I will come back again to Allah, and when I see my Lord, the same thing will happen to me. And then I will intercede and Allah will fix a limit for me to intercede whom I will let into Paradise, then I will come back for the third time; and then I will come back for the fourth time, and will say, 'None remains in Hell but those whom the Quran has imprisoned (in Hell) and who have been destined to an eternal stay in Hell.'"

Bukhari 60.3

The Prophet died a rich man. He was a Gandhi only to the extent that he spent a large part of his wealth in Allah's Cause i.e. waging war on unbelievers. As God's Messenger he was not only entitled to 20 percent of what was taken by force from Allah's purported enemies, but 100 percent of what he absconded with without a fight, and that included the valuable Jewish farms of Khaibar and the property of the Banu Nadir Jews of Medina who he forced into exile.

Narrated 'Umar:

The properties of Bani An-Nadir which Allah had transferred to His Apostle as Fai Booty were not gained by the Muslims with their horses and camels. The properties therefore, belonged especially to Allah's Apostle who used to give his family their yearly expenditure and spend what remained thereof on arms and horses to be used in Allah's Cause.

Bukhari 52.153

The Fai booty at any one time was not insignificant, as the following hadith about plunder obtained from the Hawazin (today a scattered Arab tribe) will attest, and caused resentment when the Prophet distributed some of his exclusive booty to guarantee the loyalty of recent converts.

Narrated Anas bin Malik:

When Allah favored His Apostle with the properties of Hawazin tribe as Fai (booty obtained without a fight), he started giving to some Quraish men even up to one-hundred camels each, whereupon some Ansari men said about Allah's Apostle, "May Allah forgive His Apostle! He is giving to (men of) Quraish and leaves us, in spite of the fact that our swords are still dropping blood (of the infidels)"

When Allah's Apostle was informed of what they had said, he called the Ansar (men from Medina who joined the Prophet's crusade against the unbelievers) and gathered them in a leather tent and did not call anybody else along, with them. When they gathered, Allah's Apostle came to them and said, "What is the statement which, I have been informed, and that which you have said?"

The learned ones among them replied, "O Allah's Apostle! The wise ones amongst us did not say anything, but the youngsters amongst us said, 'May Allah forgive His Apostle; he gives the Quarish and leaves the Ansar, in spite of the fact that our swords are still dribbling (wet) with the blood of the infidels.'"

Allah's Apostle replied, I give to such people as are still close to the period of Infidelity (i.e. they have recently embraced Islam and Faith is still weak in their hearts). Won't you be pleased to see people go with fortune, while you return with Allah's Apostle to your houses? By Allah, what you will return with, is better than what they are returning with."

The Ansar replied, "Yes, O Allah's Apostle, we are satisfied."

Then the Prophet said to them." You will find after me, others being preferred to you. Then be patient till you meet Allah and meet His Apostle at Al-Kauthar (*i.e. a fount in Paradise*)."

(Anas added:) But we did not remain patient.

Bukhari 53.375

His wealth, which he did not flaunt, and the fact that at the time of his death, Jews were pariahs whom a Muslim could kill on a whim (Tabari [838–923] in his Muslim history writes that the Prophet after he exiled the Banu Qaynuqa Jewish tribe from Medina announced that "Whoever of the Jews falls into your hands, kill him") means it is highly unlikely the Prophet's armour was still mortgaged to a Jew.

Narrated 'Aisha:

Allah's Apostle died while his (iron) armor was mortgaged to a Jew for thirty Sas of barley.

Bukhari 52.165

The alleged mortgage may have more to do with justifying the

Prophet's dying curse.

Narrated 'Aisha and Ibn 'Abbas:

On his death-bed Allah's Apostle put a sheet over his-face and when he felt hot, he would remove it from his face. When in that state (of putting and removing the sheet) he said, "May Allah's Curse be on the Jews and the Christians for they build places of worship at the graves of their prophets." (By that) he intended to warn (the Muslim) from what they (i.e. Jews and Christians) had done.

Bukhari 56.660

The last gathering:

Narrated Ibn Abbas:

Once the Prophet ascended the pulpit and it was the last gathering in which he took part. He was covering his shoulder with a big cloak and binding his head with an oily bandage. He glorified and praised Allah and said, "O people! Come to me."

So the people came and gathered around him and he then said, "Amma ba'du." "From now onward the Ansar (*i.e. helpers, mainly Medinan Muslims*) Muhammad will decrease and other people will increase. So anybody who becomes a ruler of the followers of Muhammad and has the power to harm or benefit people then he should accept the good from the benevolent amongst them (Ansar) and overlook the faults of their wrongdoers."

Bukhari 13.49

What may have been the cause of the Prophet's fatal affliction:

Narrated Anas bin Malik:

Allah's Apostle (p.b.u.h) fell down from a horse and his right side was either injured or scratched, so we went to inquire about his health. The time for the prayer became due and he offered the prayer while sitting and we prayed while standing.

He said, "The Imam is to be followed; so if he says Takbir, you should also say Takbir, and if he bows you should also bow; and when he lifts his head you should also do the same and if he says: Sami'a-l-lahu Liman Hamidah (Allah hears whoever sends his praises to Him) you should say: Rabbana walakal-Hamd (O our Lord! All the praises are for You.").

Bukhari 20.215

The last silent action of God's Messenger:

Narrated Anas bin Malik:

Once Allah's Apostle rode a horse and fell down and the right side (of his body) was injured. He offered one of the prayers while sitting and we also prayed behind him sitting. When he completed the prayer, he said, "The Imam is to be followed. Pray standing if he prays standing and bow when he bows; rise when he rises; and if he says, 'Sami a-l-lahu-liman hamida, say then, 'Rabbana wa Lakal-hamd' and pray standing if he prays standing and pray sitting (all of you) if he prays sitting."

Humaid said: The saying of the Prophet "Pray sitting, if he (Imam) prays sitting" was said in his former illness (during his early life) but the Prophet prayed sitting afterwards (in the last illness) and the people were praying standing behind him and the Prophet did not order them to sit. We should follow the latest actions of the Prophet.

Bukhari 11.657

The Prophet's death shroud:

Narrated 'Aisha:

When Allah's Apostle died, he was covered with a Hibra Burd (green square decorated garment).

Bukhari 72.705

The Prophet's death and Aisha:

Narrated 'Aisha:

The Prophet died while he was between my chest and chin, so I never dislike the death agony for anyone after the Prophet.

Bukhari 59.726

And chatter ensued.

Narrated Ibn 'Umar:

During the lifetime of the Prophet we used to avoid chatting leisurely and freely with our wives lest some Divine inspiration might be revealed concerning us. But when the Prophet had died, we started chatting leisurely and freely (with them).

Bukhari 62.115

Age of the Prophet when he died, and why it is important.

Narrated 'Aisha:

The Prophet died when he was sixty three years old.

Bukhari B 56.736

Narrated Abu Huraira:

The Prophet said, "Allah will not accept the excuse of any person whose instant of death is delayed till he is sixty years of age."

Bukhari 76.428

Love, hate and death.

Narrated 'Ubada bin As-Samit:

The Prophet said, "Whoever loves to meet Allah, Allah (too) loves to meet him and whoever hates to meet Allah, Allah (too) hates to meet him".

'Aisha, or some of the wives of the Prophet said, "But we dislike death."

He said: "It is not like this, but it is meant that when the time of the death of a believer approaches, he receives the good news of Allah's pleasure with him and His blessings upon him, and so at that time nothing is dearer to him than what is in front of him. He therefore loves the meeting with Allah, and Allah (too) loves the meeting with him. But when the time of the death of a disbeliever approaches, he receives the evil news of Allah's torment and His Requital, whereupon nothing is more hateful to him than what is before him. Therefore, he hates the meeting with Allah, and Allah too, hates the meeting with him."

Bukhari 76.514

The last Prophet!

Narrated Abu Huraira:

The Prophet said, "The Israelis used to be ruled and guided by prophets: Whenever a prophet died, another would take over his place. There will be no prophet after me, but there will be Caliphs who will increase in number."

The people asked, "O Allah's Apostle! What do you order us (to do)?"

He said, "Obey the one who will be given the pledge of allegiance first. Fulfil their (i.e. the Caliphs) rights, for Allah will ask them about (any shortcoming) in ruling those Allah has put under their guardianship."

Bukhari 56.661

One possible reason why Ali lost the caliphate upon the death of his father-in-law.

Narrated 'Abdullah bin Abbas:

Ali bin Abu Talib came out of the house of Allah's Apostle during his fatal illness. The people asked, "O Abu Hasan (i.e. Ali)! How is the health of Allah's Apostle this morning?"

'Ali replied, "He has recovered with the Grace of Allah."

'Abbas bin 'Abdul Muttalib held him by the hand and said to him, "In three days you, by Allah, will be ruled (by somebody else), And by Allah, I feel that Allah's Apostle will die from this ailment of his, for I know how the faces of the offspring of 'Abdul Muttalib look at the time of their death. So let us go to Allah's Apostle and ask him who will take over the Caliphate. If it is given to us we will know as to it, and if it is given to somebody else, we will inform him so that he may tell the new ruler to take care of us."

'Ali said, "By Allah, if we asked Allah's Apostle for it (*the Caliphate*) and he denied it us, the people will never give it to us after that. And by Allah, I will not ask Allah's Apostle for it."

Bukhari 59.728

Aisha was no friend of Ali and vice versa. She undoubtedly feared that if Ali was appointed caliph she would be stoned for adultery. Ali hinted at this punishment to the Prophet when she was accused of cheating on her husband (see *The Necklace*). This could explain her reaction to claims that her husband had named Ali as his successor.

Narrated Al-Aswad:

It was mentioned in the presence of 'Aisha that the Prophet had appointed 'Ali as successor by will. Thereupon she said, "Who said so? I saw the Prophet, while I was supporting him against my chest. He asked for a tray, and then fell on one side and expired, and I did not feel it. So how (do the people say) he appointed 'Ali as his successor?"

Bukhari 59.736

Kind words for a successor:

Narrated Ibn 'Abbas:

Allah's Apostle in his fatal illness came out with a piece of cloth tied round his head and sat on the pulpit. After thanking and praising Allah he said, "There is no one who had done more favor to me with life and property than Abu Bakr bin Abi Quhafa. If I were to take a Khalil (*friend*), I would certainly have taken Abu-Bakr but the Islamic brotherhood is superior. Close all the small doors in this mosque except that of Abu Bakr."

Bukhari 8.456

The Official Cause of Death

The cause of the Prophet's death offered earlier challenges the official version of what incident led to the demise of God's ultimate spokesperson. As you should be aware, the Prophet Muhammad life's template borrowed heavily from that of the prophets of the Torah and Jesus of the New Testament. In the Gospels, the penultimate Messenger of Allah returned home early, but not before suffering a gruesome death on the cross, because of the Jews.

For the arbiters of Islamic dogma, it may have seemed only logical that their Savior's passing, like that of Jesus, had been expedited by a Jew, and a female to boot. Definitely better than the man who flew bareback on a winged horse to Paradise, to have a confab with God (see section Prayers - Negotiating the Prayers), dying from wounds sustained from falling off an ordinary horse.

In the official version, the Prophet's fate was sealed at Khaibar (also spelled Khaybar), a Jewish settlement God's Messenger attacked without provocation or warning (see chapter Khaibar) after Allah postponed the assault on Mecca.

Most of the leadership of the Jews of Khaibar, and the male members of their immediate and extended family were beheaded; one leader who went by the name of Kinana was almost tortured to death in the hope he would reveal the existence of any buried treasures before he too was decapitated.

A Jewish women by the name of Zaynab may have been his daughter in the account by respected Islamic scholar Ibn Sa'd [784-845] of the attempt on the Prophet's life after the taking of Khaibar. Zaynab put poison in a carcass of lamb (some say it was goat) she was asked to cook for God's Messenger and his henchmen after the slaughter of all the killable males (those showing any growth of public hair) of her household, including her husband. She was brought before the Prophet to answer for her cooking.

"The apostle of Allah sent for Zaynab and said to her, "What induced you to do what you have done?"

She replied, "You have done to my people what you have done. You have killed my father, my uncle and my husband, so I said to myself, 'If you are a prophet, the foreleg will inform you'; and others have said, 'If you are a king we will get rid of you.'"

The leg did inform God's Messenger that it had been poisoned, but not before he had taken a bite.

Narrated Jabir ibn Abdullah:

Ibn Shihab said: Jabir ibn Abdullah used to say that a jewess from the inhabitants of Khaybar poisoned a roasted sheep and presented it to the Apostle of Allah (peace be upon him) who took its foreleg and ate from it. A group of his companions also ate with him. The Apostle of Allah (peace be upon him) then said: Take your hands away (from the food).

The Apostle of Allah (peace be upon him) then sent someone to the jewess and he called her. He said to her: Have you poisoned this sheep?

The jewess replied: Who has informed you?

He said: This foreleg which I have in my hand has informed me.

She said: Yes.

He said: What did you intend by it?

She said: I thought if you were a prophet, it would not harm you; if you were not a prophet, we should rid ourselves of him (i.e. the Prophet).

The Apostle of Allah (peace be upon him) then forgave her, and did not punish her. But some of his companions who ate it, died.

The Apostle of Allah (peace be upon him) had himself cupped on his shoulder on account of that which he had eaten from the sheep. Abu Hind cupped him with the horn and knife. He was a client of Banu Bayadah from the Ansar (Medinan helpers).

Abu Dawud 39.4495

In other hadiths, including the following, the Prophet had her killed; and it may not so much have been the leg of lamb spilling the beans that alerted God's Messenger that the food was poisoned, but one of his dining companion falling over dead.

Narrated Abu Salamah:

A jewess presented a roasted sheep to the Apostle of Allah (peace be upon him) at Khaybar. He then mentioned the rest of the tradition like that of Jabir (No. 4495).

He said: Then Bashir ibn al-Bara' ibn Ma'rur al-Ansari died.

He sent someone to call on the jewess, and said to her (when she came): What motivated you to do the work you have done? He then mentioned the rest of the tradition similar to the one mentioned by Jabir (No. 4495).

The Apostle of Allah (peace be upon him) then ordered regarding her and she was killed. But he (Abu Salamah) did not mention the matter of cupping.

Abu Dawud 39.4496

The believers often refer to the Prophet Muhammad as the Prophet of Mercy. The hadiths would belie that appellation.

Narrated Ali ibn AbuTalib:

A jewess used to abuse the Prophet (peace be upon him) and disparage him. A man strangled her till she died. The Apostle of Allah (peace be upon him) declared that no recompense was payable for her blood.

Abu Dawud 38.4349

What does the Prophet ingesting a minute amount of poison, not enough to have the desired effect or causing any visible discomfort at the time, have to do with his death four years later? It all has to do with something Aisha said her husband uttered before he died.

Narrated 'Aisha:

The Prophet in his ailment in which he died, used to say, "O 'Aisha! I still feel the pain caused by the food I ate at Khaibar, and at this time, I feel as if my aorta is being cut from that poison."

Bukhari 59.713

It is not clear in the following whether he said these exact words after he ordered Zaynab to be killed.

Narrated Abu Salamah:

Muhammad ibn Amr said on the authority of Abu Salamah, and he did not mention the name of Abu Hurayrah: The Apostle of Allah (peace be upon him) used to accept presents but not alms (sadaqah *i.e. charity*).

This version adds: So a jewess presented him at Khaybar with a roasted sheep which she had poisoned. The Apostle of Allah (peace be upon him) ate of it and the people also ate. He then said: Take away your hands (from the food), for it has informed me that it is poisoned.

Bishr ibn al-Bara' ibn Ma'rur al-Ansari died. So he (the Prophet) sent for the jewess (and said to her): What motivated you to do the work you have done?

She said: If you were a prophet, it would not harm you; but if you were a king, I should rid the people of you.

The Apostle of Allah (peace be upon him) then ordered regarding her and she was killed. He then said about the pain of which he died: I continued to feel pain from the morsel which I had eaten at Khaybar. This is the time when it has cut off my aorta.

Abu Dawud 39.4498

No matter. From credible accounts of a Jewish woman attempting to poison God's Messenger, Islamic scholars, and I use the word advisably here, have reached the implausible conclusion that it was this attempt on their Prophet's life which caused his death four years later.

The Church by blaming the Jews for the death of Jesus made it easier for those who perpetrated the holocaust to go about their business with a clear conscience. The Christians churches have learned their lessons, and the Romans of antiquity are now correctly identified as those who caused the death of the Christian's Jewish Messiah. Islam should do the same and admit, based on more credible hadith evidence, that their Messiah's death was an accident and not a Jew's fault. It might even prevent another holocaust.

If you are a religious person you may want to spare a prayer for Zaynab if she is the Jewess the Prophet mentioned is being tortured in her grave.

Narrated 'Aisha:

Once Allah's Apostle passed by (the grave of) a jewess whose relatives were weeping over her. He said, "They are weeping over her and she is being tortured in her grave."

Bukhari 23.376

Dining Does and Don'ts

As a general rule, God's Messenger did everything starting on the right. Even for those who do not consider toilet paper an abomination because it was not the way the Prophet cleaned himself after answering the call of nature, the following still applies, even for left-handed people.

Narrated 'Umar bin Abi Salama:

I was a boy under the care of Allah's Apostle and my hand used to go around the dish while I was eating. So Allah's Apostle said to me, "O boy! Mention the Name of Allah and eat with your right hand, and eat of the dish what is nearer to you."

Since then I have applied those instructions when eating.

Bukhari 65.288

Vegetarians are not Muslims!

Narrated Anas bin Malik:

Allah's Apostle said, "Whoever prays like us and faces our Quibla and eats our slaughtered animals is a Muslim and is under Allah's and His Apostle's protection. So do not betray Allah by betraying those who are in His protection."

Bukhari 8.386

You can take the boy out of the desert but you can't take the desert out of the boy; besides, imagine lugging china all over the desert, even a folding table would have been an unnecessary hardship.

Narrated Anas bin Malik:

The Prophet never took his meals at a dining table, nor in small plates, and he never ate thin well-baked bread.

The sub-narrator asked Qatada, "Over what did they use to take their meals?"

Qatada said, "On leather dining sheets."

Bukhari 65.326

The Prophet did not eat at a dining table and did not lean against anything when eating standing up, and neither should you.

Narrated Abu Juhaifa:

Allah's Apostle said, "I do not take my meals while leaning (against something)."

Bukhari 65.310

Finger licking is good!

Narrated Ibn 'Abbas:

The Prophet said, "When you eat, do not wipe your hands till you have licked it, or had it licked by somebody else."

Bukhari 65.366

As you can imagine, in one of the hottest spot on earth, you could not appreciate enough the one who quenched your thirst.

Narrated Abu Umama:

Whenever the Prophet finished his meals (or when his dining sheet was taken away), he used to say. "Praise be to Allah Who has satisfied our needs and quenched our thirst. Your favor cannot be compensated or denied."

Once he said, "Praise be to You, O our Lord! Your favor cannot be compensated, nor can be left, nor can be dispensed with, O our Lord!"

Bukhari 65.369

Utensils as an abomination in this world and an amenity in the next.

Narrated 'Abdur-Rahman bin Abi Laila:

We were sitting in the company of Hudhaifa who asked for water and a Magian brought him water. But when he placed the cup in his hand, he threw it at him and said, "Had I not forbidden him to do so more than once or twice?"

He wanted to say, "I would not have done so," adding, "but I heard the Prophet saying, "Do not wear silk or Dibaja, and do not drink in silver or golden vessels, and do not eat in plates of such metals, for such things are for the unbelievers in this worldly life and for us in the Hereafter."

Bukhari 65.337

It's never a bad idea to wash your utensils whether you got them from a friend or an enemy before using them. Don't snicker at the questions asked God's Messenger about eating game killed by an arrow or brought down by a trained or untrained dog, but consider how successful was the Prophet in getting his followers not to think for themselves no matter the activity. It's quite astounding, really!

Narrated Abu Tha'laba Al-Khushani:

I said, "O Allah's Prophet! We are living in a land ruled by the people of the Scripture; Can we take our meals in their utensils? In that land there is plenty of game and I hunt the game with my bow and with my hound that is not trained and with my trained hound. Then what is lawful for me to eat?"

He said, "As for what you have mentioned about the people of the Scripture, if you can get utensils other than theirs, do not eat out of theirs, but if you cannot get other than theirs, wash their utensils and eat out of it. If you hunt an animal with your bow after mentioning Allah's Name, eat of it, and if you hunt something with your trained hound after mentioning Allah's Name, eat of it, and if you hunt something with your untrained hound (and get it before it dies) and slaughter it, eat of it."

Bukhari 67.387

I am not sure I would want to eat from a dish in which a mouse, or any creature has died. You might say it depends how long since it drew its last breath i.e. in what state of decay is it? Perhaps, but death often causes an evacuation of the bowels and bladder which will remain in the dish after you have removed the corpse.

Narrated Maimuna:

The Prophet was asked about a mouse that had fallen into butter-fat (and died). He said, "Throw away the mouse and the portion of butter-fat around it, and eat the rest."

Bukhari 67.448

Sharing a bowl of milk in the prescribe manner from right to left as the following hadith insists, will not stop the spread of bacteria. This would have been a good time for Gabriel to show up and brief the Messenger on how many of Allah's afflictions are spread from mouth to mouth.

Narrated Anas bin Malik:

I saw Allah's Apostle drinking milk. He came to my house and I milked a sheep and then mixed the milk with water from the well for Allah's Apostle. He took the bowl and drank while on his left there was sitting Abu Bakr, and on his right there was a Bedouin.

He then gave the remaining milk to the Bedouin and said, "The right! The right (first)."

Bukhari 69.516

In the following hadith, I suspect for all the wrong reasons, the Prophet insists that you do not put your lips on the mouth of a water filed water skin; and of course, if a neighbour wants to stick a peg in a wall of his house, it's none of your business.

Narrated Abu Huraira:

Allah's Apostle forbade drinking directly from the mouth of a water skin or other leather containers and forbade preventing one's neighbor from fixing a peg in (the wall of) one's house.

Bukhari 69.531

It's okay to drink standing up.

Narrated An-Nazzal:

Ali came to the gate of the courtyard (of the Mosque) and drank (water) while he was standing and said, "Some people dislike to drink while standing, but I saw the Prophet doing (drinking water) as you have seen me doing now."

Bukhari 69.519

If offered a choice between a glass of milk or a glass of wine, or a choice between a bowl of milk, a bowl honey or a bowl of wine always pick the milk.

Narrated Abu Huraira:

On the night Allah's Apostle was taken on a night journey (Miraj) two cups, one containing wine and the other milk, were presented to him at Jerusalem. He looked at it and took the cup of milk.

Gabriel said, "Praise be to Allah Who guided you to Al-Fitra (the right path); if you had taken (the cup of) wine, your nation would have gone astray."

Bukhari 69.482

Narrated Ibn 'Abbas:

Allah's Apostle drank milk and then rinsed his mouth and said, "It contains fat."

The Prophet added: "I was raised to the Lote Tree and saw four rivers, two of which were coming out and two going in. Those which were coming out were the Nile and the Euphrates, and those which were going in were two rivers in

Paradise. Then I was given three bowls, one containing milk, and another containing honey, and a third containing wine. I took the bowl containing milk and drank it."

It was said to me, "You and your followers will be on the right path (of Islam)."

Bukhari 69.514

A drunk and disorderly believer will not always do as he is told and might even think for himself. An excellent reason for a man who wants to control every aspect of his followers' existence so they don't do anything which will see them burning in Hell, to band intoxicating beverages.

Narrated Aisha:

The Prophet said, "All drinks that produce intoxication are Haram (forbidden to drink).

Bukhari 4:243

Should you not be clear on the concept:

Narrated Abu Al-Juwairiyya:

I asked Ibn 'Abbas about Al-Badhaq. He said, "Muhammad prohibited alcoholic drinks before It was called Al-Badhaq (by saying), 'Any drink that intoxicates is unlawful.'"

I said, "What about good lawful drinks?"

He said, "Apart from what is lawful and good, all other things are unlawful and not good (unclean Al-Khabith)."

Bukhari 69.503

The Prophet extended Allah's prohibition of alcoholic beverages to the containers in which it was served, but had second thoughts about prohibiting jars altogether, except green jars.

Narrated 'Abdullah bin 'Amr:

When the Prophet forbade the use of certain containers (that were used for preparing alcoholic drinks), somebody said to the Prophet. "But not all the people can find skins." So he allowed them to use clay jars not covered with pitch.

Bukhari 69.497

Narrated Ash-Shaibani:

I heard 'Abdullah bin Abi Aufa saying, "The Prophet forbade the use of green jars."

I said, "Shall we drink out of white jars?"

He said, "No."

Bukhari 69.501

Domesticated donkey is forbidden but not the wild variety e.g. onager.

Narrated Salama bin Al-Akwa:

On the day of Khaibar the Prophet saw fires being lighted. He asked, "Why are these fires being lighted?"

The people replied that they were cooking the meat of donkeys.

He said, "Break the pots and throw away their contents."

The people said, "Shall we throw away their contents and wash the pots (rather than break them)?"

He said, "Wash them."

Bukhari B 43.657

Horse meat is okay.

Narrated Jabir bin Abdullah:

On the day of Khaibar, Allah's Apostle forbade the eating of donkey meat and allowed the eating of horse meat.

Bukhari 59.530

If you have eaten any of the prohibited meats or even drank alcohol before Allah's new dietary restrictions came to affect, you will not be assessed any sins, just don't do it again!

Narrated Anas:

I used to offer alcoholic drinks to the people at the residence of Abu Talha. Then the order of prohibiting alcoholic drinks was revealed, and the Prophet ordered somebody to announce that.

Abu Talha said to me, "Go out and see what this voice (this announcement) is."

I went out and (on coming back) said, "This is somebody announcing that alcoholic beverages have been prohibited."

Abu Talha said to me, "Go and spill it (i.e. the wine)," Then it (alcoholic drinks) was seen flowing through the streets of Medina. At that time the wine was Al-Fadikh.

The people said, "Some people (Muslims) were killed (during the battle of Uhud) while wine was in their stomachs."

So Allah revealed: "On those who believe and do good deeds there is no blame for what they ate (in the past)." (5:93)

Bukhari 60.144

If you are unsure about whether Allah's name has been mentioned over what you are about to eat, do the obvious!

Narrated 'Aisha:

Some people said, "O Allah's Apostle! Meat is brought to us by some people and we are not sure whether the name of Allah has been mentioned on it or not (at the time of slaughtering the animals)."

Allah's Apostle said (to them), "Mention the name of Allah and eat it."

Bukhari 34.273

Be sure to also thank God for the hunting dog which caught that day's dinner if you do not want to commit a sin by eating it.

Narrated 'Adi bin Hatim:

... I asked, "O Allah's Apostle! I release my dog by the name of Allah and find with it at the game, another dog on which I have not mentioned the name of Allah, and I do not know which one of them caught the game."

Allah's Apostle said (to him), "Don't eat it as you have mentioned the name of Allah on your dog and not on the other dog."

Bukhari 34.270

A dog has caught the game "for itself" if it takes one or more bites out of it, thereby making it unlawful to eat; the same for game taken down by a pack. It is however lawful to eat carrion (meat that has been dead a number of days) if it has been killed by an arrow and the animal has not wandered into the water to die.

Narrated Adi bin Hatim:

The Prophet said, "If you let loose your hound after a game and mention Allah's Name on sending it, and the hound catches the game and kills it, then you can eat of it. But if the hound eats of it, then you should not eat thereof, for the hound has caught it for itself.

And if along with your hound, join other hounds, and Allah's Name was not mentioned at the time of their sending, and they catch an animal and kill it, you should not eat of it, for you will not know which of them has killed it.

And if you have thrown an arrow at the game and then find it (dead) two or three days later and, it bears no mark other than the wound inflicted by your arrow, then you can eat of it. But if the game is found (dead) in water, then do not eat of it."

And it has also been narrated by 'Adi bin Hatim that he asked the Prophet "If a hunter throws an arrow at the game and after tracing it for two or three days he finds it dead but still bearing his arrow, (can he eat of it)?"

The Prophet replied, "He can eat if he wishes."

Bukhari 67.393

The meat may be halal, but perhaps not the hide.

Narrated Ibn Abbas:

The Prophet saw a dead sheep which had been given in charity to a freed slave girl of Maimuna, the wife of the Prophet.

The Prophet said, "Why don't you get the benefit of its hide?"

They said, "It is dead."

He replied, "Only to eat (its meat) is illegal."

Bukhari 24.569

A hadith you may remember from *Bible Stories – Eve's Burden* as to why meat goes bad and women cheat on their husbands:

Narrated Abu Huraira:

The Prophet said, "Were it not for Bani (children of) Israel, meat would not decay; and were it not for Eve, no woman would ever betray her husband."

Bukhari 55.611

The Prophet as chef:

Narrated Abu Qatada:

The Prophet forbade the mixing of ripe and unripe dates and also the mixing of dates and raisins (for preparing a syrup) but the syrup of each kind of fruit should be prepared separately. (One may have such drinks as long as it is fresh)

Bukhari 69.507

Dreams

The Koran is all over the place as to when it was revealed. In one instance, it is during one night, the night of power (97:1); in another it is during an entire month, the month of Ramadan (2:185); and in still another instance, it was revealed "piecemeal" (17:106).

Nowhere in His Book does Allah mention revealing what He revealed of His Koran in dreams; yet, this is how the Prophet's companions remember God's Messenger receiving many of God's communications, most if not all, from the angel Gabriel,

Narrated Safwan bin Ya'la bin Umaiya from his father who said:

"A man came to the Prophet while he was at Ji'rana. The man was wearing a cloak which had traces of Khaluq or Sufra (a kind of perfume). The man asked (the Prophet), 'What do you order me to perform in my 'Umra (*the lesser pilgrimage*)?' So, Allah inspired the Prophet divinely and he was screened by a place of cloth.

I wished to see the Prophet being divinely inspired.

'Umar said to me, 'Come! Will you be pleased to look at the Prophet while Allah is inspiring him?'

I replied in the affirmative.

'Umar lifted one corner of the cloth and I looked at the Prophet who was snoring. (The sub-narrator thought that he said: The snoring was like that of a camel).

When that state was over, the Prophet asked, "Where is the questioner who asked about 'Umra? Put off your cloak and wash away the traces of Khaluq from your body and clean the Sufra (yellow color) and perform in your Umra what you perform in your Hajj (i.e. the Tawaf round the Ka'ba and the Sa'i between Safa and Marwa)."

Bukhari 27.17

Allah's Messenger to the Messenger. Communications from Paradise sent while the Prophet slept would explain the horrific descriptions of Judgement Day and Hell which mere words could not have conveyed.

Aisha, the Prophet's child-bride and the most trusted of the narrators of what God's Messenger said and did remembered her husband receiving "(the Devine Inspiration) in the form of true dreams in his sleep."

Narrated Aisha:

The commencement (of the Divine Inspiration) to Allah's Apostle was in the form of true dreams in his sleep, for he never had a dream but it turned out to be true and clear as the bright daylight. Then he began to like seclusions, so he used to go in seclusion in the cave of Hira where he used to worship Allah continuously for many nights before going back to his family to take the necessary provision (of food) for the stay.

Bukhari 60.478

The first communication made by Allah via dreams may not have been about the Koran but about Aisha. It was in dreams, you may remember, that Allah gave his blessing to a pedophiliac relationship which set the precedent for men of whatever age to legally marry and have intercourse with children i.e. girls as young as nine years of age.

Dreams, the Prophet explained, convey religious knowledge. What is the Koran if not religious knowledge?

Narrated Ibn 'Umar:

I heard Allah's Apostle saying, "While I was sleeping, I was given a bowl full of milk (in a dream), and I drank of it to my fill until I noticed its wetness coming out of my nails, and then I gave the rest of it to 'Umar."

They (the people) asked, "What have you interpreted (about the dream) O Allah's Apostle?"

He said, "(It is Religious) knowledge."

Bukhari 87.134

And what is Islam, if not "The Religion"!

Narrated Abu Sa'id Al-Khudri:

Allah's Apostle said, "While I was sleeping, some people were displayed before me (in a dream). They were wearing shirts, some of which were merely covering their breasts, and some a bit longer. Then there passed before me, 'Umar bin Al-Khattab wearing a shirt he was dragging it (on the ground behind him.)"

They (the people) asked, "What have you interpreted (about the dream) O Allah's Apostle?"

He said, "The Religion."

Bukhari 87.136

Interpreting dreams as real-world predictions is very much what a Prophet does.

Narrated Abu Huraira:

I heard Allah's Apostle saying, "Nothing is left of the prophetism except Al-Mubashshirat."

They asked, "What are Al-Mubashshirat?"

He replied, "The true good dreams (that conveys glad tidings)."

Bukhari 87.119

None dared wake up the Prophet less he interrupt a transmission from Paradise.

Narrated 'Imran:

Once we were traveling with the Prophet and we carried on traveling till the last part of the night and then we (halted at a place) and slept (deeply). There is nothing sweeter than sleep for a traveler in the last part of the night. So it was only the heat of the sun that made us to wake up and the first to wake up was so and so, then so and so and then so and so (the narrator 'Auf said that Abu Raja' had told him their names but he had forgotten them) and the fourth person to wake up was 'Umar bin Al-Khattab.

And whenever the Prophet used to sleep, nobody would wake him up till he himself used to get up as we did not know what was happening (being revealed) to him in his sleep ...

Bukhari 7.340

Nothing gets Allah's and His Messenger's dander up like the mention of paying interest, therefore the Prophet having dreams where riba-eaters figure prominently is to be expected.

Narrated Samura bin Jundab:

The Prophet said, "This night I dreamt that two men came and took me to a Holy land whence we proceeded on till we reached a river of blood, where a man was standing, and on its bank was standing another man with stones in his hands. The man in the middle of the river tried to come out, but the other threw a stone in his mouth and forced him to go back to his original place. So, whenever he tried to come out, the other man would throw a stone in his mouth and force him to go back to his former place."

I asked, "Who is this?"

I was told, "The person in the river was a Riba-eater (*a lender who insist on charging interest on borrowed money*)."

Bukhari 34.298

It was in a dream that the Prophet was given the keys to the treasures of the earth.

Narrated Abu Huraira:

The Prophet said, "I have been given the keys of eloquent speech and given victory with awe (cast into the hearts of the enemy), and while I was sleeping last night, the keys of the treasures of the earth were brought to me till they were put in my hand."

Abu Huraira added: "Allah's Apostle left (this world) and now you people are carrying those treasures from place to place."

Bukhari 87.127

Unless God's Messenger was a somnambulist and fixed himself a snack while in REM sleep, in dreams you can have real food and drinks if you are a Prophet, or important enough to have your dreams catered.

'Narrated Abu Sa'id:

That he had heard the Prophet saying, "Do not fast continuously (practise Al-Wisal), and if you intend to lengthen your fast, then carry it on only till the Suhur (before the following dawn)."

The people said to him, "But you practice (Al-Wisal), O Allah's Apostle!"

He replied, "I am not similar to you, for during my sleep I have One Who makes me eat and drink."

Bukhari 31.184

It was fortunate that the crescent moon marking the first day of the month of Shawwal, meaning "lift or carry" (so named because this is the month she-camels normally would be carrying a fetus) appeared when it did, or some believers whose dreams were not being catered and who wanted to fast like their Prophet might have starved themselves to death. The first day of Shawwal is the feast of Eid al-Fitr where all fasting must stop.

Narrated Abu Huraira:

Allah's Apostle forbade Al-Wisal in fasting. So, one of the Muslims said to him, "But you practice Al-Wisal. O Allah's Apostle!"

The Prophet replied, "Who amongst you is similar to me? I am given food and drink during my sleep by my Lord."

So, when the people refused to stop Al-Wisal (fasting continuously), the Prophet fasted day and night continuously along with them for a day and then another day and then they saw the crescent moon (of the month of Shawwal).

The Prophet said to them (angrily), "If it (the crescent) had not appeared, I would have made you fast for a longer period."

That was as a punishment for them when they refused to stop (practising Al-Wisal).

Bukhari 31.186

The difference between a dream and a nightmare:

Narrated Abu Qatada:

The Prophet said, "A true good dream is from Allah, and a bad dream is from Satan."

Bukhari 87.113

Next time you have a nightmare, the Prophet recommends you don't mention it to anyone.

Narrated Abu Sa'id Al-Khudri:

The Prophet said, "If anyone of you sees a dream that he likes, then it is from Allah, and he should thank Allah for it and narrate it to others; but if he sees something else, i.e., a dream that he dislikes, then it is from Satan, and he should seek refuge with Allah from its evil, and he should not mention it to anybody, for it will not harm him."

Bukhari 87.114

When waking up from a bad dream, spit or blow your nose three times.

Narrated Abu Qatada:

The Prophet said, "A good dream that comes true is from Allah, and a bad dream is from Satan, so if anyone of you sees a bad dream, he should seek refuge with Allah from Satan and should spit on the left, for the bad dream will not harm him."

Bukhari 87.115

Perhaps as precaution against spraying saliva on a person next to you in bed and making a bad dream even worse, the Prophet recommended it be a dry spit, maybe just even clearing your throat.

Narrated Abu Qatada:

The Prophet said, "A good dream is from Allah, and a bad dream is from Satan. So whoever has seen (in a dream) something he dislike, then he should spit without saliva, thrice on his left and seek refuge with Allah from Satan, for it will not harm him, and Satan cannot appear in my shape."

Bukhari 87.124

Waking up from a nightmare about Gog and Magog:

Narrated Zainab bint Jahsh:

The Prophet got up from his sleep with a flushed red face and said, "None has the right to be worshipped but Allah. Woe to the Arabs, from the Great evil that is nearly approaching them. Today a gap has been made in the wall of Gog and Magog like this." (Sufyan illustrated by this forming the number 90 or 100 with his fingers.)

It was asked, "Shall we be destroyed though there are righteous people among us?"

The Prophet said, "Yes, if evil increased."

Bukhari 88.181

Unless you are a bonafide Prophet of God you should be very careful about looking for cures to what ails you in your dreams, even if you suspect that what ails you is a result of someone's malevolent magic.

Narrated 'Aisha:

The Prophet continued for such-and-such period imagining that he has slept (had sexual relations) with his wives, and in fact he did not.

One day he said, to me, "O 'Aisha! Allah has instructed me regarding a matter about which I had asked Him. There came to me two men, one of them sat near my feet and the other near my head. The one near my feet, asked the one near my head (pointing at me), 'What is wrong with this man?'

The latter replied, 'He is under the effect of magic.'

The first one asked, 'Who had worked magic on him?'

The other replied, 'Lubaid bin Asam.'

The first one asked, 'What material (did he use)?'

The other replied, 'The skin of the pollen of a male date tree with a comb and the hair stuck to it, kept under a stone in the well of Dharwan.'"

Then the Prophet went to that well and said, "This is the same well which was shown to me in the dream. The tops of its date-palm trees look like the heads of the devils, and its water looks like the henna infusion." Then the Prophet ordered that those things be taken out.

I said, "O Allah's Apostle! Won't you disclose (the magic object)?"

The Prophet said, "Allah has cured me and I hate to circulate the evil among the people."

'Aisha added, "(The magician) Lubaid bin Asam was a man from Bani Zuraiq, an ally of the Jews."

Bukhari 73.89

It is from lucid visions and from a dream of the Prophet that we have the only known eyewitness description of what Jesus looked like.

Narrated 'Abdullah bin 'Umar:

Allah's Apostle said, "I saw myself (in a dream) near the Ka'ba last night, and I saw a man with whitish red complexion, the best you may see amongst men of that complexion having long hair reaching his earlobes which was the best hair of its sort, and he had combed his hair and water was dropping from it, and he was performing the Tawaf around the Ka'ba while he was leaning on two men or on the shoulders of two men.

I asked, 'Who is this man?'

Somebody replied, '(He is) Messiah, son of Mary.'

Then I saw another man with very curly hair, blind in the right eye which looked like a protruding out grape. I asked, 'Who is this?'

Somebody replied, '(He is the false) Messiah, Ad-Dajjal.'"

Bukhari 72.789

Communications from Allah via dreams sometimes included visions of good and bad things.

Narrated Um Salama:

The Prophet woke up and said, "Glorified be Allah: What great (how many) treasures have been sent down, and what great (how many) afflictions have been sent down!"

Bukhari 87.128

Many who had dreams where the Prophet was a figurant were not sure if it was God's Messenger who was paying them a visit while they slept, or Satan. The Prophet assured them that it could not be Satan and why.

Narrated Anas:

The Prophet said, "Whoever has seen me in a dream, then no doubt, he has seen me, for Satan cannot imitate my shape."

Bukhari 87.123

Narrated Abu Sa'id Al-Khudri:

The Prophet said, "Whoever sees me (in a dream) then he indeed has seen the truth, as Satan cannot appear in my shape."

Bukhari 87.126

The Prophet told his male followers not to name themselves after his first-born son (who died in infancy), followed by another reminder that Satan cannot take his shape in a dream. I could only conjecture what one has to do with the other.

Narrated Abu Huraira:

The Prophet said, "Name yourselves after me (by my name), but do not call yourselves by my Kuniya (*part of an Arabic name which usually begins with "abu" and refers to a father's first-born son*), and whoever sees me in a dream, he surely sees me, for Satan cannot impersonate me (appear in my figure). And whoever intentionally ascribes something to me falsely, he will surely take his place in the (Hell) Fire."

Bukhari 73.217

If enough ordinary men have the same dream then it has to be true.

Narrated Ibn 'Umar:

Some men amongst the companions of the Prophet were shown in their dreams that the night of Qadr (Night of Power) was in the last seven nights of Ramadan.

Allah's Apostle said, "It seems that all your dreams agree that (the Night of Qadr) is in the last seven nights, and whoever wants to search for it (i.e. the Night of Qadr) should search in the last seven (nights of Ramadan)."

Bukhari 32.232

The reward of true belief as revealed in a dream:

Narrated Abu Musa:

The Prophet said, "In a dream I saw myself migrating from Mecca to a place having plenty of date trees. I thought that it was Al-Yamama or Hajar, but it came to be Medina i.e. Yathrib. In the same dream I saw myself moving a sword and its blade got broken. It came to symbolize the defeat which the Muslims suffered from, on the Day of Uhud. I moved the sword again, and it became normal as before, and that was the symbol of the victory Allah bestowed upon Muslims and their gathering together. I saw cows in my dream, and by Allah, that was a blessing, and they symbolized the believers on the Day of Uhud. And the blessing was the good Allah bestowed upon us and the reward of true belief which Allah gave us after the day of Badr."

Bukhari 56.818

The reward was of course the booty, but I digress. Wells played a big role in many of the Prophet's dreams; living in a desert environment, that is understandable.

Narrated Abu Huraira:

I heard Allah's Apostle saying, "While I was sleeping, I saw myself standing at a well, on it there was a bucket. I drew water from the well as much as Allah wished. Then Ibn Abi Quhafa (i.e. Abu Bakr) took the bucket from me and brought out one or two buckets (of water) and there was weakness in his drawing the water. May Allah forgive his weakness for him. Then the bucket turned into a very big one and Ibn Al-Khattab took it over and I had never seen such a mighty person amongst the people as him in performing such hard work, till the people drank to their satisfaction and watered their camels that knelt down there."

Bukhari 57.16

Many of the Prophet's dream were about Paradise. If you have read *A Palace in the Sky* you know what the following is all about.

Narrated Samura bin Jundab:

Allah's Apostle said, "Tonight two (visitors) came to me (in my dream) and took me to a town built with gold bricks and silver bricks. There we met men who, half of their bodies, look like the most-handsome human beings you have ever seen, and the other half, the ugliest human beings you have ever seen. Those two visitors said to those men, 'Go and dip yourselves in that river. So they dipped themselves therein and then came to us, their ugliness having disappeared and they were in the most-handsome shape. The visitors said, 'The first is the Garden of Eden and that is your dwelling place.' Then they added, 'As for those people who were half ugly and half handsome, they were those who mixed good deeds and bad deeds, but Allah forgave them.'"

Bukhari 60.196

Be careful what you wish for!

Narrated Anas bin Malik:

Allah's Apostle used to visit Um Haram bint Milhan she was the wife of 'Ubada bin As-Samit. One day the Prophet visited her and she provided him with food and started looking for lice in his head. Then Allah's Apostle slept and afterwards woke up smiling. Um Haram asked, "What makes you smile, O Allah's Apostle?"

He said, "Some of my followers were presented before me in my dream as fighters in Allah's Cause, sailing in the middle of the seas like kings on the thrones or like kings sitting on their thrones." (The narrator Ishaq is not sure as to which expression was correct).

Um Haram added, I said, "O Allah's Apostle! Invoke Allah, to make me one of them."

So Allah's Apostle invoked Allah for her and then laid his head down (and slept). Then he woke up smiling (again). (Um Haram added): I said, "What makes you smile, O Allah's Apostle?"

He said, "Some people of my followers were presented before me (in a dream) as fighters in Allah's Cause." He said the same as he had said before.

I said, "O Allah's Apostle! Invoke Allah to make me one of them." He said, "You are among the first ones."

Then Um Haram sailed over the sea during the Caliphate of Muawiya bin Abu Sufyan, and she fell down from her riding animal after coming ashore, and died.

Bukhari 87.130

Before Freud, there was the Prophet Muhammad:

Narrated 'Abdullah bin Salam:

(In a dream) I saw myself in a garden, and there was a pillar in the middle of the garden, and there was a handhold at the top of the pillar. I was asked to climb it. I said, "I cannot." Then a servant came and lifted up my clothes and I climbed (the pillar), and then got hold of the handhold, and I woke up while still holding it.

I narrated that to the Prophet who said, "The garden symbolizes the garden of Islam, and the handhold is the firm Islamic handhold which indicates that you will be adhering firmly to Islam until you die."

Bukhari 87.142

Narrated 'Abdullah:

The Prophet said, "I saw (in a dream) a black woman with unkempt hair going out of Medina and settling at Mahai'a, i.e., Al-Juhfa. I interpreted that as a symbol of epidemic of Medina being transferred to that place (Al-Juhfa)."

Bukhari 87.161

You did not swear if you wanted the Prophet to let you know what you got wrong in interpreting a dream. It may also have been his way of avoiding giving an explanation.

Narrated Ibn 'Abbas:

A man came to Allah's Apostle and said, "I saw in a dream, a cloud having shade. Butter and honey were dropping from it and I saw the people gathering it in their hands, some gathering much and some a little. And behold, there was a rope extending from the earth to the sky, and I saw that you (the Prophet) held it and went up, and then another man held it and went up and (after that) another (third) held it and went up, and then after another (fourth) man held it, but it broke and then got connected again."

Abu Bakr said, "O Allah's Apostle! Let my father be sacrificed for you! Allow me to interpret this dream."

The Prophet said to him, "Interpret it."

Abu Bakr said, "The cloud with shade symbolizes Islam, and the butter and honey dropping from it, symbolizes the Quran, its sweetness dropping and some people learning much of the Qur'an and some a little. The rope which is extended from the sky to the earth is the Truth which you (the Prophet) are following. You follow it and Allah will raise you high with it, and then another man will follow it and will rise up with it and another person will follow it and then another man will follow it but it will break and then it will be connected for him and he will rise up with it. O Allah's Apostle! Let my father be sacrificed for you! Am I right or wrong?"

The Prophet replied, "You are right in some of it and wrong in some."

Abu Bakr said, "O Allah's Prophet! By Allah, you must tell me in what I was wrong."

The Prophet said, "Do not swear."

Bukhari 87.170

When your dreams will come true:

Narrated Abu Huraira:

Allah's Apostle said, "When the Day of Resurrection approaches, the dreams of a believer will hardly fail to come true, and a dream of a believer is one of forty-six parts of prophetism, and whatever belongs to prothetism can never be false."

Bukhari 87.144

The worst lie you can tell is about a dream you have not dreamt.

Narrated Ibn 'Umar:

Allah's Apostle said, "The worst lie is that a person claims to have seen a dream which he has not seen."

Bukhari 87.167

Lying about a dream you have not dreamt is not the only worse lie you can tell!

Narrated Wathila bin Al-Asqa:

Allah's Apostle said, "Verily, one of the worst lies is to claim falsely to be the son of someone other than one's real father, or to claim to have had a dream one has not had, or to attribute to me what I have not said."

Bukhari 56.712

Whatever you do, don't lie about having a dream unless you have very nimble fingers which will be put to the test on Judgement Day.

Narrated Ibn Abbas:

The Prophet said, "Whoever claims to have seen a dream which he did not see, will be ordered to make a knot between two barley grains which he will not be able to do; and if somebody listens to the talk of some people who do not like him (to listen) or they run away from him, then molten lead will be poured into his ears on the Day of Resurrection; and whoever makes a picture, will be punished on the Day of Resurrection and will be ordered to put a soul in that picture, which he will not be able to do."

Bukhari 87.165

A dream announcing the coming of two liars:

Narrated Ibn Abbas:

Musailama-al-Kadhdhab (i.e. the liar) came in the life-time of Allah's Apostle with many of his people (to Medina) and said, "If Muhammad makes me his successor, I will follow him."

Allah's Apostle went up to him with Thabit bin Qais bin Shams; and Allah's Apostle was carrying a piece of a date-palm leaf in his hand. He stood before Musailama (and his companions) and said, "If you asked me even this piece (of a leaf), I would not give it to you. You cannot avoid the fate you are destined to, by Allah. If you reject Islam, Allah will destroy you. I think that you are most probably the same person whom I have seen in the dream."

Abu Huraira told me that Allah's Apostle; said, "While I was sleeping, I saw (in a dream) two gold bracelets round my arm, and that worried me too much. Then I was instructed divinely in my dream, to blow them off and so I blew them off, and they flew away. I interpreted the two bracelets as symbols of two liars who would appear after me. And so one of them was Al-Ansi and the other was Musailama Al-Kadhdhab from Al-Yamama."

Bukhari 56.817

A dream where apostates, some of them close collaborators of God's Messenger, are sent to Hell.

Narrated Abu Huraira:

The Prophet said, "While I was sleeping, a group (of my followers were brought close to me), and when I recognized them, a man (an angel) came out from amongst (us) me and them, he said (to them), 'Come along.'

I asked, 'Where?'

He said, 'To the (Hell) Fire, by Allah.'

I asked, 'What is wrong with them?'

He said, 'They turned apostate as renegades after you left.'

Then behold! (Another) group (of my followers) were brought close to me, and when I recognized them, a man (an angel) came out from (me and them) he said (to them); Come along.'

I asked, 'Where?'

He said, 'To the (Hell) Fire, by Allah.'

I asked, 'What is wrong with them?'

He said, 'They turned apostate as renegades after you left.'

So I did not see anyone of them escaping except a few who were like camels without a shepherd."

Bukhari 76.587

Eclipses

Most, if not all believers, are familiar with the Prophet's flight to heaven on a Pegasus-like flying horse. His stopover in Jerusalem, before getting back on al-Burak the wonder horse for the short flight to Paradise, consecrated the rock from which he took off as the third holiest site in Islam after Mecca and Medina. Paradise, in the Koran, is just above the clouds held up by invisible pillars. It would have taken only a few flaps of the wings of the powerful animal that was al-Burak to get there, the lowest level anyway.

Jerusalem is about 762 miles (1,235.82 km) as a flying-horse flies. The Prophet said, "The animal's step (was so wide that it) reached the farthest point within the reach of the animal's sight." Even so, with God's Messenger hanging on for dear life, it would have taken some time to reach Jerusalem (the irony is that the Prophet undoubtedly died from injuries sustained from falling off a horse, one without wings).

We know that Gabriel showed up with al-Burak after the Prophet had turned in for the night. Taking into account the return trip, this did not leave much time to meet with his counterparts from the Bible (in ethereal form it is assumed), negotiate the prayers, and take a guided tour of the seven levels of Paradise and the seven levels of Allah's Hell, which are described in some detail in the Koran, details that could only have come from an eyewitness.

Religious scholars have argued the trip probably occurred in a dream which would negate any flying time (if in a dream, why the horse?). Still, there was so much to do and see that the Prophet could not have taken it all in with just a few hours of sleep, or even fewer hours if he was awake, especially considering the expanse of Paradise and the formidable, forbidding territory of Hell. So why do we know so much about both places? The answer is in the hadiths. We now know from the sayings of the Prophet that Allah projected visions of Heaven and Hell, which only His Messenger could see, at various times during the day, most often during eclipses; and that at night He took His Messenger on out-of-this-world tours of both places in palpable dreams.

Theoretically, when unbelievers die, they are not sent to Hell until Judgement Day; in the meantime, they are left to be tormented in their graves (read *The Islamic Hereafter - Life in the Grave,* Boreal Books 2013). However, in many of the Prophet's visions, like in the following, God's Messenger reports seeing an unbeliever burning in Hell, instead of being tormented in his grave. Lahai is from what

Islam calls the Time of Ignorance i.e. the time before Islam. Luhai had the temerity to free animals as offering to his god, as opposed to cutting their throats and letting them bleed to death as is the Muslim tradition.

Narrated 'Aisha:

Once the sun eclipsed and Allah's Apostle stood up for the prayer and recited a very long Sura and then bowed for a long while and then raised his head and started reciting another Sura. Then he bowed, and after finishing, he prostrated and did the same in the second Raka and then said, "These (lunar and solar eclipses) are two of the signs of Allah and if you see them, pray till the eclipse is over. No doubt, while standing at this place I saw everything promised to me by Allah and I saw (Paradise) and I wanted to pluck a bunch (of grapes) therefrom, at the time when you saw me stepping forward. No doubt, I saw Hell with its different parts destroying each other when you saw me retreating and in it I saw 'Amr bin Luhai who started the tradition of freeing animals (set them free) in the name of idols."

Bukhari 22.303

Lahai, instead of awaiting Judgement Day and due process in the cramp confines of his tomb underground, is, according to the Prophet, dragging his intestines through Hell.

Narrated Said bin Al-Musaiyab:

Al-Bahira was an animal whose milk was spared for the idols and other deities, and so nobody was allowed to milk it. As-Saiba was an animal which they (i.e. infidels) used to set free in the names of their gods so that it would not be used for carrying anything.

Abu Huraira said, "The Prophet said, 'I saw Amr bin 'Amir bin Luhai Al-Khuzai dragging his intestines in the (Hell) Fire, for he was the first man who started the custom of releasing animals (for the sake of false gods).'"

Bukhari 76.723

During a solar eclipse God's Messenger mentions the interrogation that takes place in the grave where Amr bin Luhai should have been.

Narrated Asma' bint Abu Bakr:

I came to 'Aisha the wife of the Prophet during the solar eclipse. The people were standing and offering the prayer and she was also praying. I asked her, "What is wrong with the people?" She beckoned with her hand towards the sky and said, "Subhan Allah (Glorious is God)."

I asked her, "Is there a sign?"

She pointed out, "Yes." So I, too, stood for the prayer till I fell unconscious and later on I poured water on my head.

After the prayer, Allah's Apostle praised and glorified Allah and said, "Just now I have seen something which I never saw before at this place of mine, including Paradise and Hell. I have been inspired (and have understood) that you will be put to trials in your graves and these trials will be like the trials of Ad-Dajjal (the false messiah), or nearly like it (the sub narrator is not sure of what Asma' said). Angels will come to every one of you and ask, 'What do you know about this man?'

A believer will reply, 'He is Muhammad, Allah's Apostle, and he came to us with self-evident truth and guidance. So we accepted his teaching, believed and followed him.'

Then the angels will say to him to sleep in peace as they have come to know that he was a believer. On the other hand a hypocrite or a doubtful person will reply, 'I do not know but heard the people saying something and so I said the same.'"

Bukhari 4:184

During a solar eclipse the Prophet reached for some fruit from a most unlikely place, then thought better of it. The following may also be an indication that what God's Messenger was experiencing was akin to an all-encompassing illusion for him to think he could grab a bite to eat from a garden in Paradise during the eclipse prayer.

Narrated 'Abdullah bin 'Abbas:

One solar eclipse occurred during the lifetime of Allah's Apostle. He offered the eclipse prayer. His companions asked, "O Allah's Apostle! We saw you trying to take something while standing at your place and then we saw you retreating."

The Prophet said, "I was shown Paradise and wanted to have a bunch of fruit from it. Had I taken it, you would have eaten from it as long as the world remains."

Bukhari 12.715

A short narration about visions and eclipses:

Narrated 'Abdullah bin 'Abbas:

The sun eclipsed and Allah's Apostle offered the eclipse prayer and said, "I have been shown the Hellfire (now) and I never saw a worse and horrible sight than the sight I have seen today."

Bukhari 8.423

One of the horrors that the Prophet saw during the eclipse of the sun was women who, like Lahai, should have been in their abysmal graves, not burning in Hell (expect more hadiths about women burning in Hell, undeniably a favourite topic of the Prophet).

Narrated 'Abdullah bin Abbas:

During the lifetime of Allah's Apostle, the sun eclipsed. Allah's Apostle offered the prayer of (the) eclipse) and so did the people along with him. He performed a long Qiyam (standing posture) during which Surat-al-Baqara could have been recited; then he performed a prolonged bowing, then raised his head and stood for a long time which was slightly less than that of the first Qiyam (and recited Qur'an).

Then he performed a prolonged bowing again but the period was shorter than the period of the first bowing, then he stood up and then prostrated. Again he stood up, but this time the period of standing was less than the first standing.

Then he performed a prolonged bowing but of a lesser duration than the first, then he stood up again for a long time but for a lesser duration than the first.

Then he performed a prolonged bowing but of lesser duration than the first, and then he again stood up, and then prostrated and then finished his prayer. By then the sun eclipse had cleared.

The Prophet then said, "The sun and the moon are two signs among the signs of Allah, and they do not eclipse because of the death or birth of someone, so when you observe the eclipse, remember Allah (offer the eclipse prayer)."

They (the people) said, "O Allah's Apostle! We saw you stretching your hand to take something at this place of yours, then we saw you stepping backward."

He said, "I saw Paradise (or Paradise was shown to me), and I stretched my hand to pluck a bunch (of grapes), and had I plucked it, you would have eaten of it as long as this world exists. Then I saw the (Hell) Fire, and I have never before, seen such a horrible sight as that, and I saw that the majority of its dwellers were women."

The people asked, "O Allah's Apostle! What is the reason for that?"

He replied, "Because of their ungratefulness."

It was said. "Do they disbelieve in Allah (are they ungrateful to Allah)?"

He replied, "They are not thankful to their husbands and are ungrateful for the favors done to them. Even if you do good to one of them all your life, when she seems some harshness from you, she will say, 'I have never seen any good from you.'"

Bukhari 62.125

(For more or less the same story told by a different narrator see *A Palice in the Sky.*)

God's Messenger was not fond of man's best friend. He almost had them all exterminated when Gabriel did not show up when expected and the Prophet blamed a puppy.

A'isha reported that Gabriel (peace be upon him) made a promise with Allah's Messenger (may peace be upon him) to come at a definite hour; that hour came but he did not visit him. And there was in his hand (in the hand of Allah's Apostle) a staff. He threw it from his hand and said: Never has Allah or His messengers (angels) ever broken their promise. Then he cast a glance (and by chance) found a puppy under his cot and said: 'A'isha, when did this dog enter here?

She said: By Allah, I don't know He then commanded and it was turned out.

Then Gabriel came and Allah's Messenger (may peace be upon him) said to him: You promised me and I waited for you, but you did not come, whereupon he said: It was the dog in your house which prevented me (to come), for we (angels) do not enter a house in which there is a dog or a picture.

Sahih Muslim 24.5246

Cats, however, don't appear to have been a problem considering what he saw in another eclipse-inspired vision. Also, returning to the idea that God's Messenger may have been hallucinating, in the following hadith, the Prophet asks (God or Gabriel, it has to be assumed) why the woman in Hell is being lacerated by a cat.

Narrated Asma' bint Abi Bakr:

The Prophet once offered the eclipse prayer. He stood for a long time and then did a prolonged bowing. He stood up straight again and kept on standing for a long time, then bowed a long bowing and then stood up straight and then prostrated a prolonged prostration and then lifted his head and prostrated a prolonged prostration. And then he stood up for a long time and then did a prolonged bowing and then stood up straight again and kept on standing for a long time. Then he bowed a long bowing and then stood up straight and then prostrated a prolonged prostration and then lifted his head and went for a prolonged prostration.

On completion of the prayer, he said, "Paradise became so near to me that if I had dared, I would have plucked one of its bunches for you and Hell became so near to me that [I] said, 'O my Lord I will be among those people?' Then suddenly I saw a woman and a cat was lacerating her with it claws. On inquiring, it was said that the woman had imprisoned the cat till it died of starvation and she neither fed it nor freed it so that it could feed itself."

Bukhari 12.712

In the absence of eclipses, God's Messenger was often distracted at the most opportune or inopportune times depending on your point of view, such as during question and answer sessions about Islam.

Narrated Anas bin Malik:

Allah's Apostle came out as the sun declined at mid-day and offered the Zuhr prayer. He then stood on the pulpit and spoke about the Hour (Day of Judgment) and said that in it there would be tremendous things. He then said, "Whoever likes to ask me about anything he can do so and I shall reply as long as I am at this place of mine."

Most of the people wept and the Prophet said repeatedly, "Ask me."

Abdullah bin Hudhafa As-Sahmi stood up and said, "Who is my father?"

The Prophet said, "Your father is Hudhafa."

The Prophet repeatedly said, "Ask me."

Then Umar knelt before him and said, "We are pleased with Allah as our Lord, Islam as our religion, and Muhammad as our Prophet."

The Prophet then became quiet and said, "Paradise and Hell-fire were displayed in front of me on this wall just now and I have never seen a better thing (than the former) and a worse thing (than the latter)."

Bukhari 10.515

In another hadith, perhaps a variation of the previous one, it is clear that the Prophet was not always pleased to be pelted with questions.

Narrated Anas:

Once the people started asking Allah's Apostle questions, and they asked so many questions that he became angry and ascended the pulpit and said, "I will answer whatever questions you may ask me today."

I looked right and left and saw everyone covering his face with his garment and weeping. Behold! There was a man who, on quarreling with the people, used to be called as a son of a person other than his father. He said, "O Allah's Apostle! Who is my father?"

The Prophet replied, "Your father is Hudhaifa."

And then 'Umar got up and said, "We accept Allah as our Lord, and Islam as (our) religion, and Muhammad as (our) Apostle; and we seek refuge with Allah from the afflictions."

Allah's Apostle said, "I have never seen a day like today in its good and its evil for Paradise and the Hell Fire were displayed in front of me, till I saw them just beyond this wall."

Bukhari 75.373

Even prayers were not free from Divine interruptions.

Narrated Anas bin Malik:

The Prophet led us in prayer and then went up to the pulpit and beckoned with both hands towards the Qibla of the mosque and then said, "When I started leading you in prayer, I saw the display of Paradise and Hell on the wall of the mosque (facing the Qibla). I never saw good and bad as I have seen today." He repeated the last statement thrice.

Bukhari 12. 716

The sun eclipsed on the day Ibrahim, the son of God's Messenger, died

Narrated Al-Mughira bin Shu'ba:

"The sun eclipsed in the life-time of Allah's Apostle on the day when (his son) Ibrahim died. So the people said that the sun had eclipsed because of the death of Ibrahim. Allah's Apostle said, "The sun and the moon do not eclipse because of the death or life (i.e. birth) of some-one. When you see the eclipse pray and invoke Allah."

Bukhari 17.153

Eclipses are just one more way Allah frightens the ones He loves; frightens them into offering even more prayers.

Narrated Abu Bakra:

Allah's Apostle said: "The sun and the moon are two signs amongst the signs of Allah and they do not eclipse because of the death of someone but Allah frightens His devotees with them."

Bukhari 17.158

Narrated Abu Bakra:

The solar eclipse occurred while we were sitting with the Prophet. He got up dragging his garment (on the ground) hurriedly till he reached the mosque. The people turned (to the mosque) and he offered a two-Rak'at prayer whereupon the eclipse was over and he traced us and said, "The sun and the moon are two signs among the signs of Allah, so if you see a thing like this (eclipse) then offer the prayer and invoke Allah till He removes that state,"

Bukhari 72.676

Gabriel - Messenger to the Messenger

God's Messenger to the Messenger, the angel Gabriel, is even more prominent in the hadiths than he is in the Koran. In the hadiths the Prophet seems not be constrained by issues of credibility in talking about his unique relationship with God's go-to angel-confidant. The angel Gabriel is the only angel mentioned, by two different narrators, as having 600 wings. The fact that the Prophet, an alleged illiterate, stayed calm and took the time to count them, during their first or perhaps their second meeting, while memorizing the Koran is even more impressive.

Narrated Abu Ishaq-Ash-Shaibani:

I asked Zir bin Hubaish regarding the Statement of Allah: "And was at a distance of but two bow-lengths or (even) nearer; So did (Allah) convey The Inspiration to His slave (Gabriel) and then he (Gabriel) Conveyed (that to Muhammad)." (53:9-10)

On that, Zir said, "Ibn Mas'ud informed us that the Prophet had seen Gabriel having 600 wings."

Bukhari 54.455

Narrated Abdullah:

Regarding the Verses: 'And was at a distance of but two bow-lengths or (even) nearer; So did (Allah) convey the Inspiration to His slave (Gabriel) and then he Gabriel) conveyed (that to Muhammad...' (53:9-10)

Ibn Mas'ud narrated to us that the Prophet had seen Gabriel with six hundred wings.

Bukhari 60.379

Gabriel is also the only angel that, at least once, appeared before the Prophet seated on a chair; a very, very large chair with a low back is assumed.

Narrated Jabir bin 'Abdullah:

That he heard the Prophet saying, "The Divine Inspiration was delayed for a short period but suddenly, as I was walking I heard a voice in the sky, and when I looked up towards the sky, to my surprise, I saw the angel who had come to me in the Hira Cave, and he was sitting on a chair in between the sky and the earth. I was so frightened by him that I fell on the ground and came to my family and said (to them), 'Cover me! (with a blanket), cover me!' Then Allah sent the Revelation: 'O, You wrapped up (In a blanket)! (Arise and warn! And your Lord magnify And keep pure your garments, And desert the idols.'"(74:1-5)

Bukhari 54.461

Gabriel often took the form of a man.

Narrated Aisha:

Al Harith bin Hisham asked the Prophet, "How does the divine inspiration come to you?"

He replied, "In all these ways: The Angel sometimes comes to me with a voice which resembles the sound of a ringing bell, and when this state abandons me, I remember what the Angel has said, and this type of Divine Inspiration is the hardest on me; and sometimes the Angel comes to me in the shape of a man and talks to me, and I understand and remember what he says."

Bukhari 54.438

Gabriel once appeared to the Prophet as a mountain of a man.

Narrated Masruq:

I asked Aisha "What about His Statement: 'Then he (Gabriel) approached and came closer, and was at a distance of but two bow-lengths or (even) nearer? '" (53:8-9)

She replied, "It was Gabriel who used to come to the Prophet in the figure of a man, but on that occasion, he came in his actual and real figure and (he was so huge) that he covered the whole horizon."

Bukhari 54.458

Only the Prophet could see Allah's super angel, but that did not stop God's Messenger from observing the common courtesies, and introducing Gabriel to anyone who might be in the same room, such as his child-bride Aisha.

Narrated Abu Salama:

'Aisha said that the Prophet said to her "O 'Aisha! This is Gabriel and he sends his (greetings) salutations to you."

'Aisha said, "Salutations (Greetings) to him, and Allah's Mercy and Blessings be on him," and addressing the Prophet she said, "You see what I don't see."

Bukhari 54.440

It must have been difficult for the Prophet, on occasion, that none could see or hear what he could see and hear.

Narrated 'Aisha:

Allah's Apostle said, "O Aisha! This is Gabriel sending his greetings to you."

I said, "Peace, and Allah's Mercy be on him."

'Aisha added: "The Prophet used to see things which we used not to see."

Bukhari 73.220

Aisha's statement notwithstanding, some would claim to have seen Gabriel in conversation with the Prophet but did not realize it at the time.

Narrated Abu Uthman:

I got the news that Gabriel came to the Prophet while Um Salama was present. Gabriel started talking (to the Prophet and then left. The Prophet said to Um Salama, "(Do you know) who it was?" (or a similar question).

She said, "It was Dihya (a handsome person amongst the companions of the Prophet)."

Later on Um Salama said, "By Allah! I thought he was none but Dihya, till I heard the Prophet talking about Gabriel in his sermon."

Bukhari 56.827

It may have been Gabriel, in the form of a "well-shaped human being", who impregnated Mary, the Mother of Jesus. (you will find the relevant revelations in *Shared Prophets - Jesus Conceived*, Boreal Books, 2012).

Sometimes it was just a voice that someone heard. Of course, the overheard conversations were all one-sided, even the one where an incredulous Prophet asks Gabriel three times about believing men going to Paradise even if they "committed theft or committed illegal sexual intercourse" (the exclusion of women is deliberate; females who commit illegal intercourse are not entitled to Allah's Mercy and Compassion).

Narrated Abu Dhar:

Once I went out at night and found Allah's Apostle walking all alone accompanied by nobody, and I thought that perhaps he disliked that someone should accompany him. So I walked in the shade, away from the moonlight, but the Prophet looked behind and saw me and said, "Who is that?"

I replied, "Abu Dhar, let Allah get me sacrificed for you!"

He said, "O Abu Dhar, come here!"

So I accompanied him for a while and then he said, "The rich are in fact the poor (little rewarded) on the Day of Resurrection except him whom Allah gives wealth which he gives (in charity) to his right, left, front and back, and does good deeds with it."

I walked with him a little longer. Then he said to me, "Sit down here." So he made me sit in an open space surrounded by rocks, and said to me, "Sit here till I come back to you."

He went towards Al-Harra till I could not see him, and he stayed away for a long period, and then I heard him saying, while he was coming, "Even if he had committed theft, and even if he had committed illegal sexual intercourse?"

When he came, I could not remain patient and asked him, "O Allah's Prophet! Let Allah get me sacrificed for you! Whom were you speaking to by the side of Al-Harra? I did not hear anybody responding to your talk."

He said, "It was Gabriel who appeared to me beside Al-Harra and said, 'Give the good news to your followers that whoever dies without having worshipped anything besides Allah, will enter Paradise.'

I said, 'O Gabriel! Even if he had committed theft or committed illegal sexual intercourse?'

He said, 'Yes.'

I said, 'Even if he has committed theft or committed illegal sexual intercourse?'

He said, 'Yes.'

I said, 'Even if he has committed theft or committed illegal sexual intercourse?'

He said, 'Yes.'"

Bukhari 76.450

The Prophet repeating himself in the previous hadith is no accident.

Narrated Anas:

Whenever the Prophet spoke a sentence (said a thing), he used to repeat it thrice so that the people could understand it properly from him and whenever he asked permission to enter, (he knocked [at] the door) thrice with greeting.

Bukhari 3.95

A shorter narration about theft and illegal sexual intercourse not being a barrier to Paradise for males who worship only Allah:

Narrated Abu Dharr:

The Prophet said, "Gabriel came to me and gave me the glad tidings that anyone who died without worshipping anything besides Allah, would enter Paradise."

I asked (Gabriel), "Even if he committed theft, and even if he committed illegal sexual intercourse?"

He said, "(Yes), even if he committed theft, and even if he committed illegal sexual intercourse."

Bukhari 93.579

The Prophet would have loved to see his beloved Gabriel more often as I am sure Gabriel would have loved to spend more time with Allah's beloved Messenger, but it was not the angel's decision to make.

Narrated Ibn Abbas:

Allah's Apostle asked Gabriel, "Why don't you visit us more often than you do?" Then the following Holy Verse was revealed (in this respect): "And we (angels) descend not but by the order of your Lord. To Him belong what is before us and what is behind us, and what is between those two and your Lord was never forgetful." (19:64)

Bukhari 54.441

A typical English translation of the Koran contains 6,346 verses if you include the 112 unnumbered Basmalahs, the formula-invocation "in the name of Allah, the Compassionate, the Merciful" which appears at the beginning of every chapter except the first and the ninth. This means that the Prophet, as publicized in the following hadiths, in effect memorized, or at least listened to the equivalent of 44,422 revelations. Quite a feat for both messengers.

Narrated Ibn Abbas:

Allah's Apostle said, "Gabriel read the Qur'an to me in one way (i.e. dialect) and I continued asking him to read it in different ways till he read it in seven different ways."

Bukhari 54.442

Narrated 'Abdullah bin 'Abbas:

Allah's Apostle said, "Gabriel recited the Qur'an to me in one way. Then I requested him (to read it in another way), and continued asking him to recite it in other ways, and he recited it in several ways till he ultimately recited it in seven different ways."

Bukhari 61.513

It was Gabriel who first informed the Prophet about angels' aversion to pictures and dogs, including a picture of a dog.

Narrated Salim's father:

Once Gabriel promised the Prophet (that he would visit him, but Gabriel did not come) and later on he said, "We, angels, do not enter a house which contains a picture or a dog."

Bukhari 54.450

Narrated Salim's father:

Once Gabriel promised to visit the Prophet but he delayed and the Prophet got worried about that. At last he came out and found Gabriel and complained to him of his grief (for his delay). Gabriel said to him, "We do not enter a place in which there is a picture or a dog."

Bukhari 72.843

Narrated Abu Talha:

I heard Allah's Apostle saying; "Angels (of Mercy) do not enter a house wherein there is a dog or a picture of a living creature (a human being or an animal)."

Bukhari 54.448

God's Messenger was so mad at the puppy which caused Gabriel to skip his meeting with him, that he initially ordered all dogs to be killed.

Maimuna (another of the Prophet's wives) reported that one morning Allah's Messenger was silent with grief. Maimuna said: "Allah's Messenger, I find a change in your mood today."

Allah's Messenger said: "Gabriel had promised me that he would meet me tonight, but he did not meet me. By Allah, he never broke his promises," and Allah's Messenger spent the day in this sad mood. Then it occurred to him that there

had been a puppy under their cot. He commanded and it
was turned out. He then took some water in his hand and
sprinkled it at that place. When it was evening Gabriel met
him and he said to him: "You promised me that you would
meet me the previous night."

He said: "Yes, but we do not enter a house in which there is
a dog or a picture."

Then on that very morning he commanded the killing of the
dogs until he announced that the dog kept for the orchards
should also be killed, but he spared the dog meant for the
protection of extensive fields or big gardens.

Sahih Muslim 24.5248

He later amended his order and decreed that only black dogs be
killed, and still later, that only black dogs with spots over their eyes
be slaughtered.

Narrated Abdullah ibn Mughaffal:

The Prophet (peace be upon him) said: Were dogs not a
species of creature I should command that they all be killed;
but kill every pure black one.

Abu Dawud 16.2839

Abu Zubair heard Jabir Abdullah saying:

Allah's messenger ordered us to kill dogs and we carried out
this order so much so that we also killed the dog roaming
with a woman from the desert. Then Allah's apostle forbade
their killing. He said: "It is your duty to kill the jet-black
(dog) having two spots (on the eyes) for it is a devil."

Sahih Muslim 10.3813

Gabriel once appeared in a cloud, with an unlikely angel, to cheer up
a depressed Prophet. Only a real friend would show up with an angel
capable of lifting mountains and offer to drop one on some tribal
chiefs who had caused his buddy grief by refusing to become Muslims
when he asked them to do so.

Narrated 'Aisha:

That she asked the Prophet, "Have you encountered a day
harder than the day of the battle of Uhud?"

The Prophet replied, "Your tribes have troubled me a lot,
and the worse trouble was the trouble on the day of 'Aqaba
when I presented myself to Ibn 'Abd-Yalail bin 'Abd-Kulal
and he did not respond to my demand. So I departed,
overwhelmed with excessive sorrow, and proceeded on, and
could not relax till I found myself at Qarnath-Tha-alib where

I lifted my head towards the sky to see a cloud shading me unexpectedly. I looked up and saw Gabriel in it. He called me saying, 'Allah has heard your people's saying to you, and what they have replied back to you, Allah has sent the Angel of the Mountains to you so that you may order him to do whatever you wish to these people.' The Angel of the Mountains called and greeted me, and then said, 'O Muhammad! Order what you wish. If you like, I will let Al-Akh-Shabain (i.e. two mountains) fall on them.'"

The Prophet said, "No but I hope that Allah will let them beget children who will worship Allah Alone, and will worship None besides Him."

Bukhari 54.454

Rather than wake his good friend, Gabriel would meet him in his dreams, such as the time he introduced the angel Michael to the Prophet.

Narrated Samura:

The Prophet said, "Last night I saw (in a dream) two men coming to me. One of them said, 'The person who kindles the fire is Malik, the gate-keeper of the (Hell) Fire, and I am Gabriel, and this is Michael.'"

Bukhari 54.459

Not all people were convinced that it was an angel who was in regular communication with their kin.

Narrated Jundab bin 'Abdullah:

Gabriel did not come to the Prophet (for some time) and so one of the Quraish women said, "His Satan has deserted him."

So came the Divine Revelation: "By the forenoon And by the night When it is still! Your Lord (O Muhammad) has neither Forsaken you Nor hated you." (93:1-3)

Bukhari 21.225

During the month of Ramadan, Gabriel visited the Prophet every day; visits during which their roles seemed to be reversed.

Narrated Ibn 'Abbas:

The Prophet was the most generous amongst the people, and he used to be more so in the month of Ramadan when Gabriel visited him, and Gabriel used to meet him on every night of Ramadan till the end of the month. The Prophet used to recite the Holy Qur'an to Gabriel, and when Gabriel met him, he used to be more generous than a fast wind (which causes rain and welfare).

Bukhari 31.126

What did I say about Gabriel being Allah's go-to angel for just about everything.

Narrated Abu Huraira:

The Prophet said, "If Allah loves a person, He calls Gabriel saying, 'Allah loves so and-so; O Gabriel! Love him.' Gabriel would love him and make an announcement amongst the inhabitants of the Heaven. 'Allah loves so-and-so, therefore you should love him also,' and so all the inhabitants of the Heaven would love him, and then he is granted the pleasure of the people on the earth."

Bukhari 54.431

Of course Gabriel was the Prophet's guide and companion during the night he visited with God in Paradise and his counterparts from the Bible. The narrators, like God's Messenger, assumed that the heart, not the brain, was where the mind i.e. consciousness and unconsciousness (dreaming) manifested themselves.

Narrated Sharik bin 'Abdullah bin Abi Namr:

I heard Anas bin Malik telling us about the night when the Prophet was made to travel from the Ka'ba Mosque. Three persons (i.e. angels) came to the Prophet before he was divinely inspired, while he was sleeping in Al Masjid-ul-Haram.

The first (of the three angels) said, "Which of them is he?"

The second said, "He is the best of them."

That was all that happened then, and he did not see them till they came at another night and he perceived their presence with his heart, for the eyes of the Prophet were closed when he was asleep, but his heart was not asleep (not unconscious). This is characteristic of all the prophets: Their eyes sleep but their hearts do not sleep.

Then Gabriel took charge of the Prophet and ascended along with him to the Heaven.

Bukhari 56.770

Gabriel not only delivered Allah's revelations but also personal messages such as the one for his first wife Khadija who would die penniless in a ditch outside Mecca. This was before her husband achieved fame and fortune after seeking refuge in Medina.

Narrated Abu Huraira:

The Prophet said that Gabriel said, "Here is Khadija coming to you with a dish of food or a tumbler containing something to drink. Convey to her a greeting from her Lord (Allah) and give her the glad tidings that she will have a palace in Paradise built of Qasab wherein there will be neither any noise nor any fatigue (trouble)."

Bukhari 93.588

Of course, Gabriel accompanied the Prophet in all his battles dressed ready for the occasion, in this instance the battle of Badr.

Narrated Ibn 'Abbas:

The Prophet said on the day (of the battle) of Badr, "This is Gabriel holding the head of his horse and equipped with arms for the battle."

Bukhari 59.330

The Prophet would have most, if not all the poets who mocked him killed when he got the chance; this does not mean that he was reticent in enlisting his own rhymesters, perhaps even Gabriel, to mock his enemies.

Narrated Al-Bara:

The Prophet said to Hassan, "Lampoon them (the pagans) in verse, and Gabriel is with you."

Bukhari 73.174

After all is said and done, did Gabriel reveal the Koran to the Prophet, or did he just listen to what Allah had already inputted directly into His Messenger's brain?

Narrated Ibn Abbas:

(as regards) Allah's Statement: "Move not your tongue concerning (the Quran) to make haste therewith." (75:16) When Gabriel revealed the Divine Inspiration in Allah's Apostle, he (Allah's Apostle) moved his tongue and lips, and that state used to be very hard for him, and that movement indicated that revelation was taking place. So Allah revealed in Surat Al-Qiyama which begins: "I do swear by the Day of Resurrection... " (75) the Verses: "Move not your tongue concerning (the Quran) to make haste therewith. It is for Us to collect it (Quran) in your mind, and give you the ability to recite it by heart." (75:16-17)

Ibn Abbas added: It is for Us to collect it (Qur'an) (in your mind), and give you the ability to recite it by heart means, "When We reveal it, listen. Then it is for Us to explain it," means, "It is for us to explain it through your tongue."

So whenever Gabriel came to Allah's Apostle he would keep quiet (and listen), and when the Angel left, the Prophet would recite that revelation as Allah promised him.

Bukhari 60.451

The Most Influential Christian of All Time

Jewish hospitality ensured that Islam had a future, but it was a Christian kin of the future Prophet Muhammad who convinced him that he was indeed called upon to be God's Messenger, and not to be afraid. We are again indebted to Aisha for the story of her future husband's first encounter with the Angel Gabriel and how Waraqa convinced him that the angel had been sent by Allah.

Narrated 'Aisha:

The commencement of the Divine Inspiration to Allah's Apostle was in the form of good dreams which came true like bright day light, and then the love of seclusion was bestowed upon him.

He used to go in seclusion in the cave of Hira where he used to worship (Allah alone) continuously for many days before his desire to see his family.

He used to take with him the journey food for the stay and then come back to (his wife) Khadija to take his food like-wise again till suddenly the Truth descended upon him while he was in the cave of Hira. The angel came to him and asked him to read. The Prophet replied, "I do not know how to read."

The Prophet added, "The angel caught me (forcefully) and pressed me so hard that I could not bear it any more. He then released me and again asked me to read and I replied, 'I do not know how to read.' Thereupon he caught me again and pressed me a second time till I could not bear it any more. He then released me and again asked me to read but again I replied, 'I do not know how to read (or what shall I read)?'

Thereupon he caught me for the third time and pressed me, and then released me and said, 'Read in the name of your Lord, who has created (all that exists) has created man from a clot. Read! And your Lord is the Most Generous.' (96:1, 96:2, 96:3) Then Allah's Apostle returned with the Inspiration and with his heart beating severely. Then he went to Khadija bint Khuwailid and said, 'Cover me! Cover me!'"

They covered him till his fear was over and after that he told her everything that had happened and said, "I fear that something may happen to me."

Khadija replied, "Never! By Allah, Allah will never disgrace you. You keep good relations with your kith and kin, help the poor and the destitute, serve your guests generously and assist the deserving calamity-afflicted ones."

Khadija then accompanied him to her cousin Waraqa bin Naufal bin Asad bin 'Abdul 'Uzza, who, during the pre-Islamic period became a Christian and used to write the writing with Hebrew letters. He would write from the Gospel in Hebrew as much as Allah wished him to write. He was an old man and had lost his eyesight.

Khadija said to Waraqa, "Listen to the story of your nephew, O my cousin!"

Waraqa asked, "O my nephew! What have you seen?"

Allah's Apostle described whatever he had seen.

Waraqa said, "This is the same one who keeps the secrets (angel Gabriel) whom Allah had sent to Moses. I wish I were young and could live up to the time when your people would turn you out."

Allah's Apostle asked, "Will they drive me out?"

Waraqa replied in the affirmative and said, "Anyone (man) who came with something similar to what you have brought was treated with hostility; and if I should remain alive till the day when you will be turned out then I would support you strongly." But after a few days Waraqa died and the Divine Inspiration was also paused for a while.

Narrated Jabir bin:

'Abdullah Al-Ansari while talking about the period of pause in revelation reporting the speech of the Prophet "While I was walking, all of a sudden I heard a voice from the sky. I looked up and saw the same angel who had visited me at the cave of Hira' sitting on a chair between the sky and the earth. I got afraid of him and came back home and said, 'Wrap me (in blankets).' And then Allah revealed the following Holy Verses (of Quran): 'O you (i.e. Muhammad)! wrapped up in garments!' Arise and warn (the people against Allah's Punishment),... up to 'and desert the idols.' (74:1-5) After this the revelation started coming strongly, frequently and regularly."

Bukhari 1.3

Hell

The following should be read in conjunction with *The Islamic Hereafter – Hell, Boreal Books (2012)* or *Pain, Pleasure and Prejudice - Hell, Boreal Books (2012)*.

One quarter to a one third of the Koran is about Paradise and Hell. With so many verses about Allah's out-of-this world carrot and stick, hadiths about Hell, and how you get there might appear superfluous. Nonetheless, following are a few which may hold some interest. Hell, in both the Koran and the Hadiths is an enormous living thing which will have to be dragged to its appointed place on Judgement Day.

> Abu Huraira reported Allah's Messenger (may peace be upon him) as saying: The Hell would he brought on that day (the Day of judgment) with seventy thousand bridles and every bridle would be controlled by seventy thousand angels.

> *Sahih Muslim 40.6810*

From what he saw of Hell, God's Messenger drew interesting conclusions; for instance, that Hell's Fire has an impact on the weather. The Prophet may not have been aware that in the southern hemisphere the seasons are reversed when he made the following observation:

> **Narrated Abu Huraira:**
>
> The Prophet said, "In very hot weather delay the Zuhr prayer till it becomes (a bit) cooler because the severity of heat is from the raging of Hell-fire. The Hell-fire of Hell complained to its Lord saying: O Lord! My parts are eating (destroying) one another. So Allah allowed it to take two breaths, one in the winter and the other in the summer. The breath in the summer is at the time when you feel the severest heat and the breath in the winter is at the time when you feel the severest cold."

> *Bukhari 10.512*

How hot is Hell's Fire?

> **Narrated Abu Huraira:**
>
> Allah's Apostle said, "Your (ordinary) fire is one of 70 parts of the (Hell) Fire."

Someone asked, "O Allah's Apostle this (ordinary) fire would have been sufficient (to torture the unbelievers)."

Allah's Apostle said, "The (Hell) Fire has 69 parts more than the ordinary (worldly) fire, each part is as hot as this (worldly) fire."

Bukhari 54.487

Is it Allah or His Messenger who can't pass up an opportunity to denigrate women? His Messenger reaches for some fruit from a tree in Paradise and gets a appalling vision of women burning in Hell. It is not known if it was Allah who provided His Messenger with an explanation as to why these women needed to suffer horribly for an eternity, or did the Prophet assume the punishment based on the difficulties he faced managing a household of more than a dozen mostly young wives (thirteen at one time) for whom he could have been a father. It may be telling that on a number of occasions, as Allah reveals in His Koran, His Messenger had to call on Him to discipline some of his more boisterous young spouses (the relevant revelations are in *Women and the Koran*, Boreal Books 2012). The experience may have tainted their views about women to such an extent that both would see most of them burn in Hell for an eternity. The following hadith is quoted in its entirety in the chapter *Women*:

Narrated 'Abdullah bin Abbas:

...

The people say, "O Allah's Apostle! We saw you taking something from your place and then we saw you retreating."

The Prophet replied, "I saw Paradise and stretched my hands towards a bunch (of its fruits) and had I taken it, you would have eaten from it as long as the world remains.

I also saw the Hell-fire and I had never seen such a horrible sight. I saw that most of the inhabitants were women."

The people asked, "O Allah's Apostle! Why is it so?"

The Prophet replied, "Because of their ungratefulness."

Bukhari 18.161

Both murdered and murderer in a fight go to Hell.

Al-Ahnaf bin Qais:

While I was going to help this man ('Ali Ibn Abi Talib), Abu Bakra met me and asked, "Where are you going?"

I replied, "I am going to help that person."

He said, "Go back for I have heard Allah's Apostle saying, 'When two Muslims fight (meet) each other with their swords, both the murderer as well as the murdered will go to the Hell-fire.'"

I said, "O Allah's Apostle! It is all right for the murderer but what about the murdered one?"

Allah's Apostle replied, "He surely had the intention to kill his companion."

Bukhari 2.30

What about one dead child saving a mother from Hell's Fire?

Narrated Abu Said Al-Khudri:

Some women requested the Prophet to fix a day for them as the men were taking all his time. On that he promised them one day for religious lessons and commandments. Once during such a lesson the Prophet said, "A woman whose three children die will be shielded by them from the Hell fire."

On that a woman asked, "If only two die?"

He replied, "Even two (will shield her from the Hell-fire)."

Bukhari 3.101

Be kind to your cat, and let it eat all the insects it wants.

Narrated 'Abdullah bin 'Umar:

Allah's Apostle said, "A woman was tortured and was put in Hell because of a cat which she had kept locked till it died of hunger."

Allah's Apostle further said, "(Allah knows better) Allah said (to the woman), 'You neither fed it nor watered when you locked it up, nor did you set it free to eat the insects of the earth.'"

Bukhari 40.553

To be on the safe side, I would get rid of the silverware.

Narrated Um Salama (the wife of the Prophet):

Allah's Apostle said, "He who drinks in silver utensils is only filling his abdomen with Hell Fire."

Bukhari 69.538

Was there ever any doubt?

Narrated 'Ali:

The Prophet said, "Do not tell a lie against me for whoever tells a lie against me (intentionally) then he will surely enter the Hell-fire."

Bukhari 3:106

Always be careful what you say. Better still, be quiet!

Narrated Abu Huraira:

The Prophet; said, "A slave (of Allah) may utter a word which pleases Allah without giving it much importance, and because of that Allah will raise him to degrees (of reward): a slave (of Allah) may utter a word (carelessly) which displeases Allah without thinking of its gravity and because of that he will be thrown into the Hell-Fire."

Bukhari 76.485

Adoptive parents, fathers actually for it is their decision, be warned. Make sure the child you adopt does not confuse you with his natural father. If he does, your pride and joy is going to Hell (for how this came about read *Women and the Koran, Boreal Books 2012*).

Narrated Abu Dhar:

The Prophet said, "If somebody claims to be the son of any other than his real father knowingly, he but disbelieves in Allah, and if somebody claims to belong to some folk to whom he does not belong, let such a person take his place in the (Hell) Fire."

Bukhari 56.711

If you cause God's Messenger to make a bad decision you will pay for it later.

Narrated Um Salama (the wife of the Prophet):

Allah's Apostle heard some people quarreling at the door of his dwelling. He came out and said, "I am only a human being, and opponents come to me (to settle their problems); maybe someone amongst you can present his case more eloquently than the other, whereby I may consider him true and give a verdict in his favor. So, If I give the right of a Muslim to another by mistake, then it is really a portion of (Hell) Fire, he has the option to take or give up (before the Day of Resurrection)."

Bukhari 43.638

One of the more substantial benefits of fasting (a camel's journey is assumed):

Narrated Abu Said:

I heard the Prophet saying, "Indeed, anyone who fasts for one day for Allah's Pleasure, Allah will keep his face away from the (Hell) fire for (a distance covered by a journey of) seventy years."

Bukhari 52.93

That fever you are experiencing ...

Narrated Aisha:

The Prophet said, "Fever is from the heat of the (Hell) Fire, so cool it with water."

Bukhari 54.485

Another besides Lahai (see *Eclipses*) who will be dragging his intestines around Hell:

Narrated Abu Wail:

Somebody said to Usama, "Will you go to so-and-so (i.e. 'Uthman) and talk to him (i.e. advise him regarding ruling the country)?"

He said, "You see that I don't talk to him. Really I talk to (advise) him secretly without opening a gate (of affliction), for neither do I want to be the first to open it (i.e. rebellion), nor will I say to a man who is my ruler that he is the best of all the people after I have heard something from Allah's Apostle."

They said, "What have you heard him saying?"

He said, "I have heard him saying, a man will be brought on the Day of Resurrection and thrown in the (Hell) Fire, so that his intestines will come out, and he will go around like a donkey goes around a millstone. The people of (Hell) Fire will gather around him and say: 'O so-and-so! What is wrong with you? Didn't you use to order us to do good deeds and forbid us to do bad deeds?' He will reply: 'Yes, I used to order you to do good deeds, but I did not do them myself, and I used to forbid you to do bad deeds, yet I used to do them myself.'"

Bukhari 54.489

The Koran is okay with you killing yourself in Allah's Cause, and for your sacrifice you will be granted instant access to Paradise no questions asked. The following is for those who would contemplate leaving this world at a time of their choosing for no good reason.

Narrated Abu Huraira:

The Prophet said, "Whoever purposely throws himself from a mountain and kills himself, will be in the (Hell) Fire falling down into it and abiding therein perpetually forever; and whoever drinks poison and kills himself with it, he will be carrying his poison in his hand and drinking it in the (Hell) Fire wherein he will abide eternally forever; and whoever kills himself with an iron weapon, will be carrying that weapon in his hand and stabbing his abdomen with it in the (Hell) Fire wherein he will abide eternally forever."

Bukhari 71.670

Who will be in Hell with his brain boiling away after Judgement Day? That would be the Prophet's uncle Abu-Talib who took in the infant Muhammad whose own father died before he was born, looked after him, loved and sheltered him, protected him from his enemies when he grew into Prophethood. It is just too bad that he refused his nephew's entreaties to become a Muslim and died an unbeliever.

Narrated Abu Said Al-Khudri:

That he heard the Prophet when somebody mentioned his uncle (i.e. Abu Talib), saying, "Perhaps my intercession will be helpful to him on the Day of Resurrection so that he may be put in a shallow fire reaching only up to his ankles. His brain will boil from it."

Bukhari 58.224

Rubbing it in!

Narrated Anas:

The Prophet said, "Allah will say to that person of the (Hell) Fire who will receive the least punishment, 'If you had everything on the earth, would you give it as a ransom to free yourself (i.e. save yourself from this Fire)?' He will say, 'Yes.' Then Allah will say, 'While you were in the backbone of Adam, I asked you much less than this, i.e. not to worship others besides Me, but you insisted on worshipping others besides me.'"

Bukhari 55.551

Heraclius

As oral histories, the hadiths leave a lot to be desired. Western scholarship considers oral histories valid accounts of what may or may not have happened, until archeological evidence (physical proof) is discovered that contradicts what was revealed in stories often told around a camp fire and passed down from generation to generation. But how do you contradict a revealed truth? You can't, by definition, and where Islam is concerned, a very dangerous thing to do!

Much research has been done and written about the life and times of Byzantine emperors from Constantine I to Constantine XI who died, along with thousands of his subjects, in a forlorn defence of Constantinople against Ottoman Muslim attackers on the 29th of May 1453. If a hadith attributed to a companion of the Prophet is to be believed, God's Messenger came close to obtaining the bloodless surrender of the Byzantine Empire about 800 years earlier. Then, a confident Prophet, who was now in control of most of the Arabian Peninsula, sent a letter to all the kingdoms which bordered his domain demanding they become Muslims or else.

A hadith recounts how, after receiving the Prophet's ultimatum and meeting with a kin and sometimes enemy of God's Messenger, Abu Sufyan, the Byzantine emperor, Heraclius decided to surrender his kingdom to the Prophet until a mob convinced him otherwise. The following is a long hadith – a testimony to the prodigious memory of those who were present at the Court of Heraclius and those who transmitted it:

Narrated 'Abdullah bin 'Abbas:

Abu Sufyan bin Harb informed me that Heraclius had sent a messenger to him while he had been accompanying a caravan from Quraish. They were merchants doing business in Sham (Syria, Palestine, Lebanon and Jordan), at the time when Allah's Apostle had truce with Abu Sufyan and Quraish infidels. So Abu Sufyan and his companions went to Heraclius at Ilya (Jerusalem).

Heraclius called them in the court and he had all the senior Roman dignitaries around him. He called for his translator who, translating Heraclius's question said to them, "Who amongst you is closely related to that man who claims to be a Prophet?"

Abu Sufyan replied, "I am the nearest relative to him (amongst the group)."

Heraclius said, "Bring him (Abu Sufyan) close to me and make his companions stand behind him."

Abu Sufyan added, "Heraclius told his translator to tell my companions that he wanted to put some questions to me regarding that man (The Prophet) and that if I told a lie they (my companions) should contradict me."

Abu Sufyan added, "By Allah! Had I not been afraid of my companions labeling me a liar, I would not have spoken the truth about the Prophet.

The first question he asked me about him was: 'What is his family status amongst you?'

I replied, 'He belongs to a good (noble) family amongst us.'

Heraclius further asked, 'Has anybody amongst you ever claimed the same (i.e. to be a Prophet) before him?'

I replied, 'No.'

He said, 'Was anybody amongst his ancestors a king?'

I replied, 'No.'

Heraclius asked, 'Do the nobles or the poor follow him?'

I replied, 'It is the poor who follow him.'

He said, 'Are his followers increasing decreasing (day by day)?'

I replied, 'They are increasing.'

He then asked, 'Does anybody amongst those who embrace his religion become displeased and renounce the religion afterwards?'

I replied, 'No.'

Heraclius said, 'Have you ever accused him of telling lies before his claim (to be a Prophet)?'

I replied, 'No.'

Heraclius said, 'Does he break his promises?'

I replied, 'No. We are at truce with him but we do not know what he will do in it.'

I could not find opportunity to say anything against him except that. Heraclius asked, 'Have you ever had a war with him?'

I replied, 'Yes.'

Then he said, 'What was the outcome of the battles?'

I replied, 'Sometimes he was victorious and sometimes we.'

Heraclius said, 'What does he order you to do?'

I said, 'He tells us to worship Allah and Allah alone and not to worship anything along with Him, and to renounce all that our ancestors had said. He orders us to pray, to speak the truth, to be chaste and to keep good relations with our Kith and kin.'

Heraclius asked the translator to convey to me the following, I asked you about his family and your reply was that he belonged to a very noble family. In fact all the Apostles come from noble families amongst their respective peoples. I questioned you whether anybody else amongst you claimed such a thing, your reply was in the negative. If the answer had been in the affirmative, I would have thought that this man was following the previous man's statement.

Then I asked you whether anyone of his ancestors was a king. Your reply was in the negative, and if it had been in the affirmative, I would have thought that this man wanted to take back his ancestral kingdom.

I further asked whether he was ever accused of telling lies before he said what he said, and your reply was in the negative. So I wondered how a person who does not tell a lie about others could ever tell a lie about Allah.

I, then asked you whether the rich people followed him or the poor. You replied that it was the poor who followed him. And in fact all the Apostle have been followed by this very class of people.

Then I asked you whether his followers were increasing or decreasing. You replied that they were increasing, and in fact this is the way of true faith, till it is complete in all respects.

I further asked you whether there was anybody, who, after embracing his religion, became displeased and discarded his religion. Your reply was in the negative, and in fact this is (the sign of) true faith, when its delight enters the hearts and mixes with them completely.

I asked you whether he had ever betrayed. You replied in the negative and likewise the Apostles never betray.

Then I asked you what he ordered you to do. You replied

that he ordered you to worship Allah and Allah alone and not to worship anything along with Him and forbade you to worship idols and ordered you to pray, to speak the truth and to be chaste.

If what you have said is true, he will very soon occupy this place underneath my feet and I knew it (from the scriptures) that he was going to appear but I did not know that he would be from you, and if I could reach him definitely, I would go immediately to meet him and if I were with him, I would certainly wash his feet.'

Heraclius then asked for the letter addressed by Allah's Apostle which was delivered by Dihya to the Governor of Busra, who forwarded it to Heraclius to read. The contents of the letter were as follows:

"In the name of Allah the Beneficent, the Merciful (This letter is) from Muhammad the slave of Allah and His Apostle to Heraclius the ruler of Byzantine. Peace be upon him, who follows the right path. Furthermore I invite you to Islam, and if you become a Muslim you will be safe, and Allah will double your reward, and if you reject this invitation of Islam you will be committing a sin by misguiding your Arisiyin (peasants). (And I recite to you Allah's Statement:) 'O people of the scripture! Come to a word common to you and us that we worship none but Allah and that we associate nothing in worship with Him, and that none of us shall take others as Lords beside Allah. Then, if they turn away, say: Bear witness that we are Muslims (those who have surrendered to Allah).' (3:64).

Abu Sufyan then added, "When Heraclius had finished his speech and had read the letter, there was a great hue and cry in the Royal Court. So we were turned out of the court.

I told my companions that the question of Ibn-Abi-Kabsha (the Prophet Muhammad) has become so prominent that even the King of Bani Al-Asfar (Byzantine) is afraid of him. Then I started to become sure that he (the Prophet) would be the conqueror in the near future till I embraced Islam (i.e. Allah guided me to it)."

The sub narrator adds, "Ibn An-Natur was the Governor of Ilya' (Jerusalem) and Heraclius was the head of the Christians of Sham. Ibn An-Natur narrates that once while Heraclius was visiting ilya' (Jerusalem), he got up in the morning with a sad mood. Some of his priests asked him why he was in that mood? Heraclius was a foreteller and an astrologer. He replied, 'At night when I looked at the stars, I saw that the leader of those who practice circumcision had appeared (become the conqueror). Who are they who practice circumcision?'

The people replied, 'Except the Jews nobody practices circumcision, so you should not be afraid of them (Jews). 'Just Issue orders to kill every Jew present in the country.'

While they were discussing it, a messenger sent by the king of Ghassan to convey the news of Allah's Apostle to Heraclius was brought in. Having heard the news, he (Heraclius) ordered the people to go and see whether the messenger of Ghassan was circumcised.

The people, after seeing him, told Heraclius that he was circumcised. Heraclius then asked him about the Arabs. The messenger replied, 'Arabs also practice circumcision.'

(After hearing that) Heraclius remarked that sovereignty of the 'Arabs had appeared.

Heraclius then wrote a letter to his friend in Rome who was as good as Heraclius in knowledge. Heraclius then left for Homs (a town in Syrian) and stayed there till he received the reply of his letter from his friend who agreed with him in his opinion about the emergence of the Prophet and the fact that he was a Prophet.

On that Heraclius invited all the heads of the Byzantines to assemble in his palace at Homs. When they assembled, he ordered that all the doors of his palace be closed. Then he came out and said, 'O Byzantines! If success is your desire and if you seek right guidance and want your empire to remain then give a pledge of allegiance to this Prophet (i.e. embrace Islam).'

(On hearing the views of Heraclius) the people ran towards the gates of the palace like onagers but found the doors closed.

Heraclius realized their hatred towards Islam and when he lost the hope of their embracing Islam, he ordered that they should be brought back in audience.

(When they returned) he said, 'What already said was just to test the strength of your conviction and I have seen it.'

The people prostrated before him and became pleased with him, and this was the end of Heraclius's story (in connection with his faith)."

Bukhari 1.6

A Muslim who does not believe that this authenticated Sunni Cannon hadith is a faithful account of what transpired at the court of

Heraclius, and that the Byzantine Emperor would have surrendered his empire to the Prophet had it not been for a mob outside the palace gate is, by definition, a heretic. The punishment for heresy is crucifixion, after having an arm and a leg on opposite sides lopped off.

Jews

Just like in the Koran, Jews figure prominently in the hadiths, but seldom in a good way. It took the Holocaust to bring Christians to their senses and come to the aid of the Jews e.g. Israel instead of inciting hatred against them, much of it implicit, because of an unfortunate allegation in the gospels, that they are responsible for another Jew's death, that Jew being Jesus. The hatred of Jews in the Koran and the hadiths is largely explicit, virulent and pervasive. It is an invitation for a repeat of the holocaust on a more expansive, more horrific scale in which every Muslim will be expected to do his or her duty, and that is to kill Jews wherever they find them. Unlike the NAZI's attempt at genocide, there will be no place to hide.

Narrated 'Abdullah bin 'Umar:

Allah's Apostle said, "You (i.e. Muslims) will fight with the Jews till some of them will hide behind stones. The stones will (betray them) saying, 'O 'Abdullah (i.e. slave of Allah)! There is a Jew hiding behind me; so kill him.'"

Bukhari 52.176

It is only a matter of time, Allah does not break a promise.

Narrated 'Abdullah bin 'Umar:

I heard Allah's Apostle saying, "The Jews will fight with you, and you will be given victory over them so that a stone will say, 'O Muslim! There is a Jew behind me; kill him!'"

Bukhari 56.791

The Jews did not start this war, that, in the absence of a miracle, may see them exterminated. From the beginning, the Prophet and his followers were the aggressors, but you would not be aware of that from reading either the hadiths or the Koran. If it had not been for the Jews of Medina who welcomed and sheltered the budding Prophet whose Meccan kin wanted to kill him for promoting what they considered a hateful intolerant religion, Islam would have been stillborn (read *Pain, Pleasure and Prejudice – Jews of Medina, Boreal Books*) or *Allah's War Against the Unbelievers – The Battle for Medina, Boreal Books*).

Relations between the Muslims and the Jews of Medina cooled considerably after the Jews refused to accept Muhammad as a legitimate intervener with the Almighty. That role being reserved for the chosen people. The disagreement first led to the trading of insults.

Narrated 'Aisha:

Once the Jews came to the Prophet and said, "Death be upon you." So I cursed them.

The Prophet said, "What is the matter?"

I said, "Have you not heard what they said?"

The Prophet said, "Have you not heard what I replied (to them)? (I said), ('The same is upon you.')"

Bukhari 42.186

It did not help that the Jews began asking questions of the Prophet to which the answer was not readily forthcoming; that is, until Allah came up with a blanket solution to the problem.

Narrated 'Abdullah:

While I was going with the Prophet through the ruins of Medina and he was reclining on a date-palm leaf stalk, some Jews passed by. Some of them said to the others: Ask him (the Prophet) about the spirit. Some of them said that they should not ask him that question as he might give a reply which would displease them. But some of them insisted on asking, and so one of them stood up and asked, "O Aba-l-Qasim ! What is the spirit?"

The Prophet remained quiet. I thought he was being inspired Divinely. So I stayed till that state of the Prophet (while being inspired) was over. The Prophet then said, "And they ask you (O Muhammad) concerning the spirit -- Say: The spirit -- its knowledge is with my Lord. And of knowledge you (mankind) have been given only a little)." (17:85)

Bukhari 3:127

As the dispute escalated, the Arabs went from emulating the Jews to doing the exact opposite of what they did, including what they did with their hair, or did not do.

Narrated Abu Huraira:

The Prophet said, "Jews and Christians do not dye their hair so you should do the opposite of what they do.

Bukhari 56.668

It was a bit more complicated where Jewish scripture was concerned. The Koran was being revealed piecemeal, and what it said was not unlike what was written in the Torah, except in briefness. The Torah was very much the guide to Allah's laws for mankind for the early Muslim e.g. talion law, one god etc. With an incomplete Koran, should they continue to follow what was revealed to the Jews?

Narrated Abu Huraira:

The people of the Scripture (Jews) used to recite the Torah in Hebrew and they used to explain it in Arabic to the Muslims. On that Allah's Apostle said, "Do not believe the people of the Scripture or disbelieve them, but say: 'We believe in Allah and what is revealed to us.'" (2:136)

Bukhari 60.12

At one point in time, perhaps before the interdiction about hair, the dispute started to turn ugly with the Prophet explicitly invoking Allah's curse on the Jews for what we would consider a petty offence; but in the black and white world in which Islam was finding its bearings, nothing was petty where Allah and His Messenger and the Jews were concerned.

Narrated Jabir bin 'Abdullah:

I heard Allah's Apostle, in the year of the Conquest of Mecca, saying, "Allah and His Apostle made illegal the trade of alcohol, dead animals, pigs and idols."

The people asked, "O Allah's Apostle! What about the fat of dead animals, for it was used for greasing the boats and the hides; and people use it for lights?"

He said, "No, it is illegal."

Allah's Apostle further said, "May Allah curse the Jews, for Allah made the fat (of animals) illegal for them, yet they melted the fat and sold it and ate its price."

Bukhari 34.438

From being a people to emulate, the Jews became a people to despise; a tribe of liars and cheaters who distorted Allah's instructions to the point of ridicule.

Narrated Abu Huraira:

Allah's Apostle said, "It was said to Bani Israel, enter the gate (of the town) with humility (prostrating yourselves) and saying: 'Repentance', but they changed the word and entered the town crawling on their buttocks and saying: 'A wheat grain in the hair (*one meaning: 'A wheat grain in the hair means greedy and wasting'*).'"

Bukhari 55.615

From there, it was a short interval to exile and mass murder.

Narrated Abu Huraira:

While we were in the mosque, Allah's Apostle came out to us and said, "Let us proceed to the Jews." So we went along with him till we reached Bait-al-Midras (a place where the Torah used to be recited and all the Jews of the town used to gather).

The Prophet stood up and addressed them, "O Assembly of Jews! Embrace Islam and you will be safe!"

The Jews replied, "O Aba-l-Qasim! You have conveyed Allah's message to us."

The Prophet said, "That is what I want (from you)."

He repeated his first statement for the second time, and they said, "You have conveyed Allah's message, O Aba-l-Qasim."

Then he said it for the third time and added, "You should know that the earth belongs to Allah and His Apostle, and I want to exile you from this land, so whoever among you owns some property, can sell it, otherwise you should know that the earth belongs to Allah and His Apostle."

Bukhari 85.77

One of the Jewish tribes of Medina chose to ignore the Prophet's invitation to get out of town, and instead sought an alliance with the Meccans who were marching on Medina. The Bani Quraiza (also spelled Qurayzah) could not bring themselves to attack the Muslims who, without Allah's intervention, would probably have been easily defeated, unable to defend themselves on two fronts. For their reluctance to engage the Muslims while they were most vulnerable they expected mercy from God's Messenger. It was not to be.

As you read the following hadith, remember what I said earlier, that the Muslims were the aggressors from the outset. The Jews of Medina's downfall was largely due to their reluctance to do what the Muslims did and fight for their lives. The following hadith may also be disingenuous in asserting that some of the seven hundred or so men and boys of the Bani Quraiza were not killed because they accepted to become Muslims. The only males of the Bani Quraiza who were not beheaded were those who had yet to grow pubic hair i.e. children.

Narrated Ibn Umar:

Bani An-Nadir and Bani Quraiza fought (against the Prophet violating their peace treaty), so the Prophet exiled Bani An-Nadir and allowed Bani Quraiza to remain at their places (in Medina) taking nothing from them till they fought against the Prophet again). He then killed their men and distributed their women, children and property among the Muslims, but some of them came to the Prophet and he granted them safety, and they embraced Islam. He exiled all the Jews from Medina. They were the Jews of Bani Qainuqa', the tribe of 'Abdullah bin Salam and the Jews of Bani Haritha and all the other Jews of Medina.

Bukhari 59.362

Jihad

Jihad should be read in conjunction with *Allah's War on the Unbelievers, Boreal Books (2012)* or *Pain, Pleasure and Prejudice - Civil War, Boreal Books (2012)*.

Narrated 'Abdullah bin Abi Aufa:

Allah's Apostle said, "Know that Paradise is under the shades of swords."

Bukhari 52.73

Narrated Abu Musa:

A man came to the Prophet and asked, "O Allah's Apostle! What kind of fighting is in Allah's cause? (I ask this), for some of us fight because of being enraged and angry and some for the sake of his pride and haughtiness."

The Prophet raised his head (as the questioner was standing) and said, "He who fights so that Allah's Word (Islam) should be superior, then he fights in Allah's cause."

Bukhari 3:125

You have to be at least fifteen years of age before you can volunteer to kill and die in Allah's Cause.

Narrated Ibn 'Umar:

That the Prophet inspected him on the day of Uhud while he was fourteen years old, and the Prophet did not allow him to take part in the battle. He was inspected again by the Prophet on the day of Al-Khandaq (i.e. battle of the Trench) while he was fifteen years old, and the Prophet allowed him to take Part in the battle.

Bukhari 59.423

The Prophet and his followers returned to Mecca as conquerors after seeking refuge in Medina to escape their Meccan kin who wanted to kill them because their hate-filled religious beliefs would have transformed ecumenical, welcoming-to-all-religions Mecca into an intolerant host. Their worst fears were realised when they surrendered Mecca without a fight to God's Messenger after obtaining assurances – which Allah repudiated the very next day – that they could continue to worship three cherished female deities. The taking of Mecca did not mean peace as the Prophet makes clear in the following hadith. Universal Jihad was on.

Narrated Ibn 'Abbas:

Allah's Apostle said, "There is no Hijra (i.e. migration) (from Mecca to Medina) after the Conquest (of Mecca), but Jihad and good intention remain; and if you are called (by the Muslim ruler) for fighting, go forth immediately."

Bukhari 52.42

According to a former Mujahideen refuge from the Iraq/Iran war, in the War on Civilization, the example of the Prophet is more important than Allah's sanctioning of that war. My Iranian friend uses the expression *War on Civilization* instead of the more common, politically correct *War of Civilizations* because he does not consider Islam, a product of the Dark Ages, a civilization but its antithesis; an annihilator of critical thinking and progress, the hallmark of any civilization worthy of the name.

Allah, in the Koran, gives the green light to kill those who would think for themselves and fight the encroaching darkness; but, it is the example and sayings of His alleged Messenger, the Prophet Muhammad, he says which stokes the passion of his followers to kill and die in this ultimate war between reason and its nemesis.

Narrated Abu Huraira:

The Prophet said, "By Him in Whose Hands my life is! Were it not for some men amongst the believers who dislike to be left behind me and whom I cannot provide with means of conveyance, I would certainly never remain behind any Sariya' (army-unit) setting out in Allah's Cause. By Him in Whose Hands my life is! I would love to be martyred in Allah's Cause and then get resurrected and then get martyred, and then get resurrected again and then get martyred and then get resurrected again and then get martyred."

Bukhari 52.54

Narrated Samura:

The Prophet said, "Last night two men came to me (in a dream) and made me ascend a tree and then admitted me into a better and superior house, better of which I have never seen. One of them said, 'This house is the house of martyrs.'"

Bukhari 52.49

The example of the Prophet was not lost on boys as young as 12 years old, perhaps even younger who were used, in a tactic sanctioned by

Khomeini, to clear minefields or in suicidal attacks to expose Iraqi positions (experience soldiers were too valuable to risk in such enterprises) before the tanks rolled forward running over the bodies of the dead and dying children. The children were given small plastic keys made in China or Japan to hang around their necks, and told this key would let them into Paradise. Before the actual advance across a minefield, or a swamp to be electrocuted, or a field to be shredded by enemy artillery, a man on a charger brandishing a saber and pointing at the Iraqi positions would appear on the horizon urging them on. The children were told this was the Prophet Muhammad, and their hero would be there to welcome them into Paradise should they be martyred.

Holy War as conceived by Allah and His Messenger also did away with the moral imperative against killing your fellow man except in self-defence, making killing people for their religious beliefs or lack thereof, a good thing.

Narrated Abdullah bin Masud:

I asked Allah's Apostle, "O Allah's Apostle! What is the best deed?"

He replied, "To offer the prayers at their early stated fixed times."

I asked, "What is next in goodness?"

He replied, "To be good and dutiful to your parents."

I further asked, "What is next in goodness?"

He replied, "To participate in Jihad in Allah's Cause."

I did not ask Allah's Apostle anymore and if I had asked him more, he would have told me more.

Bukhari 52.41

For the killer in Allah's Cause it's a win-win situation whether he lives or dies.

Narrated Abu Huraira:

I heard Allah's Apostle saying, "The example of a Mujahid (Muslim fighter) in Allah's Cause—and Allah knows better who really strives in His Cause—is like a person who fasts and prays continuously. Allah guarantees that He will admit the Mujahid in His Cause into Paradise if he is killed, otherwise He will return him to his home safely with rewards and war booty."

Bukhari 52.46

The immorality of killing those who refuse to believe that your scriptures are superior plumbed new depths of depravity in Allah and

His Messenger. Islam is the only mainstream religion which promises unrestrained, limitless fornication opportunities with sexually-adept spirits made flesh, the infamous houris, for the murder of its detractors.

Narrated Anas:

The Prophet said, "A single endeavor (of fighting) in Allah's Cause in the afternoon or in the forenoon is better than all the world and whatever is in it. A place in Paradise as small as the bow or lash of one of you is better than all the world and whatever is in it. And if a houri from Paradise appeared to the people of the earth, she would fill the space between Heaven and the Earth with light and pleasant scent and her head cover is better than the world and whatever is in it."

Bukhari 52.53

It does not have to be mass-murder to be amply rewarded.

Narrated Al-Bara:

A man whose face was covered with an iron mask (i.e. clad in armor) came to the Prophet and said, "O Allah's Apostle! Shall I fight or embrace Islam first?"

The Prophet said, "Embrace Islam first and then fight."

So he embraced Islam, and was martyred. Allah's Apostle said, "A little work, but a great reward. (He did very little (after embracing Islam), but he will be rewarded in abundance)."

Bukhari 52.63

If a believer is killed in Allah's Cause he goes to Paradise to enjoy an eternity of orgiastic sex as part of what the Prophet refers to as "the dignity he receives (from Allah)" while those he has killed in Allah's Cause will burn in Hell forever. This is giving dignity a whole new meaning.

Narrated Anas bin Malik:

The Prophet said, "Nobody who enters Paradise likes to go back to the world even if he got everything on the earth, except a Mujahid who wishes to return to the world so that he may be martyred ten times because of the dignity he receives (from Allah)."

Narrated Al-Mughira bin Shu'ba:

Our Prophet told us about the message of our Lord that "Whoever amongst us is killed will go to Paradise."

Umar asked the Prophet, "Is it not true that our men who

are killed will go to Paradise and their's (i.e. those of the Pagan's) will go to the (Hell) fire?"

The Prophet said, "Yes."

Bukhari 52.72

An old-fashion killer who has killed, but not in Allah's Cause, can still be rewarded with Paradise if before he dies he kills in Allah's Cause (a hadith to that effect quoted elsewhere).

Narrated Abu Huraira:

Allah's Apostle said, "Allah welcomes two men with a smile; one of whom kills the other and both of them enter Paradise. One fights in Allah's Cause and gets killed. Later on Allah forgives the killer who also get martyred (in Allah's Cause)."

Bukhari 52.80

All this killing is for one reason and one reason only!

Narrated Abu Musa:

A man came to the Prophet and asked, "A man fights for war booty; another fights for fame and a third fights for showing off; which of them fights in Allah's Cause?"

The Prophet said, "He who fights that Allah's Word (i.e. Islam) should be superior, fights in Allah's Cause."

Bukhari 52.65

Terrorism in Allah's Cause is not a modern invention.

Narrated Abu Huraira:

Allah's Apostle said, "I have been sent with the shortest expressions bearing the widest meanings, and I have been made victorious with terror (cast in the hearts of the enemy) ..."

Bukhari 52.220

An example on how the Prophet terrorized those he was about to annihilate in Allah's Cause – from the assault on Khaibar.

Narrated Anas:

Allah's Apostle reached Khaibar at night and it was his habit that, whenever he reached the enemy at night, he will not attack them till it was morning. When it was morning, the Jews came out with their spades and baskets, and when they saw him(i.e. the Prophet), they said, "Muhammad! By Allah! Muhammad and his army!"

The Prophet said, "Khaibar is destroyed, for whenever we approach a (hostile) nation (to fight), then evil will be the morning for those who have been warned."

Bukhari 59.510

If you have a horse, use it for Jihad and get an even bigger reward.

Narrated 'Urwa Al-Bariqi:

The Prophet said, "Good will remain (as a permanent quality) in the foreheads of horses (for Jihad) till the Day of Resurrection, for they bring about either a reward (in the Hereafter) or booty (in this world)."

Bukhari 52.104

Narrated Abu Huraira:

The Prophet said, "If somebody keeps a horse in Allah's Cause motivated by his faith in Allah and his belief in His Promise, then he will be rewarded on the Day of Resurrection for what the horse has eaten or drunk and for its dung and urine."

Bukhari 52.105

The one day festival of Eid ul-Fitr (also spelt al-Fitr), the Festival of Breaking the Fast, marks the end of Ramadan. It was during this festival, and that of ul-Adha which commemorates the end of the Hajj, that the Prophet usually gave his army its marching orders.

Narrated Abu Sa'id Al-Khudri:

The Prophet used to proceed to the Musalla (*open space outside a mosque that is mainly used for praying, Encyclopedia of Islam*) on the days of Id-ul-fitr and Id-ul-Adha; the first thing to begin with was the prayer and after that he would stand in front of the people and the people would keep sitting in their rows.

Then he would preach to them, advise them and give them orders, (i.e. Khutba). And after that if he wished to send an army for an expedition, he would do so ...

Bukhari 15.76

The army was to attack without regards for the lives of the women and children of the unbelievers and no place was to be considered sacred i.e. Hima in the following revelation where unbelievers could seek refuge e.g. a church, synagogue or temple and not be killed.

Narrated As-Sab bin Jaththama:

The Prophet passed by me at a place called Al-Abwa or

Waddan, and was asked whether it was permissible to attack the pagan warriors at night with the probability of exposing their women and children to danger.

The Prophet replied, "They (i.e. women and children) are from them (i.e. pagans)."

I also heard the Prophet saying, "The institution of Hima (inviolate place) is invalid except for Allah and His Apostle."

Bukhari 52.256

Whom Allah has ordained to be your masters!

Narrated Jubair bin Haiya:

'Umar sent the Muslims to the great countries to fight the pagans ... 'Umar sent us (to Khosrau i.e. a king of Persia) appointing An-Numan bin Muqrin as our commander. When we reached the land of the enemy, the representative of Khosrau came out with forty-thousand warriors, and an interpreter got up saying, "Let one of you talk to me!"

Al-Mughira replied, "Ask whatever you wish."

The other asked, "Who are you?"

Al-Mughira replied, "We are some people from the Arabs; we led a hard, miserable, disastrous life: we used to suck the hides and the date stones from hunger; we used to wear clothes made up of fur of camels and hair of goats, and to worship trees and stones. While we were in this state, the Lord of the Heavens and the Earths, elevated in His Remembrance and Majesty is His Highness, sent to us from among ourselves a Prophet whose father and mother are known to us. Our Prophet, the Messenger of our Lord, has ordered us to fight you till you worship Allah Alone or give Jizya (i.e. tribute); and our Prophet has informed us that our Lord says: 'Whoever amongst us is killed (i.e. martyred), shall go to Paradise to lead such a luxurious life as he has never seen, and whoever amongst us remain alive, shall become your master ...'"

Bukhari 53.386

To be relegated to mere servants of the practitioners of the superior religion may be the fate reserved for all unbelievers, the Prophet's predictions about the course of the war to establish Allah's Kingdom on earth having proven, in many instances, remarkably accurate.

Narrated Jabir bin Samura:

The Prophet said, "When Khosrau perishes (the last great king of the Sasanian Empire, 590 to 628), there will be no more Khosrau after him, and when Caesar perishes, there will be no more Caesar after him,"

The Prophet also said, "You will spend the treasures of both of them in Allah's Cause."

Bukhari 56.816

If you are going to fight the unbelievers during Dhul Hijja, the month of the Hajj pilgrimage, make it a suicide mission.

Narrated Ibn Abbas:

The Prophet said, "No good deeds done on other days are superior to those done on these (first ten days of Dhul Hijja)."

Then some companions of the Prophet said, "Not even Jihad?"

He replied, "Not even Jihad, except that of a man who does it by putting himself and his property in danger (for Allah's sake) and does not return with any of those things."

Bukhari 14.86

Jihad is, of course, only superior to the goods deeds done during the first ten days of Dhul Hijja if you die while killing unbelievers.

Narrated Abu Huraira:

A man came to Allah's Apostle and said, "Instruct me as to such a deed as equals Jihad (in reward)."

He replied, "I do not find such a deed ..."

Bukhari 52.44

At the Battle for Medina, the Medinan expressed what could be a holy warrior's credo "We are those who have given a pledge ..."

Narrated Anas:

Allah's Apostle went towards the Khandaq (i.e. trench) and saw the Emigrants (from Mecca) and the Ansar (*Medinan helpers*) digging in a very cold morning as they did not have slaves to do that for them. When he noticed their fatigue and hunger he said, "O Allah! The real life is that of the Hereafter, (so please) forgive the Ansar and the Emigrants."

In its reply the Emigrants and the Ansar said, "We are those who have given a pledge of allegiance to Muhammad that we will carry on Jihad as long as we live."

Bukhari 52.87

Just a few more encouragements to kill and die for Allah from an overabundance of appeals to maim and murder:

Narrated Abu Said Al-Khudri:

Somebody asked, "O Allah's Apostle! Who is the best among the people?"

Allah's Apostle replied "A believer who strives his utmost in Allah's Cause with his life and property."

They asked, "Who is next?"

He replied, "A believer who stays in one of the mountain paths worshipping Allah and leaving the people secure from his mischief."

Bukhari 52.45

Narrated Abu Abs:

Allah's Apostle said," Anyone whose both feet get covered with dust in Allah's Cause will not be touched by the (Hell) fire."

Bukhari 52.66

Narrated Sahl bin Sad As-Sa'di:

Allah's Apostle said, "To guard Muslims from infidels in Allah's Cause for one day is better than the world and whatever is on its surface, and a place in Paradise as small as that occupied by the whip of one of you is better than the world and whatever is on its surface; and a morning's or an evening's journey which a slave (person) travels in Allah's Cause is better than the world and whatever is on its surface."

Bukhari 52.142

Narrated Abu Said Al-Khudri

The Prophet said, "A time will come when groups of people will go for Jihad and it will be asked, 'Is there anyone amongst you who has enjoyed the company of the Prophet?'

The answer will be, 'Yes.' Then they will be given victory (by Allah) (because of him).

Then a time will come when it will be asked. 'Is there anyone amongst you who has enjoyed the company of the companions of the Prophet?'

It will be said, 'Yes,' and they will be given victory (by Allah).

Then a time will come when it will be said. 'Is there anyone amongst you who has enjoyed the company of the companions of the companions of the Prophet?'

It will be said, 'Yes,' and they will be given victory (by Allah)."

Bukhari 52.146

Narrated Abu Huraira:

Allah's Apostle said, "I have been ordered to fight with the people till they say, 'None has the right to be worshipped but Allah,' and whoever says, 'None has the right to be worshipped but Allah,' his life and property will be saved by me except for Islamic law, and his accounts will be with Allah, (either to punish him or to forgive him.)"

Bukhari 52.196

Narrated Ibn Abbas:

When the Verse: 'If there are twenty steadfast amongst you (Muslims), they will overcome two-hundred (non-Muslims)' was revealed, it became hard on the Muslims when it became compulsory that one Muslim ought not to flee (in war) before ten (non-Muslims).

So (Allah) lightened the order by revealing: '(But) now Allah has lightened your (task) for He knows that there is weakness in you. So if there are of you one-hundred steadfast, they will overcome (two-hundred (non-Muslims).' (8:66)

So when Allah reduced the number of enemies which Muslims should withstand, their patience and perseverance against the enemy decreased as much as their task was lightened for them.

Bukhari 60.176

Firdaus

Unless you have a good reason to stay at home, if you want the best Allah has to offer, go out and kill and die in His Cause.

Narrated Sahl bin Sad As-Sa'idi:

I saw Marwan bin Al-Hakam sitting in the Mosque. So I came forward and sat by his side. He told us that Zaid bin Thabit had told him that Allah's Apostle had dictated to him the Divine Verse: "Not equal are those believers who sit (at home) and those who strive hard and fight in the Cause of Allah with their wealth and lives." (4:95)

Zaid said, "Ibn-Maktum came to the Prophet while he was dictating to me that very Verse."

On that Ibn Um Maktum said, "O Allah's Apostle! If I had power, I would surely take part in Jihad." He was a blind man. So Allah sent down revelation to His Apostle while his thigh was on mine and it became so heavy for me that I feared that my thigh would be broken. Then that state of the Prophet was over after Allah revealed "...except those who are disabled (by injury or are blind or lame etc.)" (4:95)

Bukhari 52.85

The best Allah has to offer is the Firdaus. Upon reaching Paradise, a holy warrior who has died slaughtering unbelievers in Allah's Cause e.g. a suicide bomber, should take the Prophet's advice and insist on staying there, he has <u>earned</u> it.

Narrated Abu Huraira:

The Prophet said, "Whoever believes in Allah and His Apostle, offer prayer perfectly and fasts the month of Ramadan, will rightfully be granted Paradise by Allah, no matter whether he fights in Allah's Cause or remains in the land where he is born."

The people said, "O Allah's Apostle! Shall we acquaint the people with the good news?"

He said, "Paradise has one-hundred grades which Allah has reserved for the Mujahidin who fight in His Cause, and the distance between each of two grades is like the distance between the Heaven and the Earth. So, when you ask Allah (for something), ask for Al-Firdaus which is the best and highest part of Paradise."

Bukhari 52.48

Are you mad?

Narrated Anas:

Um (the mother of) Haritha came to Allah's Apostle after Haritha had been martyred on the Day (of the battle) of Badr by an arrow thrown by an unknown person. She said, "O Allah's Apostle! You know the position of Haritha in my heart (i.e. how dear to me he was), so if he is in Paradise, I will not weep for him, or otherwise, you will see what I will do."

The Prophet said, "Are you mad? Is there only one Paradise? There are many Paradises, and he is in the highest Paradise of Firdaus."

The Prophet added, "A forenoon journey or an afternoon journey in Allah's Cause is better than the whole world and whatever is in it; and a place equal to an arrow bow of anyone of you, or a place equal to a foot in Paradise is better than the whole world and whatever is in it; and if one of the women of Paradise looked at the earth, she would fill the whole space between them (the earth and the heaven) with light, and would fill whatever is in between them, with perfume, and the veil of her face is better than the whole world and whatever is in it."

Bukhari 76.572

Never-Ending Wars

War is endemic in Islam, whether it is the never-ending war against unbelievers or believers killing believers in brutal civil wars over leadership and dogma. The Prophet started it, the war to rid the world of all who refused to submit to the Will of God, as he understood it, after escaping to Medina. As an enticement to kill until none was left who did not accept Islam as his or her religion, God's Messenger, after consulting with his Mentor, revealed that the property of an unbeliever, including his wives and daughters, belonged to the Muslim who killed him.

His strategy was successful and in a few short years the entire Arab population of the Peninsula had converted to Islam or had been killed or taken into slavery. This overwhelming victory over the unbelievers was quickly followed, after his death, by three civil wars under the four so-called Righty Guided Caliphs (Bakr, Umar, Uthman and Ali), the last three assassinated by unhappy believers, heralding an often violent tradition of settling leadership issues, benefitting a religion where violence and the threat of violence is pervasive.

Both types of wars, the general war against unbelievers and the bloody pitiless conflicts between believers continue in one form or another to this day, with the second type – civil strife in the following hadith – expected to continue indefinitely, even if Islam is successful in ridding the world of all of those who refuse to submit to the Will of Allah.

Narrated Jubair bin Mut'im:

I heard the Prophet reciting Surat-at-Tur in Maghrib prayer, and that was at a time when belief was first planted in my heart. The Prophet while speaking about the war prisoners of Badr, said, "Were Al-Mutim bin Adi alive and interceded with me for these filthy people, I would definitely forgive them for his sake."

Narrated Said bin Al-Musaiyab: When the first civil strife (in Islam) took place because of the murder of 'Uthman, it left none of the Badr warriors alive. When the second civil strife, that is the battle of Al-Harra, took place, it left none of the Hudaibiya treaty companions alive. Then the third civil strife took place and it did not subside till it had exhausted all the strength of the people.

Bukhari 59.358

A saying of God's Messenger to ease the conscience of those, who, in their zeal to rid the world of Allah's enemies, slaughter the innocent, in ever increasing numbers, even those who have submitted to the Will of Allah hoping to save themselves:

Narrated 'Aisha:

Allah's Apostle said, "An army will invade the Ka'ba and when the invaders reach Al-Baida', all the ground will sink and swallow the whole army."

I said, "O Allah's Apostle! How will they sink into the ground while amongst them will be their markets (the people who worked in business and not invaders) and the people not belonging to them?"

The Prophet replied, "all of those people will sink but they will be resurrected and judged according to their intentions."

Bukhari 34.329

Judgement Day - Omens

Judgement Day Omens should be read in conjunction with *The Islamic Hereafter - Judgement Day (2012)* or *Pain, Pleasure and Prejudice - Judgement Day, Boreal Books (2012)* for the Koran's extensive coverage of that most ominous of days.

Of all the apparent absurdities that Muslims have to believe to avoid spending an eternity on fire in Hell none are stranger than Allah's and His Messenger accounts of Judgement Day, with the portents of that most ominous of days coming in a close second for incongruity and plain weirdness.

The old Persia is today the Islamic Republic of Iran and much of the former Byzantine Empire is now under Muslim rule. The modern example of autocratic, theocratic government which the Prophet warned against in the following hadith is very much a fixture of countries like Iran and the type of rule that Islamists would like to see everywhere. Will they now be the example that bring on the End Times?

Narrated Abu Huraira:

The Prophet said, "The Hour will not be established till my followers copy the deeds of the previous nations and follow them very closely, span by span, and cubit by cubit (i.e., inch by inch)."

It was said, "O Allah's Apostle! Do you mean by those (nations) the Persians and the Byzantines?"

The Prophet said, "Who can it be other than they?"

Bukhari 92.421

The Byzantine Empire was a Christian Empire therefore the following warning in the same vein as the first makes some sense:

Narrated Abu Sa'id Al-Khudri:

The Prophet said, "You will follow the ways of those nations who were before you, span by span and cubit by cubit (i.e., inch by inch) so much so that even if they entered a hole of a mastigure (*large spiny-tailed lizard*), you would follow them."

We said, "O Allah's Apostle! (Do you mean) the Jews and the Christians?"

He said, "Whom else?"

Bukhari 92.422

The Prophet expected the End Times to occur during his lifetime or shortly after his death (this is also confirmed in the Koran, see *From Merchant to Messenger, Boreal Books 2012* for the relevant revelations) before the collapse of the Byzantine and Persian Empires.

Narrated Sahl bin Sad As-Sa'idi (a companion of Allah's Apostle):

Allah's Apostle, holding out his middle and index fingers, said, "My advent and the Hour are like this (or like these)," namely, the period between his era and the Hour is like the distance between those two fingers, i.e. very short.

Bukhari 63.221

The believers will have to fight and slaughter the Jews, with Allah helping out in His own inimitable way, before the blessed Hour which will see killing on an even more monstrous scale, is established.

Narrated Abu Huraira:

Allah's Apostle said, "The Hour will not be established until you fight with the Jews, and the stone behind which a Jew will be hiding will say, "O Muslim! There is a Jew hiding behind me, so kill him."

Bukhari 52.177

The following hadiths may be a reference to the Huns and other newcomers from the East who challenged Roman rule. Many became Muslims and are no longer a factor as far as the Prophet's End Time prophesies are concerned, leaving only the Jews as the people to be ruthlessly dealt with before Allah calls it quits for the human race.

Narrated 'Amr bin Taghlib:

The Prophet said, "One of the portents of the Hour is that you will fight with people wearing shoes made of hair; and one of the portents of the Hour is that you will fight with broad-faced people whose faces will look like shields coated with leather."

Bukhari 52.178

Narrated Abu Huraira:

Allah's Apostle said, "The Hour will not be established until you fight with the Turks; people with small eyes, red faces, and flat noses. Their faces will look like shields coated with leather. The Hour will not be established till you fight with people whose shoes are made of hair."

Bukhari 52.179

Narrated Abu Huraira:

The Prophet said, "The Hour will not be established till you fight with the Khudh and the Kirman from among the non-Arabs. They will be of red faces, flat noses and small eyes; their faces will look like flat shields, and their shoes will be of hair."

Bukhari 56.788

Judgement Day won't happen until all the good people have died.

Narrated Mirdas Al-Aslami:

The Prophet said, "The righteous (pious people will depart (die) in succession one after the other, and there will remain (on the earth) useless people like the useless husk of barley seeds or bad dates."

Bukhari 75.442

Faith is believing that the whole thing won't start until a slave gives birth to her master and "shepherds of black camels" have developed an interest in erecting tall buildings.

Narrated Abu Huraira:

One day while the Prophet was sitting in the company of some people, (The angel) Gabriel came and asked, "What is faith?"

Allah's Apostle replied, "Faith is to believe in Allah, His angels, (the) meeting with Him, His Apostles, and to believe in Resurrection."

Then he further asked, "What is Islam?"

Allah's Apostle replied, "To worship Allah Alone and none else, to offer prayers perfectly to pay the compulsory charity (Zakat) and to observe fasts during the month of Ramadan."

Then he further asked, "What is Ihsan (perfection)?"

Allah's Apostle replied, "To worship Allah as if you see Him, and if you cannot achieve this state of devotion then you must consider that He is looking at you."

Then he further asked, "When will the Hour be established?"

Allah's Apostle replied, "The answerer has no better knowledge than the questioner. But I will inform you about its portents. 1. When a slave (lady) gives birth to her master. 2. When the shepherds of black camels start boasting and competing with others in the construction of higher buildings. And the Hour is one of five things which nobody knows except Allah."

The Prophet then recited: "Verily, with Allah (Alone) is the knowledge of the Hour." (31:34)

Then that man (Gabriel) left and the Prophet asked his companions to call him back, but they could not see him.

Then the Prophet said, "That was Gabriel who came to teach the people their religion."

Abu 'Abdullah said: He (the Prophet) considered all that as a part of faith.

Bukhari 2.47

Judgement Day will not start until a large fire is visible throughout the Hijaz (also spelled Hejaz) a more than 100,000 square miles area of present day Saudi Arabia centered on Mecca and Medina where Islam was born.

Narrated Abu Huraira:

Allah's Apostle said, "The Hour will not be established till a fire will come out of the land of Hijaz, and it will throw light on the necks of the camels at Busra."

Bukhari 88.234

Before or after the onset of the inferno a man from Yemen (Qahtan) will be seen driving people like sheep.

Narrated Abu Huraira:

Allah's Apostle said, "The Hour will not be established till a man from Qahtan appears, driving the people with his stick."

Bukhari 88.233

For some, rational women-loving men, end times will be the best of times, except for the earthquakes and an increase in homicides.

Narrated Abu Musa:

The Prophet (p.b.u.h) said, "A time will come upon the people when a person will wander about with gold as Zakat and will not find anybody to accept it, and one man will be seen followed by forty women to be their guardian because of scarcity of men and great number of women."

Bukhari 24.495

Narrated Abu Huraira:

The Prophet said, "The Hour (Last Day) will not be established until (religious) knowledge will be taken away (by the death of religious learned men), earthquakes will be very frequent, time will pass quickly, afflictions will appear, murders will increase and money will overflow amongst you."

Bukhari 17.146

Narrated Anas:

I will narrate to you a Hadith and none other than I will tell you about after it. I heard Allah's Apostle saying: From among the portents of the Hour are (the following):

1. Religious knowledge will decrease (by the death of religious learned men).

2. Religious ignorance will prevail.

3. There will be prevalence of open illegal sexual intercourse.

4. Women will increase in number and men will decrease in number so much so that fifty women will be looked after by one man.

Bukhari 3.81

At least four of the following six signs have come to pass:

Narrated Auf bin Mali:

I went to the Prophet during the Ghazwa (battle) of Tabuk while he was sitting in a leather tent. He said, "Count six signs that indicate the approach of the Hour: my death, the conquest of Jerusalem, a plague that will afflict you (and kill you in great numbers) as the plague that afflicts sheep, the increase of wealth to such an extent that even if one is given one hundred Dinars, he will not be satisfied; then an affliction which no Arab house will escape, and then a truce between you and Bani Al-Asfar (i.e. the Byzantines) who will betray you and attack you under eighty flags. Under each flag will be twelve thousand soldiers."

Bukhari 53.401

More signs of which you may already be aware:

Narrated Abu Huraira:

Allah's Apostle said, "The Hour will not be established

(1) till two big groups fight each other whereupon there will be a great number of casualties on both sides and they will be following one and the same religious doctrine,

(2) till about thirty Dajjals (liars) appear, and each one of them will claim that he is Allah's Apostle,

(3) till the religious knowledge is taken away (by the death of religious scholars)

(4) earthquakes will increase in number

(5) time will pass quickly,

(6) afflictions will appear,

(7) Al-Harj, (i.e. killing) will increase,

(8) till wealth will be in abundance - so abundant that a wealthy person will worry lest nobody should accept his Zakat (charity), and whenever he will present it to someone, that person (to whom it will be offered) will say, 'I am not in need of it,

(9) till the people compete with one another in constructing high buildings,

(10) till a man when passing by a grave of someone will say, 'Would that I were in his place,

(11) and till the sun rises from the West. So when the sun will rise and the people will see it (rising from the West) they will all believe (embrace Islam) but that will be the time when: (As Allah said,) 'No good will it do to a soul to believe then, if it believed not before, nor earned good (by deeds of righteousness) through its Faith.' (6:158)

And the Hour will be established while two men spreading a garment in front of them but they will not be able to sell it, nor fold it up;

and the Hour will be established when a man has milked his she-camel and has taken away the milk but he will not be able to drink it;

and the Hour will be established before a man repairing a tank (for his livestock) is able to water (his animals) in it;

and the Hour will be established when a person has raised a morsel (of food) to his mouth but will not be able to eat it."

Bukhari 88.237

To save yourself and your religion during the End Times, flee to the mountains and the valleys with your sheep.

Narrated Abu Said Al-Khudri:

Allah's Apostle said, "A time will come that the best property of a Muslim will be sheep which he will take on the top of mountains and the places of rainfall (valleys) so as to flee with his religion from afflictions."

Bukhari 2.18

Where the afflictions will come from:

Narrated 'Abdullah bin 'Umar:

I saw Allah's Apostle pointing towards the east saying, "Lo! Afflictions will verily emerge hence; afflictions will verily emerge hence where the (side of the head of) Satan appears."

Bukhari 54.499

Could suicide bombers be a harbinger of Judgement Day?

Narrated Abu Huraira:

Allah's Apostle said, "Time will pass rapidly, good deeds will decrease, and miserliness will be thrown (in the hearts of the people), and the Harj (will increase)."

They asked, "What is the Harj?"

He replied, "(It is) killing (murdering), (it is) murdering (killing)."

Bukhari 73.63

Many of those murdered will undoubtedly be young people, young believers in fact, killed on orders from an old man.

Narrated 'Ali:

I heard the Prophet saying, "In the last days (of the world) there will appear young people with foolish thoughts and ideas. They will give good talks, but they will go out of Islam as an arrow goes out of its game, their faith will not exceed their throats. So, wherever you find them, kill them, for there will be a reward for their killers on the Day of Resurrection."

Bukhari 61.577

In the Koran, the moon and the sun, which occupy the same orbit, will collide during Allah's End Times extravaganza: "He asks: 'When is the Day of Resurrection coming?' Then, when the sight is dazzled;

And the moon is eclipsed; And the sun and the moon are joined together;" (75:6-9). This may explain the Prophet's alarm at the onset of eclipses.

Narrated Abu Musa:

The sun eclipsed and the Prophet got up, being afraid that it might be the Hour (i.e. Day of Judgment). He went to the Mosque and offered the prayer with the longest Qiyam, bowing and prostration that I had ever seen him doing. Then he said, "These signs which Allah sends do not occur because of the life or death of somebody, but Allah makes His worshipers afraid by them. So when you see anything thereof, proceed to remember Allah, invoke Him and ask for His forgiveness."

Bukhari 17.167

Visions of a breach in the wall between Gog and Magog, another harbinger of Judgement Day mentioned in the Koran, also caused the Prophet to panic believing the Hour was at hand.

Narrated Zainab bint Jahsh:

That the Prophet once came to her in a state of fear and said, "None has the right to be worshipped but Allah. Woe unto the Arabs from a danger that has come near. An opening has been made in the wall of Gog and Magog like this," making a circle with his thumb and index finger.

Zainab bint Jahsh said, "O Allah's Apostle! Shall we be destroyed even though there are pious persons among us?"

He said, "Yes, when the evil person will increase."

Bukhari 54.565

Narrated Ibn Abbas:

Allah's Apostle performed the Tawaf (around the Ka'ba while riding his camel, and every time he reached the corner (of the Black Stone) he pointed at it with his hand and said, "Allahu Akbar." (Zainab said: The Prophet said, "An opening has been made in the wall of Gog and Magog like this and this," forming the number 90 (with his thumb and index finger).

Bukhari 63.215

The Doctor Dolittle effect!

Narrated Abu Huraira:

Once Allah's Apostle; offered the morning prayer and then faced the people and said, "While a man was driving a cow, he suddenly rode over it and beat it. The cow said, 'We have not been created for this, but we have been created for sloughing.' On that the people said astonishingly, 'Glorified be Allah! A cow speaks! '"

The Prophet said, "I believe this, and Abu Bakr and 'Umar too, believe it, although neither of them was present there. While a person was amongst his sheep, a wolf attacked and took one of the sheep. The man chased the wolf till he saved it from the wolf, where upon the wolf said, 'You have saved it from me; but who will guard it on the day of the wild beasts when there will be no shepherd to guard them except me (because of riots and afflictions)?'"

The people said surprisingly, "Glorified be Allah! A wolf speaks!"

The Prophet said, "But I believe this, and Abu Bakr and 'Umar too, believe this, although neither of them was present there."

Bukhari 56.677

Take precautions to avoid surprises when the big Day comes, such as being accused of the sins of your brother.

Narrated Abu Huraira:

Allah's Apostle said, "Whoever has wronged his brother, should ask for his pardon (before his death), as (in the Hereafter) there will be neither a Dinar nor a Dirham. (He should secure pardon in this life) before some of his good deeds are taken and paid to his brother, or, if he has done no good deeds, some of the bad deeds of his brother are taken to be loaded on him (in the Hereafter)."

Bukhari 76.541

An unmistakable clue that Judgement Day is at hand is the sun rising in the West, but it will be too late to believe.

Narrated Abu Huraira:

Allah's Apostle said, "The Hour will not be established until the sun rises from the West: and when the people see it, then whoever will be living on the surface of the earth will have faith, and that is (the time) when no good will it do to a soul to believe then, if it believed not before."

Bukhari 60.159

The sun will rise in the West to be replaced by a big head where it used to make an appearance every morning since the formation of the solar system.

Narrated Abu Masud:

The Prophet pointed with his hand towards Yemen and said twice, "Faith is there," and then pointed towards the East, and said, "Verily, sternness and mercilessness are the qualities of those who are busy with their camels and pay no attention to their religion, where the two sides of the head of Satan will appear," namely, the tribes of Rabl'a and Muqar.

Bukhari 63.223

Things will be so bad that you will wish you were dead ...

Narrated Abu Huraira:

The Prophet said, "The Hour will not be established till a man passes by a grave of somebody and says, 'Would that I were in his place.'"

Bukhari 88.231

... but perhaps not before witnessing the most bizarre spectacle that will signal the Hour is at hand, the jiggling of women's buttocks.

Narrated Abu Huraira:

Allah's Apostle said, "The Hour will not be established till the buttocks of the women of the tribe of Daus move while going round Dhi-al-Khalasa." Dhi-al-Khalasa was the idol of the Daus tribe which they used to worship in the pre Islamic Period of Ignorance.

Bukhari 88.232

The appearance of a thin legged black Ethiopian man who has come to destroy the holiest shrine in Islam may also be a precursor of Judgement Day.

Narrated Abu Huraira:

Allah's Apostle said, "DhusSuwaiqatain (the thin legged man) from Ethiopia will demolish the Ka'ba."

Bukhari 26.666

Narrated Ibn Abbas:

The Prophet said, "As if I were looking at him, a black person with thin legs plucking the stones of the Ka'ba one after another."

Bukhari 26.665

The last to die:

Narrated Abu Huraira:

I heard Allah's Apostle saying, "The people will leave Medina in spite of the best state it will have, and none except the wild birds and the beasts of prey will live in it, and the last persons who will die will be two shepherds from the tribe of Muzaina, who will be driving their sheep towards Medina, but will find nobody in it, and when they reach the valley of Thaniyat-al-Wada', they will fall down on their faces dead."

Bukhari 30.98

Ad-Dajjal and Jesus

No narration about the End Times would be complete without mentioning the coming of the false messiah, Ad-Dajjal. The appearance of Ad-Dajjal during the chaos that will be the End Times cannot be doubted. The Prophet, who, in the hadiths and the Koran expects the End Times to occur in his lifetime or shortly thereafter, sought protection in his prayers from the malevolent messiah's influence.

Narrated 'Aisha:

The Prophet used to say, "O Allah! I seek refuge with You from laziness and geriatric old age, from all kinds of sins and from being in debt; from the affliction of the Fire and from the punishment of the Fire and from the evil of the affliction of wealth; and I seek refuge with You from the affliction of poverty, and I seek refuge with You from the affliction of Al-Mesiah Ad-Dajjal. O Allah! Wash away my sins with the water of snow and hail, and cleanse my heart from all the sins as a white garment is cleansed from the filth, and let there be a long distance between me and my sins, as You made East and West far from each other."

Bukhari 75.379

God's Messenger would have us believe that he is the first Prophet to mention that the false messiah is one-eyed.

Narrated Abdullah bin Umar:

Allah's Apostle stood up amongst the people and then praised and glorified Allah as He deserved and then he mentioned Ad-Dajjal, saying, "I warn you of him, and there was no prophet but warned his followers of him; but I will tell you something about him which no prophet has told his followers: Ad-Dajjal is one-eyed whereas Allah is not."

Bukhari 88.241

Ad-Dajjal has two eyes, actually but is blind in one eye. For a false messiah he is not very bright, leaving a clear message between his seeing and blind eye that he is not who he pretends to be.

Narrated Anas:

The Prophet said, "Allah did not send any prophet but that he warned his nation of the one-eyed liar (Ad-Dajjal). He is one-eyed while your Lord is not one-eyed. The word 'Kafir' (unbeliever) is written between his two eyes."

Bukhari 93.505

In one hadith, Ad-Dajjal sets up residence on salt flats next to Medina. How he will get there, having been forbidden access to the mountain passes leading to the city, is not explained. He will try to impress his audience by killing a man then bringing him back to life, until Allah intervenes when he tries the same trick again.

Narrated Abu Sa'id:

One day Allah's Apostle narrated to us a long narration about Ad-Dajjal and among the things he narrated to us, was: "Ad-Dajjal will come, and he will be forbidden to enter the mountain passes of Medina. He will encamp in one of the salt areas neighboring Medina and there will appear to him a man who will be the best or one of the best of the people. He will say 'I testify that you are Ad-Dajjal whose story Allah's Apostle has told us.'

Ad-Dajjal will say (to his audience), 'Look, if I kill this man and then give him life, will you have any doubt about my claim?'

They will reply, 'No,'

Then Ad-Dajjal will kill that man and then will make him alive.

The man will say, 'By Allah, now I recognize you more than ever!'

Ad-Dajjal will then try to kill him (again) but he will not be given the power to do so."

Bukhari 88.246

Allah will limits Ad-Dajjal's influence in other ways.

Narrated Al-Mughira bin Shu'ba:

Nobody asked the Prophet as many questions as I asked regarding Ad-Dajjal. The Prophet said to me, "What worries you about him?"

I said, "Because the people say that he will have a mountain of bread and a river of water with him (i.e. he will have abundance of food and water)"

The Prophet said, "Nay, he is too mean to be allowed such a thing by Allah"' (but it is only to test mankind whether they believe in Allah or in Ad-Dajjal.)

Bukhari 88.238

When you see Ad-Dajjal and he asks you to choose between the fire and the water he is carrying, chose fire. The following two hadiths explain why:

Narrated Hudhaifa:

The Prophet said about Ad-Dajjal that he would have water and fire with him: (what would seem to be) fire, would be cold water and (what would seem to be) water, would be fire.

Bukhari 88.244

Narrated Abu Huraira:

Allah's Apostle said, "Shall I not tell you about the Dajjal a story of which no prophet told his nation? The Dajjal is one-eyed and will bring with him what will resemble Hell and Paradise, and what he will call Paradise will be actually Hell; so I warn you (against him) as Noah warned his nation against him."

Bukhari 55.554

It's hard to believe that there will still be unbelievers in Medina when Ad-Dajjal shows up, for even today, only Muslims are allowed into the second most holy site in all of Islam after Mecca.

Narrated Anas bin Malik:

The Prophet said, "Ad-Dajjal will come and encamp at a place close to Medina and then Medina will shake thrice whereupon every Kafir (disbeliever) and hypocrite will go out (of Medina) towards him."

Bukhari 88.239

The safest place to be during the End Times battle between good and evil will be Medina in present day Saudi Arabia.

Narrated Abu Huraira:

Allah's Apostle said, "There are angels at the mountain passes of Medina (so that) neither plague nor Ad-Dajjal can enter it."

Bukhari 88.247

Narrated Abu Bakra:

The Prophet said, "The terror caused by Al-Masih Ad-Dajjal will not enter Medina and at that time Medina will have seven gates and there will be two angels at each gate (guarding them)."

Bukhari 88.240

Road access to both Mecca and Medina will also be denied Ad-Dajjal.

Narrated Anas bin Malik:

The Prophet said, "There will be no town which Ad-Dajjal will not enter except Mecca and Medina, and there will be no entrance (road) (of both Mecca and Medina) but the angels will be standing in rows guarding it against him, and then Medina will shake with its inhabitants thrice (i.e. three earth-quakes will take place) and Allah will expel all the nonbelievers and the hypocrites from it."

Bukhari 30.105

Before, or after defeating Ad-Dajjal in the final battle of the End-Times, Jesus, among other things, will kill all the pigs.

Narrated Abu Huraira:

Allah's Apostle said, "The Hour will not be established until the son of Mary (i.e. Jesus) descends amongst you as a just ruler, he will break the cross, kill the pigs, and abolish the Jizya tax. Money will be in abundance so that nobody will accept it (as charitable gifts)."

Bukhari 43.656

During the End Times, Jesus will judge the living according to the Koran.

Narrated Abu Huraira:

Allah's Apostle said "How will you be when the son of Mary (i.e. Jesus) descends amongst you and he will judge people by the Law of the Quran and not by the law of Gospel."

Bukhari 55.658

Judgement Day

Judgement Day should be read in conjunction with *The Islamic Hereafter - Judgement Day (2012)* or *Pain, Pleasure and Prejudice - Judgement Day, Boreal Books (2012)* for the Koran's extensive coverage of that most ominous of days. For an entertaining, if ultimately depressing short play about the Day, you cannot do better than *Alice Visits a Mosque to Learn About Judgment Day, Boreal Books (2013)*

Of all the apparent absurdities that Muslims have to believe to avoid spending an eternity on fire in Hell none are stranger than Allah's and His Messenger's accounts of what will take place on Judgement Day.

It will be a dark day!

Narrated Abu Huraira:

The Prophet said, "The sun and the moon will be folded up (deprived of their light) on the Day of Resurrection."

Bukhari 54.422

The first person to be resurrected on Judgement Day will be the Prophet, or maybe Moses.

Narrated Abu Said Al-Khudri:

The Prophet said, "The people will fall unconscious on the Day of Resurrection, then suddenly I will see Moses holding one of the pillars of the Throne."

Abu Huraira said: The Prophet said, "I will be the first person to be resurrected and will see Moses holding the Throne."

Bukhari 93.524

The colour and texture of the land on which all people that ever lived and died will be gathered to be judge:

Narrated Sahl bin Sa'd:

I heard the Prophet saying, "The people will be gathered on the Day of Resurrection on reddish white land like a pure loaf of bread (made of pure fine flour)."

Bukhari 76.528

Pity the camel with the ten riders!

Narrated Abu Huraira:

The Prophet said, "The people will be gathered in three ways: (The first way will be of) those who will wish or have a hope (for Paradise) and will have a fear (of punishment). (The second batch will be those who will gather) riding two on a camel or three on a camel or ten on a camel. (The third batch) the rest of the people will be urged to gather by the Fire which will accompany them at the time of their afternoon nap and stay with them where they will spend the night, and will be with them in the morning wherever they may be then, and will be with them in the afternoon wherever they may be then."

Bukhari 76.529

The tail bone of the dead and decomposed will be used to recreate their bodies on Judgement Day according to the Prophet's primary narrator, who must have heard it from God's Messenger at one time or another.

Narrated Abu Huraira:

The Prophet said, "Between the two blowing of the trumpet there will be forty."

The people said, "O Abu Huraira! Forty days?"

I refused to reply. They said, "Forty years?"

I refused to reply and added: Everything of the human body will decay except the coccyx bone (of the tail) and from that bone Allah will reconstruct the whole body.

Bukhari 60.338

No tail bone, no problem!

Narrated Abu Sa'id:

The Prophet said, "Amongst the people preceding your age, there was a man whom Allah had given a lot of money. While he was in his death-bed, he called his sons and said, 'What type of father have I been to you? They replied, 'You have been a good father.' He said, 'I have never done a single good deed; so when I die, burn me, crush my body, and scatter the resulting ashes on a windy day.' His sons did accordingly, but Allah gathered his particles and asked (him), 'What made you do so?' He replied, "Fear of you.' So Allah bestowed His Mercy upon him. (forgave him)."

Bukhari 56.684

The first to be dressed on Judgment Day will be Abraham.

Narrated Ibn Abbas:

The Prophet said, "You will be gathered (on the Day of Judgment), bare-footed, naked and not circumcised."

He then recited: 'As We began the first creation, We, shall repeat it: A Promise We have undertaken: Truly we shall do it.' (21:104)

He added, "The first to be dressed on the Day of Resurrection, will be Abraham, and some of my companions will be taken towards the left side (i.e. to the (Hell) Fire), and I will say: 'My companions! My companions!' It will be said: 'They renegade from Islam after you left them.'"

Then I will say as the Pious slave of Allah (i.e. Jesus) said. "And I was a witness over them while I dwelt amongst them. When You took me up You were the Watcher over them, And You are a witness to all things. If You punish them. They are Your slaves and if You forgive them, Verily you, only You are the All-Mighty, the All-Wise."

Bukhari 55.568

The first to be called on Judgment Day will be Adam.

Narrated Abu Huraira:

The Prophet said, "The first man to be called on the Day of Resurrection will be Adam who will be shown his offspring, and it will be said to them, 'This is your father, Adam.' Adam will say (responding to the call), 'Labbaik ((*here I am*) and Sa'daik (*I am obedient*).' Then Allah will say (to Adam), 'Take out of your offspring, the people of Hell.' Adam will say, 'O Lord, how many should I take out?' Allah will say, 'Take out ninety-nine out of every hundred.'"

They (the Prophet's companions) said, "O Allah's Apostle! If ninety-nine out of every one hundred of us are taken away, what will remain out of us?"

He said, "My followers in comparison to the other nations are like a white hair on a black ox."

Bukhari 76.536

The Ram of Death will make an appearance only to be slaughtered.

Narrated Abu Said Al-Khudri:

Allah's Apostle said, "On the Day of Resurrection Death will be brought forward in the shape of a black and white ram. Then a call maker will call, 'O people of Paradise!' Thereupon they will stretch their necks and look carefully. The caller will say, 'Do you know this?'

They will say, 'Yes, this is Death.' By then all of them will have seen it.

Then it will be announced again, 'O people of Hell!' They will stretch their necks and look carefully.

The caller will say, 'Do you know this?'

They will say, 'Yes, this is Death.' And by then all of them will have seen it.

Then it (that ram) will be slaughtered and the caller will say, 'O people of Paradise! Eternity for you and no death. O people of Hell! Eternity for you and no death.'"

Then the Prophet, recited: "And warn them of the Day of distress when the case has been decided, while (now) they are in a state of carelessness (i.e. the people of the world) and they do not believe." (19:39)

Bukhari 60.254

The appearance of a weightless fat man on Judgement Day does not mean that you will all be floating about like balloons waiting to be judged. It is about Allah ignoring unbelievers, as understood in a modern complete translation of revelation 18:105 "Those who disbelieve in the Revelations of their Lord and in meeting Him. Their works are in vain and We will not take any account of them on the Day of Resurrection."

Narrated Abu Huraira:

Allah's Apostle said, "On the Day of Resurrection, a huge fat man will come who will not weigh, the weight of the wing of a mosquito in Allah's Sight, and then the Prophet added, 'We shall not give them any weight on the Day of Resurrection'" (18:105)

Bukhari 60.253

Judgement Day is the day Allah will sort out the good people He has indiscriminately killed.

Narrated Ibn 'Umar:

Allah's Apostle said, "If Allah sends punishment upon a nation then it befalls upon the whole population indiscriminately and then they will be resurrected (and judged) according to their deeds."

Bukhari 88.224

The earth will be part of the entertainment; on that both Muslims and Jews are in agreement.

Narrated Abu Said Al-Khudri:

The Prophet said, "The earth will be a bread on the Day of Resurrection, and the [ir]resistible (Allah) will topple turn it with His Hand like anyone of you topple turns a bread with his hands while (preparing the bread) for a journey, and that bread will be the entertainment for the people of Paradise."

A man from the Jews came (to the Prophet) and said, "May The Beneficent (Allah) bless you, O Abul Qasim! Shall I tell you of the entertainment of the people of Paradise on the Day of Resurrection?"

The Prophet said, "Yes."

The Jew said, "The earth will be a bread," as the Prophet had said. Thereupon the Prophet looked at us and smiled till his premolar tooth became visible. Then the Jew further said, "Shall I tell you of the udm (additional food taken with bread) they will have with the bread?" He added, "That will be Balam and Nun."

The people asked, "What is that?"

He said, "It is an ox and a fish, and seventy thousand people will eat of the caudate lobe (i.e. extra lobe) of their livers."

Bukhari 76.527

Unbelievers will be subjected to some face time, but it won't be fun.

Narrated Anas bin Malik:

A man said, "O Allah's Prophet! Will Allah gather the non-believers on their faces on the Day of Resurrection?"

He said, "Will not the One Who made him walk on his feet in this world, be able to make him walk on his face on the Day of Resurrection?"

Bukhari 60.283

Men will not pay attention to all that naked female flesh milling about and vice versa, and for good reason.

Narrated 'Aisha:

Allah's Apostle said, "The people will be gathered barefooted, naked, and uncircumcised."

I said, "O Allah's Apostle! Will the men and the women look at each other?"

He said, "The situation will be too hard for them to pay attention to that."

Bukhari 76.534

Pity the pregnant mothers on Judgement Day!

Narrated Abu Said Al-Khudri:

The Prophet said, "On the day of Resurrection Allah will say, 'O Adam!' Adam will reply, 'Labbaik (*here I am*) our Lord, and Sa'daik (*I am obedient*)'

Then there will be a loud call (saying), 'Allah orders you to take from among your offspring a mission for the (Hell) Fire.'

Adam will say, 'O Lord! Who are the mission for the (Hell) Fire?'

Allah will say, 'Out of each thousand, take out 999.'

"At that time every pregnant female shall drop her load (have a miscarriage) and a child will have grey hair. And you shall see mankind as in a drunken state, yet not drunk, but severe will be the torment of Allah." (22:2)

(When the Prophet mentioned this), the people were so distressed (and afraid) that their faces got changed (in color) whereupon the Prophet said, "From Gog and Magog nine-hundred ninety-nine will be taken out and one from you. You Muslims (compared to the large number of other people) will be like a black hair on the side of a white ox, or a white hair on the side of a black ox, and I hope that you will be one-fourth of the people of Paradise."

On that, we said, "Allahu-Akbar!"

Then he said, "I hope that you will be) one-third of the people of Paradise."

We again said, "Allahu-Akbar!"

Then he said, "(I hope that you will be) one-half of the people of Paradise."

So we said, "Allahu Akbar."

Bukhari 60.265

Some of the people will not be able to prostrate themselves on Judgement Day.

Narrated Abu Said:

I heard the Prophet saying, "Allah will bring forth the severest Hour, and then all the Believers, men and women, will prostrate themselves before Him, but there will remain those who used to prostrate in the world for showing off and for gaining good reputation. Such people will try to prostrate (on the Day of Judgment) but their back will be as stiff as if it is one bone (a single vertebra)."

Bukhari 60.441

No amount of deodorant will mask the fear or being too close to the sun.

Narrated Abu Huraira:

Allah's Apostle said, "The people will sweat so profusely on the Day of Resurrection that their sweat will sink seventy cubits deep into the earth, and it will rise up till it reaches the people's mouths and ears."

Bukhari 76.539

Giving "losing face" a whole new meaning.

Narrated 'Abdullah bin 'Umar

The Prophet said, "A man keeps on asking others for something till he comes on the Day of Resurrection without any piece of flesh on his face."

The Prophet added, "On the Day of Resurrection, the Sun will come near (to, the people) to such an extent that the sweat will reach up to the middle of the ears, so, when all the people are in that state, they will ask Adam for help, and then Moses, and then Muhammad (p.b.u.h) ."

The sub-narrator added "Muhammad will intercede with Allah to judge amongst the people. He will proceed on till he will hold the ring of the door (of Paradise) and then Allah will exalt him to Maqam Mahmud (the privilege of intercession, etc.). And all the people of the gathering will send their praises to Allah.

Bukhari 24.553

The people with whom Allah will be angry:

Narrated Ibn Mas'ud:

The Prophet said, "Whoever takes a (false) oath in order to grab (others) property, then Allah will be angry with him when he will meet Him."

Bukhari 48.839

The worst people in Allah's Sight on Judgement Day will be the hypocrites.

Narrated Abu Huraira:

The Prophet said, "The worst people in the Sight of Allah on the Day of Resurrection will be the double faced people who appear to some people with one face and to other people with another face."

Bukhari 73.84

Those for whom Allah will provide shade on Judgement Day:

Narrated Abu Huraira:

The Prophet said, "Seven (people) will be shaded by Allah by His Shade on the Day of Resurrection when there will be no shade except His Shade. (They will be), a just ruler, a young man who has been brought up in the worship of Allah, a man who remembers Allah in seclusion and his eyes are then flooded with tears, a man whose heart is attached to mosques (offers his compulsory congregational prayers in the mosque), two men who love each other for Allah's Sake, a man who is called by a charming lady of noble birth to commit illegal sexual intercourse with her, and he says, 'I am afraid of Allah,' and (finally), a man who gives in charity so secretly that his left hand does not know what his right hand has given."

Bukhari 82.798

Some of the people Allah will ignore on Judgement Day:

Narrated Abu Huraira:

Allah's Apostle said, "There will be three types of people whom Allah will neither speak to them on the Day of Resurrection nor will purify them from sins, and they will have a painful punishment: They are, (1) a man possessed superfluous water (more than he needs) on a way and he withholds it from the travelers. (2) a man who gives a pledge of allegiance to an Imam (ruler) and gives it only for worldly benefits, if the Imam gives him what he wants, he abides by his pledge, otherwise he does not fulfill his pledge; (3) and a man who sells something to another man after the 'Asr prayer and swears by Allah (a false oath) that he has been offered so much for it whereupon the buyer believes him."

Bukhari 89.319

The Prophet said that the first cases to be adjudicated on Judgement Day will be those where blood was shed, one has to assume not in Allah's Cause.

Narrated 'Abdullah:

The Prophet said, "The cases which will be decided first (on the Day of Resurrection) will be the cases of blood-shedding."

Bukhari 76.540

On Judgement Day, God's Messenger will receive people on the banks of his private river in Paradise, but not all will be welcomed.

Narrated Abu Huraira:

The Prophet said, "By Him in Whose Hands my soul is, I will drive some people out from my (sacred) Fount on the Day of Resurrection as strange camels are expelled from a private trough."

Bukhari 40.555

Do not assume that the Prophet, in the following hadith, does not know exactly how many people will hold hands and enter Paradise as a group glittering like the moon on Judgement Day:

Narrated Sahl bin Sa'd:

The Prophet said, "Seventy-thousand or seven-hundred thousand of my followers (the narrator is in doubt as to the correct number) will enter Paradise holding each other till the first and the last of them enter Paradise at the same time, and their faces will have a glitter like that of the moon at night when it is full."

Bukhari 76.551

Believers will enter Paradise via the gate that best corresponds to what Allah considers the good they did.

Narrated Abu Huraira:

Allah's Apostle said, "Whoever gives two kinds (of things or property) in charity for Allah's Cause, will be called from the gates of Paradise and will be addressed, 'O slaves of Allah! Here is prosperity.' So, whoever was amongst the people who used to offer their prayers, will be called from the gate of the prayer; and whoever was amongst the people who used to participate in Jihad, will be called from the gate of Jihad; and whoever was amongst those who used to observe fasts, will be called from the gate of Ar-Raiyan; whoever was amongst those who used to give in charity, will be called from the gate of charity."

Abu Bakr said, "Let my parents be sacrificed for you, O Allah's Apostle! No distress or need will befall him who will be called from those gates. Will there be any one who will be called from all these gates?"

The Prophet replied, "Yes, and I hope you will be one of them."

Bukhari 31.121

On a bridge between Hell and Paradise believers will be held in check before being purified of their sins in a ritual which involves settling old arguments among themselves the old fashion way.

Narrated Abu Said Al-Khudri:

Allah's Apostle said, "When the believers pass safely over (the bridge across) Hell, they will be stopped at a bridge in between Hell and Paradise where they will retaliate upon each other for the injustices done among them in the world, and when they get purified of all their sins, they will be admitted into Paradise. By Him in Whose Hands the life of Muhammad is everybody will recognize his dwelling in Paradise better than he recognizes his dwelling in this world."

Bukhari 43.620

Believers may still need up to four witnesses to attest to their good deeds before being admitted into Paradise.

Narrated Abu Al-Aswad:

Once I went to Medina where there was an outbreak of disease and the people were dying rapidly. I was sitting with 'Umar and a funeral procession passed by. The people praised the deceased. 'Umar said, "It has been affirmed" (Paradise).

Then another funeral procession passed by. The people praised the deceased. 'Umar said, "It has been affirmed." (Paradise).

Then another funeral procession passed by. The people praised the deceased. 'Umar said, "It has been affirmed (Paradise)."

Then a third funeral procession passed by and the people talked badly of the deceased. 'Umar said, "It has been affirmed (Hell)."

I asked Umar, "O chief of the believers! What has been affirmed?"

He said, "I have said what the Prophet said. He said, 'Allah will admit into paradise any Muslim whose good character is attested by four persons.'"

We asked the Prophet, 'If there were three witnesses only?'

He said, 'Even three.'

We asked, 'If there were two only?'

He said, 'Even two.'

But we did not ask him about one witness."

Bukhari 48.811

Those who shed their blood in a jihad will smell particularly good on Judgement Day if, like the Prophet, you like the smell of musk.

Narrated Abu Huraira:

The Prophet said, "A wound which a Muslim receives in Allah's cause will appear on the Day of Resurrection as it was at the time of infliction; blood will be flowing from the wound and its color will be that of the blood but will smell like musk."

Bukhari 4:238

Muslims will, of course, be foremost on Judgement Day.

Narrated Abu Huraira:

Allah's Apostle said, "We (Muslims) are the last (people to come in the world) but (will be) the foremost (on the Day of Resurrection)."

The same narrator told that the Prophet had said, "You should not pass urine in stagnant water which is not flowing then (you may need to) wash in it."

Bukhari 4:239

Seven heavens, seven hells and now seven earths! It there a pattern here?

Narrated Salim's father (i.e. 'Abdullah):

The Prophet said, "Whoever takes a piece of the land of others unjustly, he will sink down the seven earths on the Day of Resurrection."

Bukhari 43.634

Show-offs beware!

Narrated Jundub:

The Prophet said, "He who lets the people hear of his good deeds intentionally, to win their praise, Allah will let the people know his real intention (on the Day of Resurrection), and he who does good things in public to show off and win the praise of the people, Allah will disclose his real intention (and humiliate him).

Bukhari 76.506

Land speculators beware!

Narrated Said bin Zaid:

Allah's Apostle said, "Whoever usurps the land of somebody unjustly, his neck will be encircled with it down the seven earths (on the Day of Resurrection)."

Bukhari 43.632

Traitors beware!

Narrated Ibn Umar:

The Prophet said, "Every betrayer will have a flag which will be fixed on the Day of Resurrection, and the flag's prominence will be made in order to show the betrayal he committed."

Bukhari 53.411

Liars beware!

Narrated Samura bin Jundub:

The Prophet said, "I saw (in a dream), two men came to me."

Then the Prophet narrated the story (saying), "They said, 'The person, the one whose cheek you saw being torn away (from the mouth to the ear) was a liar and used to tell lies and the people would report those lies on his authority till they spread all over the world. So he will be punished like that till the Day of Resurrection.'"

Bukhari 73.118

Rich people beware!

Narrated Abu Huraira:

Allah's Apostle said, "Anyone whom Allah has given wealth but he does not pay its Zakat, then, on the Day of Resurrection, his wealth will be presented to him in the shape of a bald-headed poisonous male snake with two poisonous glands in its mouth and it will encircle itself round his neck and bite him over his cheeks and say, 'I am your wealth; I am your treasure.'"

Then the Prophet recited this Divine Verse: "And let not those who covetously withhold of that which Allah has bestowed upon them of His Bounty." (3.180)

Bukhari 60.88

Those rich in livestock may fare slightly better than those with a snake around their neck for not remitting the required Zakat.

Narrated Abu Dhar:

Once I went to him (the Prophet) and he said, "By Allah in Whose Hands my life is (or probably said, 'By Allah, except Whom none has the right to be worshipped) whoever had camels or cows or sheep and did not pay their Zakat, those animals will be brought on the Day of Resurrection far bigger and fatter than before and they will tread him under their hooves, and will butt him with their horns, and (those animals will come in circle): When the last does its turn, the first will start again, and this punishment will go on till Allah has finished the judgments amongst the people."

Bukhari 24.539

Choose your baby's name well.

Narrated Abu Huraira:

Allah's Apostle said, "The most awful name in Allah's sight on the Day of Resurrection, will be (that of) a man calling himself Malik Al-Amlak (the king of kings)."

Bukhari 73.224

Don't steal from the collection plate, for I am sure Allah will also have a way of making you stand out for that transgression on Judgement Day.

Narrated Abu Humaid Al-Sa'idi:

The Prophet appointed a man from the tribe of Al-Azd, called Ibn 'Utbiyya for collecting the Zakat. When he returned he said, "This (i.e. the Zakat) is for you and this has been given to me as a present."

The Prophet said, "Why hadn't he stayed in his father's or mother's house to see whether he would be given presents or not? By Him in Whose Hands my life is, whoever takes something from the resources of the Zakat (unlawfully) will be carrying it on his neck on the Day of Resurrection; if it be a camel, it will be grunting; if a cow, it will be mooing; and if a sheep, it will be bleating."

The Prophet then raised his hands till we saw the whiteness of his armpits, and he said thrice, "O Allah! Haven't I conveyed Your Message (to them)?"

Bukhari 47.769

Zakat was very much a tax in Allah's Cause, which you could not avoid paying if you did not want the Prophet's and later the Caliph's troops showing up your door, thereby elevating charitable donations to the equivalent of protection money. The Prophet, of course, preferred putting the fear of God in recalcitrant charity givers.

Narrated Abu Huraira:

Allah's Apostle said, "On the Day of Resurrection the Kanz (Treasure or wealth of which, Zakat has not been paid) of anyone of you will appear in the shape of a huge bald headed poisonous male snake and its owner will run away from it, but it will follow him and say, 'I am your Kanz.'"

The Prophet added, "By Allah, that snake will keep on following him until he stretches out his hand and let the snake swallow it."

Allah's Apostle added, "If the owner of camels does not pay their Zakat, then, on the Day of Resurrection those camels will come to him and will strike his face with their hooves ..."

Bukhari 86.89

Taking more than your fair share of the war booty (ghulul) will incur similar debasing treatment on Judgement Day as inflicted on those caught stealing from Allah's mandatory charitable contribution.

Narrated Abu Huraira:

The Prophet got up amongst us and mentioned Al Ghulul, emphasized its magnitude and declared that it was a great sin saying, "Don't commit Ghulul for I should not like to see anyone amongst you on the Day of Resurrection, carrying over his neck a sheep that will be bleating, or carrying over his neck a horse that will be neighing.

Such a man will be saying: 'O Allah's Apostle! Intercede with Allah for me,' and I will reply, 'I can't help you, for I have conveyed Allah's Message to you.'

Nor should I like to see a man carrying over his neck, a camel that will be grunting.

Such a man will say, 'O Allah's Apostle! Intercede with Allah for me, and I will say, 'I can't help you for I have conveyed Allah's Message to you,' or one carrying over his neck gold and silver and saying, 'O Allah's Apostle! Intercede with Allah for me,' and I will say, I can't help you for I have conveyed Allah's Message to you,' or one carrying clothes that will be fluttering, and the man will say, 'O Allah's Apostle! Intercede with Allah for me.' And I will say, 'I can't help you, for I have conveyed Allah's Message to you.'"

Bukhari 52.307

Narrated 'Abdullah bin 'Amr:

There was a man who looked after the family and the belongings of the Prophet and he was called Karkara. The man died and Allah's Apostle said, "He is in the (Hell) Fire."

The people then went to look at him and found in his place, a cloak he had stolen from the war booty.

Bukhari 52.308

The least punishment one can expect:

Narrated An-Nu'man bin Bashir:

I heard the Prophet saying, "The least punished person of the (Hell) Fire people on the Day of Resurrection will be a man under whose arch of the feet two smoldering embers will be placed, because of which his brain will boil just like Al-Mirjal (copper vessel) or a Qum-qum (narrow-necked vessel) is boiling with water."

Bukhari 76.567

Another hadith about a nephew's love!

Narrated Abu Said Al-Khudri:

I heard Allah's Apostles when his uncle, Abu Talib had been mentioned in his presence, saying, "May be my intercession will help him (Abu Talib) on the Day of Resurrection so that he may be put in a shallow place in the Fire, with fire reaching his ankles and causing his brain to boil."

Bukhari 76.569

Expect no mercy if you did not worship Allah and only Allah. What could have been easier!

Narrated Anas bin Malik:

The Prophet said, "Allah will say to the person who will have the minimum punishment in the Fire on the Day of Resurrection, 'If you had things equal to whatever is on the earth, would you ransom yourself (from the punishment) with it?' He will reply, 'Yes.' Allah will say, 'I asked you a much easier thing than this while you were in the backbone of Adam, that is, not to worship others besides Me, but you refused and insisted to worship others besides Me."'

Bukhari 76.562

Purgatory anyone?

Narrated Abu Said Al-Khudri:

Allah's Apostle said, "When the people of Paradise have entered Paradise, and the people of the Fire have entered the Fire, Allah will say. 'Take out (of the Fire) whoever has got faith equal to a mustard seed in his heart.' They will come out, and by that time they would have burnt and became like coal, and then they will be thrown into the river of Al-Hayyat (life) and they will spring up just as a seed grows on the bank of a rainwater stream."

The Prophet said, "Don't you see that the germinating seed comes out yellow and twisted?"

Bukhari 76.565

Narrated Anas bin Malik:

The Prophet said, "Some people will come out of the Fire after they have received a touch of the Fire, changing their color, and they will enter Paradise, and the people of Paradise will name them 'Al-Jahannamiyin the (Hell) Fire people."

Bukhari 76.564

The last thing you will be shown before you take your place in Paradise, or are cast into Hell:

Narrated Abu Huraira:

The Prophet said, "None will enter Paradise but will be shown the place he would have occupied in the (Hell) Fire if he had rejected faith, so that he may be more thankful; and none will enter the (Hell) Fire but will be shown the place he would have occupied in Paradise if he had faith, so that may be a cause of sorrow for him."

Bukhari 76.573

Horses will undergo a transformation on Judgement Day.

Narrated 'Abdullah bin 'Umar:

Allah's Apostle said, "Good will remain (as a permanent quality) in the foreheads of horses till the Day of Resurrection."

Bukhari 52.102

Narrated 'Urwa-al-Bariqi:

The Prophet said, "Horses are always the source of good, namely, rewards (in the Hereafter) and booty, till the Day of Resurrection."

Bukhari 53.348

The last person to enter Paradise:

Narrated 'Abdullah:

The Prophet said, "I know the person who will be the last to come out of the (Hell) Fire, and the last to enter Paradise. He will be a man who will come out of the (Hell) Fire crawling, and Allah will say to him, 'Go and enter Paradise.'

He will go to it, but he will imagine that it had been filled, and then he will return and say, 'O Lord, I have found it full.'

Allah will say, 'Go and enter Paradise, and you will have what equals the world and ten times as much (or, you will have as much as ten times the like of the world).'

On that, the man will say, 'Do you mock at me (or laugh at me) though You are the King?'"

I saw Allah's Apostle (while saying that) smiling that his premolar teeth became visible.

It is said that will be the lowest in degree amongst the people of Paradise.

Bukhari 76.575

No longer an angry God.

Narrated Abu Said Al-Khudri:

Allah's Apostle said, "Allah will say to the people of Paradise, 'O the people of Paradise!'

They will say, 'Labbaik, O our Lord, and Sa'daik!'

Allah will say, 'Are you pleased?'

They will say, 'Why should we not be pleased since You have given us what You have not given to anyone of Your creation?'

Allah will say, 'I will give you something better than that.'

They will reply, 'O our Lord! And what is better than that?'

Allah will say, 'I will bestow My pleasure and contentment upon you so that I will never be angry with you after forever.'"

Bukhari 76.557

The last announcement:

Narrated Ibn 'Umar:

The Prophet; said, "The people of Paradise will enter Paradise, and the people of the (Hell) Fire will enter the (Hell) Fire: then a call-maker will get up (and make an announcement) among them, 'O the people of the (Hell) Fire! No death anymore ! And O people of Paradise! No death (anymore) but Eternity."

Bukhari 76.552

Hell will then be closed, but not before It and Paradise have a short discussion about what has just happened.

Narrated Abu Huraira:

The Prophet said: "Paradise and the Fire (Hell) argued, and the Fire (Hell) said, 'I have been given the privilege of receiving the arrogant and the tyrants.'

Paradise said, 'What is the matter with me? Why do only the weak and the humble among the people enter me?'

On that, Allah said to Paradise, 'You are My Mercy which I bestow on whoever I wish of my servants.' Then Allah said to the (Hell) Fire, 'You are my (means of) punishment by which I punish whoever I wish of my slaves. And each of you will have its fill.'

As for the Fire (Hell), it will not be filled till Allah puts His Foot over it whereupon it will say, 'Qati! Qati!'

At that time it will be filled, and its different parts will come closer to each other; and Allah will not wrong any of His created beings. As regards Paradise, Allah will create a new creation to fill it with."

Bukhari 6:373

Paradise will remain open for business.

Narrated Anas:

The Prophet said, "(The people will be thrown into Hell (Fire) and it will keep on saying, 'Is there any more?' till the Lord of the Worlds puts His Foot over it, whereupon its different sides will come close to each other, and it will say, 'Qad!

Qad! (enough! enough!) By Your 'Izzat (Honor and Power) and YOUR KARAM (Generosity)!' Paradise will remain spacious enough to accommodate more people

Bukhari 93.481

A Fistful of Prophets

Muhammad will be a witness for Noah on Judgement Day:

Narrated Abu Said:

Allah's Apostle said, "Noah and his nation will come (on the Day of Resurrection and Allah will ask (Noah), 'Did you convey (the Message)?' He will reply, 'Yes, O my Lord!'

Then Allah will ask Noah's nation, 'Did Noah convey My Message to you?'

They will reply, 'No, no prophet came to us.'

Then Allah will ask Noah, 'Who will stand a witness for you?'

He will reply, 'Muhammad and his followers (will stand witness for me).' So, I and my followers will stand as witnesses for him (that he conveyed Allah's Message)."

That is, (the interpretation) of the Statement of Allah: "Thus we have made you a just and the best nation that you might be witnesses Over mankind .." (2.143)

Bukhari 55.555

Moses may be the exemption to the rule that all must die on Judgement Day, then resurrected.

Narrated Abu Huraira:

Two men, a Muslim and a Jew, abused each other. The Muslim said, "By Him Who gave superiority to Muhammad over all the people."

On that, the Jew said, "By Him Who gave superiority to Moses over all the people." The Muslim became furious at that and slapped the Jew in the face. The Jew went to Allah's Apostle and informed him of what had happened between him and the Muslim.

Allah's Apostle said, "Don't give me superiority over Moses, for the people will fall unconscious on the Day of Resurrection and I will be the first to gain consciousness, and behold ! Moses will be there holding the side of Allah's Throne. I will not know whether Moses has been among those people who have become unconscious and then has regained consciousness before me, or has been among those exempted by Allah from falling unconscious."

Bukhari 76.524

Abraham will get a vicious demonstration of what Allah thinks about unbelievers.

Narrated Abu Huraira:

The Prophet said, "On the Day of Resurrection Abraham will meet his father Azar whose face will be dark and covered with dust. (The Prophet Abraham will say to him): 'Didn't I tell you not to disobey me?'

His father will reply: 'Today I will not disobey you.'

Abraham will say: 'O Lord! You promised me not to disgrace me on the Day of Resurrection; and what will be more disgraceful to me than cursing and dishonoring my father?'

Then Allah will say (to him): 'I have forbidden Paradise for the disbelievers.' Then he will be addressed, 'O Abraham! Look! What is underneath your feet?'

He will look and there he will see a Dhabh (an animal,) blood-stained, which will be caught by the legs and thrown in the (Hell) Fire."

Bukhari 55.569

Unbelievers, like Abraham's father, will be easy to identify on Judgement day.

Narrated Abu Huraira:

The Prophet said, "On the Day of Resurrection Abraham will see his father covered with Qatara and Ghabara. (i.e. having a dark face)."

Bukhari 60.292

Who will save us?

Narrated Abu Huraira:

Some (cooked) meat was brought to Allah Apostle and the meat of a forearm was presented to him as he used to like it. He ate a morsel of it and said, "I will be the chief of all the people on the Day of Resurrection. Do you know the reason for it?

Allah will gather all the human being of early generations as well as late generation on one plain so that the announcer will be able to make them all-hear his voice and the watcher will be able to see all of them.

The sun will come so close to the people that they will suffer such distress and trouble as they will not be able to bear or stand. Then the people will say, 'Don't you see to what state you have reached? Won't you look for someone who can intercede for you with your Lord'

Some people will say to some others, 'Go to Adam.' So they will go to Adam and say to him. 'You are the father of mankind; Allah created you with His Own Hand, and breathed into you of His Spirit (meaning the spirit which he created for you); and ordered the angels to prostrate before you; so (please) intercede for us with your Lord. Don't you see in what state we are? Don't you see what condition we have reached?'

Adam will say, 'Today my Lord has become angry as He has never become before, nor will ever become thereafter. He forbade me (to eat of the fruit of) the tree, but I disobeyed Him. Myself! Myself! Myself! (has more need for intercession). Go to someone else; go to Noah.'

So they will go to Noah and say (to him), 'O Noah! You are the first (of Allah's Messengers) to the people of the earth, and Allah has named you a thankful slave; please intercede for us with your Lord. Don't you see in what state we are?'

He will say. 'Today my Lord has become angry as He has never become nor will ever become thereafter. I had (in the world) the right to make one definitely accepted invocation, and I made it against my nation. Myself! Myself! Myself! Go to someone else; go to Abraham.'

They will go to Abraham and say, 'O Abraham! You are Allah's Apostle and His Khalil from among the people of the earth; so please intercede for us with your Lord. Don't you see in what state we are?'

He will say to them, 'My Lord has today become angry as He has never become before, nor will ever become thereafter. I had told three lies (Abu Haiyan (the sub-narrator) mentioned them in the Hadith) Myself! Myself! Myself! Go to someone else; go to Moses.'

The people will then go to Moses and say, 'O Moses! You art Allah's Apostle and Allah gave you superiority above the others with this message and with His direct Talk to you; (please) intercede for us with your Lord Don't you see in what state we are?'

Moses will say, 'My Lord has today become angry as He has never become before, nor will become thereafter, I killed a person whom I had not been ordered to kill. Myself! Myself!

Myself! Go to someone else; go to Jesus.'

So they will go to Jesus and say, 'O Jesus! You are Allah's Apostle and His Word which He sent to Mary, and a superior soul created by Him, and you talked to the people while still young in the cradle. Please intercede for us with your Lord. Don't you see in what state we are?'

Jesus will say. 'My Lord has today become angry as He has never become before nor will ever become thereafter. Jesus will not mention any sin, but will say, 'Myself! Myself! Myself! Go to someone else; go to Muhammad.'

So they will come to me and say, 'O Muhammad ! You are Allah's Apostle and the last of the prophets, and Allah forgave your early and late sins. (Please) intercede for us with your Lord. Don't you see in what state we are?'"

The Prophet added, "Then I will go beneath Allah's Throne and fall in prostration before my Lord. And then Allah will guide me to such praises and glorification to Him as He has never guided anybody else before me.

Then it will be said, 'O Muhammad Raise your head. Ask, and it will be granted. Intercede it (your intercession) will be accepted.'

So I will raise my head and Say, 'My followers, O my Lord! My followers, O my Lord'.

It will be said, 'O Muhammad! Let those of your followers who have no accounts, enter through such a gate of the gates of Paradise as lies on the right; and they will share the other gates with the people.'"

The Prophet further said, "By Him in Whose Hand my soul is, the distance between every two gate-posts of Paradise is like the distance between Mecca and Busra (in Sham)."

Bukhari 60.236

A slightly different version where Jesus is not mentioned can be found in *The Islamic Hereafter - Life in the Grave II)*

The Bridge Over Hell

The bridge over Hell adds another layer of confusion to Judgement Day – as if there was not enough already – by introducing still another way that the resurrected dead will be judged, in this instance on bridge instead of in a large gathering somewhere on earth. The bridge over Hell, variation number one; watch out for the hooks.

Narrated Abu Huraira:

Some people said, "O Allah's Apostle! Shall we see our Lord on the Day of Resurrection?"

He said, "Do you crowd and squeeze each other on looking at the sun when it is not hidden by clouds?"

They replied, "No, Allah's Apostle."

He said, "Do you crowd and squeeze each other on looking at the moon when it is full and not hidden by clouds?"

They replied, "No, O Allah's Apostle!"

He said, "So you will see Him (your Lord) on the Day of Resurrection similarly Allah will gather all the people and say, 'Whoever used to worship anything should follow that thing.' So, he who used to worship the sun, will follow it, and he who used to worship the moon will follow it, and he who used to worship false deities will follow them; and then only this nation (i.e., Muslims) will remain, including their hypocrites.

Allah will come to them in a shape other than they know and will say, 'I am your Lord.'

They will say, 'We seek refuge with Allah from you. This is our place; (we will not follow you) till our Lord comes to us, and when our Lord comes to us, we will recognize Him.'

Then Allah will come to then in a shape they know and will say, 'I am your Lord.'

They will say, '(No doubt) You are our Lord,' and they will follow Him. Then a bridge will be laid over the (Hell) Fire."

Allah's Apostle added, "I will be the first to cross it. And the invocation of the Apostles on that Day, will be 'Allahukka Sallim, Sallim (O Allah, save us, save us!),' and over that bridge there will be hooks Similar to the thorns of As Sa'dan (a thorny tree). Didn't you see the thorns of As-Sa'dan?"

The companions said, "Yes, O Allah's Apostle."

He added, "So the hooks over that bridge will be like the thorns of As-Sa-dan except that their greatness in size is only known to Allah. These hooks will snatch the people according to their deeds. Some people will be ruined because of their evil deeds, and some will be cut into pieces and fall down in Hell, but will be saved afterwards, when Allah has finished the judgments among His slaves, and intends to take out of the Fire whoever He wishes to take out from among those who used to testify that none had the right to be worshipped but Allah.

We will order the angels to take them out and the angels will know them by the mark of the traces of prostration (on their foreheads) for Allah banned the fire to consume the traces of prostration on the body of Adam's son. So they will take them out, and by then they would have burnt (as coal), and then water, called Maul Hayat (water of life) will be poured on them, and they will spring out like a seed springs out on the bank of a rainwater stream, and there will remain one man who will be facing the (Hell) Fire and will say, 'O Lord! It's (Hell's) vapor has poisoned and smoked me and its flame has burnt me; please turn my face away from the Fire.'

He will keep on invoking Allah till Allah says, 'Perhaps, if I give you what you want), you will ask for another thing?'

The man will say, 'No, by Your Power, I will not ask You for anything else.'

Then Allah will turn his face away from the Fire. The man will say after that, 'O Lord, bring me near the gate of Paradise.'

Allah will say (to him), 'Didn't you promise not to ask for anything else? Woe to you, O son of Adam ! How treacherous you are!'

The man will keep on invoking Allah till Allah will say, 'But if I give you that, you may ask me for something else.'

The man will say, 'No, by Your Power. I will not ask for anything else.' He will give Allah his covenant and promise not to ask for anything else after that.

So Allah will bring him near to the gate of Paradise, and when he sees what is in it, he will remain silent as long as Allah will, and then he will say, 'O Lord! Let me enter Paradise.'

Allah will say, 'Didn't you promise that you would not ask Me for anything other than that? Woe to you, O son of Adam ! How treacherous you are!'

On that, the man will say, 'O Lord! Do not make me the most wretched of Your creation,' and will keep on invoking Allah till Allah will smile and when Allah will smile because of him, then He will allow him to enter Paradise, and when he will enter Paradise, he will be addressed, 'Wish from so-and-so.' He will wish till all his wishes will be fulfilled, then

Allah will say, 'All this (i.e. what you have wished for) and as much again therewith are for you.'"

Abu Huraira added: "That man will be the last of the people of Paradise to enter (Paradise)."

Narrated 'Ata (while Abu Huraira was narrating): Abu Said was sitting in the company of Abu Huraira and he did not deny anything of his narration till he reached his saying: "All this and as much again therewith are for you." Then Abu Sa'id said, "I heard Allah's Apostle saying, 'This is for you and ten times as much.'"

Abu Huraira said, "In my memory it is 'as much again therewith.'"

Bukhari 76.577

The bridge over Hell, variation number two; not quite as bad except for Jews and Christians.

Narrated Abu Sa'id Al-Khudri:

The Prophet then said, "Somebody will then announce, 'Let every nation follow what they used to worship.' So the companions of the cross will go with their cross, and the idolaters (will go) with their idols, and the companions of every god (false deities) (will go) with their god, till there remain those who used to worship Allah, both the obedient ones and the mischievous ones, and some of the people of the Scripture. Then Hell will be presented to them as if it were a mirage.

Then it will be said to the Jews, 'What did you use to worship?'

They will reply, 'We used to worship Ezra, the son of Allah.'

It will be said to them, 'You are liars, for Allah has neither a wife nor a son. What do you want (now)?'

They will reply, 'We want You to provide us with water.'

Then it will be said to them 'Drink,' and they will fall down in Hell (instead).

Then it will be said to the Christians, 'What did you use to worship?'

They will reply, 'We used to worship Messiah, the son of Allah.'

It will be said, 'You are liars, for Allah has neither a wife nor a son. What: do you want (now)?'

They will say, 'We want You to provide us with water.' It will be said to them, 'Drink,' and they will fall down in Hell (instead).

When there remain only those who used to worship Allah (Alone), both the obedient ones and the mischievous ones, it will be said to them, 'What keeps you here when all the people have gone?'

They will say, 'We parted with them (in the world) when we were in greater need of them than we are today, we heard the call of one proclaiming, 'Let every nation follow what they used to worship,' and now we are waiting for our Lord.'

Then the Almighty will come to them in a shape other than the one which they saw the first time, and He will say, 'I am your Lord,' and they will say, 'You are not our Lord.' And none will speak: to Him then but the Prophets, and then it will be said to them, 'Do you know any sign by which you can recognize Him?'

They will say. 'The Shin,' and so Allah will then uncover His Shin whereupon every believer will prostrate before Him and there will remain those who used to prostrate before Him just for showing off and for gaining good reputation. These people will try to prostrate but their backs will be rigid like one piece of a wood (and they will not be able to prostrate). Then the bridge will be laid across Hell."

We, the companions of the Prophet said, "O Allah's Apostle! What is the bridge?"

He said, "It is a slippery (bridge) on which there are clamps and (Hooks like) a thorny seed that is wide at one side and narrow at the other and has thorns with bent ends. Such a thorny seed is found in Najd and is called As-Sa'dan. Some of the believers will cross the bridge as quickly as the wink of an eye, some others as quick as lightning, a strong wind, fast horses or she-camels. So some will be safe without any harm; some will be safe after receiving some scratches, and some will fall down into Hell (Fire). The last person will cross by being dragged (over the bridge)."

The Prophet said, "You (Muslims) cannot be more pressing in claiming from me a right that has been clearly proved to be yours than the believers in interceding with Almighty for their (Muslim) brothers on that Day, when they see themselves safe. They will say, 'O Allah! (Save) our brothers (for they) used to pray with us, fast with us and also do good deeds with us.'

Allah will say, 'Go and take out (of Hell) anyone in whose

heart you find faith equal to the weight of one (gold) Dinar.' Allah will forbid the Fire to burn the faces of those sinners. They will go to them and find some of them in Hell (Fire) up to their feet, and some up to the middle of their legs. So they will take out those whom they will recognize and then they will return, and Allah will say (to them), 'Go and take out (of Hell) anyone in whose heart you find faith equal to the weight of one half Dinar.'

They will take out whomever they will recognize and return, and then Allah will say, 'Go and take out (of Hell) anyone in whose heart you find faith equal to the weight of an atom* (or a smallest ant), and so they will take out all those whom they will recognize."

Abu Sa'id said: If you do not believe me then read the Holy Verse: 'Surely! Allah wrongs not even of the weight of an atom (or a smallest ant) but if there is any good (done) He doubles it.' (4:40)

The Prophet added, "Then the prophets and Angels and the believers will intercede, and (last of all) the Almighty (Allah) will say, 'Now remains My Intercession'. He will then hold a handful of the Fire from which He will take out some people whose bodies have been burnt, and they will be thrown into a river at the entrance of Paradise, called the water of life. They will grow on its banks, as a seed carried by the torrent grows. You have noticed how it grows beside a rock or beside a tree, and how the side facing the sun is usually green while the side facing the shade is white.

Those people will come out (of the River of Life) like pearls, and they will have (golden) necklaces, and then they will enter Paradise whereupon the people of Paradise will say, 'These are the people emancipated by the Beneficent. He has admitted them into Paradise without them having done any good deeds and without sending forth any good (for themselves).' Then it will be said to them, 'For you is what you have seen and its equivalent as well.'"

Bukhari 93.532s

----

* Atom comes from the Greek átomos and was used by the ancient Greeks to describe something infinitely small, so the use of the word by the translator's may not imply that the Prophet was familiar with the atomic structure of matter.

Khaibar

Khaibar should be read in conjunction with *Allah's War Against the Unbelievers - Khaybar (2012)* or *Pain, Pleasure and Prejudice - Khaybar, Boreal Books (2012).*

Khaibar is not just another of the many bloody pitiless battles waged by the Prophet Muhammad to establish his rule on the Arabian Peninsula. After Badr, no battle gets more mention in the hadiths than that of Khaibar (also spelled Khaybar). The horde of wholly warriors descending on the villages and towns of the Peninsula intent on slaughter, destruction and plunder, with God's Messenger announcing to their inhabitants their imminent annihilation in his god's name, as he does at Khaibar must have been terrifying.

Narrated Anas bin Malik:

Allah's Apostle reached Khaibar in the early morning and the people of Khaibar came out with their spades, and when they saw the Prophet they said, "Muhammad and his army!" and returned hurriedly to take refuge in the fort.

The Prophet raised his hands and said, "Allah is Greater! Khaibar is ruined! If we approach a nation, then miserable is the morning of those who are warned."

Bukhari 56.840

The call to prayer only delayed the inevitable.

Narrated Humaid:

Anas bin Malik said, "Whenever the Prophet went out with us to fight (in Allah's cause) against any nation, he never allowed us to attack till morning and he would wait and see: if he heard Adhan (the call to prayer) he would postpone the attack and if he did not hear Adhan he would attack them ..."

Bukhari 11.584

Dawn was when the unbelievers could expect the holy horde's onslaught.

Narrated Anas:

The Prophet set out for Khaibar and reached it at night. He used not to attack if he reached the people at night, till the day broke. So, when the day dawned, the Jews came out with their bags and spades. When they saw the Prophet; they said, "Muhammad and his army!"

The Prophet said, "Allahu Akbar! (Allah is Greater) and Khaibar is ruined, for whenever we approach a nation (i.e. enemy to fight) then it will be a miserable morning for those who have been warned."

Bukhari 52.195

In another hadith, which includes the Prophet's ban on eating the meat of domesticated donkey, God's Messenger reached Khaibar in the morning.

Narrated Anas:

The Prophet reached Khaibar in the morning, while the people were coming out carrying their spades over their shoulders. When they saw him they said, "This is Muhammad and his army! Muhammad and his army!" So, they took refuge in the fort.

The Prophet raised both his hands and said, "Allahu Akbar, Khaibar is ruined, for when we approach a nation (i.e. enemy to fight) then miserable is the morning of the warned ones."

Then we found some donkeys which we (killed and) cooked. The announcer of the Prophet announced: "Allah and His Apostle forbid you to eat donkey's meat." So, all the pots including their contents were turned upside down.

Bukhari 52.234

You could still however fill your belly with the flesh of the onager, a wild variety of donkey.

Narrated Abu Qatada:

We were in the company of the Prophet at a place called Al-Qaha (which is at a distance of three stages of journey from Medina) ...

I noticed that some of my companions were watching something, so I looked up and saw an onager. (I rode my horse and took the spear and whip) but my whip fell down (and I asked them to pick it up for me) but they said, "We will not help you by any means as we are in a state of Ihram (*sacred state*)." So, I picked up the whip myself and attacked the onager from behind a hillock and slaughtered it and brought it to my companions.

Some of them said, "Eat it." While some others said, "Do not eat it." So, I went to the Prophet who was ahead of us and asked him about it, He replied, "Eat it as it is Halal (i.e. it is legal to eat it)."

Bukhari 29.49

On the day of the battle, the eating of horse flesh was made lawful.

Narrated Jabir bin 'Abdullah:

On the Day of the battle of Khaibar, Allah's Apostle made donkey's meat unlawful and allowed the eating of horse flesh.

Bukhari 67.429

You should not however spice up your wild donkey or horse meat dish with garlic if you intended to go to mosque before or after the battle.

Narrated Ibn 'Umar:

During the holy battle of Khaibar the Prophet said, "Whoever ate from this plant (i.e. garlic) should not enter our mosque."

Bukhari 12.812

On the day of the battle temporary marriages were forbidden, or so it would seem.

Narrated Muhammad bin 'Ali:

'Ali was told that Ibn 'Abbas did not see any harm in the Mut'a marriage. 'Ali said, "Allah's Apostle forbade the Mut'a marriage on the Day of the battle of Khaibar and he forbade the eating of donkey's meat."

Some people said, "If one, by a tricky way, marries temporarily, his marriage is illegal."

Others said, "The marriage is valid but its condition is illegal."

Bukhari 86.91

The taking of a town or village was as straightforward as it was pitiless. First prayers, then an assault on the unbelievers' position. If successful, as most of these massacres were, then came the plunder and apportioning of the property of the men killed including their wives, daughters and sons which were taken into slavery. Young women and girls were especially prized as slave-girls. At Khaibar, God's Messenger obtained the seventeen year old Safiya (also spelled Safiyya) for his troubles. She would become his eleventh wife.

Narrated Anas bin Malik:

Allah's Apostle (p.b.u.h) offered the Fajr prayer when it was still dark, then he rode and said, "Allah Akbar! Khaibar is ruined. When we approach near to a nation, the most unfortunate is the morning of those who have been warned."

The people came out into the streets saying, "Muhammad and his army."

Allah's Apostle vanquished them by force and their warriors were killed; the children and women were taken as captives. Safiya was taken by Dihya Al-Kalbi and later she belonged to Allah's Apostle who married her and her Mahr (dowry) was her manumission.

Bukhari 14.68

Ali, the Prophet's son-in-law and future Caliph (Leader of the Believers) may have been reluctant to join the fight due to an eye ailment which his father-in-law cured with a dab of saliva.

Narrated Sahl bin Sad:

That he heard the Prophet on the day (of the battle) of Khaibar saying, "I will give the flag to a person at whose hands Allah will grant victory." So, the companions of the Prophet got up, wishing eagerly to see to whom the flag will be given, and every one of them wished to be given the flag. But the Prophet asked for 'Ali. Someone informed him that he was suffering from eye-trouble. So, he ordered them to bring 'Ali in front of him.

Then the Prophet spat in his eyes and his eyes were cured immediately as if he had never any eye-trouble.

'Ali said, "We will fight with them (i.e. infidels) till they become like us (i.e. Muslims)."

The Prophet said, "Be patient, till you face them and invite them to Islam and inform them of what Allah has enjoined upon them. By Allah! If a single person embraces Islam at your hands (i.e. through you), that will be better for you than the red camels."

Bukhari 52.192

Another account of Ali's lateness in joining the assault on Khaibar.

Narrated Salama bin Al-Akwa:

Ali remained behind the Prophet during the battle of Khaibar as he was suffering from some eye trouble but then he said, "How should I stay behind Allah's Apostle?" So, he set out till he joined the Prophet.

On the eve of the day of the conquest of Khaibar, Allah's Apostle said, "(No doubt) I will give the flag or, tomorrow, a man whom Allah and His Apostle love or who loves Allah and His apostle will take the flag. Allah will bestow victory upon him."

Suddenly 'Ali joined us though we were not expecting him. The people said, "Here is 'Ali." So, Allah's Apostle gave the flag to him and Allah bestowed victory upon him.

Bukhari 52.219

During the battle of Khaibar, a camel driver and storyteller by the name of Amir apparently committed suicide; but not before dispatching an undetermined number of unbelievers. In the first of two narrations about the circumstances surrounding Amir's demise, it's again donkey meat which gets most of the Prophet's attention.

Narrated Salama bin Al-Akwa':

We went out with the Prophet to Khaibar. A man among the people said, "O 'Amir! Will you please recite to us some of your poetic verses?" So 'Amir got down and started chanting among them, saying, "By Allah! Had it not been for Allah, we would not have been guided." 'Amir also said other poetic verses which I do not remember.

Allah's Apostle said, "Who is this (camel) driver?"

The people said, "He is 'Amir bin Al-Akwa."

He said, "May Allah bestow His Mercy on him."

A man from the People said, "O Allah's Apostle! Would that you let us enjoy his company longer."

When the people (Muslims) lined up, the battle started, and 'Amir was struck with his own sword (by chance) by himself and died.

In the evening, the people made a large number of fires (for cooking meals).

Allah's Apostle said, "What is this fire? What are you making the fire for?"

They said, "For cooking the meat of donkeys."

He said, "Throw away what is in the pots and break the pots!"

A man said, "O Allah's Prophet! May we throw away what is in them and wash them?"

He said, "Never mind, you may do so."

Bukhari 75.343

In the second narration, the preoccupation is thankfully no longer about donkey meat but about Amir's death, and whether the way he died – by his own hand or by accident – means that he has voided Allah's guarantee of a reward i.e. Paradise for whomever dies killing unbelievers.

Narrated Salama:

We went out with the Prophet to Khaibar. A man (from the companions) said, "O 'Amir! Let us hear some of your Huda (camel-driving songs.)" So he sang some of them (i.e. a lyric in harmony with the camels walk).

The Prophet said, "Who is the driver (of these camels)?"

They said, "Amir."

The Prophet said, "May Allah bestow His Mercy on him!"

The people said, "O Allah's Apostle! Would that you let us enjoy his company longer!" Then 'Amir was killed the following morning.

The people said, "The good deeds of 'Amir are lost as he has killed himself."

I returned at the time while they were talking about that. I went to the Prophet and said, "O Allah's Prophet! Let my father be sacrificed for you! The people claim that 'Amir's good deeds are lost."

The Prophet said, "Whoever says so is a liar, for 'Amir will have a double reward as he exerted himself to obey Allah and fought in Allah's Cause. No other way of killing would have granted him greater reward."

Bukhari 83.29

The Prophet Muhammad, as God's Messenger, was not only entitled to one fifth of the booty obtained the hard way, but all the booty that was obtained without a fight, the Fai'. Technically, the valuable farmland surrounding Khaibar had not been fought over therefore under the doctrine of Fai' (see *Booty and the Unbelievers*) it belonged to God's Messenger exclusively.

What made the land around the oasis of Khaibar extraordinarily valuable was the Jewish farmers who worked the land; something the Messenger's holy warriors would not have cared to do, even if they had known how to grow dates and such, for absconding with the belongings of the unbelievers was a much more profitable enterprise. The Prophet let the Jewish farmers of Khaibar continue to work the land in return for half of what they produced.

Narrated Abdullah bin Umar:

Allah's Apostle gave the land of Khaibar to the Jews to work on and cultivate and take half of its yield. Ibn 'Umar added, "The land used to be rented for a certain portion (of its yield)." Nafi mentioned the amount of the portion but I forgot it.

Rafi' bin Khadij said, "The Prophet forbade renting farms."

Narrated 'Ubaid-Ullah Nafi' said: Ibn 'Umar said: (The contract of Khaibar continued) till 'Umar evacuated the Jews (from Khaibar).

Bukhari 36.485

Some of the Jewish farmers were not grateful, or simply wanted to test the Prophet's claim to being God's Messenger, therefore under His Protection.

Narrated Abu Huraira:

When Khaibar was conquered, a roasted poisoned sheep was presented to the Prophets as a gift (by the Jews). The Prophet ordered, "Let all the Jews who have been here, be assembled before me."

The Jews were collected and the Prophet said (to them), "I am going to ask you a question. Will you tell the truth?"

They said, "Yes."

The Prophet asked, "Who is your father?"

They replied, "So-and-so."

He said, "You have told a lie; your father is so-and-so."

They said, "You are right."

He said, "Will you now tell me the truth, if I ask you about something?"

They replied, "Yes, O Abu Al-Qasim; and if we should tell a lie, you can realize our lie as you have done regarding our father."

On that he asked, "Who are the people of the (Hell) Fire?"

They said, "We shall remain in the (Hell) Fire for a short period, and after that you will replace us."

The Prophet said, "You may be cursed and humiliated in it!

By Allah, we shall never replace you in it." Then he asked, "Will you now tell me the truth if I ask you a question?"

They said, "Yes, O Abu Al-Qasim."

He asked, "Have you poisoned this sheep?"

They said, "Yes."

He asked, "What made you do so?"

They said, "We wanted to know if you were a liar in which case we would get rid of you, and if you are a prophet then the poison would not harm you."

Bukhari 53.394

What the Jewish farmers of Khaibar produced was one of the most profitable acquisition of the Prophet and may explain his successor's unilateral takeover of God's Messenger's interests.

Narrated 'Aisha:

Fatima sent somebody to Abu Bakr asking him to give her her inheritance from the Prophet from what Allah had given to His Apostle through Fai (i.e. booty gained without fighting). She asked for the Sadaqa (i.e. wealth assigned for charitable purposes) of the Prophet at Medina, and Fadak, and what remained of the Khumus (i.e., one-fifth) of the Khaibar booty.

Abu Bakr said, "Allah's Apostle said, 'We (Prophets), our property is not inherited, and whatever we leave is Sadaqa, but Muhammad's Family can eat from this property, i.e. Allah's property, but they have no right to take more than the food they need.' By Allah! I will not bring any change in dealing with the Sadaqa of the Prophet (and will keep them) as they used to be observed in his (i.e. the Prophet's) life-time, and I will dispose with it as Allah's Apostle used to do,"

Then 'Ali said, "I testify that None has the right to be worshipped but Allah, and that Muhammad is His Apostle," and added, "O Abu Bakr! We acknowledge your superiority." Then he (i.e. 'Ali) mentioned their own relationship to Allah's Apostle and their right.

Abu Bakr then spoke saying, "By Allah in Whose Hands my life is. I love to do good to the relatives of Allah's Apostle rather than to my own relatives"

Abu Bakr added: Look at Muhammad through his family (i.e. if you are not good to his family you are not good to him).

Bukhari 57.60

Fatima the Prophet's daughter and mother of his grandsons confronted Bakr, but was unsuccessful in getting him to give her what should have been her due. Bakr's excuse was that he needed her father's legacy for charitable works and to feed his now destitute widows who were also denied a share of their husband's estate.

Narrated 'Aisha:

Fatima and Al 'Abbas came to Abu Bakr, seeking their share from the property of Allah's Apostle and at that time, they were asking for their land at Fadak and their share from Khaibar.

Abu Bakr said to them, "I have heard from Allah's Apostle saying, 'Our property cannot be inherited, and whatever we leave is to be spent in charity, but the family of Muhammad may take their provisions from this property."

Abu Bakr added, "By Allah, I will not leave the procedure I saw Allah's Apostle following during his lifetime concerning this property."

Therefore Fatima left Abu Bakr and did not speak to him till she died.

Bukhari 80.718

Bakr, by absconding with the Prophet's estate and Allah by forbidding any man to marry His Messenger's wives after his passing (33:53 ... You should never hurt the Messenger of Allah, nor take his wives in marriage after him ...), meant that they were reduced to the status of beggars, dependent on the whims of the parsimonious acquisitive Bakr for their survival.

Umar, Bakr's successor would return some of the Prophet's property which was allegedly meant for charity to Ali, Fatima's husband. The property had probably lost much of its value after Umar exiled the Jews who farmed the land, justifying his actions in a hadith, that it was always the Prophet's intention to expel the Jews of Khaibar.

Narrated Ibn 'Umar:

Umar expelled the Jews and the Christians from Hijaz. When Allah's Apostle had conquered Khaibar, he wanted to expel the Jews from it as its land became the property of Allah, His Apostle, and the Muslims. Allah's Apostle intended to expel the Jews but they requested him to let them stay there on the condition that they would do the labor and get half of the fruits.

Allah's Apostle told them, "We will let you stay on thus condition, as long as we wish." So, they (i.e. Jews) kept on living there until 'Umar forced them to go towards Taima' and Ariha'.

Bukhari 39.531

Umar accused the Jews of harming a believer, then used what the Jews thought was a joke made at their expense by the Prophet (Abu-l-Qasim in the following hadith) to nullify God's Messenger's agreement.

Narrated Ibn Umar:

When the people of Khaibar dislocated Abdullah bin Umar's hands and feet, Umar got up delivering a sermon saying, "No doubt, Allah's Apostle made a contract with the Jews concerning their properties, and said to them, 'We allow you (to stand in your land) as long as Allah allows you.' Now Abdullah bin Umar went to his land and was attacked at night, and his hands and feet were dislocated, and as we have no enemies there except those Jews, they are our enemies and the only people whom we suspect, I have made up my mind to exile them."

When Umar decided to carry out his decision, a son of Abu Al-Haqiq's came and addressed 'Umar, "O chief of the believers, will you exile us although Muhammad allowed us to stay at our places, and made a contract with us about our properties, and accepted the condition of our residence in our land?"

'Umar said, "Do you think that I have forgotten the statement of Allah's Apostle: 'What will your condition be when you are expelled from Khaibar and your camel will be carrying you night after night?'"

The Jew replied, "That was a joke from Abu-l-Qasim."

'Umar said, "O the enemy of Allah! You are telling a lie."

'Umar then drove them out and paid them the price of their properties in the form of fruits, money, camel saddles and ropes, etc.

Bukhari 50.890

Umar would eventually expel all Jews and Christians from the Hejaz, the so-called holy land of Islam, which comprises most of the western part of modern-day Saudi Arabia and is centered on Mecca and Medina.

Narrated Ibn 'Umar:

Umar bin Al-Khattab expelled all the Jews and Christians from the land of Hijaz. Allah's Apostle after conquering Khaibar, thought of expelling the Jews from the land which, after he conquered it belonged to Allah, Allah's Apostle and the Muslims. But the Jews requested Allah's Apostle to leave them there on the condition that they would do the labor and get half of the fruits (the land would yield).

Allah's Apostle said, "We shall keep you on these terms as long as we wish." Thus they stayed till the time of 'Umar's Caliphate when he expelled them to Taima and Ariha.

Bukhari 53.380

Safiya, Juwairiya and Rayhanah

Narrated Anas:

Amongst the captives was Safiya. First she was given to Dihya Al-Kalbi and then to the Prophet.

Bukhari 34.431

Under normal circumstances, Islamic law, backed by the Koran, demands that a man give his bride a dowry before marrying her. This is meant to give the wife-to-be some means of looking after herself, if only for a short period, should her husband divorce her with those three little words you probably have all heard about "I divorce you" repeated three time before sending her packing after ascertaining she is not pregnant with <u>his</u> child. A wife's dowry is her only possession, everything else including the family home is exclusively her husband's. Her dowry is also one of the few means she has of "ransoming herself" i.e. foregoing her diary to obtain a divorce from an abusive husband. The Prophet essentially got his eleventh wife cost-free, deeming that his setting her free before marrying her was the equivalent of a dowry.

Narrated 'Abdul 'Aziz:

Anas said, "When Allah's Apostle invaded Khaibar, we offered the Fajr prayer there early in the morning) when it was still dark. The Prophet rode and Abu Talha rode too and I was riding behind Abu Talha. The Prophet passed through the lane of Khaibar quickly and my knee was touching the thigh of the Prophet. He uncovered his thigh and I saw the whiteness of the thigh of the Prophet. When he entered the town, he said, 'Allahu Akbar! Khaibar is ruined. Whenever we approach near a (hostile) nation (to fight) then evil will be the morning of those who have been warned.'

He repeated this thrice. The people came out for their jobs and some of them said, 'Muhammad (has come).' (Some of our companions added, "With his army.") We conquered Khaibar, took the captives, and the booty was collected. Dihya came and said, 'O Allah's Prophet! Give me a slave girl from the captives.'

The Prophet said, 'Go and take any slave girl.' He took Safiya bint Huyai.

A man came to the Prophet and said, 'O Allah's Apostles! You gave Safiya bint Huyai to Dihya and she is the chief mistress of the tribes of Quraiza and An-Nadir and she befits none but you.'

So the Prophet said, 'Bring him along with her.'

So Dihya came with her and when the Prophet saw her, he said to Dihya, 'Take any slave girl other than her from the captives.'"

Anas added: "The Prophet then manumitted her and married her."

Thabit asked Anas, "O Abu Hamza! What did the Prophet pay her (as Mahr i.e. dowry)?"

He said, "Herself was her Mahr for he manumitted her and then married her."

Anas added, "While on the way, Um Sulaim dressed her for marriage (ceremony) and at night she sent her as a bride to the Prophet. So the Prophet was a bridegroom and he said, 'Whoever has anything (food) should bring it.' He spread out a leather sheet (for the food) and some brought dates and others cooking butter. (I think he (Anas) mentioned As-SawTq). So they prepared a dish of Hais (a kind of meal). And that was Walrma (the marriage banquet) of Allah's Apostle ."

Bukhari 8.367

It is not clear in the hadiths consulted if the Prophet's broad interpretation of Allah's decree concerning a dowry became a precedent where any men could now take a slave-girl as a wife without spending a penny on a dowry. The Prophet may also have been looking at saving money, in Allah's Cause I am sure, in having a very frugal marriage banquet.

Narrated Anas bin Malik:

The Prophet came to Khaibar and when Allah made him victorious and he conquered the town by breaking the enemy's defense, the beauty of Safiya bint Huyai bin Akhtab was mentioned to him and her husband had been killed while she was a bride. Allah's Apostle selected her for himself and he set out in her company till he reached Sadd-ar-Rawha' where her menses were over and he married her.

Then Hais (a kind of meal) was prepared and served on a small leather sheet (used for serving meals). Allah's Apostle then said to me, "Inform those who are around you (about the wedding banquet)."

So that was the marriage banquet given by Allah's Apostle for (his marriage with) Safiya. After that we proceeded to Medina and I saw that Allah's Apostle was covering her with a cloak while she was behind him. Then he would sit beside his camel and let Safiya put her feet on his knees to ride (the camel).

Bukhari 34.437

A hadith on how believers ascertained if the Prophet had taken a wife or a slave-girl (Safiya is spelled Saffiyya in the following hadith):

Narrated Anas:

The Prophet stayed for three days between Khaibar and Medina, and there he consummated his marriage to Safiyya bint Huyai.

I invited the Muslims to the wedding banquet in which neither meat nor bread was offered. He ordered for leather dining-sheets to be spread, and dates, dried yoghurt and butter were laid on it, and that was the Prophet's wedding banquet.

The Muslims wondered, "Is she (Saffiyya) considered as his wife or his slave girl?" Then they said, "If he orders her to veil herself, she will be one of the mothers of the Believers; but if he does not order her to veil herself, she will be a slave girl."

So when the Prophet proceeded from there, he spared her a space behind him (on his she-camel) and put a screening veil between her and the people.

Bukhari 62.22

Safiya was not the first valued war prize to become the wife of God's Messenger after another of the Prophet's many, mostly unprovoked merciless attacks on the unbelievers.

Narrated Ibn Aun:

I wrote a letter to Nafi and Nafi wrote in reply to my letter that the Prophet had suddenly attacked Bani Mustaliq without warning while they were heedless and their cattle were being watered at the places of water. Their fighting men were killed and their women and children were taken as captives; the Prophet got Juwairiya on that day.

Nafi said that Ibn 'Umar had told him the above narration and that Ibn 'Umar was in that army.

Bukhari 46.717

The most doleful story of a woman whom the Prophet took into his household is that of Rayhanah (also spelled Rayhana). God's Messenger had the audacity to ask her to marry him after overseeing the slaughter of the more than seven hundred men and boys of her tribe, including her father and husband. From *From Merchant to Messenger - Wives of the Messenger, Boreal Books (2012)*:

> Rayhanah is "not usually listed as a wife" of God's Messenger. She agreed to become his concubine, seeing it as unseemly to accept the Prophet's marriage proposal after he had just ordered the beheading of all the men and boys (males with traces of pubic hair) of her tribe after the battle of the Ditch (also referred to as the battle of the Trench) ...
>
> > After the battle of the Trench [Rayhanah was] marched into the courtyard with the several hundred other women and their children to be claimed as a reward by the Muslim soldiers, while the Qurayzah man were led away to be executed.
>
> Rayhanah was not only a beautiful young woman. "Rayhana's name means 'extremely flagrant' and Muhammad loved perfumes" making her even more irresistible to God's Messenger. Rayhanah's life with the Prophet was short and tumultuous: some say she converted to Islam, others that she died as a slave of Muhammad, and still others that she was allowed to rejoin her Jewish community, which is somewhat unlikely as she is buried, along with other wives of God's Messenger, in Baqi cemetery of Medina.
>
> > She died a short two years after the massacre of the men and boys of her tribe. Her age and how she died remains a mystery; all that we know is that the beautiful, tragic Rayhanah died young. I would not exclude suicide. It must have been difficult to be intimate with a man, even an extraordinary man, who was responsible for the death of your father, your husband, your male relatives and the enslavement of your female kin.

Life in the Grave

Much of the following is from *The Islamic Hereafter - Life in in Grave,* *Boreal Books, (2012).*

Narrated Anas bin Malik:

The Prophet used to say, "O Allah! I seek refuge with You from helplessness, laziness, cowardice and feeble old age; I seek refuge with You from afflictions of life and death and seek refuge with You from the punishment in the grave."

Bukhari 52.77

For most of what Islam has to say about what happens to a human being after he or she passes away we must look to the sayings (Traditions) of the Prophet Muhammad and his extraordinary insights into what happens after everything fades to black. If you thought the Compassionate's description of what He intends to do to unbelievers and sinners when he gets His hands on them was about as bad as it could get, you haven't read His Messenger's account of what will be done to them when they die. Don't try to make sense of what you are about to read, and don't let it give you nightmares.

According to the Traditions the whole death thing starts innocently enough. Forty days before a person dies, a leaf with the soon-to-be-deceased's name on it falls from a tree in Paradise just beneath Allah's throne. 'Izra'il, the angel of death picks it up and schedules a pick-up forty days hence. Even believers, the Prophet said, will be taken aback when 'Izra'il comes a knocking. When he shows up on their doorstep, even after they have been warned of his coming by the Messenger of God, they will still ask him: "Who are you?"

Be that as it may, the last person the soon-to-be-departed will see is not the angel of death, but two angels who have been patiently and anonymously recording his or her bad and good deeds. These two angels, in the blink of an eye, will present the soon-to-be-deceased with their lifetime of good and bad deeds. With this-was-your-life formalities out of the way, the person's living, thinking, seeing, able-to-feel-pain soul will sink into the ground where they died; but not before 'Izra'il has finished extracting it from the still warm body, drawing it out like rough cotton through the eye sockets.

Like birth, death in Islamic traditions is meant to be a painful transition. Satan will offer a believer in Allah's good books to relieve him or her of some of the pain caused by 'Izra'il appalling soul extraction method. On the threshold of Paradise, if the poor tormented soul can't stand the pain and accepts Satan's offer to reduce its suffering, it's a U-turn to Hell for it and its owner come Judgement Day. It will be sorry it could not stand the pain just a while longer.

If the extracted soul is meant to go to Hell it will be given a glimpse of life in the grave and its final destination on Judgement Day. The horror-struck soul will then briefly escape 'Izra'il's grip and will fly to heaven and try all seven doors to the seven levels of heaven only to be turned back by the angels guarding the entrances to Paradise. It will be forced to return to 'Izra'il who will then stuff it back into the already decaying corpse and the reconstituted soul-body combo will begin its new life in the grave. The believers who died literally in Allah's good books will be provided with a spacious grave complete with curtains and a bed. An unbeliever, or a believer who died while in Allah's bad books, will be confined to a cramped space with walls constantly closing in on them making every breath a laboured one.

After the living dead have settled into their zombie-like existence, two black-skin, blue-eyed angels by the name of Munkar and Nakir will burst into their graves and start questioning the decaying remains, which will sit up, as to its religious beliefs for forty days non-stop.

Narrated Al-Bara' bin 'Azib:

The Prophet (p.b.u.h) said, "When a faithful believer is made to sit in his grave, then (the angels) come to him and he testifies that none has the right to be worshipped but Allah and Muhammad is Allah's Apostle. And that corresponds to Allah's statement: 'Allah will keep firm those who believe with the word that stands firm ... '" (14.27).

Bukhari 23.450

The point of this questioning is lost on many since the Koran states that a believer enters Paradise based on their records of good and bad deeds, or at Allah's discretion. The corpse will not only be asked about Allah's Revelations but also whether it ever said anything bad about the Prophet. If it only said good things about him during its living breathing life above ground, God's Messenger said, all is forgiven (or so it would seem).

Narrated Anas:

Prophet Muhammad said, "When a human being is laid in his grave and his companions return and he even hears their footsteps, two angels come to him and make him sit and ask him: 'What did you use to say about this man, Muhammad?' He will say: 'I testify that he is Allah's slave and His Apostle.' Then it will be said to him, 'Look at your place in the Hell-Fire. Allah has given you a place in Paradise instead of it.'"

Prophet Muhammad added, "The dead person will see both his places. But a non-believer or a hypocrite will say to the angels, 'I do not know, but I used to say what the people used to say!' It will be said to him, 'Neither did you know nor did you take the guidance (by reciting the Quran).' Then he will be hit with an iron hammer between his two ears, and he will cry and that cry will be heard by whatever approaches him except human beings and jinns."

Bukhari 23.422

The interrogation over, the occupant of the grave will continue to get twice daily visits, until Judgement Day, from another angel. He has not come to chat, but to open those curtains with that pleasing or horrifying view.

Narrated 'Abdullah bin 'Umar:

Allah's Apostle said, "When anyone of you dies, he is shown his place both in the morning and in the evening. If he is one of the people of Paradise; he is shown his place in it, and if he is from the people of the Hell-Fire; he is shown his place there-in. Then it is said to him, 'This is your place till Allah resurrect you on the Day of Resurrection.'"

Bukhari 23.461

Life in the grave for unbelievers and other sinners will be uncomfortable in the extreme. God's Messenger said that "we would faint in terror if we could hear the screams of those being tormented" in their graves. Even a minor sin, or a sin that is only in the mind of the observer such as an involuntary discharge of urine, can lead to an agonizing life in the grave?

Narrated Ibn 'Abbas:

Allah's Apostle passed by two graves and said, "Both of them (persons in the grave) are being tortured, and they are not being tortured for a major sin. This one used not to save himself from being soiled with his urine, and the other used to go about with calumnies (among the people to rouse hostilities, e.g., one goes to a person and tells him that so-and-so says about him such-and-such evil things)."

The Prophet then asked for a green leaf of a date-palm tree, split it into two pieces and planted one on each grave and said, "It is hoped that their punishment may be abated till those two pieces of the leaf get dried."

Bukhari 73.78

Why dogs sometimes howl for no apparent reason and, is it possible that it was two little old Jewish ladies who first put the idea in the Prophet's head about the undead. It was after "the Jewish ladies" told the story to Aisha and she, in turn, repeated it to her husband thinking it was a lie (he obviously had never mentioned it before), that God's Messenger began to seek refuge from life as an undead in his prayers.

Narrated 'Aisha:

Two old ladies from among the Jewish ladies entered upon me and said, "The dead are punished in their graves," but I thought they were telling a lie and did not believe them in the beginning. When they went away and the Prophet entered upon me, I said, "O Allah's Apostle! Two old ladies" and told him the whole story.

He said, "They told the truth; the dead are really punished, to the extent that all the animals hear (the sound resulting from) their punishment."

Since then I always saw him seeking refuge with Allah from the punishment of the grave in his prayers.

Bukhari 75.377

As to the trial i.e. interrogation conducted by Munkar and Nakir, this too seems to have come from Jewish folklore. Initially, the Prophet believed that only Jews would be put on trial in their graves. Later, Allah set him straight.

'A'isha reported:

The Holy Prophet (may peace be upon him) entered my house when a jewess was with me and she was saying: Do you know that you would be put to trial in the grave?

The Messenger of Allah (may peace be upon him) trembled (on hearing this) and said: It is the Jews only who would-be put to trial.

'A'isha said: We passed some nights and then the Messenger of Allah (may peace be upon him) said: Do you know that it has been revealed to me:" You would be put to trial in the grave"?

'A'isha said: 1 heard the Messenger of Allah (may peace be upon him) seeking refuge from the torment of the grave after this.

Sahih Muslim 4.1212

Medicine

The hadiths, along with the Koran make up the immutable laws of Islam, if not the universe. When it comes to treating what ails you, it is a law that is often broken with impunity. The reason that Saudi Arabia is ruled by a gerontology is more a result of modern medicine, especially advances and innovations in the treatment of coronary and heart disease, than whatever God's Messenger prescribed.

A concerted effort was made, after the ban on innovation, to set up a school of "Prophetic Medicine" based on the sayings and example of the Prophet and His Companions.

> ... an attempt was made to create an alternative system of medical science, 'prophetic medicine' (tibb mabawi). This represented a reaction against the tradition which came from Galen. Its system was built upon what the Hadith recorded of the practices of the Prophet and his companions in regards to health and sickness. It was not created by medical men, however, but by lawyers and traditionalists who held the strict view that the Qur'an and Hadith contained all that was necessary for the conduct of human life. It was the view of a minority, even among religious scholars, and a critical opinion was expressed, with his robust good sense, by Ibn Khaldun. This kind of medicine, he asserted, could occasionally and accidently be correct, but it was based on no rational principle.
>
> *A History of the Arab People*, Albert Hourani, Harvard University Press 1991, p. 203

It did not meet with the expected success, and the laws governing Prophetic Medicine remain the most flouted of Islamic laws; and for good reason.

Cupping was a favourite therapy of God's Messenger for whatever ailed him, and it's a therapy that comes highly recommended in the hadiths.

Narrated Jabir bin 'Abdullah:

That he paid Al-Muqanna a visit during his illness and said, "I will not leave till he gets cupped, for I heard Allah's Apostle saying, 'There is healing in cupping.'"

Bukhari 71.600

Cupping therapy is an ancient Chinese form of alternative medicine in which a local suction is created on the skin, The Prophet's cupping treatment would likely have involved heating the cup and/or the air inside it, then quickly placing the cup on the skin. As the air inside the cup cooled it would have created a small vacuum which would have exerted a small tug on the skin. Conventional medicine has not found cupping to be effective in the treatment of any disease

In a Abu Dawood hadith the Prophet recommended cupping for a headache and dying your legs with henna to relieve the pain.

Narrated Salmah:

The maid-servant of the Apostle of Allah (peace be upon him), said: No one complained to the Apostle of Allah (peace be upon him) of a headache but he told him to get himself cupped, or of a pain in his legs but he told him to dye them with henna.

Abu Dawood 28.3849

The Prophet would even recommend cupping for a headache, when even achieving a sacred state did not relieve that persistent migraine.

Narrated Ibn 'Abbas:

The Prophet was cupped on his head for an ailment he was suffering from while he was in a state of Ihram ("*a sacred state which a Muslim must enter in order to perform the major pilgrimage (Hajj) or the minor pilgrimage (Umrah)*Wiki) at a water place called Lahl Jamal.

Ibn 'Abbas further said: Allah's Apostle was cupped on his head for unilateral headache while he was in a state of Ihram.

Bukhari 71.602

Fasting was not an impediment to cupping:

Narrated Ibn Abbas:

The Prophet was cupped while he was in the state of Ihram, and also while he was observing a fast.

Bukhari 31.159

Of course, cupping was what you paid medical professional to have done to you. For the squeamish, or those who could not afford it, there was always sea incense.

Narrated Anas:

That he was asked about the wages of the one who cups others. He said, "Allah's Apostle was cupped by Abd Taiba, to whom he gave two Sa of food and interceded for him with his masters who consequently reduced what they used to charge him daily. Then the Prophet said, 'The best medicines you may treat yourselves with are cupping and sea incense.'"

He added, "You should not torture your children by treating tonsillitis by pressing the tonsils or the palate with the finger, but use incense."

Bukhari 71.599

Incense is not mentioned in the following saying of the Prophet as one of the three things with the best healing properties, but I am sure it is an oversight.

Narrated Ibn 'Abbas:

(The Prophet said), "Healing is in three things: A gulp of honey, cupping, and branding with fire (cauterizing). But I forbid my followers to use (cauterization) branding with fire."

Bukhari 71.584

A substitute for cauterization with a hot poker:

Narrated Sahl bin Saud As-Sa'idi:

When the helmet broke on the head of the Prophet and his face became covered with blood and his incisor tooth broke (i.e. during the battle of Uhud), 'Ali used to bring water in his shield while Fatima was washing the blood off his face. When Fatima saw that the bleeding increased because of the water, she took a mat (of palm leaves), burnt it, and stuck it (the burnt ashes) on the wound of Allah's Apostle, whereupon the bleeding stopped.

Bukhari 71.618

What is this about black cumin being a cure for every disease except death?

Narrated Khalid bin Sad:

We went out and Ghalib bin Abjar was accompanying us. He fell ill on the way and when we arrived at Medina he was still sick. Ibn Abi 'Atiq came to visit him and said to us, "Treat him with black cumin. Take five or seven seeds and crush them (mix the powder with oil) and drop the resulting mixture into both nostrils, for 'Aisha has narrated to me that she heard the Prophet saying, 'This black cumin is healing for all diseases except As-Sam.' Aisha said, 'What is As-Sam?' He said, 'Death.'"

Bukhari 71.591

When your stomach lies, the answer is honey.

Narrated Abu Said Al-Khudri:

A man came to the Prophet and said, "My brother has some abdominal trouble."

The Prophet said to him "Let him drink honey."

The man came for the second time and the Prophet said to him, "Let him drink honey."

He came for the third time and the Prophet said, "Let him drink honey."

He returned again and said, "I have done that."'

The Prophet then said, "Allah has said the truth, but your brother's abdomen has told a lie. Let him drink honey."

So he made him drink honey and he was cured.

Bukhari 71.588

Milk I can understand, but camel piss?

Narrated Anas:

The climate of Medina did not suit some people, so the Prophet ordered them to follow his shepherd, i.e. his camels, and drink their milk and urine (as a medicine).

So they followed the shepherd that is the camels and drank their milk and urine till their bodies became healthy. Then they killed the shepherd and drove away the camels.

When the news reached the Prophet he sent some people in their pursuit. When they were brought, he cut their hands and feet and their eyes were branded with heated pieces of iron.

Bukhari 71.590

Sweets will cause a release of feel-good endorphins, therefore the following recipe may have some merit in curing depression.

Narrated 'Ursa:

Aisha used to recommend At-Talbina (a meal made from barley flour, formed by adding milk and honey to the dried barley powder) for the sick and for such a person as grieved over a dead person.

She used to say, "I heard Allah's Apostle saying, 'At-Talbina gives rest to the heart of the patient and makes it active and relieves some of his sorrow and grief.'"

Bukhari 71.593

If black cumin is not the answer, then it's back to incense.

Narrated Um Qais bint Mihsan:

I heard the Prophet saying, "Treat with the Indian incense, for it has healing for seven diseases; it is to be sniffed by one having throat trouble, and to be put into one side of the mouth of one suffering from pleurisy."

Bukhari 71.596

An unusual cure for lice:

Narrated Ka'b bin Ujrah:

The Prophet came to me during the period of Al-Hudaibiya, while I was lighting fire underneath a cooking pot and lice were falling down my head. He said, "Do your lice hurt you?"

I said, "Yes."

He said, "Shave your head and fast for three days or feed six poor persons or slaughter a sheep as a sacrifice."

Bukhari 71.604

Kohl is an ancient eye cosmetic which was thought to have medicinal properties. In Islam, only men can use cosmetics in public therefore the Prophet, who was a user of khol, was correct, if somewhat insensitive to the woman's discomfort, in ignoring her request to use the eyeliner.

Narrated Um Salama:

The husband of a lady died and her eyes became sore and the people mentioned her story to the Prophet. They asked him whether it was permissible for her to use kohl as her eyes were exposed to danger.

He said, "Previously, when one of you was bereaved by a husband she would stay in her dirty clothes in a bad unhealthy house (for one year), and when a dog passed by, she would throw a globe of dung. No, (she should observe the prescribed period Idda i.e. waiting period) for four months and ten days."

Bukhari 71.607

Collyrium is an eye cleanser which God's Messenger also denied a grieving widow.

Narrated Umm Salamah, Ummul Mu'minin:

The Prophet (peace be upon him) said: A woman whose husband has died must not wear clothes dyed with safflower (usfur) or with red ochre (mishq) and ornaments. She must not apply henna and collyrium.

Abu Dawud 12.2297

Something else for the eyes, mushroom secretions:

Narrated Said bin Zaid:

I heard the Prophet saying, "Truffles are like Manna (i.e. they grow naturally without man's care) and their water heals eye diseases."

Bukhari 71.609

Allah is responsible for spreading contagious disease, but that does not mean you should not try to avoid what He may be attempting to infect you with.

Narrated Abu Huraira:

Allah's Apostle said, '(There is) no 'Adwa (no contagious disease is conveyed without Allah's permission) nor is there any bad omen (from birds), nor is there any Hamah, nor is there any bad omen in the month of Safar, and one should run away from the leper as one runs away from a lion'

Bukhari 71.608

Then again, during a plague, God's Messenger recommends you stay put.

Narrated 'Aisha:

I asked Allah's Apostle about the plague. He said, "That was a means of torture which Allah used to send upon whom-so-ever He wished, but He made it a source of mercy for the believers, for anyone who is residing in a town in which this disease is present, and remains there and does not leave that town, but has patience and hopes for Allah's reward, and knows that nothing will befall him except what Allah has written for him, then he will get such reward as that of a martyr."

Bukhari 77.616

Only a death cult would consider a plague a good thing!

Narrated 'Aisha:

That she asked Allah's Apostle about plague, and Allah's Apostle informed her saying, "Plague was a punishment which Allah used to send on whom He wished, but Allah made it a blessing for the believers. None (among the believers) remains patient in a land in which plague has broken out and considers that nothing will befall him except what Allah has ordained for him, but that Allah will grant him a reward similar to that of a martyr."

Bukhari 71.630

That fever you are experiencing ...

Narrated Nazi':

Abdullah bin 'Umar said, "The Prophet said, 'Fever is from the heat of Hell, so put it out (cool it) with water.'"

Nafi' added: 'Abdullah used to say, "O Allah! Relieve us from the punishment," (when he suffered from fever).

Bukhari 71.619

Debilitating fevers like those associated with cholera epidemics became a common occurrence after the Prophet and his followers made Medina their home, and Hell may have had nothing to do with it.

Narrated AbuSa'id al-Khudri:

I heard that the people asked the Prophet of Allah (peace be upon him): Water is brought for you from the well of Buda'ah. It is a well in which dead dogs, menstrual clothes and excrement of people are thrown.

The Messenger of Allah (peace be upon him) replied: Verily water is pure and is not defiled by anything.

Abu Dawud 1.0067

Narrated Abu Sa'id al-Khudri:

The people asked the Messenger of Allah (peace be upon him): Can we perform ablution out of the well of Buda'ah, which is a well into which menstrual clothes, dead dogs and stinking things were thrown?

He replied: Water is pure and is not defiled by anything.

Sahih Muslim 1.0066

The fly carries both the disease and its cure if handled properly.

Narrated Abu Huraira:

Allah's Apostle said, "If a fly falls in the vessel of any of you, let him dip all of it (into the vessel) and then throw it away, for in one of its wings there is a disease and in the other there is healing (antidote for it) i e. the treatment for that disease."

Bukhari 71.673

What about a mouse?

Narrated Maimuna:

Allah's Apostle was asked regarding ghee (cooking butter) in which a mouse had fallen. He said, "Take out the mouse and throw away the ghee around it and use the rest."

Bukhari 4.236

Some dates eaten as part of a balanced breakfast will make you immune to poison and spells.

Narrated Saud:

The Prophet said, "If somebody takes some 'Ajwa dates every morning, he will not be effected by poison or magic on that day till night." (Another narrator said seven dates).

Bukhari 71.663

Prayer, but not just any prayer, is the cure for snake bites and a scorpion's sting.

Narrated Abu Said:

Some of the companions of the Prophet went on a journey till they reached some of the 'Arab tribes (at night). They asked the latter to treat them as their guests but they refused. The chief of that tribe was then bitten by a snake (or stung by a scorpion) and they tried their best to cure him but in vain.

Some of them said (to the others), "Nothing has benefited him, will you go to the people who resided here at night, it may be that some of them might possess something (as treatment)."

They went to the group of the companions (of the Prophet) and said, "Our chief has been bitten by a snake (or stung by a scorpion) and we have tried everything but he has not benefitted. Have you got anything (useful)?"

One of them replied, "Yes, by Allah! I can recite a Ruqya (*not unlike an exorcism where repeating over and over specific verses from the Koran figure prominently*), but as you have refused to accept us as your guests, I will not recite the Ruqya for you unless you fix for us some wages for it."

They agreed to pay them a flock of sheep. One of them then went and recited (Suratul-Fatiha): "All the praises are for the Lord of the Worlds" and puffed over the chief who became all right as if he was released from a chain, and got up and started walking, showing no signs of sickness.

They paid them what they agreed to pay. Some of them (i.e. the companions) then suggested to divide their earnings among themselves, but the one who performed the recitation said, "Do not divide them till we go to the Prophet and narrate the whole story to him, and wait for his order."

So, they went to Allah's Apostle and narrated the story. Allah's Apostle asked, "How did you come to know that Surat-ul-Fatiha was recited as Ruqya?"

Then he added, "You have done the right thing. Divide (what you have earned) and assign a share for me as well."

The Prophet smiled thereupon.

Bukhari 36.476

Narrated Al-Aswad:

I asked 'Aisha about treating poisonous stings (a snake-bite or a scorpion sting) with a Ruqya. She said, "The Prophet allowed the treatment of poisonous sting with Ruqya."

Bukhari 71.637

Ruqya could also cure diseases whose provenance was unknown.

Narrated 'Abdul 'Aziz:

Thabit and I went to Anas bin Malik. Thabit said, "O Abu Hamza! I am sick."

On that Anas said, "Shall I treat you with the Ruqya of Allah's Apostle?"

Thabit said, "Yes."

Anas recited, "O Allah! The Lord of the people, the Remover of trouble! (Please) cure (Heal) (this patient), for You are the Healer. None brings about healing but You; a healing that will leave behind no ailment."

Bukhari 71.638

Ruqya, in combination with the spit of certain people, was the best.

Narrated 'Aisha:

Allah's Apostle used to read in his Ruqya, "In the Name of Allah, the earth of our land and the saliva of some of us cure our patient with the permission of our Lord" (with a slight shower of saliva) while treating with a Ruqya.

Bukhari 71.642

Islam is a product of the Dark Ages. This is the period in our history generally accepted to be between 400 and 1000 CE when irrational beliefs and fears overwhelmed common sense and reason. The Prophet, if not typical of his generation, was a product of his time, as his belief in an evil eye will attest.

Narrated Um Salama:

That the Prophet saw in her house a girl whose face had a black spot. He said. "She is under the effect of an evil eye; so treat her with a Ruqya."

Bukhari 71.635

Ablutions are always good for whatever ails you, just be careful where you get your water.

Narrated 'Ali:

I used to get the emotional urethral discharge frequently so I requested Al-Miqdad to ask the Prophet about it. Al-Miqdad asked him and he replied, "One has to perform ablution (after it)."

Bukhari 3.134

Musk

No smell in the hadiths gets more mention than the scent of musk. It is everywhere, it will even be the smell of Paradise. It is obvious that the powerful aromatic substance extracted since ancient times from the gland of the male musk deer was a favourite fragrance of the Prophet. A good pious person smells of musk, and if he has any to share, he will give you some free of charge or you will be willing to pay him for it.

Narrated Abu Musa:

The Prophet said, "The example of a good pious companion and an evil one is that of a person carrying musk and another blowing a pair of bellows. The one who is carrying musk will either give you some perfume as a present, or you will buy some from him, or you will get a good smell from him, but the one who is blowing a pair of bellows will either burn your clothes or you will get a bad smell from him."

Bukhari 67.442

It may still hurt, but it will smell nice, the blood of a martyr that is on Judgement Day.

Narrated Abu Huraira:

The Prophet said, "A wound which a Muslim receives in Allah's cause will appear on the Day of Resurrection as it was at the time of infliction; blood will be flowing from the wound and its color will be that of the blood but will smell like musk."

Bukhari 4.238

Rubbing the "the place soiled with blood" with a cloth scented with musk three times was part of God's Messenger's prescribed purification ritual after the end of "menses".

Narrated 'Aisha:

A woman asked the Prophet about the bath which is take[n] after finishing from the menses. The Prophet told her what to do and said, "Purify yourself with a piece of cloth scented with musk."

The woman asked, "How shall I purify myself with it?"

He said, "Subhan Allah (*Glorious is God*)! Purify yourself (with it)."

I pulled her to myself and said, "Rub the place soiled with blood with it."

Bukhari 6.311

Narrated 'Aisha:

An Ansari woman asked the Prophet how to take a bath after finishing from the menses. He replied, "Take a piece a cloth perfumed with musk and clean the private parts with it thrice."

The Prophet felt shy and turned his face. So I pulled her to me and told her what the Prophet meant.

Bukhari 6.312

A fasting person's breath is one of the few odours mentioned in the hadiths that is better than the smell of musk.

Narrated Abu Huraira:

Allah's Apostle said, "Allah said, 'All the deeds of Adam's sons (people) are for them, except fasting which is for Me, and I will give the reward for it.' Fasting is a shield or protection from the fire and from committing sins. If one of you is fasting, he should avoid sexual relation with his wife and quarreling, and if somebody should fight or quarrel with him, he should say, 'I am fasting.' By Him in Whose Hands my soul is, the unpleasant smell coming out from the mouth of a fasting person is better in the sight of Allah than the smell of musk. There are two pleasures for the fasting person, one at the time of breaking his fast, and the other at the time when he will meet his Lord; then he will be pleased because of his fasting."

Bukhari 31.128

Near the Prophet's palace in the sky there is a river whose smell is nicer than musk and whose banks and/or river bed smells like musk.

Narrated 'Abdullah bin 'Amr:

The Prophet said, "My Lake-Fount is (so large that it takes) a month's journey to cross it. Its water is whiter than milk, and its smell is nicer than musk (a kind of Perfume), and its drinking cups are (as numerous) as the (number of) stars of the sky; and whoever drinks from it, will never be thirsty."

Bukhari 76.581

The Prophet's cold hands, it was said, smelled nicer than musk.

Narrated Abu Juhaifa:

Once Allah's Apostle went to Al-Batha at noon, performed the ablution and offered' a two Rakat Zuhr prayer and a two-Rak'at 'Asr prayer while a spearheaded stick was planted before him and the passersby were passing in front of it. (After the prayer), the people got up and held the hands of the Prophet and passed them on their faces. I also took his hand and kept it on my face and noticed that it was colder than ice, and its smell was nicer than musk.

Bukhari 56.753

The sweat from eating spicy food of those lucky enough to make it into Paradise will smell like musk.

Jabir reported:

I heard Allah's Apostle (may peace be upon him) as saying that the inmates of Paradise would eat and drink but would neither spit, nor pass water, nor void excrement, nor suffer catarrah. It was said: Then, what would happen with food? Thereupon he said: They would belch and sweat (and it would be over with their food), and their sweat would be that of musk and they would glorify and praise Allah as easily as you breathe.

Sahih Muslim 40.6798

Paradise

The following should be read in conjunction with *The Islamic Hereafter - Paradise, Boreal Books (2012)* or *Pain, Pleasure and Prejudice - Heaven, Boreal Books (2012)*.

One quarter to a one third of the Koran is about Paradise and Hell. With so many verses about Allah's out-of-this world carrot and stick, hadiths about Paradise, and how you might get there may be superfluous. Nonetheless, following are a few which may hold some interest.

Paradise, only Muslims allowed!

Narrated 'Abdullah:

While we were in the company of the Prophet in a tent he said, "Would it please you to be one fourth of the people of Paradise?"

We said, "Yes."

He said, "Would It please you to be one-third of the people of Paradise?"

We said, "Yes."

He said, "Would it please you to be half of the people of Paradise?"

We said, "Yes."

Thereupon he said, "I hope that you will be one half of the people of Paradise, for none will enter Paradise but a Muslim soul, and you people, in comparison to the people who associate others in worship with Allah, are like a white hair on the skin of a black ox, or a black hair on the skin of a red ox."

Bukhari 76.535

The privileged seventy thousand!

Narrated Ibn 'Abbas:

Allah's Apostle said, "Nations were displayed before me; one or two prophets would pass by along with a few followers. A prophet would pass by accompanied by nobody. Then a big crowd of people passed in front of me and I asked, "Who are they, are they my followers?' It was said, 'No. It is Moses and his followers.' It was said to me, 'Look at the horizon.' Behold! There was a multitude of people filling the horizon. Then it was said to me, 'Look there and there about the stretching sky!' Behold! There was a multitude filling the horizon,' It was said to me, 'This is your nation out of whom seventy thousand shall enter Paradise without reckoning.'"

Then the Prophet entered his house without telling his companions who they (the 70,000) were. So the people started talking about the issue and said, "It is we who have believed in Allah and followed His Apostle; therefore those people are either ourselves or our children who are born m the Islamic era, for we were born in the pre-Islamic Period of Ignorance."

When the Prophet heard of that, he came out and said. "Those people are those who do not treat themselves with Ruqya, nor do they believe in bad or good omen (from birds etc.) nor do they get themselves branded (cauterized) but they put their trust (only) in their Lord "

On that 'Ukasha bin Muhsin said. "Am I one of them, O Allah's Apostle?"

The Prophet said, "Yes."

Then another person got up and said, "Am I one of them?"

The Prophet said, "'Ukasha has anticipated you."

Bukhari 71.606

During his one night visit to Paradise to discuss with Allah important aspects of his religion, such as the number of prayers, the Prophet describes what Moses, Jesus and Abraham looked like, but not Allah. The following hadith about Allah being veiled may explain why:

Narrated Abdullah bin Qais:

Allah's Apostle said, "Two gardens, the utensils and the contents of which are of silver, and two other gardens, the utensils and contents of which are of gold. And nothing will prevent the people who will be in the Garden of Eden from seeing their Lord except the curtain of Majesty over His Face."

Bukhari 60.401

The Prophet mentions two Paradises of silver and two of gold? I wonder if he cleared that one with Allah?

Narrated 'Abdullah bin Qais:

The Prophet said, "(There will be) two Paradises of silver and all the utensils and whatever is therein (will be of silver);

and two Paradises of gold, and its utensils and whatever therein (will be of gold), and there will be nothing to prevent the people from seeing their Lord except the Cover of Majesty over His Face in the Paradise of Eden (eternal bliss)."

Bukhari 93.536

The tents of Paradise:

Narrated 'Abdullah bin Qais Al-Ashari:

The Prophet said, "A tent (in Paradise) is like a hollow pearl which is thirty miles in height and on every corner of the tent the believer will have a family that cannot be seen by the others."

Bukhari 54.466

The biggest pearl you will ever see:

Narrated Abdullah bin Qais:

Allah's Apostle said, "In Paradise there is a pavilion made of a single hollow pearl sixty miles wide, in each corner of which there are wives who will not see those in the other corners; and the believers will visit and enjoy them. And there are two gardens, the utensils and contents of which are made of silver; and two other gardens, the utensils and contents of which are made of so-and-so (i.e. gold) and nothing will prevent the people staying in the Garden of Eden from seeing their Lord except the curtain of Majesty over His Face."

Bukhari 60.402

There is a tree in Paradise that is even bigger than the biggest tent.

Narrated Anas bin Malik:

The Prophet said: "There is a tree in Paradise (which is so big and huge that) if a rider travels in its shade for one hundred years, he would not be able to cross it."

Bukhari 54:474

The first meal of the people of Paradise will be a slice of fish liver.

Narrated Anas:

When 'Abdullah bin Salam heard the arrival of the Prophet at Medina, he came to him and said, "I am going to ask you about three things which nobody knows except a prophet: What is the first portent of the Hour? What will be the first meal taken by the people of Paradise? Why does a child resemble its father, and why does it resemble its maternal uncle?"

Allah's Apostle said, "Gabriel has just now told me of their answers."

'Abdullah said, "He (i.e. Gabriel), from amongst all the angels, is the enemy of the Jews."

Allah's Apostle said, "The first portent of the Hour will be a fire that will bring together the people from the east to the west; the first meal of the people of Paradise will be Extra-lobe (caudate lobe) of fish-liver ..."

Bukhari 55.546

What about alcoholic drinks?

Narrated Ibn 'Umar:

Allah's Apostle said, "Whoever drinks alcoholic drinks in the world and does not repent (before dying), will be deprived of it in the Hereafter."

Bukhari 69.481

In the Hereafter you will get all the sex you can handle, if you abstain from sex in the here-and-now, and that includes oral sex.

Narrated Sahl bin Sa'd:

Allah's Apostle said, "Whoever can guarantee (the chastity of) what is between his two jaw-bones and what is between his two legs (i.e. his tongue and his private parts), I guarantee Paradise for him."

Bukhari 76.481

The pettiness of One who would deny Paradise for the paltriest of imagined crimes never fails to amaze.

Narrated Sa'd:

I heard the Prophet saying, "Whoever claims to be the son of a person other than his father, and he knows that person is not his father, then Paradise will be forbidden for him."

I mentioned that to Abu Bakra, and he said, "My ears heard that and my heart memorized it from Allah's Apostle."

Bukhari 80.758

All that glitters!

Narrated Abu Huraira:

Allah's Apostle said, "The first group of people who will enter

Paradise, will be glittering like the full moon and those who will follow them, will glitter like the most brilliant star in the sky. They will not urinate, relieve nature, spit, or have any nasal secretions. Their combs will be of gold, and their sweat will smell like musk. The aloe wood will be used in their centers. Their wives will be houris. All of them will look alike and will resemble their father Adam (in stature), sixty cubits tall."

Bukhari 55.544

The Prophet's visions of the Hereafter included visions into the future and visions of women's leg bones through their flesh, which would indicate that women will be naked in Paradise.

Narrated Abu Huraira:

Allah's Apostle said, "The first group (of people) who will enter Paradise will be [glittering] like the moon when it is full. They will not spit or blow their noses or relieve nature. Their utensils will be of gold and their combs of gold and silver; in their centers the aloe wood will be used, and their sweat will smell like musk. Every one of them will have two wives; the marrow of the bones of the wives' legs will be seen through the flesh out of excessive beauty. They (i.e. the people of Paradise) will neither have differences nor hatred amongst themselves; their hearts will be as if one heart and they will be glorifying Allah in the morning and in the evening."

Bukhari 54:468

Specials abodes in Paradise are called Ghuraf.

Narrated Sahl:

The Prophet said, "The people of Paradise will see the Ghuraf (special abodes) in Paradise as you see a star in the sky."

Bukhari 76.561

You can smell Paradise from quite a distance in time.

Narrated 'Abdullah bin 'Amr:

The Prophet said, "Whoever killed a person having a treaty with the Muslims, shall not smell the smell of Paradise though its smell is perceived from a distance of forty years."

Bukhari 53.391

From a distance Paradise may look like Hell and vice versa

Narrated Abu Huraira:

Allah's Apostle said, "The (Hell) Fire is surrounded by all kinds of desires and passions, while Paradise is surrounded by all kinds of disliked undesirable things."

Bukhari 76.494

So near, and yet so far.

Narrated 'Abdullah:

The Prophet said, "Paradise is nearer to any of you than the Shirak (leather strap) of his shoe, and so is the (Hell) Fire.

Bukhari 76.495

The Prophet, in his description of Paradise would remind his listeners that there are ways to ensure your admittance no questions asked.

Narrated Abu Huraira:

The Prophet said: "The person who participates in (Holy battles) in Allah's cause and nothing compels him to do so except belief in Allah and His Apostles, will be recompensed by Allah either with a reward, or booty (if he survives) or will be admitted to Paradise (if he is killed in the battle as a martyr)...'"

Bukhari 2:35

Narrated Al-Mughira:

Our Prophet has informed us our Lord's Message that whoever of us is martyred, will go to Paradise.

Bukhari 93.621

A less drastic and more civilized way then martyrdom and killing unbelievers to obtain a ticket to Paradise was learning the 99 names of Allah.

Narrated Abu Huraira:

Allah's Apostle said: "Allah has ninety-nine names, i.e. one-hundred minus one, and whoever knows them will go to Paradise."

Bukhari 50:894

Goat herders probably have the easiest less demanding method of being assured of Paradise.

Narrated 'Abdullah bin 'Amr:

That Allah's Apostle said, "There are forty virtuous deeds and the best of them is the Maniha of a she-goat (*"a gift in the form of a she-camel or a sheep which is given temporarily so that its milk may be used and then it is returned to the owner*"), and anyone who does one of these virtuous deeds hoping for Allah's reward with firm confidence that he will get it, then Allah will make him enter Paradise ...

Hassan (a sub-narrator) said, "We tried to count those good deeds below the Maniha; we mentioned replying to the sneezer, removing harmful things from the road, etc., but we failed to count even fifteen."

Bukhari 47.800

The easiest way to get into Paradise, if you want to risk it, is saying the following before you die:

Narrated 'Abdullah:

The Prophet said one statement and I said another. The Prophet said "Whoever dies while still invoking anything other than Allah as a rival to Allah, will enter Hell (Fire)."

And I said, "Whoever dies without invoking anything as a rival to Allah, will enter Paradise."

Bukhari 60.24

Build a mosque in the here-and-now, and Allah will build you a mosque in the Hereafter. Is it any wonder minarets have become a ubiquitous feature of the urban landscape.

Narrated 'Ubdaidullah Al-Khaulani:

I heard 'Uthman bin 'Affan saying, when people argued too much about his intention to reconstruct the mosque of Allah's Apostle, "You have talked too much. I heard the Prophet saying, 'Whoever built a mosque ... Allah would build for him a similar place in Paradise.'"

Bukhari 8.441

If you can't afford to build a mosque ...

Narrated Abu Huraira:

The Prophet said, "Allah will prepare for him who goes to the mosque (every) morning and in the afternoon (for the congregational prayer) an honorable place in Paradise with good hospitality for (what he has done) every morning and afternoon goings."

Bukhari 11.631

The injured in Allah's Cause will not be granted Paradise if they choose to end their lives rather than keep on fighting.

Narrated Jundub:

Allah's Apostle said, "Amongst the nations before you there was a man who got a wound and growing impatient (with its pain), he took a knife and cut his hand with it and the blood did not stop till he died. Allah said, 'My Slave hurried to bring death upon himself so I have forbidden him (to enter) Paradise.'"

Bukhari 56.669

The value of a sliver of Paradise and an afternoon's journey in Allah's Cause:

Narrated Sahl:

I heard the Prophet saying, "A (small) place equal to an area occupied by a whip in Paradise is better than the (whole) world and whatever is in it; and an undertaking (journey) in the forenoon or in the afternoon for Allah's Cause, is better than the whole world and whatever is in it."

Bukhari 76.424

A Jew in Paradise:

Narrated Sad bin Abi Waqqas:

I have never heard the Prophet saying about anybody walking on the earth that he is from the people of Paradise except 'Abdullah bin Salam. The following Verse was revealed concerning him: "And a witness from the children of Israel testifies that this Qur'an is true" (46:10)

Bukhari 58.157

A palace in Paradise for the deserving first wife of Allah's Messenger:

Narrated 'Aisha:

I did not feel jealous of any of the wives of the Prophet as much as I did of Khadija (although) she died before he married me, for I often heard him mentioning her, and Allah had told him to give her the good tidings that she would have a palace of Qasab (i.e. pipes of precious stones and pearls in Paradise), and whenever he slaughtered a sheep, he would send her women-friends a good share of it.

Bukhari 58.164

Nursing infants who need one, will be provided with a wet nurse.

Narrated Al-Bara:

When Ibrahim (the son of the Prophet) died, Allah's Apostle said, "There is a wet nurse for him in Paradise."

Bukhari 73.215

Upon entering Heaven's gates, remember to ask for the Firdaus, if you have been an exemplary believer.

Narrated Abu Huraira:

The Prophet said, "Whoever believes in Allah and His Apostle offers prayers perfectly and fasts (the month of) Ramadan then it is incumbent upon Allah to admit him into Paradise, whether he emigrates for Allah's cause or stays in the land where he was born."

They (the companions of the Prophet) said, "O Allah's Apostle! Should we not inform the people of that?"

He said, "There are one-hundred degrees in Paradise which Allah has prepared for those who carry on Jihad in His Cause. The distance between every two degrees is like the distance between the sky and the Earth, so if you ask Allah for anything, ask Him for the Firdaus, for it is the last part of Paradise and the highest part of Paradise, and at its top there is the Throne of Beneficent, and from it gush forth the rivers of Paradise."

Bukhari 93.519

No, we have not lost our senses!

Narrated Anas:

Haritha was martyred on the day (of the battle) of Badr, and he was a young boy then. His mother came to the Prophet and said, "O Allah's Apostle! You know how dear Haritha is to me. If he is in Paradise, I shall remain patient, and hope for reward from Allah, but if it is not so, then you shall see what I do?"

He said, "May Allah be merciful to you! Have you lost your senses? Do you think there is only one Paradise? There are many Paradises and your son is in the (most superior) Paradise of Al-Firdaus."

Bukhari 59.318

Prayers

45:20 This (Qur'an) is an illumination for mankind, a guidance and mercy unto a people who believe with certainty.

In Allah's Universe, you may not even speculate about what He tells you is the absolute truth, no matter the incongruity. The disincentive that is Allah's blanket embargo against seeking knowledge that might contradict what He has revealed in His Koran may be partly responsible for the Muslims world, which constitutes 21 percent of the world's population (2011), having produced only 10 Nobel Prize laureates, with only two in the physical sciences (1979 physics, 1999 chemistry).

Not to be overlooked is the requirements of an Islamic education where priority is given to learning Arabic and attempting to memorize the Koran in its entirety; the negative impact on critical thinking just as damaging, if not more, than the time not available to non-religious subjects which Islamists consider very much a pre-occupation of the ignorant as is the time not spent at prayer and glorifying Allah. If excessive worship is the answer, than the world may eventually owe Islam an enormous debt.

There are a lot of hadiths about what prayer the Prophet said at a specific time of the day and on special occasions e.g. the Hajj; and perhaps, more important, how he did them e.g. how many rakats did he perform (one rakat = one complete set of prayers including prostrations).

The five daily compulsory prayer and their approximate start times:

Fajr - dawn prayer.

Zuhr - not before noon (sun must have reached or passed its zenith).

Asr - late afternoon when the "shadow of a vertical stick equals its length".

Maghrib - sunset prayer.

'Isha - night prayer, the sun must have completely set, often offered at midnight.

Other terms related to prayer:

Adhan - call to prayer.

Al-Fatiha – the first chapter of the Koran, its seven revelations i.e. verses must be repeated at the beginning of each prayer unit of the compulsory prayers.

Fard – compulsory prayers.

Iqama - the second and last call to prayer.

rak'a = one cycle of prostrations, also spelled rakat.

Taslim - the conclusion of worship, where one recites 'Assalaamu 'alaykum wa rahmatu-Allah (Peace and blessings of God be unto you).

Witr - odd number prayer.

Negotiating the Obligatory Prayers

The third holiest site in Islam is a rock underneath the Dome of the Rock, which is part of the Al-Aqsa Mosque complex on Temple Mount in Jerusalem. Muslims believe that this is the rock from which the Prophet ascended to heaven on a magical night in 621 on the back of a winged-horse named Al-Buraq (also spelled al-Burak) to meet with the Boss. It was during this meeting with God that the number of prayers a believer must perform every day was established.

Following are three lengthy hadiths about this seminal event in the history of both Islam and Paradise. In the first hadith there is no mention of a stopover in Jerusalem. In the second: no al-Buraq and no Jerusalem. The third hadith, probably the most significant, contains both a reference to the winged Pegasus-like horse and Jerusalem.

Narrated Abbas bin Malik:

Malik bin Sasaa said that Allah's Apostle described to them his Night Journey saying, "While I was lying in Al-Hatim or Al-Hijr, suddenly someone came to me and cut my body open from here to here."

I asked Al-Jarud who was by my side, "What does he mean?"

He said, "It means from his throat to his pubic area," or said, "From the top of the chest."

The Prophet further said, "He then took out my heart. Then a gold tray of Belief was brought to me and my heart was washed and was filled (with Belief) and then returned to its original place*. Then a white animal which was smaller than a mule and bigger than a donkey was brought to me."

(On this Al-Jarud asked, "Was it the buraq, O Abu Hamza?"

I (i.e. Anas) replied in the affirmative).

The Prophet said, "The animal's step (was so wide that it) reached the farthest point within the reach of the animal's sight. I was carried on it, and Gabriel set out with me till we reached the nearest heaven. When he asked for the gate to be opened, it was asked, 'Who is it?'

Gabriel answered, 'Gabriel.'

It was asked, 'Who is accompanying you?'

Gabriel replied, 'Muhammad.'

It was asked, 'Has Muhammad been called?'

Gabriel replied in the affirmative. Then it was said, 'He is welcomed. What an excellent visit his is!' The gate was opened, and when I went over the first heaven, I saw Adam there.

Gabriel said (to me). 'This is your father, Adam; pay him your greetings.' So I greeted him and he returned the greeting to me and said, 'You are welcomed, O pious son and pious Prophet.'

Then Gabriel ascended with me till we reached the second heaven. Gabriel asked for the gate to be opened.

It was asked, 'Who is it?'

Gabriel answered, 'Gabriel.'

It was asked, 'Who is accompanying you?'

Gabriel replied, 'Muhammad.'

It was asked, 'Has he been called?'

Gabriel answered in the affirmative.

Then it was said, 'He is welcomed. What an excellent visit his is!' The gate was opened. When I went over the second heaven, there I saw Yahya (i.e. John) and 'Isa (i.e. Jesus) who were cousins of each other.

Gabriel said (to me), 'These are John and Jesus; pay them your greetings.'

So I greeted them and both of them returned my greetings to me and said, 'You are welcomed, O pious brother and pious Prophet.'

Then Gabriel ascended with me to the third heaven and asked for its gate to be opened.

It was asked, 'Who is it?'

Gabriel replied, 'Gabriel.'

It was asked, 'Who is accompanying you?'

Gabriel replied, 'Muhammad.'

It was asked, 'Has he been called?'

Gabriel replied in the affirmative. Then it was said, 'He is welcomed, what an excellent visit his is!' The gate was opened, and when I went over the third heaven there I saw Joseph. Gabriel said (to me), 'This is Joseph; pay him your greetings.' So I greeted him and he returned the greeting to me and said, 'You are welcomed, O pious brother and pious Prophet.'

Then Gabriel ascended with me to the fourth heaven and asked for its gate to be opened.

It was asked, 'Who is it?'

Gabriel replied, 'Gabriel'

It was asked, 'Who is accompanying you?'

Gabriel replied, 'Muhammad.'

It was asked, 'Has he been called?'

Gabriel replied in the affirmative.

Then it was said, 'He is welcomed, what an excellent visit his is!' The gate was opened, and when I went over the fourth heaven, there I saw Idris. Gabriel said (to me), 'This is Idris; pay him your greetings.' So I greeted him and he returned the greeting to me and said, 'You are welcomed, O pious brother and pious Prophet.'

Then Gabriel ascended with me to the fifth heaven and asked for its gate to be opened.

It was asked, 'Who is it?'

Gabriel replied, 'Gabriel.'

It was asked. 'Who is accompanying you?'

Gabriel replied, 'Muhammad.'

It was asked, 'Has he been called?'

Gabriel replied in the affirmative.

Then it was said He is welcomed, what an excellent visit his is! So when I went over the fifth heaven, there I saw Harun (i.e. Aaron), Gabriel said, (to me). This is Aaron; pay him your greetings.' I greeted him and he returned the greeting to me and said, 'You are welcomed, O pious brother and pious Prophet.'

Then Gabriel ascended with me to the sixth heaven and asked for its gate to be opened.

It was asked. 'Who is it?'

Gabriel replied, 'Gabriel.'

It was asked, 'Who is accompanying you?'

Gabriel replied, 'Muhammad.'

It was asked, 'Has he been called?'

Gabriel replied in the affirmative.

It was said, 'He is welcomed. What an excellent visit his is!'

When I went (over the sixth heaven), there I saw Moses. Gabriel said (to me),' This is Moses; pay him your greeting. So I greeted him and he returned the greetings to me and said, 'You are welcomed, O pious brother and pious Prophet.'

When I left him (i.e. Moses) he wept. Someone asked him, 'What makes you weep?'

Moses said, 'I weep because after me there has been sent (as Prophet) a young man whose followers will enter Paradise in greater numbers than my followers.'

Then Gabriel ascended with me to the seventh heaven and asked for its gate to be opened.

It was asked, 'Who is it?'

Gabriel replied, 'Gabriel.'

It was asked,' Who is accompanying you?'

Gabriel replied, 'Muhammad.'

It was asked, 'Has he been called?'

Gabriel replied in the affirmative.

Then it was said, 'He is welcomed. What an excellent visit his is!' So when I went (over the seventh heaven), there I saw Abraham. Gabriel said (to me), 'This is your father; pay your greetings to him.' So I greeted him and he returned the greetings to me and said, 'You are welcomed, O pious son and pious Prophet.'

Then I was made to ascend to Sidrat-ul-Muntaha (i.e. the Lote Tree of the utmost boundary [of Paradise]) Behold! Its fruits were like the jars of Hajr (i.e. a place near Medina) and its leaves were as big as the ears of elephants.

Gabriel said, 'This is the Lote Tree of the utmost boundary). Behold ! There ran four rivers, two were hidden and two were visible, I asked, 'What are these two kinds of rivers, O Gabriel?'

He replied, 'As for the hidden rivers, they are two rivers in Paradise and the visible rivers are the Nile and the Euphrates.'

Then Al-Bait-ul-Ma'mur** (i.e. the Sacred House was shown to me and a container full of wine and another full of milk and a third full of honey were brought to me. I took the milk. Gabriel remarked, 'This is the Islamic religion which you and your followers are following.' Then the prayers were enjoined on me: They were fifty prayers a day.

When I returned, I passed by Moses who asked (me), 'What have you been ordered to do?'

I replied, 'I have been ordered to offer fifty prayers a day.'

Moses said, 'Your followers cannot bear fifty prayers a day, and by Allah, I have tested people before you, and I have tried my level best with Bani (*Children of*) Israel (in vain). Go back to your Lord and ask for reduction to lessen your followers' burden.'

So I went back, and Allah reduced ten prayers for me. Then again I came to Moses, but he repeated the same as he had said before. Then again I went back to Allah and He reduced ten more prayers.

When I came back to Moses he said the same, I went back to Allah and He ordered me to observe ten prayers a day.

When I came back to Moses, he repeated the same advice, so I went back to Allah and was ordered to observe five prayers a day.

When I came back to Moses, he said, 'What have you been ordered?'

I replied, 'I have been ordered to observe five prayers a day.'

He said, 'Your followers cannot bear five prayers a day, and no doubt, I have got an experience of the people before you, and I have tried my level best with Bani Israel, so go back to your Lord and ask for reduction to lessen your follower's burden.'

I said, 'I have requested so much of my Lord that I feel

ashamed, but I am satisfied now and surrender to Allah's Order.'

When I left, I heard a voice saying, 'I have passed My Order and have lessened the burden of My Worshipers."

Bukhari 58.227

----

* In a Sahih Muslim hadith the washing of the Prophet's heart occurred when God's Messenger was a boy.

Anas b. Malik reported that Gabriel came to the Messenger of Allah (may peace be upo him) while he was playing with his playmates. He took hold of him and lay him prostrate on the ground and tore open his breast and took out the heart from it and then extracted a blood-clot out of it and said: That was the part of Satan in thee. And then he washed it with the water of Zamzam in a golden basin and then it was joined together and restored to it place. The boys came running to his mother, i. e. his nurse, and said: Verily Muhammad has been murdered. They all rushed toward him (and found him all right) His color was changed, Anas said. I myself saw the marks of needle on his breast.

Sahih Muslim 1.311

** Bait-ul-Ma'mur is a replica of the Ka'ba in Mecca, and is situated directly above it. Like Muslims on earth, angels are required to make a pilgrimage to this Ka'ba in the sky at least once in their lifetime as immortals, and seventy thousand angels do so every day. The Ka'ba in the sky may or may not have two doors.

Narrated Aswad:

Ibn Az-Zubair said to me, "Aisha used to tell you secretly a number of things. What did she tell you about the Ka'ba?"

I replied, "She told me that once the Prophet said, 'O 'Aisha! Had not your people been still close to the pre-Islamic period of ignorance (infidelity)! I would have dismantled the Ka'ba and would have made two doors in it; one for entrance and the other for exit."

Later on Ibn Az-Zubair did the same.

Bukhari 3:128

The hadith where the horse al-Buraq is not mentioned. In this account it is Adam who is seen weeping, not Moses. Because it is quite similar to the previous hadith, I have omitted large portions.

Narrated Abu Dhar:

Allah's Apostle said, "While I was at Mecca the roof of my house was opened and Gabriel descended, opened my chest, and washed it with Zam-zam water.

Then he brought a golden tray full of wisdom and faith and having poured its contents into my chest, he closed it.

Then he took my hand and ascended with me to the nearest heaven, when I reached the nearest heaven, Gabriel said to the gatekeeper of the heaven, 'Open (the gate).'

...

The gatekeeper asked, 'Who is it?'

Gabriel answered: 'Gabriel.'

He asked, 'Is there anyone with you?'

Gabriel replied, 'Yes, Muhammad is with me.'

He asked, 'Has he been called?'

Gabriel said, 'Yes.'

So the gate was opened and we went over the nearest heaven and there we saw a man sitting with some people on his right and some on his left. When he looked towards his right, he laughed and when he looked toward his left he wept. Then he said, 'Welcome! O pious Prophet and pious son.'

I asked Gabriel, 'Who is he?'

He replied, 'He is Adam and the people on his right and left are the souls of his offspring. Those on his right are the people of Paradise and those on his left are the people of Hell and when he looks towards his right he laughs and when he looks towards his left he weeps.'

...

So I returned to Allah and requested for further reduction and half of it was reduced. I again passed by Moses and he said to me: 'Return to your Lord, for your followers will not be able to bear it.

So I returned to Allah and He said, 'These are five prayers and they are all (equal to) fifty (in reward) for My Word does not change.' I returned to Moses and he told me to go back once again.

I replied, 'Now I feel shy of asking my Lord again.'

Then Gabriel took me till we reached Sidrat-il-Muntaha

(Lote tree of; the utmost boundary [of Paradise]) which was shrouded in colors, indescribable.

Then I was admitted into Paradise where I found small (tents or) walls (made) of pearls and its earth was of musk."

Bukhari 6.345

The most important account, the one with a stopover in Jerusalem, is actually a hadith recorded by the second most respected hadith collector, Sahih Muslim. In this hadith the Prophet is offered a choice of wine, milk or honey at the beginning of the journey rather than towards the end of his sojourn in Paradise. (Please note, Sahih Muslim does not use quotes.)

It is narrated on the authority of Anas b. Malik that the Messenger of Allah (may peace be upon him) said: I was brought al-Buraq Who is an animal white and long, larger than a donkey but smaller than a mule, who would place his hoof a distance equal to the range of version.

I mounted it and came to the Temple (Bait Maqdis in Jerusalem), then tethered it to the ring used by the prophets.

I entered the mosque and prayed two rak'ahs in it, and then came out and Gabriel brought me a vessel of wine and a vessel of milk. I chose the milk, and Gabriel said: You have chosen the natural thing. Then he took me to heaven.

Gabriel then asked the (gate of heaven) to be opened and he was asked who he was. He replied: Gabriel.

He was again asked: Who is with you?

He (Gabriel) said: Muhammad.

It was said: Has he been sent for?

Gabriel replied: He has indeed been sent for. And (the door of the heaven) was opened for us and lo! we saw Adam. He welcomed me and prayed for my good.

Then we ascended to the second heaven. Gabriel (peace be upon him) (asked the door of heaven to be opened), and he was asked who he was. He answered: Gabriel; and was again asked: Who is with you?

He replied: Muhammad.

It was said: Has he been sent for?

He replied: He has indeed been sent for. The gate was opened.

When I entered 'Isa b. Maryam and Yahya b. Zakariya (peace be upon both of them), cousins from the maternal side. welcomed me and prayed for my good.

Then I was taken to the third heaven and Gabriel asked for the opening (of the door).

He was asked: Who are you?

He replied: Gabriel.

He was (again) asked: Who is with you?

He replied Muhammad (may peace be upon him).

It was said: Has he been sent for?

He replied He has indeed been sent for. (The gate) was opened for us and I saw Yusuf (peace of Allah be upon him) who had been given half of (world) beauty. He welcomed me prayed for my well-being. Then he ascended with us to the fourth heaven.

Gabriel (peace be upon him) asked for the (gate) to be opened, and it was said: Who is he?

He replied: Gabriel.

It was (again) said: Who is with you?

He said: Muhammad.

It was said: Has he been sent for?

He replied: He has indeed been sent for.

The (gate) was opened for us, and lo! Idris was there. He welcomed me and prayed for my well-being (About him) Allah, the Exalted and the Glorious, has said:" We elevated him (Idris) to the exalted position" (Qur'an 19:57).

Then he ascended with us to the fifth heaven and Gabriel asked for the (gate) to be opened.

It was said: Who is he?

He replied Gabriel.

It was (again) said: Who is with thee?

He replied: Muhammad.

It was said Has he been sent for?

He replied: He has indeed been sent for. (The gate) was opened for us and then I was with Harun (Aaron-peace of Allah be upon him). He welcomed me prayed for my well-being. Then I was taken to the sixth heaven.

Gabriel (peace be upon him) asked for the door to be opened.

It was said: Who is he?

He replied: Gabriel.

It was said: Who is with thee?

He replied: Muhammad.

It was said: Has he been sent for?

He replied: He has indeed been sent for. (The gate) was opened for us and there I was with Musa (Moses peace be upon him) He welcomed me and prayed for my well-being.

Then I was taken up to the seventh heaven.

Gabriel asked the (gate) to be opened.

It was said: Who is he?

He said: Gabriel

It was said. Who is with thee?

He replied: Muhammad (may peace be upon him.)

It was said: Has he been sent for?

He replied: He has indeed been sent for. (The gate) was opened for us and there I found Ibrahim (Abraham peace be upon him) reclining against the Bait-ul-Ma'mur and there enter into it seventy thousand angels every day, never to visit (this place) again.

Then I was taken to Sidrat-ul-Muntaha whose leaves were like elephant ears and its fruit like big earthenware vessels. And when it was covered by the Command of Allah, it underwent such a change that none amongst the creation has the power to praise its beauty.

Then Allah revealed to me a revelation and He made obligatory for me fifty prayers every day and night.

Then I went down to Moses (peace be upon him) and he said: What has your Lord enjoined upon your Ummah?

I said: Fifty prayers.

He said: Return to thy Lord and beg for reduction (in the number of prayers), for your community shall not be able to bear this burden. as I have put to test the children of Israel and tried them (and found them too weak to bear such a heavy burden).

He (the Holy Prophet) said: I went back to my Lord and said: My Lord, make things lighter for my Ummah.

(The Lord) reduced five prayers for me. I went down to Moses and said. (The Lord) reduced five (prayers) for me, He said: Verily thy Ummah shall not be able to bear this burden; return to thy Lord and ask Him to make things lighter.

I then kept going back and forth between my Lord Blessed and Exalted and Moses, till He said: There are five prayers every day and night. O Muhammad, each being credited as ten, so that makes fifty prayers. He who intends to do a good deed and does not do it will have a good deed recorded for him; and if he does it, it will be recorded for him as ten; whereas he who intends to do an evil deed and does not do, it will not be recorded for him; and if he does it, only one evil deed will be recorded.

I then came down and when I came to Moses and informed him, he said: Go back to thy Lord and ask Him to make things lighter.

Upon this the Messenger of Allah remarked: I returned to my Lord until I felt ashamed before Him.

Sahih Muslim book 1 hadith 309

There were no eyewitnesses to the Prophet's departure from Mecca, his landing in Jerusalem, his takeoff for heaven or his return flight to Mecca the following morning; and of course there is no historical or archaeological evidence of any kind to back up his story which may explain why Islamic scholars have speculated that the journey never took place in reality but occurred in a dream. For the Prophet and his Host, it was not a dream. God's Messenger described this journey to sceptical Meccans the next day. Even with Allah providing visual aids to help His Messenger recall what he had seen, many believed he had gone insane.

Narrated Jabir bin 'Abdullah:

That he heard Allah's Apostle saying, "When the people of Quraish did not believe me (i.e. the story of my Night Journey), I stood up in Al-Hijr (the unroofed portion of the Ka'ba) and Allah displayed Jerusalem in front of me, and I began describing it to them while I was looking at it."

Bukhari 58.226

It was only after he remembered seeing a caravan from the air (which shortly arrived in Mecca) that some of the accusations of insanity were withdrawn.

It is from this one visit to Paradise that we have the only eyewitness account of what Jesus and Moses may have looked like. In one hadith Jesus has the "lank hair"; in another it is Moses.

Narrated Ibn Abbas:

The Prophet said, "On the night of my ascent to the Heaven, I saw Moses who was a tall brown curly-haired man as if he was one of the men of Shan'awa tribe, and I saw Jesus, a man of medium height and moderate complexion inclined to the red and white colors and of lank hair ..."

Bukhari 54.462

Narrated Abu Huraira:

Allah's Apostle said, "On the night of my Ascension to Heaven, I saw (the prophet) Moses who was a thin person with lank hair, looking like one of the men of the tribe of Shanua; and I saw Jesus who was of average height with red face as if he had just come out of a bathroom. And I resemble prophet Abraham more than any of his offspring does. Then I was given two cups, one containing milk and the other wine. Gabriel said, 'Drink whichever you like.' I took the milk and drank it. Gabriel said, 'You have accepted what is natural, (True Religion i.e. Islam) and if you had taken the wine, your followers would have gone astray.'"

Bukhari 55.607

Narrated Ibn 'Abbas:

The Prophet said, "One should not say that I am better than Jonah (i.e. Yunus) bin Matta." So, he mentioned his father Matta. The Prophet mentioned the night of his Ascension and said, "The prophet Moses was brown, a tall person as if from the people of the tribe of Shanu'a. Jesus was a curly-haired man of moderate height." He also mentioned Malik, the gate-keeper of the (Hell) Fire, and Ad-Dajjal.

Bukhari 55.608

The Call to Prayer

A number of options were considered to announce to the believers that it was again time to pray, before settling on the Adhan i.e. the call to prayer.

Narrated Ibn 'Umar:

When the Muslims arrived at Medina, they used to assemble for the prayer, and used to guess the time for it. During those days, the practice of Adhan for the prayers had not been introduced yet. Once they discussed this problem regarding the call for prayer. Some people suggested the use of a bell like the Christians, others proposed a trumpet like the horn used by the Jews, but 'Umar was the first to suggest that a man should call (the people) for the prayer; so Allah's Apostle ordered Bilal to get up and pronounce the Adhan for prayers.

Bukhari 11.578

Narrated Anas bin Malik:

When the number of Muslims increased they discussed the question as to how to know the time for the prayer by some familiar means. Some suggested that a fire be lit (at the time of the prayer) and others put forward the proposal to ring the bell. Bilal was ordered to pronounce the wording of Adhan twice and of the Iqama once only.

Bukhari 11.580

You can do your own Adhan if necessary, but it may annoy the neighbours if they are not believers, but not those who will bear witness on Judgement Day that you did what Allah and His Messenger expected you to do, even when you thought no one was watching.

Narrated 'Abdul Rahman:

Abu Sa'id Al-Khudri told my father, "I see you liking sheep and the wilderness. So whenever you are with your sheep or in the wilderness and you want to pronounce Adhan for the prayer raise your voice in doing so, for whoever hears the Adhan, whether a human being, a jinn or any other creature, will be a witness for you on the Day of Resurrection."

Abu Said added, "I heard it (this narration) from Allah's Apostle."

Bukhari 11.583

After listening to your own shouting of the Adhan, or the Muezzin from his minaret, you can increase your odds that it will not only be a jinn or some other creature that will interceded on your behalf on Judgement Day, but the Prophet Muhammad himself.

Narrated Jabir bin 'Abdullah:

Allah's Apostle said, "Whoever after listening to the Adhan says, 'Allahumma Rabba hadhihi-d-da' watit-tammati was-salatil qa'imati, ati Muhammadan al-wasilata wal-fadilata, wab' athhu maqaman mahmudan-il-ladhi wa' adtahu (O Allah! Lord of this perfect call (of not ascribing partners to You) and of the regular prayer which is going to be established! Kindly give Muhammad the right of intercession and superiority and send him (on the Day of Judgment) to the best and the highest place in Paradise which You promised him)', then intercession for me will be permitted for him on the Day of Resurrection").

Bukhari 11.588

Preparing for Prayer - Ablution

Performing ablution the Prophet's way:

Narrated 'Ata' bin Yasar:

Ibn 'Abbas performed ablution and washed his face (in the following way): He ladled out a handful of water, rinsed his mouth and washed his nose with it by putting in water and then blowing it out. He then, took another handful (of water) and did like this (gesturing) joining both hands, and washed his face, took another handful of water and washed his right forearm. He again took another handful of water and washed his left forearm, and passed wet hands over his head and took another handful of water and poured it over his right foot (up to his ankles) and washed it thoroughly and similarly took another handful of water and washed thoroughly his left foot (up to the ankles) and said, "I saw Allah's Apostle performing ablution in this way."

Bukhari 4.142

People used to fight over the Prophet's leftover water from ablution, some would even drink the water.

Narrated Ibn Shihab:

Mahmud bin Ar-Rabi' who was the person on whose face the Prophet had ejected a mouthful of water from his family's well while he was a boy, and 'Urwa (on the authority of Al-Miswar and others) who testified each other, said, "Whenever the Prophet, performed ablution, his companions were nearly fighting for the remains of the water."

Bukhari 4:188

Narrated As-Sa'ib bin Yazid:

My aunt took me to Allah's Apostle and said, "O Allah's Apostle! My sister's son is sick." So he passed his hand over my head and invoked for Allah's blessing upon me and then performed the ablution. I drank from the water of his ablution and I stood behind him and looked at his Khatam (the seal of Prophethood) between his shoulders (and its size was) like the button of a tent.

Bukhari 75.363

Revelation 4:43 is often referred to as the Verse of Tayammum and is about performing ablution when water is not available: " ... And if you are sick or on a journey, or if anyone of you has relieved himself, or you have touched women and could not find water, you might rub yourself with clean earth, wiping your faces and hands with it. Allah is indeed All Pardoning, All-Forgiving."

The verse was revealed when the Prophet and his party, because of Aisha, had to spend time in the desert where no water was available and could not perform ablution in the prescribed manner. The long and the short of it:

Narrated 'Aisha:

We went out with Allah's Apostle on one of his journeys till we reached Al-Baida or Dhatul-Jaish where my necklace got broken (and lost).

Allah's Apostle stopped to search for it and the people too stopped with him. There was no water at that place and they had no water with them. So they went to Abu Bakr and said, "Don't you see what 'Aisha has done? She has made Allah's Apostle and the people stop where there is no water and they have no water with them."

Abu Bakr came while Allah's Apostle was sleeping with his head on my thigh and said, "You detained Allah Apostle and the people where there is no water and they have no water." He then admonished me and said what Allah wished and pinched me at my flanks with his hands, but I did not move because the head of Allah's Apostle was on my thigh. Allah's Apostle kept on sleeping till be got up in the morning and found no water. Then Allah revealed the Divine Verse of Tayammum, and the people performed Tayammum.

Usaid bin AlHudair said. "O family of Abu Bakr! This is not the first blessings of yours." We urged the camel on which I was sitting to get up from its place and the necklace was found under it.

Bukhari 57.21

Narrated 'Aisha:

That she borrowed a necklace from Asma' and it was lost. Allah's Apostle sent some of his companions to look for it. During their journey the time of prayer was due and they prayed without ablution.

When they returned to the Prophet they complained about it. So the Divine Verse of Tayammum was revealed.

Bukhari 57.117

As usual, for the Prophet there is only one right way to do things, and Allah is always there to punish anyone who dares deviate from His Messenger's example.

Narrated 'Abdullah bin 'Amr:

Once the Prophet remained behind us in a journey. He joined us while we were performing ablution for the prayer which was over-due. We were just passing wet hands over our feet (and not washing them properly) so the Prophet addressed us in a loud voice and said twice or thrice: "Save your heels from the fire."

Bukhari 3.57

When a fart is not a fart:

Narrated 'Abbas bin Tamim:

That his uncle said: "The Prophet was asked: If a person feels something during his prayer; should one interrupt his prayer?"

The Prophet said: "No! You should not give it up unless you hear a sound or smell something."

Narrated Ibn Abi Hafsa: Az-Zuhri said, "There is no need of repeating ablution unless you detect a smell or hear a sound."

Bukhari 34.272

How To, When, Etc.

A change of direction:

Narrated Al-Bara' (bin 'Azib):

When the Prophet came to Medina, he stayed first with his grandfathers or maternal uncles from Ansar. He offered his prayers facing Baitul-Maqdis (Jerusalem) for sixteen or seventeen months, but he wished that he could pray facing the Ka'ba (at Mecca).

The first prayer which he offered facing the Ka'ba was the 'Asr prayer in the company of some people. Then one of those who had offered that prayer with him came out and passed by some people in a mosque who were bowing during their prayers (facing Jerusalem).

He said addressing them, "By Allah, I testify that I have prayed with Allah's Apostle facing Mecca (Ka'ba)."

Hearing that, those people changed their direction towards the Ka'ba immediately.

Jews and the people of the scriptures used to be pleased to see the Prophet facing Jerusalem in prayers but when he changed his direction towards the Ka'ba, during the prayers, they disapproved of it.

Al-Bara' added, "Before we changed our direction towards the Ka'ba (Mecca) in prayers, some Muslims had died or had been killed and we did not know what to say about them (regarding their prayers.) Allah then revealed: 'And Allah would never make your faith (prayers) to be lost (i.e. the prayers of those Muslims were valid).'" (2:143).

Bukhari 2.37

How to pray properly was something the Prophet took upon himself to demonstrate after being told by God, at one time or another, how He wanted it done.

Narrated Ibn 'Abbas:

The Prophet said, "I have been ordered to prostrate on seven bones i.e. on the forehead along with the tip of the nose and the Prophet pointed towards his nose, both hands, both knees and the toes of both feet and not to gather the clothes or the hair."

Bukhari 12.776

Narrated Anas bin Malik:

The Prophet said, "Be straight in the prostrations and none of you should put his forearms on the ground (in the prostration) like a dog."

Bukhari 12.785

Countless hadiths recall how God's Messenger performed this or that prayer. A hadith about how he performed three rak'as upon declaring that "God is Great" i.e. the Takbir, which must be said on six separate occasions during a session for the prayer to be valid.

Narrated Muhammad bin 'Amr bin 'Ata':

I was sitting with some of the companions of Allah's Apostle and we were discussing about the way of praying of the Prophet.

Abu Humaid As-Saidi said, "I remember the prayer of Allah's Apostle better than any one of you. I saw him raising both his hands up to the level of the shoulders on saying the Takbir; and on bowing he placed his hands on both knees and bent his back straight, then he stood up straight from bowing till all the vertebrate took their normal positions. In prostrations, he placed both his hands on the ground with the forearms away from the ground and away from his body, and his toes were facing the Qibla. On sitting in the second Rak'a he sat on his left foot and propped up the right one; and in the last Rak'a he pushed his left foot forward and kept the other foot propped up and sat over the buttocks "

Bukhari 12.791

An equal time interval was observed between rituals.

Narrated Al-Bara:

The time taken by the Prophet in prostrations, bowing, and the sitting interval between the two prostrations was about the same.

Bukhari 12.783

The Prophet was very much a petty perfectionist and into controlling every detail of everyone's existence, and prayer was no exception. Allah obviously agreed with His Messenger's obsession:

Narrated An-Nu'man bin 'Bashir:

The Prophet said, "Straighten your rows or Allah will alter your faces."

Bukhari 11.685

You could not have straight rows if you did not have crowds and straight rows, as the Prophet reminded his followers, were an important part of a "correct prayer".

Narrated Anas bin Malik:

The Prophet said, "Straighten your rows as the straightening of rows is essential for a perfect and correct prayer."

Bukhari 11.690

And whatever you do, don't look at the sky during prayer!

Narrated Anas bin Malik:

The Prophet said, "What is wrong with those people who look towards the sky during the prayer?" His talk grew stern while delivering this speech and he said, "They should stop (looking towards the sky during the prayer); otherwise their eye-sight would be taken away."

Bukhari 12.717

No talking!

Narrated Zaid bin Arqam:

In the lifetime of the Prophet we used to speak while praying, and one of us would tell his needs to his companions, till the verse, "Guard strictly your prayers" (2:238) was revealed. After that we were ordered to remain silent while praying.

Bukhari 22.292

Get up and give me two!

Narrated Jabir bin 'Abdullah:

A person entered the mosque while the Prophet was delivering the Khutba on a Friday. The Prophet said to him, "Have you prayed?"

The man replied in the negative.

The Prophet said, "Get up and pray two Rakat."

Bukhari 13.52

Make sure your shoulders are covered!

Narrated Abu Huraira:

The Prophet said, "None of you should offer prayer in a single garment that does not cover the shoulders."

Bukhari 8.355

Narrated Abu Huraira:

Allah's Apostle said, "Whoever prays in a single garment must cross its ends (over the shoulders)."

Bukhari 8.356

Everyone has had a teacher like the Prophet, I am sure. You know the one who said she had eyes in the back of her head.

Narrated Anas bin Malik:

Once the Iqama was pronounced and Allah's Apostle faced us and said, "Straighten your rows and stand closer together, for I see you from behind my back."

Bukhari 11.687

Narrated Abu Huraira:

Allah's Apostle said, "You see me facing the Qibla; but, by Allah, nothing is hidden from me regarding your bowing and submissiveness and I see you from behind my back."

Bukhari 12:708

If you must spit during prayer:

Narrated Anas:

The Prophet said, "Whenever anyone of you offers his prayer he is speaking in private to his Lord. So he should not spit to his right but under his left foot."

Qatada said, "He should not spit in front of him but to his left or under his feet."

And Shu'ba said, "He should not spit in front of him, nor to his right but to his left or under his foot."

Anas said: The Prophet said, "He should neither spit in the direction of his Qibla nor to his right but to his left or under his foot."

Bukhari 10.508

Not reciting the seven verses that make up the first chapter of the Koran as part of the prayer ritual renders a prayer meaningless.

Narrated 'Ubada bin As-Samit:

Allah's Apostle said, "Whoever does not recite Al-Fatiha in his prayer, his prayer is invalid."

Bukhari 12.723

The first thing you should do before even thinking of sitting after entering a mosque:

Narrated Abu Qatada bin Rabi Al-Ansari:

The Prophet said, "If anyone of you enters a Mosque, he should not sit until he has offered a two-Rakat prayer."

Bukhari 21.264

Mixing it up!

Narrated Abu Huraira:

Allah's Apostle forbade two kinds of sales, two kinds of dresses, and two prayers. He forbade offering prayers after the Fajr prayer till the rising of the sun and after the 'Asr prayer till its setting.

He also forbade "Ishtimal-Assama" and "al-Ihtiba" in one garment in such a way that one's private parts are exposed towards the sky. He also forbade the sales called "Munabadha" and "Mulamasa."

Bukhari 10.558

Narrated Abu Huraira:

Allah's Apostle said, "While a man was going on a way, he saw a thorny branch and removed it from the way and Allah became pleased by his action and forgave him for that." Then the Prophet said, "Five are martyrs: One who dies of plague, one who dies of an abdominal disease, one who dies of drowning, one who is buried alive (and) dies and one who is killed in Allah's cause."

(The Prophet further said, "If the people knew the reward for pronouncing the Adhan and for standing in the first row (in the congregational prayer) and found no other way to get it except by drawing lots they would do so, and if they knew the reward of offering the Zuhr prayer early (in its stated time), they would race for it and [if] they knew the reward for 'Isha' and Fajr prayers in congregation, they would attend them even if they were to crawl')

Bukhari 11.624

This Prophet had a fondness for odd numbers, and that extended to prayers and the number of stones he used to clean himself after answering the call of nature (see *Call of Nature*) to the number of dates he ate at one time.

Narrated Nafi':

Ibn 'Umar said, "While the Prophet was on the pulpit, a man asked him how to offer the night prayers. He replied, 'Pray two Rakat at a time and then two and then two and so on, and if you are afraid of the dawn (the approach of the time of the Fajr prayer) pray one Rak'a and that will be the witr for all the Rakat which you have offered."

Ibn 'Umar said, "The last Rakat of the night prayer should be odd for the Prophet ordered it to be so."

Bukhari 8.461

Narrated Anas bin Malik:

Allah's Apostle never proceeded (for the prayer) on the Day of 'Id-ul-Fitr unless he had eaten some dates. Anas also narrated: The Prophet used to eat odd number of dates.

Bukhari 15.73

Could you repeat that?

Narrated Ibn Umar:

Once a person asked Allah's Apostle about the night prayer. llah's Apostle replied, "The night prayer is offered as two Rakat followed by two Rakat and so on and if anyone is afraid of the approaching dawn (Fajr prayer) he should pray one Raka and this will be a W:tr for all the Rakat which he has prayed before."

Nafi' told that 'Abdullah bin 'Umar used to say Taslim between (the first) two Rakat and (the third) odd one in the Witr prayer, when he wanted to attend to a certain matter (during that interval between the Rakat).

Bukhari 16.105

It's pray now or pray later.

Narrated Anas:

The Prophet said, "If anyone forgets a prayer he should pray that prayer when he remembers it. There is no expiation except to pray the same." Then he recited: "Establish prayer for My (i.e. Allah's) remembrance." (20:14).

Bukhari 10.571

If you plan on having sex, or have had a nocturnal emission before the call to prayer, make sure to take a bath and avoid being impure i.e. Junub for the purpose of praying.

Narrated Abu Huraira:

Once iqama was pronounced and the people had straightened the rows, Allah's Apostle went forward (to lead the prayer) but he was Junub, so he said, "Remain in your places." And he went out, took a bath and returned with water trickling from his head. Then he led the prayer.

Bukhari 11.613

When not taking a bath is not an option, although brushing your teeth and perfuming yourself (men only) may be optional:

Narrated Abu Said Al-Khudri:

The Prophet said, "Ghusl (taking a bath) on Friday is compulsory for every Muslim reaching the age of puberty."

Bukhari 12.817

Narrated Abu Said:

I testify that Allah's Apostle said, "The taking of a bath on Friday is compulsory for every male Muslim who has attained the age of puberty and (also) the cleaning of his teeth with Siwak, and the using of perfume if it is available."

Amr (a sub-narrator) said, "I confirm that the taking of a bath is compulsory, but as for the Siwak and the using of perfume, Allah knows better whether it is obligatory or not, but according to the Hadith it is as above."

Bukhari 13.5

At one time, the Prophet considered having his followers brush their teeth five times a day.

Narrated Abu Huraira:

Allah's Apostle said, "If I had not found it hard for my followers or the people, I would have ordered them to clean their teeth with Siwak for every prayer."

Bukhari 13.12

The end of worship for women:

Narrated Um Salama:

"The Prophet after finishing the prayer with Taslim used to stay at his place for a while."

Ibn Shihab said, "I think (and Allah knows better), that he used to wait for the departure of the women who had prayed."

Ibn Shihab wrote that he had heard it from Hind bint Al-Harith Al-Firasiya from Um Salama, the wife of the Prophet (Hind was from the companions of Um Salama) who said, "When the Prophet finished the prayer with Taslim, while facing the right then facing left), the women would depart and enter their houses before Allah's Apostle departed."

Bukhari 12.809

Narrated 'Aisha:

When Allah's Apostle finished the Fajr prayer, the women would leave covered in their sheets and were not recognized owing to the darkness.

Bukhari 12.826

Instructions from the Prophet on how a woman should clean her dress if it has been soiled by menstrual discharge before she can pray in it:

Narrated Asma':

A woman came to the Prophet and said, "If anyone of us gets menses in her clothes then what should she do?"

He replied, "She should (take hold of the soiled place), rub it and put it in the water and rub it in order to remove the traces of blood and then pour water over it. Then she can pray in it."

Bukhari: 4.227

Another warning for those who would sleep in and miss the first compulsory prayer:

Narrated Samura bin Jundab:

The Prophet said in his narration of a dream that he saw, "He whose head was being crushed with a stone was one who learnt the Quran but never acted on it, and slept ignoring the compulsory prayers."

Bukhari 21.244

You can delay the Zuhr prayer if Hell is in the process of exhaling.

Narrated Abu Huraira:

The Prophet said, "In very hot weather delay the Zuhr prayer till it becomes (a bit) cooler because the severity of heat is from the raging of Hell-fire. The Hell-fire of Hell complained to its Lord saying: O Lord! My parts are eating (destroying) one another. So Allah allowed it to take two breaths, one in the winter and the other in the summer. The breath in the summer is at the time when you feel the severest heat and the breath in the winter is at the time when you feel the severest cold."

Bukhari 10.512

No pressure!

Narrated Ibn 'Umar:

Allah's Apostle said, "Whoever misses the 'Asr prayer (intentionally) then it is as if he lost his family and property."

Bukhari 10.527

Narrated Abu Al-Mahh:

We were with Buraida in a battle on a cloudy day and he said, "Offer the 'Asr prayer early as the Prophet said, "Whoever leaves the 'Asr prayer, all his (good) deeds will be annulled."

Bukhari 10.528

Do not let your attention wonder. A warning from both Allah and His Messenger:

Narrated Jabir bin 'Abdullah:

While we were praying (Jumua Khutba & prayer) with the Prophet (p.b.u.h), some camels loaded with food, arrived (from Sham). The people diverted their attention towards the camels (and left the mosque), and only twelve persons remained with the Prophet. So this verse was revealed: "But when they see some bargain or some amusement, They disperse headlong to it, And leave you standing." (62:11)

Bukhari 13.58

Keeping count of the rakats:

Narrated 'Abdullah bin Umar:

Allah's Apostle used to pray two Rakat before the Zuhr prayer and two Rakat after it. He also used to pray two Rakat after the Maghrib prayer in his house, and two Rakat after the 'Isha' prayer. He never prayed after Jumua prayer till he departed (from the Mosque), and then he would pray two Rakat at home.

Bukhari 13.59

Wait to eat onions or garlic if you want to join the believers in prayer at the mosque:

Narrated 'Abdul 'Aziz:

A man asked Anas, "What did you hear from the Prophet about garlic?" He said, "The Prophet said, 'Whoever has eaten this plant should neither come near us nor pray with us.'"

Bukhari 12.815

Narrated Jabir bin 'Abdullah:

The Prophet said, "Whoever eats garlic or onion should keep away from our mosque or should remain in his house."

(Jabir bin 'Abdullah, in another narration said, "Once a big pot containing cooked vegetables was brought. On finding unpleasant smell coming from it, the Prophet asked, 'What is in it?' He was told all the names of the vegetables that were in it. The Prophet ordered that it should be brought near to some of his companions who were with him. When the Prophet saw it he disliked to eat it and said, 'Eat. (I don't eat) for I converse with those whom you don't converse with (i.e. the angels)."

Bukhari 12.814

Eating a shoulder cut of mutton after performing your ablution should not require a repeat ritual purification before getting down and doing your prayers.

Narrated 'Abdullah bin 'Abbas:

Allah's Apostle ate a piece of cooked mutton from the shoulder region and prayed without repeating ablution.

Bukhari 4.206

Precautions were taken during wartime so that the enemies of the Muslims would not use the believers' praying time to their advantage. These safeguards became known as the "fear prayer".

Narrated Sahl bin Abi Hathma (describing the Fear prayer):

The Imam stands up facing the Qibla and one batch of them (i.e. the army) (out of the two) prays along with him and the other batch faces the enemy. The Imam offers one Rak'a with the first batch they themselves stand up alone and offer one bowing and two prostrations while they are still in their place, and then go away to relieve the second batch, and the second batch comes (and takes the place of the first batch in the prayer behind the Imam) and he offers the second Rak'a with them.

So he completes his two-Rak'at and then the second batch bows and prostrates two prostrations (i.e. complete their second Rak'a and thus all complete their prayer).

Bukhari 59.452

Narrated Shu'aib:

I asked Az-Zuhri, "Did the Prophet ever offer the Fear Prayer?"

Az-Zuhri said, "I was told by Salim that 'Abdullah bin Umar I had said, 'I took part in a holy battle with Allah's Apostle in Najd. We faced the enemy and arranged ourselves in rows. Then Allah's Apostle (p.b.u.h) stood up to lead the prayer and one party stood to pray with him while the other faced the enemy. Allah's Apostle (p.b.u.h) and the former party bowed and performed two prostrations. Then that party left and took the place of those who had not prayed. Allah's Apostle prayed one Raka (with the latter) and performed two prostrations and finished his prayer with Taslim. Then everyone of them bowed once and performed two prostrations individually.'"

Bukhari 14.64

When you can pray while standing:

Narrated Nafi':

Ibn Umar said something similar to Mujahid's saying: Whenever (Muslims and non-Muslims) stand face to face in battle, the Muslims can pray while standing.

Ibn Umar added, "The Prophet said, 'If the number of the enemy is greater than the Muslims, they can pray while standing or riding (individually).'"

Bukhari 14.65

The only one who could make a prayer compulsory was Allah, but not if His Messenger did not perform it at least once.

Narrated 'Aisha:

Allah's Apostle used to give up a good deed, although he loved to do it, for fear that people might act on it and it might be made compulsory for them. The Prophet never prayed the Duha prayer (mid-morning prayer), but I offer it.

Bukhari 21.228

Praying till it hurts:

Narrated Al-Mughira:

The Prophet used to stand (in the prayer) or pray till both his feet or legs swelled. He was asked why (he offered such an unbearable prayer) and he said, "should I not be a thankful slave."

Bukhari 21.230

If the Prophet was not already at prayer, it was the crowing of a cock which reminded him it was time to get up and pray ... again.

Narrated Al-Ashath:

He (the Prophet (p.b.u.h)) used to get up for the prayer on hearing the crowing of a cock.

Bukhari 21.233

When the Prophet went to perform the Istisqa, the rain prayer, he took some precautions:

Narrated 'Abbas bin Tamim's uncle:

The Prophet (p.b.u.h) went out to offer the Istisqa' prayer and turned (and put on) his cloak inside out.

Bukhari 17.119

There is no mention of a prayer to stop the rain.

Narrated Anas bin Malik:

Once in the lifetime of the Prophet (p.b.u.h) the people were afflicted with drought (famine). While the Prophet was delivering the Khutba (sermon) on a Friday, a Bedouin stood up and said, "O, Allah's Apostle! Our possessions are being destroyed and the children are hungry; Please invoke Allah (for rain)".

So the Prophet raised his hands. At that time there was not a trace of cloud in the sky. By Him in Whose Hands my soul is as soon as he lowered his hands, clouds gathered like mountains, and before he got down from the pulpit, I saw the rain falling on the beard cf the Prophet. It rained that day, the next day, the third day, the fourth day till the next Friday.

The same Bedouin or another man stood up and said, "O Allah's Apostle! The houses have collapsed, our possessions and livestock have been drowned; Please invoke Allah (to protect us)".

So the Prophet I raised both his hands and said, "O Allah! Round about us and not on us".

So, in whatever direction he pointed with his hands, the clouds dispersed and cleared away, and Medina's (sky) became clear as a hole in between the clouds. The valley of Qanat remained flooded, for one month, none came from outside but talked about the abundant rain.

Bukhari 13.55

How to do prayers when you are in a hurry.

Narrated 'Abdullah bin 'Umar:

I saw Allah's Apostle delaying the Maghrib prayer till he offered it along with the 'Isha' prayer whenever he was in a hurry during the journey.

Salim narrated, "Ibn 'Umar used to do the same whenever he was in a hurry during the journey."

And Salim added, "Ibn 'Umar used to pray the Maghrib and 'Isha' prayers together in Al-Muzdalifa."

Salim said, "Ibn 'Umar delayed the Maghrib prayer because at that time he heard the news of the death of his wife Safiya bint Abi 'Ubaid."

I said to him, "The prayer (is due)."

He said, "Go on."

Again I said, "The prayer (is due)."

He said, "Go on, till we covered two or three miles. Then he got down, prayed and said, 'I saw the Prophet praying in this way, whenever he was in a hurry during the journey.'"

Abdullah (bin 'Umar) added, "Whenever the Prophet was in a hurry, he used to delay the Maghrib prayer and then offer three Rakat (of the Maghrib) and perform Taslim, and after waiting for a short while, Iqama used to be pronounced for the 'Isha prayer when he would offer two Rakat and perform Taslim. He would never offer any optional prayer till the middle of the night (when he used to pray the Tahajjud)."

Bukhari 20.197

Why you should not pray while drowsy.

Narrated 'Aisha:

Allah's Apostle said, "If anyone of you feels drowsy while praying he should go to bed (sleep) till his slumber is over because in praying while drowsy one does not know whether one is asking for forgiveness or for a bad thing for oneself."

Bukhari 4:211

Don't interrupt the Imam!

Narrated Abu Huraira:

Allah's Apostle (p.b.u.h) said, "When the Imam is delivering the Khutba (*sermon*), and you ask your companion to keep quiet and listen, then no doubt you have done an evil act."

Bukhari 13.56

Do not raise your head before the Imam.

Narrated Abu Huraira:

The Prophet said, "Isn't he who raises his head before the Imam afraid that Allah may transform his head into that of a donkey or his figure (face) into that of a donkey?"

Bukhari 11.660

When the practice, a profitable one it would seem, of the Imam preaching separately to the women started:

Narrated Ibn Juraij:

'Ata said, "Jabir bin 'Abdullah said, 'The Prophet went out on the Day of 'Id-ul-Fitr and offered the prayer before delivering the Khutba, Ata told me that during the early days of IbnAz-Zubair, Ibn Abbas had sent a message to him telling him that the Adhan for the 'Id Prayer was never pronounced (in the life time of Allah's Apostle) and the Khutba used to be delivered after the prayer. Ata told me that Ibn Abbas and Jabir bin 'Abdullah, had said, - where was no Adhan for the prayer of '7d-ul-Fitr and 'Id-ul-Aqha."

'Ata said, "I heard Jabir bin 'Abdullah saying, 'The Prophet stood up and started with the prayer, and after it he delivered the Khutba. When the Prophet of Allah (p.b.u.h) finished (the Khutba), he went to the women and preached to them, while he was leaning on Bilal's hand. Bilal was spreading his garment and the ladies were putting alms in it.'"

I said to 'Ata, "Do you think it incumbent upon an Imam to
go to the women and preach to them after finishing the
prayer and Khutba?"

'Ata said, "No doubt it is incumbent on Imams to do so, and
why should they not do so?"

Bukhari 15.78

The Musalla is the area outside a mosque mainly used for praying.
On the day marking the end of Ramadan, "Day of 'Id" and "'Id day" in
the following hadiths, some women were allowed to pray in this area.
The following two hadiths appear to contradict each other as to which
women were granted the privilege to stand behind the men and
proclaim how great is God.

Narrated Um 'Atiya:

We used to be ordered to come out on the Day of 'Id and
even bring out the virgin girls from their houses and
menstruating women so that they might stand behind the
men and say Takbir along with them and invoke Allah along
with them and hope for the blessings of that day and for
purification from sins.

Bukhari 15.88

Narrated Muhammad:

Um 'Atiyya said: "Our Prophet ordered us to come out (on
'Id day) with the mature girls and the virgins staying in
seclusion."

Hafsa narrated the above mentioned Hadith and added,
"The mature girls or virgins staying in seclusion but the
menstruating women had to keep away from the Musalla."

Bukhari 15.91

What is most interesting about the following hadith is that both the
Prophet and his successor Abu Bakr, the father of Aisha, would be
buried in her bedroom.

Narrated Ibn 'Umar:

Allah's Apostle said, "Offer some of your prayers in your
houses and do not make them graves."

Bukhari 21.280

'Id-ul-Fitr and 'Id-ul-Adha were not just days of celebration — the first
marking the end of Ramadan, the other the Hajj — those were also
the days when the Prophet gave his army its marching orders, which
would explain the spear. Pity the unbelievers on the receiving end.

Narrated Ibn Umar:

On the day of 'Id-ul-Fitr and 'Id-ul-Adha a spear used to be planted in front of the Prophet I (as a Sutra i.e. an object which separates the worshiper from people passing in front of him for the prayer) and then he would pray.

Bukhari 15.89

Friday was also meant to be the day of worship for Christians and Jews.

Narrated Abu Huraira:

I heard Allah's Apostle (p.b.u.h) saying, "We (Muslims) are the last (to come) but (will be) the foremost on the Day of Resurrection though the former nations were given the Holy Scriptures before us. And this was their day (Friday) the celebration of which was made compulsory for them but they differed about it. So Allah gave us the guidance for it (Friday) and all the other people are behind us in this respect: the Jews' (holy day is) tomorrow (i.e. Saturday) and the Christians' (is) the day after tomorrow (i.e. Sunday)."

Bukhari 13.1

When praying, not to do exactly as the Prophet demonstrated can be fatal.

Narrated 'Abdullah bin Masud:

The Prophet recited Suratan-Najm (103) at Mecca and prostrated while reciting it and those who were with him did the same except an old man who took a handful of small stones or earth and lifted it to his forehead and said, "This is sufficient for me."

Later on, I saw him killed as a non-believer.

Bukhari 19.173

Not attending prayers carries its own risks.

Narrated Abu Huraira:

The Prophet said, "No doubt, I intended to order somebody to pronounce the Iqama of the (compulsory congregational) prayer and then I would go to the houses of those who do not attend the prayer and burn their houses over them."

Bukhari 41.602

Narrated Abu Huraira:

The Prophet said, "No prayer is harder for the hypocrites than the Fajr and the 'Isha' prayers and if they knew the reward for these prayers at their respective times, they would certainly present themselves (in the mosques) even if they had to crawl."

The Prophet added, "Certainly I decided to order the Mu'adh-dhin (call-maker) to pronounce Iqama and order a man to lead the prayer and then take a fire flame to burn all those who had not left their houses so far for the prayer along with their houses (*members of the household?*)."

Bukhari 11.626

An exception to the burn them in their houses rule:

Narrated Nafi':

Ibn 'Umar said, "Allah's Apostle said, 'If the supper is served for anyone of you and the Iqama is pronounced, start with the supper and don't be in haste (and carry on eating) till you finish it.'"

If food was served for Ibn 'Umar and Iqama was pronounced, he never came to the prayer till he finished it (i.e. food) in spite of the fact that he heard the recitation (of the Qur'an) by the Imam (in the prayer).

Narrated Ibn 'Umar: The Prophet said, "If anyone of you is having his meals, he should not hurry up till he is satisfied even if the prayer has been started."

Bukhari 11.642

What are Muslims who live in the Arctic and near-Arctic to do during the period in the summer when the sun does not set or only partially; or in the winter when it does not rise at all or not completely?

Narrated Ibn Umar:

Allah's Apostle said, "When the (upper) edge of the sun appears (in the morning), don't perform a prayer till the sun appears in full, and when the lower edge of the sun sets, don't perform a prayer till it sets completely. And you should not seek to pray at sunrise or sunset for the sun rises between two sides of the head of the devil (or Satan)."

Bukhari 54.494

For whom it is pointless to pray:

Narrated Abdullah bin 'Umar:

When Abdullah bin Ubdi (bin Salul) died, his son came to Allah's Apostle and said "O Allah's Apostle, give me your shirt so that I may shroud my father's body in it. And please offer a funeral prayer for him and invoke Allah for his forgiveness."

The Prophet gave him his shirt and said to him 'Inform us when you finish (and the funeral procession is ready) call us.

When he had finished he told the Prophet and the Prophet proceeded to order his funeral prayers but Umar stopped him and said, "Didn't Allah forbid you to offer the funeral prayer for the hypocrites when He said: 'Whether you (O Muhammad) ask forgiveness for them or ask not forgiveness for them: (and even) if you ask forgiveness for them seventy times. Allah will not forgive them.'" (9:80)

Then there was revealed: "And never (O Muhammad) pray for any of them that dies, nor stand at his grave." (9:84)

Thenceforth the Prophet did not offer funeral prayers for the hypocrites.

Bukhari 72.688

How you differentiate between a hypocrite from one who is deserving of prayers at his funeral:

Narrated 'Abdullah bin 'Amr:

The Prophet said, "Whoever has (the following) four characters will be a hypocrite, and whoever has one of the following four characteristics will have one characteristic of hypocrisy until he gives it up. These are:

(1) Whenever he talks, he tells a lie;

(2) whenever he makes a promise, he breaks it;

(3) whenever he makes a covenant he proves treacherous;

(4) and whenever he quarrels, he behaves impudently in an evil insulting manner."

Bukhari 43.639

Another who must be denied the funeral prayer is a stillborn child. In hadith 54.430 (*see Babies*) the Prophet said the soul enters the body of an embryo forty days after conception. This begs the question as to why, a child into whom Allah has "breathed" a soul is not entitled to a funeral prayer even if born dead or who dies during childbirth.

Narrated Ibn Shihab:

The funeral prayer should be offered for every child even if he were the son of a prostitute as he was born with a true faith of Islam (i.e. to worship none but Allah Alone). If his parents are Muslims, particularly the father, even if his mother were a non-Muslim, and if he after the delivery cries (even once) before his death (i.e. born alive) then the funeral prayer must be offered.

And if the child does not cry after his delivery (i.e. born dead) then his funeral prayer should not be offered, and he will be considered as a miscarriage.

Bukhari 23.440

The Prophet was not keen on offering the funeral prayer for a deceased in debt.

Narrated Salama bin Al-Akwa:

A dead person was brought to the Prophet so that he might lead the funeral prayer for him. He asked, "Is he in debt?"

When the people replied in the negative, he led the funeral prayer. Another dead person was brought and he asked, "Is he in debt?"

They said, "Yes."

He (refused to lead the prayer and) said, "Lead the prayer of your friend."

Abu Qatada said, "O Allah's Apostle! I undertake to pay his debt." Allah's Apostle then led his funeral prayer.

Bukhari 37.492

How some could tell what prayer the Prophet was uttering:

Narrated Abu Ma'mar:

We said to Khabbab "Did Allah's Apostle used to recite in Zuhr and 'Asr prayers?" He replied in the affirmative. We said, "How did you come to know about it?" He said, "By the movement of his beard."

Bukhari 12.744

The author of the Gettysburg address should have been so honoured:

Narrated Rifa'a bin Rafi AzZuraqi:

One day we were praying behind the Prophet. When he raised his head from bowing, he said, "Sami'a-l-lahu Liman hamida."

A man behind him said, "Rabbana walaka-l hamd hamdan Kathiran taiyiban mubarakan fihi" (O our Lord! All the praises are for You, many good and blessed praises).

When the Prophet completed the prayer, he asked, "Who has said these words?"

The man replied, "I."

The Prophet said, "I saw over thirty angels competing to write it first."

[The] Prophet rose (from bowing) and stood straight till all the vertebrae of his spinal column came to a natural position.

Bukhari 12.764

Angels and Rewards Based on a Point System

The more you pray the more your name gets mentioned in high places.

Narrated Abu Huraira:

Allah's Apostle said, "Angels come to you in succession by night and day and all of them get together at the time of the Fajr and 'Asr prayers. Those who have passed the night with you (or stayed with you) ascend (to the Heaven) and Allah asks them, though He knows everything about you, well, "In what state did you leave my slaves?"

The angels reply: "When we left them they were praying and when we reached them, they were praying."

Bukhari 10.530

Again, the angel will not intercede on your behalf if they smell or hear anything untoward.

Narrated Abu Huraira:

The Prophet said, "As long as any-one of you is waiting for the prayer, he is considered to be praying actually, and the angels say, 'O Allah! Be merciful to him and forgive him', (and go on saying so) unless he leaves his place of praying or passes wind (i.e. breaks his ablution)."

Bukhari 54.452

It is a good idea to arrive early for Friday prayers, not only because of who will be taking attendance, but also if you want rewards equivalent to sacrificing a camel to Allah.

Narrated Abu Huraira:

The Prophet said, "On every Friday the angels take their stand at every gate of the mosques to write the names of the people chronologically (i.e. according to the time of their arrival for the Friday prayer and when the Imam sits (on the pulpit) they fold up their scrolls and get ready to listen to the sermon."

Bukhari 54.433

Narrated Abu Huraira:

Allah's Apostle (p.b.u.h) said, "Any person who takes a bath on Friday like the bath of Janaba (ritual bathing) and then goes for the prayer (in the first hour i.e. early), it is as if he had sacrificed a camel (in Allah's cause); and whoever goes in the second hour it is as if he had sacrificed a cow; and whoever goes in the third hour, then it is as if he had sacrificed a horned ram; and if one goes in the fourth hour, then it is as if he had sacrificed a hen; and whoever goes in the fifth hour then it is as if he had offered an egg. When the Imam comes out (i.e. starts delivering the Khutba i.e. sermon), the angels present themselves to listen to the Khutba."

Bukhari 13.6

It's all about the rewards! When you see people rushing into the street to perform the obligatory prayers, it's not only because of the consequences of not praying at the decreed times and in the manner prescribed, but also for the increased rewards that come with praying with a crowd of worshippers.

Narrated Abu Huraira:

Allah's Apostle said, "If the people knew the reward for pronouncing the Adhan and for standing in the first row (in congregational prayers) and found no other way to get that except by drawing lots they would draw lots, and if they knew the reward of the Zuhr prayer (in the early moments of its stated time) they would race for it (go early) and if they knew the reward of 'Isha' and Fajr (morning) prayers in congregation, they would come to offer them even if they had to crawl."

Bukhari 11.589

How to get twenty five times the reward for a prayer ... or is it twenty seven? It may have to do with the distance from the mosque.

Narrated Abu Huraira:

The Prophet said, "The prayer offered in congregation is twenty five times more superior (in reward) to the prayer offered alone in one's house or in a business center, because if one performs ablution and does it perfectly, and then proceeds to the mosque with the sole intention of praying, then for each step which he takes towards the mosque, Allah upgrades him a degree in reward and (forgives) crosses out one sin till he enters the mosque. When he enters the mosque he is considered in prayer as long as he is waiting for the prayer and the angels keep on asking for Allah's forgiveness for him and they keep on saying: 'O Allah! Be Merciful to him, O Allah! Forgive him', as long as he keeps on sitting at his praying place and does not pass wind."

Bukhari 8.466

Narrated Abu Musa:

The Prophet said, "The people who get tremendous reward for the prayer are those who are farthest away (from the mosque) and then those who are next farthest and so on. Similarly one who waits to pray with the Imam has greater reward than one who prays and goes to bed."

Bukhari 11.623

Narrated 'Abdullah bin Umar:

Allah's Apostle said, "The prayer in congregation is twenty seven times superior to the prayer offered by person alone."

Bukhari 11.618

Why Medina and Mecca attract so many believers every year, and not only for the mandatory once-in-a-lifetime pilgrimage to Mecca, may have to do with the biggest reward of all for saying your prayer in a crowd of like-minded souls.

Narrated Abu Huraira:

Allah's Apostle said, "One prayer in my Mosque (*Medina*) is better than one thousand prayers in any other mosque excepting Al-Masjid-Al-Haram (*the Grand Mosque of Mecca*)."

Bukhari 21.282

In 2012, the Saudis began work on the Masjid an-Nabawi in Medina, where the Prophet Muhammad is buried. When completed it will not only be the largest mosque in the world, but the largest building, capable of accommodating 1.6 million ultimate-reward seekers.

It must have been difficult to restrain yourself from shouting "Amin" nonstop and disrupting the prayers.

Narrated Abu Huraira:

Allah's Apostle said, "Say Amen when the Imam says "Ghair-il-maghdubi 'alaihim wala-ddal-lin; not the path of those who earn Your Anger (such as Jews) nor of those who go astray (such as Christians); all the past sins of the person whose saying (of Amin) coincides with that of the angels, will be forgiven.

Bukhari 12.749

Narrated Abu Huraira:

Allah's Apostle said, "If any one of you says, "Amin" and the angels in the heavens say `Amin' and the former coincides with the latter, all his past sins will be forgiven."

Bukhari 12.748

A very short hour during which you can still get lucky.

Narrated Abu Huraira:

Allah's Apostle (p.b.u.h) talked about Friday and said, "There is an hour (opportune time) on Friday and if a Muslim gets it while praying and asks something from Allah, then Allah will definitely meet his demand." And he (the Prophet) pointed out the shortness of that time with his hands.

Bukhari 13.57

They also pray those who sit waiting for the prayer to start, and don't fart!

Narrated Abu Huraira:

Allah's Apostle said, "The congregational prayer of anyone amongst you is more than twenty (five or twenty seven) times in reward than his prayer in the market or in his house, for if he performs ablution completely and then goes to the mosque with the sole intention of performing the prayer, and nothing urges him to proceed to the mosque except the prayer, then, on every step which he takes towards the mosque, he will be raised one degree or one of his sins will be forgiven. The angels will keep on asking Allah's forgiveness and blessings for every one of you so long as he keeps sitting at his praying place. The angels will say, 'O Allah, bless him! O Allah, be merciful to him!' as long as he does not do Hadath (fart) or a thing which gives trouble to the other."

The Prophet further said, "One is regarded in prayer so long as one is waiting for the prayer."

Bukhari 34.330

Who gets the reward if the Imam gets it wrong.

Narrated Abu Huraira:

Allah's Apostle said, "If the Imam leads the prayer correctly then he and you will receive the rewards but if he makes a mistake (in the prayer) then you will receive the reward for the prayer and the sin will be his."

Bukhari 11.663

Do it right and even more sins will be forgiven.

Narrated Salman-Al-Farsi:

The Prophet (p.b.u.h) said, "Whoever takes a bath on Friday, purifies himself as much as he can, then uses his (hair) oil or perfumes himself with the scent of his house, then proceeds (for the Jumua i.e. Friday prayer) and does not separate two persons sitting together (in the mosque), then prays as much as (Allah has) written for him and then remains silent while the Imam is delivering the Khutba, his sins in-between the present and the last Friday would be forgiven."

Bukhari 13.8

Catching up with the rich through prayer:

Narrated Abu Huraira:

Some poor people came to the Prophet and said, "The wealthy people will get higher grades and will have permanent enjoyment and they pray like us and fast as we do. They have more money by which they perform the Hajj, and 'Umra; fight and struggle in Allah's Cause and give in charity."

The Prophet said, "Shall I not tell you a thing upon which if you acted you would catch up with those who have surpassed you? Nobody would overtake you and you would be better than the people amongst whom you live except those who would do the same. Say 'Sub-han-al-lah', 'Alhamdu-lillah' and 'Allahu Akbar' thirty three times each after every (compulsory) prayer..."

Bukhari 12.804

The value in Qirats of attending a funeral:

Narrated Abu Huraira:

Allah's Apostle said, "(A believer) who accompanies the funeral procession of a Muslim out of sincere faith and hoping to attain Allah's reward and remains with it till the funeral prayer is offered and the burial ceremonies are over, he will return with a reward of two Qirats. Each Qirat is like the size of the (Mount) Uhud. He who offers the funeral prayer only and returns before the burial, will return with the reward of one Qirat only."

Bukhari 2.45

Worried about debts?

Narrated 'Aisha:

Allah's Apostle used to invoke Allah in the prayer saying "Allahumma inni a'udhu bika min adhabil-qabri, wa a'udhu bika min fitnatil-masihid-dajjal, wa a'udhu bika min fitnatil-mahya wa fitnatil-mamati. Allahumma inni a'udhu bika minal-ma thami wal-maghrami. (O Allah, I seek refuge with You from the punishment of the grave and from the afflictions of Masi,h Ad-Dajjal (the false messiah)and from the afflictions of life and death. O Allah, I seek refuge with You from the sins and from being in debt)."

Somebody said to him, "Why do you so frequently seek refuge with Allah from being in debt?"

The Prophet replied, "A person in debt tells lies whenever he speaks, and breaks promises whenever he makes (them)."

'Aisha also narrated: I heard Allah's Apostle in his prayer seeking refuge with Allah from the afflictions of Ad-dajjal (the false messiah).

Bukhari 12.795

The value of prayer said while sitting:

Narrated 'Abdullah bin Buraida:

'Imran bin Husain had piles. Once Abu Ma mar narrated from 'Imran bin Husain had said, "I asked the Prophet (p.b.u.h) about the prayer of a person while sitting. He said, 'It is better for one to pray standing; and whoever prays sitting gets half the reward of that who prays while standing; and whoever prays while Lying gets half the reward of that who prays while sitting.'"

Bukhari 20.217

An evil deed, like kissing a woman, is erased by prayer.

Narrated Ibn Masud:

A man kissed a woman and then came to Allah's Apostle and told him of that, so this Divine Inspiration was revealed to the Prophet 'And offer Prayers perfectly at the two ends of the day, and in some hours of the night; (i.e. (five) compulsory prayers). Verily, the good deeds remove the evil deeds (small sins) That is a reminder for the mindful.' (11:114)

The man said, "Is this instruction for me only?"

The Prophet said, "It is for all those of my followers who encounter a similar situation."

Bukhari 60.209

Satan and the Devils at Prayer Time

Narrated Abu Huraira:

Allah's Apostle said, "When the call for prayer is made, Satan takes to his heels passing wind so that he may not hear the Adhan and when the call is finished he comes back, and when the Iqama is pronounced, Satan again takes to his heels, and when the Iqama is finished he comes back again and tries to interfere with the person and his thoughts and say, 'Remember this and that (which he has not thought of before the prayer)', till the praying person forgets how much he has prayed. If anyone of you does not remember whether he has offered three or four Rakat then he should perform two prostrations of Sahu (forgetfulness) while sitting."

Bukhari 22.323

The Prophet could have captured Satan (or it could have been a jinn) on one of these occasions, but thought better of it.

Narrated Abu Huraira:

The Prophet once offered the prayer and said, "Satan came in front of me and tried to interrupt my prayer, but Allah gave me an upper hand on him and I choked him. No doubt, I thought of tying him to one of the pillars of the mosque till you get up in the morning and see him. Then I remembered the statement of Prophet Solomon, 'My Lord! Bestow on me a kingdom such as shall not belong to any other after me.' Then Allah made him (Satan) return with his head down (humiliated)."

Bukhari 22.301

Narrated Abu Huraira:

The Prophet said, "A strong demon from the jinns came to me yesterday suddenly, so as to spoil my prayer, but Allah enabled me to overpower him, and so I caught him and intended to tie him to one of the pillars of the Mosque so that all of you might see him, but I remembered the invocation of my brother Solomon: 'And grant me a kingdom such as shall not belong to any other after me.' (38:35) so I let him go cursed."

Bukhari 55.634

How Satan steals a portion of a prayer:

Narrated 'Aisha:

I asked the Prophet about one's looking here and there during the prayer. He replied, "It is what Satan steals from the prayer of any one of you."

Bukhari 54.511

Satan may also be responsible for your waking up with your hair in knots, assuming you still have hair.

Narrated Abu Huraira:

Allah's Apostle said, "Satan puts three knots at the back of the head of any of you if he is asleep. On every knot he reads and exhales the following words, 'The night is long, so stay asleep.' When one wakes up and remembers Allah, one knot is undone; and when one performs ablution, the second knot is undone, and when one prays the third knot is undone and one gets up energetic with a good heart in the morning; otherwise one gets up lazy and with a mischievous heart."

Bukhari 21.243

Satan may also be responsible for the color of the wax in your ear.

Narrated 'Abdullah:

A person was mentioned before the Prophet (p.b.u.h) and he was told that he had kept on sleeping till morning and had not got up for the prayer.

The Prophet said, "Satan urinated in his ears."

Bukhari 21.245

Night of Qadr

The night of Qadr is a hit or miss sort of thing.

Narrated Abu Huraira:

Allah's Apostle said, "Whoever establishes the prayers on the night of Qadr out of sincere faith and hoping to attain Allah's rewards (not to show off) then all his past sins will be forgiven."

Bukhari 2.34

Narrated Ibn 'Umar:

Some men amongst the companions of the Prophet were shown in their dreams that the Night of Qadr was in the last seven Nights of Ramadan. Allah's Apostle said, "It seems that all your dreams agree that (the Night of Qadr) is in the last seven Nights, and whoever wants to search for it (i.e. the Night of Qadr) should search in the last seven (Nights of Ramadan)."

Bukhari 32.232

Why the Prophet may have been unable to be more accurate as to the *Night of Qadr.*

Narrated 'Ubada bin As-Samit:

Allah's Apostle went out to inform the people about the (date of the) night of decree (Al-Qadr) but there happened a quarrel between two Muslim men.

The Prophet said, "I came out to inform you about (the date of) the night of Al-Qadr, but as so and so and so and so quarrelled, its knowledge was taken away (I forgot it) and maybe it was better for you. Now look for it in the 7th, the 9th and the 5th (of the last 10 nights of the month of Ramadan)."

Bukhari 2.46

Why the night of Qadr is more propitious to getting your sins absolved than any other night during the month of Ramadan is not obvious.

Narrated Abu Huraira:

Allah's Apostle said: "Whoever establishes prayers during the nights of Ramadan faithfully out of sincere faith and hoping to attain Allah's rewards (not for showing off), all his past sins will be forgiven."

Bukhari 2.36

The Pulpit

At one point in time God's Messenger requested a pulpit. It was built out of tamarisk, a type of cedar, by the slave of a nameless woman.

Narrated Abu Hazim bin Dinar:

Some people went to Sahl bin Sad As-Sa'idi and told him that they had different opinions regarding the wood of the pulpit. They asked him about it and he said, "By Allah, I know of what wood the pulpit was made, and no doubt I saw it on thy very first day when Allah's Apostle I took his seat on it. Allah's Apostle sent for such and such an Ansari woman (and Sahl mentioned her name) and said to her, 'Order your slave-carpenter to prepare for me some pieces of wood (i.e. pulpit) on which I may sit at the time of addressing the people.' So she ordered her slave-carpenter and he made it from the tamarisk of the forest and brought it (to the woman). The woman sent that (pulpit) to Allah's Apostle who ordered it to be placed here. Then I saw Allah's Apostle praying on it and then bowed on it. Then he stepped back, got down and prostrated on the ground near the foot of the pulpit and again ascended the pulpit. After finishing the prayer he faced the people and said, 'I have done this so that you may follow me and learn the way I pray.'"

Bukhari 13.40

The new pulpit left a nearby palm stem, next to which the Prophet used to deliver his Friday sermon, in tears.

Narrated Jabir bin 'Abdullah:

The Prophet used to stand by a tree or a date-palm on Friday. Then an Ansari woman or man said. "O Allah's Apostle! Shall we make a pulpit for you?"

He replied, "If you wish." So they made a pulpit for him and when it was Friday, he proceeded towards the pulpit (for delivering the sermon). The date-palm cried like a child!

The Prophet descended (the pulpit) and embraced it while it continued moaning like a child being quietened (sic).

The Prophet said, "It was crying for (missing) what it used to hear of religious knowledge given near to it."

Bukhari 56.784

Narrated Anas bin Malik:

That he heard Jabir bin 'Abdullah saying, "The roof of the Mosque was built over trunks of date-palms working as pillars. When the Prophet delivered a sermon, he used to stand by one of those trunks till the pulpit was made for him, and he used it instead. Then we heard the trunk sending a sound like of a pregnant she-camel till the Prophet came to it, and put his hand over it, then it became quiet."

Bukhari 56.785

Nocturnal Devotions and Qunuts

Towards the end of his life, the Prophet spent many of his remaining nights on earth at prayer.

Narrated 'Aisha:

Allah's Apostle offered Witr prayer at different nights at various hours extending (from the 'Isha prayer, the night prayer, the last of the five compulsory prayers) up to the last hour of the night.

Bukhari 16.110

Narrated 'Aisha:

I did not see the Prophet reciting (the Quran) in the night prayer while sitting except when he became old; when he used to recite while sitting, and when thirty or forty verses remained from the Sura, he would get up and recite them and then bow.

Bukhari 21.249

As to how many rakats the Prophet did during the Night Prayer:

Narrated Masruq:

I asked Aisha about the night prayer of Allah's Apostle and she said, "It was seven, nine or eleven Rakat besides the two Rakat of the Fajr prayer (i.e. Sunna)."

Bukhari 21.240

Narrated 'Aisha:

The Prophet (p.b.u.h) used to offer thirteen Rakat of the night prayer and that included the Witr and two Rakat (Sunna) of the Fajr prayer.

Bukhari 21.241

His followers, in increasing numbers, like mindless automaton joined the Prophet during his nights spent worshipping Allah thinking that another round of compulsory prayers was in the offing. Not this time.

There would be no call to prayer to break the silence of the middle of the night.

Narrated Aisha:

Once in the middle of the night Allah's Apostle (p.b.u.h) went out and prayed in the mosque and some men prayed with him. The next morning the people spoke about it and so more people gathered and prayed with him (in the second night). They circulated the news in the morning, and so, on the third night the number of people increased greatly.

Allah's Apostle (p.b.u.h) came out and they prayed behind him. On the fourth night the mosque was overwhelmed by the people till it could not accommodate them.

Allah's Apostle came out only for the Fajr (the first of the obligatory prayers) prayer and when he finished the prayer, he faced the people and recited "Tashah-hud" (I testify that none has the right to be worshipped but Allah and that Muhammad is His Apostle), and then said, "Amma ba'du. Verily your presence (in the mosque at night) was not hidden from me, but I was afraid that this prayer (Prayer of Tahajjud i.e. the night prayer, a voluntary prayer) might be made compulsory and you might not be able to carry it out."

Bukhari 13.46

Some of the prayers the Prophet offered at night were Nawafil prayers i.e. prayers that are not compulsory. The type of prayer he offered when riding.

Narrated Ibn 'Umar:

The Prophet used to offer (Nawafil) prayers on his Rahila (mount) facing its direction by signals, but not the compulsory prayer. He also used to pray Witr on his (mount) Rahila.

Bukhari 16.114

During his nocturnal devotions God's Messenger may also have recited Qunuts.

Narrated Muhammad bin Sirin:

Anas was asked, "Did the Prophet recite Qunut (a prayer within a prayer, usually in the form a supplication, recited while standing) in the Fajr prayer?"

Anas replied in the affirmative.

He was further asked, "Did he recite Qunut before bowing?"

Anas replied, "He recited Qunut after bowing for some time (for one month)."

Bukhari 16.115

Narrated 'Asim:

I asked Anas bin Malik about the Qunut. Anas replied, "Definitely it was (recited)".

I asked, "Before bowing or after it?"

Anas replied, "Before bowing."

I added, "So and so has told me that you had informed him that it had been after bowing."

Anas said, "He told an untruth (i.e. "was mistaken," according to the Hijazi dialect). Allah's Apostle recited Qunut after bowing for a period of one month."

Anas added, "The Prophet sent about seventy men (who knew the Quran by heart) towards the pagans (of Najd) who were less than they in number and there was a peace treaty between them and Allah's Apostles (but the Pagans broke the treaty and killed the seventy men). So Allah's Apostle recited Qunut for a period of one month asking Allah to punish them."

Bukhari 16.116

An example of a Qunut:

Narrated Abu Huraira:

Whenever the Prophet (p.b.u.h) lifted his head from the bowing in the last Raka he used to say: "O Allah! Save 'Aiyash bin Abi Rabi'a. O Allah! Save Salama bin Hisham. O Allah! Save Walid bin Walid. O Allah! Save the weak faithful believers. O Allah! Be hard on the tribes of Mudar and send (famine) years on them like the famine years of (Prophet) Joseph ."

The Prophet further said, "Allah forgive the tribes of Ghifar and save the tribes of Aslam."

Abu Az-Zinad (a sub-narrator) said, "The Qunut used to be recited by the Prophet in the Fajr prayer."

Bukhari 17.120

The Prophet would sometimes ask members of his household, including his daughter Fatima and his son-in-law Ali, who was not impressed, to join him in his nocturnal devotions.

Narrated Um Salama:

One night the Prophet got up and said, "Subhan Allah! How many afflictions Allah has revealed tonight and how many treasures have been sent down (disclosed). Go and wake the sleeping lady occupants of these dwellings up (for prayers), perhaps a well-dressed in this world may be naked in the Hereafter."

Bukhari 21.226

Narrated 'Ali bin Abi Talib:

One night Allah's Apostle came to me and Fatima, the daughter of the Prophet and asked, "Won't you pray (at night)?"

I said, "O Allah's Apostle! Our souls are in the hands of Allah and if He wants us to get up He will make us get up."

When I said that, he left us without saying anything and I heard that he was hitting his thigh and saying, "But man is more quarrelsome than anything." (18:54)

Bukhari 21.227

Insomnia may not have been the cause for the Prophet's night time devotions.

Narrated Abu Huraira:

Allah's Apostle (p.b.u.h) said, "Our Lord, the Blessed, the Superior, comes every night down on the nearest Heaven to us when the last third of the night remains, saying: 'Is there anyone to invoke Me, so that I may respond to invocation? Is there anyone to ask Me, so that I may grant him his request? Is there anyone seeking My forgiveness, so that I may forgive him?'"

Bukhari 21.246

Satan, Devils and the Jinn

Remember the Urininator?

Narrated 'Abdullah:

It was mentioned before the Prophet that there was a man who slept the night till morning (after sunrise).

The Prophet said, "He is a man in whose ears (or ear) Satan had urinated."

Bukhari 54.492

If a donkey's braying wakes you up during the night and you feel a moist warmth in your ears, chances are Satan has paid you a visit.

Narrated Abu Huraira:

The Prophet said, "When you hear the crowing of cocks, ask for Allah's Blessings for (their crowing indicates that) they have seen an angel. And when you hear the braying of donkeys, seek Refuge with Allah from Satan for (their braying indicates) that they have seen a Satan."

Bukhari 54.522

Then again, Satan may have been keeping you company all night and you were not aware of it.

Narrated Abu Huraira:

The Prophet said, "If anyone of you rouses from sleep and performs the ablution, he should wash his nose by putting water in it and then blowing it out thrice, because Satan has stayed in the upper part of his nose all the night."

Bukhari 54.516

A single sneeze may contain over 100,000 germ-filled droplets travelling at up to 100 miles an hour. A sneeze in a large crowd can easily infect 150 people in 5 minutes; a yawn, on the other hand, is quite harmless, germ-wise. You would think a sneeze would be something that Satan would cause and that Allah would abhor.

Narrated Abu Huraira:

The Prophet said, "Allah likes sneezing and dislikes yawning, so if someone sneezes and then praises Allah, then it is obligatory on every Muslim who heard him, to say:

May Allah be merciful to you (Yar-hamuka-l-lah). But as regards yawning, it is from Satan, so one must try one's best to stop it, if one says 'Ha' when yawning, Satan will laugh at him."

Bukhari 73.242

At the risk of spoiling the mood, how to protect the child you might conceive from Satan:

Narrated Ibn 'Abbas:

The Prophet said, "If anyone of you, when having sexual relation with his wife, say: 'In the name of Allah. O Allah! Protect us from Satan and prevent Satan from approaching our offspring you are going to give us,' and if he begets a child (as a result of that relation) Satan will not harm it."

Bukhari 54.493

Protecting your unborn child from Satan by invoking Allah's protection will not stop Satan from laying two fingers on the infant, with one exception.

Narrated Abu Huraira:

The Prophet said, "When any human being is born. Satan touches him at both sides of the body with his two fingers, except Jesus, the son of Mary, whom Satan tried to touch but failed, for he touched the placenta-cover instead."

Bukhari 54.506

Believing that Satan is the cause of your anger, for some, may have been a sign of madness or insanity.

Narrated Sulaiman bin Surd:

While I was sitting in the company of the Prophet, two men abused each other and the face of one of them became red with anger, and his jugular veins swelled (i.e. he became furious).

On that the Prophet said, "I know a word, the saying of which will cause him to relax, if he does say it. If he says: 'I seek Refuge with Allah from Satan then all his anger will go away."

Somebody said to him, "The Prophet has said, 'Seek refuge with Allah from Satan.'"

The angry man said, "Am I mad?"

Bukhari 54.502

Narrated Sulaiman bin Surad:

A man from the companions of the Prophet said, "Two men abused each other in front of the Prophet and one of them became angry and his anger became so intense that his face became swollen and changed.

The Prophet said, "I know a word the saying of which will cause him to relax if he does say it."

Then a man went to him and informed him of the statement of the Prophet and said, "Seek refuge with Allah from Satan."

On that, angry man said, "Do you find anything wrong with me? Am I insane. Go away!"

Bukhari 73.74

The Prophet stopped to explain how pervasive Satan is when he was spotted with his eleventh wife out in the open, and suspected that two men who saw them might think they were not married.

Narrated Safiya bint Huyai:

The wife of the Prophet [said] that she went to Allah's Apostle while he was in Itikaf (staying in the mosque) during the last ten nights of the month of Ramadan. She spoke to him for an hour (a while) at night and then she got up to return home. The Prophet got up to accompany her, and when they reached the gate of the mosque opposite the dwelling place of Um Salama, the wife of the Prophet, two Ansari men passed by, and greeting Allah's Apostle, they quickly went ahead.

Allah's Apostle said to them, "Do not be in a hurry, she is Safiya, the daughter of Huyai."

They said, "Subhan Allah (Glorious is God)! O Allah's Apostle (how dare we suspect you)." That was a great thing for both of them.

The Prophet then said, "Satan runs in the body of Adam's son (i.e. man) as his blood circulates in it, and I was afraid that he (Satan) might insert an evil thought in your hearts."

Bukhari 73.238

Satan, an absolute liar who told the truth! Is it conceivable that the Prophet had heard of Epimenides of Crete who said "All Cretans are liars" and from whom we get the infamous Liar Paradox.

Narrated Abu Huraira:

Allah's Apostle deputed me to keep Sadaqat (al-Fitr) of

Ramadan. A comer came and started taking handfuls of the foodstuff (of the Sadaqa) (stealthily). I took hold of him and said, "By Allah, I will take you to Allah's Apostle."

He said, "I am needy and have many dependents, and I am in great need."

I released him, and in the morning Allah's Apostle asked me, "What did your prisoner do yesterday?"

I said, "O Allah's Apostle! The person complained of being needy and of having many dependents, so, I pitied him and let him go."

Allah's Apostle said, "Indeed, he told you a lie and he will be coming again."

I believed that he would show up again as Allah's Apostle had told me that he would return. So, I waited for him watchfully. When he (showed up and) started stealing handfuls of foodstuff, I caught hold of him again and said, "I will definitely take you to Allah's Apostle."

He said, "Leave me, for I am very needy and have many dependents. I promise I will not come back again."

I pitied him and let him go. In the morning Allah's Apostle asked me, "What did your prisoner do?"

I replied, "O Allah's Apostle! He complained of his great need and of too many dependents, so I took pity on him and set him free."

Allah's Apostle said, "Verily, he told you a lie and he will return."

I waited for him attentively for the third time, and when he (came and) started stealing handfuls of the foodstuff, I caught hold of him and said, "I will surely take you to Allah's Apostle as it is the third time you promise not to return, yet you break your promise and come."

He said, "(Forgive me and) I will teach you some words with which Allah will benefit you."

I asked, "What are they?"

He replied, "Whenever you go to bed, recite "Ayat al-Kursi" - 'Allahu la ilaha illa huwa-l-Haiy-ul Qaiyum' (*Allah — there is no God but He, the Living, the Self-Subsisting and All-Sustaining*) till you finish the whole verse. (If you do so), Allah will appoint a guard for you who will stay with you and no satan will come near you till morning."

So, I released him. In the morning, Allah's Apostle asked,

"What did your prisoner do yesterday?"

I replied, "He claimed that he would teach me some words by which Allah will benefit me, so I let him go."

Allah's Apostle asked, "What are they?"

I replied, "He said to me, 'Whenever you go to bed, recite Ayat al-Kursi from the beginning to the end - Allahu la ilaha illa huwa-lHaiy-ul-Qaiyum.' He further said to me, '(If you do so), Allah will appoint a guard for you who will stay with you, and no satan will come near you till morning.'"

The Prophet said, "He really spoke the truth, although he is an absolute liar. Do you know whom you were talking to, these three nights, O Abu Huraira?"

Abu Huraira said, "No."

He said, "It was Satan."

Bukhari 38.505

Satan is not afraid to ask the big question, but you should be!

Narrated Abu Huraira:

Allah's Apostle said, "Satan comes to one of you and says, 'Who created so-and-so?' till he says, 'Who has created your Lord?' So, when he inspires such a question, one should seek refuge with Allah and give up such thoughts."

Bukhari 54.496

Satan has been known to interfere in battles on the side of pagans.

Narrated 'Aisha:

On the day (of the battle) of Uhud when the pagans were defeated, Satan shouted, "O slaves of Allah! Beware of the forces at your back," and on that the Muslims of the front files fought with the Muslims of the back files (thinking they were pagans) ...

Bukhari 54.510

If you see a person talking to himself, it may not be that he is speaking into one of those hand-free cellphones, but seeking protection from Satan.

Narrated Abu Huraira:

Allah's Apostle said, "If one says one-hundred times in one day: 'None has the right to be worshipped but Allah, the Alone Who has no partners, to Him belongs Dominion and to Him belong all the Praises, and He has power over all things (i.e. Omnipotent)', one will get the reward of manumitting ten slaves, and one-hundred good deeds will be written in his account, and one-hundred bad deeds will be wiped off or erased from his account, and on that day he will be protected from the morning till evening from Satan, and nobody will be superior to him except one who has done more than that which he has done."

Bukhari 54.514

Earlier on, people were not afraid to express doubts as to who was the invisible friend with whom the Prophet met on a regular basis.

Narrated Jundub bin Sufyan:

Once Allah's Apostle became sick and could not offer his night prayer (Tahajjud) for two or three nights. Then a lady (the wife of Abu Lahab) came and said, "O Muhammad! I think that your Satan has forsaken you, for I have not seen him with you for two or three nights!"

On that Allah revealed: "By the forenoon, and by the night when it darkens, your Lord (O Muhammad) has neither forsaken you, nor hated you." (93:1-3)

Bukhari 60.475

Asking Allah to disgrace a drunk is only making Satan's job easier.

Narrated Abu Salama:

Abu Huraira said, "A man who drank wine was brought to the Prophet. The Prophet said, 'Beat him!'"

Abu Huraira added, "So some of us beat him with our hands, and some with their shoes, and some with their garments (by twisting it) like a lash, and then when we finished, someone said to him, 'May Allah disgrace you!' On that the Prophet said, 'Do not say so, for you are helping Satan to overpower him.'"

Bukhari 81.768

Is it Satan, a devil or a Jinn? Satan, like the modern vampire, does not enter a house unless he is invited, an open door is an invitation. What is less clear in the following is what is the devil doing here.

Narrated Jabir bin 'Abdullah:

Allah's Apostle said, "When night falls (or when it is evening), stop your children from going out, for the devils spread out at that time. But when an hour of the night has passed, release them and close the doors and mention Allah's Name, for Satan does not open a closed door. Tie the mouth of your water-skin and mention Allah's Name; cover your containers and utensils and mention Allah's Name. Cover them even by placing something across it, and extinguish your lamps."

Bukhari 69.527

Satan may behave like a devil, but a devil he is not, unless the preceding is not an oversight. The same cannot be said of the Jinn, a creature from the Koran from which we get the caricature of the genie. Could the Jinn and the devils be one of the same? Devils are always bad, Jinns are sometimes good; some even became Muslims after hearing the Prophet recite verses from the Koran. Would it make any sense to chain Muslims, even if they be Jinns, during the month of Ramadan?

Narrated Abu Huraira:

Allah's Apostle said, "When the month of Ramadan starts, the gates of the heaven are opened and the gates of Hell are closed and the devils are chained."

Bukhari 31.123

In the Koran, it is the Jinn who eavesdrop on Allah's conversions with His angels; in the hadiths, it is mostly the devils, unless they are one of the same.

Narrated 'Aisha:

I heard Allah's Apostle saying, "The angels descend the clouds and mention this or that matter decreed in the Heaven. The devils listen stealthily to such a matter, come down to inspire the soothsayers with it, and the latter would add to it one-hundred lies of their own."

Bukhari 54.432

In a hadith, the devil closest to the first level of Paradise who heard whatever was being discussed, passes it down to other devils who are stacked beneath him all the way to the surface of the earth. In a hadith about stacked devils, the Prophet is assisted by a fellow by the name of Sufyan who illustrates how it all works.

Narrated Abu Huraira:

The Prophet said, "When Allah has ordained some affair in the Heaven, the angels beat with their wings in obedience to His statement, which sounds like a chain dragged over a rock. Until when fear is banished from their (angels) hearts, the (angels) say, 'What was it that your Lord said?' They say, 'The truth; And He is the Most High, the Most Great.' (34:23) Then those who gain a hearing by stealing (i.e. devils) will hear Allah's Statement: 'Those who gain a hearing by stealing, (stand one over the other like this)'.

(Sufyan, to illustrate this, spread the fingers of his right hand and placed them one over the other horizontally.)

A flame may overtake and burn the eavesdropper before conveying the news to the one below him; or it may not overtake him till he has conveyed it to the one below him, who in his turn, conveys it to the one below him, and so on till they convey the news to the earth.

(Or probably Sufyan said, "Till the news reaches the earth.")

Then the news is inspired to a sorcerer who would add a hundred lies to it. His prophecy will prove true (as far as the heavenly news is concerned).

The people will say. 'Didn't he tell us that on such-and-such a day, such-and-such a thing will happen? We have found that [it] is true because of the true news heard from heaven.'"

Bukhari 60.223

So which is it? Who are the snitches who inform the soothsayers about Allah's private conversations with His angels? Is it the devils or the Jinn?

Narrated 'Aisha:

The Prophet said, "While the angels talk amidst the clouds about things that are going to happen on earth, the devils hear a word of what they say and pour it in the ears of a soothsayer as one pours something in a bottle, and they add one hundred lies to that (one word)."

Bukhari 54.508

Narrated 'Aisha:

Some people asked the Prophet regarding the soothsayers. He said, "They are nothing."

They said, "O Allah's Apostle! Some of their talks come true."

The Prophet said, "That word which happens to be true is what a Jinn snatches away by stealth (from the Heaven) and pours it in the ears of his friend (the foreteller) with a sound like the cackling of a hen. The soothsayers then mix with that word, one hundred lies."

Bukhari 93.650

Again, which is it? From whom should you hide your utensils?

Narrated Jabir bin 'Abdullah:

The Prophet said, "Cover your utensils and tie your water skins, and close your doors and keep your children close to you at night, as the Jinns spread out at such time and snatch things away. When you go to bed, put out your lights, for the mischief-doer (i.e. the rat) may drag away the wick of the candle and burn the dwellers of the house."

Ata said, "The devils." (instead of the Jinns).

Bukhari 54.533

Narrated Jabir:

The Prophet said, "When night falls, then keep your children close to you, for the devil spread out then. An hour later you can let them free; and close the gates of your house (at night), and mention Allah's Name thereupon, and cover your utensils, and mention Allah's Name thereupon, (and if you don't have something to cover your utensil) you may put across it something (e.g. a piece of wood etc.)."

Bukhari 54.500

The Prophet sought refuge from the devils and the evil eye for his grandsons in an age where devils were everywhere, and the evil eye a fact of life.

Narrated Abu Huraira:

The Prophet said, "The effect of an evil eye (*a malevolent look that many cultures believe able to cause injury or misfortune for the person at whom it is directed* ᵂⁱᵏⁱ) is a fact."

Bukhari 71.636

Narrated Ibn 'Abbas:

The Prophet used to seek Refuge with Allah for Al-Hasan and Al-Husain and say: "Your forefather (i.e. Abraham) used to seek Refuge with Allah for Ishmael and Isaac by reciting the following: 'O Allah! I seek Refuge with Your Perfect Words from every devil and from poisonous pests and from every evil, harmful, envious eye.'"

Bukhari 55.590

When he answered the call of nature in an enclosed space, it is from the Jinn that the Prophet sought refuge with Allah.

Narrated Anas bin Malik:

Whenever the Prophet went to the lavatory, he used to say: "Allahumma Inni a'udhu bika mina-lkhubthi Wal khaba'ith

(*O Allah, I seek refuge in you from the male female evil and the Jinn*)."

Bukhari 75.334

Is it possible that devils and Jinns would eat the same crud.

Narrated Abu Huraira:

That once he was in the, company of the Prophet carrying a water pot for his ablution and for cleaning his private parts. While he was following him carrying it (i.e. the pot), the Prophet said, "Who is this?"

He said, "I am Abu Huraira."

The Prophet said, "Bring me stones in order to clean my private parts, and do not bring any bones or animal dung."

Abu Huraira went on narrating: So I brought some stones, carrying them in the corner of my robe till I put them by his side and went away. When he finished, I walked with him and asked, "What about the bone and the animal dung?"

He said, "They are of the food of Jinns. The delegate of Jinns of (the city of) Nasibin came to me – and how nice those Jinns were – and asked me for the remains of the human food. I invoked Allah for them that they would never pass by a bone or animal dung but find food on them."

Bukhari 58.200

Most of us have a good idea about what devils, if they exist, look like. It is unfortunate that the Prophet did not tie up a Jinn when he had the chance, as recounted in hadith 55.634 in *Prayers - Satan and the Devils at Prayer Time*. It would have been interesting to compare their physiology with what we imagine devils look like.

Jinns, like man, will die and be resurrected on Judgement Day. Can the same be said of devils?

Narrated Ibn 'Abbas:

The Prophet used to say, "I seek refuge (with YOU) by Your 'Izzat, None has the right to be worshipped but You Who does not die while the Jinns and the human beings die."

Bukhari 93.480

Selling It!

Nowhere is Islamic law applied more selectively than in commercial transactions. To do as the Prophet demands would completely cripple the modern economy. Take money for instance:

Narrated Abu Al-Minhal:

I used to practice money exchange, and I asked Zaid bin 'Arqam about it, and he narrated what the Prophet said in the following: Abu Al-Minhal said, "I asked Al-Bara' bin 'Azib and Zaid bin Arqam about practicing money exchange. They replied, 'We were traders in the time of Allah's Apostle and I asked Allah's Apostle about money exchange. He replied, 'If it is from hand to hand, there is no harm in it; otherwise it is not permissible.'"

Bukhari 34.276

Some of what the Prophet had to say about buying and selling are benign, but these are the exception.

Narrated Abu Huraira:

I heard Allah's Apostle saying, 'The swearing (by the seller) may persuade the buyer to purchase the goods but that will be deprived of Allah's blessing."

Bukhari 34.300

Narrated Abdullah bin Umar:

A person came to the Prophet and told him that he was always betrayed in purchasing.

The Prophet told him to say at the time of buying, "No cheating."

Bukhari 34.328

God's Messenger would try to control every aspect of the selling and buying of goods, as he did with everything he came in contact with, often to the point of absurdity. There was no macro-economic thinking behind the lawmaker's decrees. From the Prophet's experience the type of bartering that occurred around him was what was done everywhere, it was a micro-economic perspective perfectly suited for the ultimate micro-manager. All that needed to be done was to modify trade and commercial practices from the time of ignorance, the world before Islam, to his and Allah's liking. In the process he made how people bought and sold stuff 1,400 years ago the equivalent of revealed truths therefore timeless and unchanging.

An example of how Allan and His Messenger's obsession with their followers not earning interest completely change the nature of barter, many would say for the worst, much worse if Islamic law was uniform in its application:

Narrated 'Umar bin Al-Khattab:

Allah's Apostle said, "The bartering of gold for silver is Riba, (usury), except if it is from hand to hand and equal in amount, and wheat grain for wheat grain is usury except if it is from hand to hand and equal in amount, and dates for dates is usury except if it is from hand to hand and equal in amount, and barley for barley is usury except if it is from hand to hand and equal in amount."

Bukhari 34.344

For a religion with global ambitions it is quite incredible how parochial its founder was in promulgating immutable laws. What is even more incredible is that his followers, Islamists in particular, would have us believe, by force and under threat of extermination if necessary, that these laws, the sayings and examples of a Dark Age trailblazer, if strictly applied will lead to a perfect world.

What if the world economy was subjected to Islamic economic laws? For one thing, futures markets would be a thing of the pass. It would also be impossible, without breaking the law, for individuals, companies, even government to negotiate large scales sales of staples such as rice, wheat, corn ... anything for that matter, on behalf of the producers.

Narrated Ibn Umar:

The Prophet said, "He who buys foodstuff should not sell it till he has received it."

Bukhari 34.343

Narrated Ibn 'Abbas:

The Prophet forbade the selling of foodstuff before receiving it. I consider that all types of sellings (sic) should be done similarly.

Bukhari 34.345

Narrated 'Abdullah bin 'Umar:

Allah's Apostle forbade the sale called 'Habal-al-Habala which was a kind of sale practiced in the pre-Islamic period of ignorance. One would pay the price of a she-camel which was not born yet ...

Bukhari 34.353

It would mean the end of food wholesalers. Say goodbye to the modern supermarket.

Narrated Tawus:

Ibn 'Abbas said, "Allah's Apostle said, 'Do not go to meet the caravans on the way (for buying their goods without letting them know the market price); a town dweller should not sell the goods of a desert dweller on behalf of the latter.'"

I asked Ibn 'Abbas, "What does he mean by not selling the goods of a desert dweller by a town dweller?"

He said, "He should not become his broker."

Bukhari 34.367

It would mean the end of electronic commerce e.g. internet and purchases made over the phone.

Narrated Haklm bin Hizam:

The Prophet said, "The buyer and the seller have the option of cancelling or confirming the deal unless they separate."

Bukhari 34.321

Why the Prophet would insist that food purchases made from a passing caravan could not be resold on the spot is a mystery to this twenty-first century consumer.

Narrated Nafi:

Ibn 'Umar told us that the people used to buy food from the caravans in the lifetime of the Prophet. The Prophet used to forbid them to sell it at the very place where they had purchased it (but they were to wait) till they carried it to the market where foodstuff was sold.

Ibn 'Umar said, "The Prophet also forbade the reselling of foodstuff by somebody who had bought it unless he had received it with exact full measure"

Bukhari 34.334

Nowhere is the micro-management obsession of the Prophet more evident than his insistence, at the that risk of a beating, that if you bought perishables without first insisting on them being measured i.e. weighted before your eyes, you had to take them home, where I assume, you had a scale of some sort, and confirm for yourself that the measure was accurate. What about modern pre-wrapped food which is weighed at the factory where it is packaged?

Narrated Ibn 'Umar:

I saw the people buy foodstuff randomly (i.e. blindly without measuring it) in the life-time of Allah's Apostle and they were punished (by beating), if they tried to sell it before carrying it to their own houses.

Bukhari 34.347

The merchant in the Messenger is everywhere evident in his obsessions with weights and measures.

Narrated Ibn 'Umar:

The Prophet forbade Muzabana; and Muzabana is the selling of fresh fruit (without measuring it) for something by measure on the basis that if that thing turns to be more than the fruit, the increase would be for the seller of the fruit, and if it turns to be less, that would be of his lot.

Narrated Ibn 'Umar from Zaid bin Thabit that the Prophet allowed the selling of the fruits on the trees after estimation (when they are ripe).

Bukhari 34.381

The Prophet's backyard was not so much a world of farmers as a world of traders and herders. God's Messenger did not even know how date growers went about their business until he left the desert trading hub of Mecca for the oasis city of Medina and was scandalized to discover that date-bearing palms were artificially pollinated and ordered the practice stopped. He re-instituted the practice the next year after date production plummeted, but insisted it be done when he wasn't around. Of course, this did not mean he could not regulate the sale of the fruits of date-palms not pollinated the old-fashion way.

Narrated Abdullah bin Umar:

Allah's Apostle said, "If someone sells pollinated date-palms, their fruits will be for the seller, unless the buyer stipulates the contrary."

Bukhari 50.877

This exposure to date production, his experience as a merchant and his access to the Creator's expert advice, meant God's Messenger was comfortable telling the growers and consumers when and how dates should be traded. Date being a staple of the Arab diet and a favorite of the Prophet, meant that the vast majority of hadiths about fruits and vegetable are about dates. A word you should get familiar with, which you will now frequently encounter is Sa. It is a unit of measurement described by Wiki as "The oldest accurate information about it is that of the qafiz of Hajjaj" which equaled one Sa' of the Prophet's (4.2125 Litres)

Narrated 'Aisha:

The family of Muhammad did not eat two meals on one day, but one of the two was of dates.

Bukhari 76.462

Narrated 'Abdullah bin 'Umar:

Allah's Apostle said, "Do not sell fruits of dates until they become free from all the dangers of being spoilt or blighted; and do not sell fresh dates for dry dates."

Narrated Salim and 'Abdullah from Zaid bin Habit "Later on Allah's Apostle permitted the selling of ripe fruits on trees for fresh dates or dried dates in Bai'-l-'Araya, and did not allow it for any other kind of sale."

Bukhari 34.389

Narrated Abu Huraira:

The Prophet allowed the sale of the dates of 'Araya provided they were about five Awsuq (singular: Wasaq which means sixty Sa's) or less (in amount).

Bukhari 34.395

Narrated Ibn 'Umar:

Allah's Apostle forbade Al-Muzabana, i.e. to sell ungathered (sic) dates of one's garden for measured dried dates or fresh ungathered grapes for measured dried grapes; or standing crops for measured quantity of foodstuff. He forbade all such bargains.

Bukhari 34.407

Narrated Abu Bakhtari At-Tai:

I asked Ibn 'Abbas about Salam for (the fruits of) date-palms. He replied "The Prophet forbade the sale of dates on the trees till they became fit for eating and could be weighed."

A man asked what to be weighed (as the dates were still on the trees). Another man sitting beside Ibn 'Abbas replied, "Till they are cut and stored."

Narrated Abu Al-Bakhtari: I heard Ibn Abbas (saying) that the Prophet forbade ... etc. as above.

Bukhari 35.450

Narrated Anas bin Malik:

Allah's Apostle forbade the sale of fruits till they are almost ripe. He was asked what is meant by 'are almost ripe.' He replied, "Till they become red."

Bukhari 34.403

Even in the trading of dates you had to be sure you were not circumventing Allah's prohibition against earning interest. Again the Prophet came to the rescue for those unclear on the concept.

Narrated Abu Said Al-Khudri and Abu Huraira:

Allah's Apostle appointed somebody as a governor of Khaibar. That governor brought to him an excellent kind of dates (from Khaibar).

The Prophet asked, "Are all the dates of Khaibar like this?"

He replied, "By Allah, no, O Allah's Apostle! But we barter one Sa of this (type of dates) for two Sas of dates of ours and two Sas of it for three of ours."

Allah's Apostle said, "Do not do so (as that is a kind of usury) but sell the mixed dates (of inferior quality) for money, and then buy good dates with that money."

Bukhari 34.405

Narrated Abu Said al-Khudri:

Once Bilal brought Barni (i.e. a kind of dates) to the Prophet and the Prophet asked him, "From where have you brought these?"

Bilal replied, "I had some inferior type of dates and exchanged two Sas of it for one Sa of Barni dates in order to give it to the Prophet to eat."

Thereupon the Prophet said, "Beware! Beware! This is definitely Riba (usury)! This is definitely Riba (Usury)! Don't do so, but if you want to buy (a superior kind of dates) sell the inferior dates for money and then buy the superior kind of dates with that money."

Bukhari 39.506

Narrated Jabir bin 'Abdullah:

The Prophet forbade the sales called Al-Mukhabara, Al-

Muhaqala and Al-Muzabana and the selling of fruits till they are free from blights. He forbade the selling of the fruits except for money, except the 'Araya.

Bukhari 40.567

For hadiths about other foodstuff you have to look to the hadiths about what the believers will eat in Paradise.

As mentioned earlier, the Prophet's world was not so much a world of farmers but a world of traders and herders until he immigrated at forty-something, with most of his followers, to the oasis city of Medina to escape his Meccan kin who now wanted to kill him for preaching what they considered a dangerous, intolerant, insulting religion.

The Prophet's knowledge of trade practices during the Dark Ages, in what we now call the Middle East, was undoubtedly unparalleled; His knowledge of animal husbandry, the science of breeding and caring for farm animals, while undoubtedly superior to that of farming, could not have been as comprehensive. What the Prophet knew about the care and feeding of domesticated animals, apart from the camels in the caravans he was part of, seems to have come from a short stint as a shepherd, which was, according to God's latest messenger, a rite of passage for all messengers of God.

Narrated Abu Huraira:

The Prophet said, "Allah did not send any prophet but shepherded sheep."

His companions asked him, "Did you do the same?"

The Prophet replied, "Yes, I used to shepherd the sheep of the people of Mecca for some Qirats."

Bukhari 36.463

We only have the Prophet's word that he worked for a short time as a shepherd in the nearly grassless inhospitable desert in which Mecca is situated. Then again if you can't trust God's Messenger to tell you the truth, who can you trust?

God's Messenger, as could be expected, considered himself an expert in animal husbandry and like dates, when and in what condition an animal could be sold or returned to the seller. And, like the focus on dates, the hadiths concerning the sale of livestock are very much about what grazed in the Prophet's neighbourhood and what sold at his local market. Note the use of dates in arriving at a fair exchange in the following hadiths about the sale and disposition of livestock.

Narrated Abu Huraira:

The Prophet said, "Don't keep camels and sheep unmilked (sic) for a long time, for whoever buys such an animal has the option to milk it and then either to keep it or return it to the owner along with one Sa of dates."

Some narrated from Ibn Sirin (that the Prophet had said), "One Sa of wheat, and he has the option for three days."

And some narrated from Ibn Sirin, "a Sa of dates," not mentioning the option for three days. But a Sa of dates is mentioned in most narrations.

Bukhari 34.358

Narrated 'Abdullah bin Mas'ud:

Whoever buys a sheep which has not been milked for a long time, has the option of returning it along with one Sa of dates; and the Prophet forbade going to meet the seller on the way (as he has no knowledge of the market price and he may sell his goods at a low price).

Bukhari 34.359

Narrated Abu Huraira:

Allah's Apostle said, "Do not go forward to meet the caravan (to buy from it on the way before it reaches the town). And do not urge buyers to cancel their purchases to sell them (your own goods) yourselves, and do not practice Najsh. A town dweller should not sell the goods for the desert dweller. Do not leave sheep unmilked for a long time, when they are on sale, and whoever buys such an animal has the option of returning it, after milking it, along with a Sa of dates or keeping it. it has been kept unmilked for a long period by the seller (to deceive others).

Bukhari 34.360

Transfer of ownership of a pregnant camel must await the birth of its offspring.

Narrated 'Abdullah:

The people used to sell camels on the basis of Habal-al-Habala. The Prophet forbade such sale. Nafi' explained Habalal-Habala by saying. "The camel is to be delivered to the buyer after the she-camel gives birth."

Bukhari 35.457

Rules for traders in precious metals:

Narrated Abu Bakra:

Allah's Apostle said, "Don't sell gold for gold unless equal in weight, nor silver for silver unless equal in weight, but you could sell gold for silver or silver for gold as you like."

Bukhari 34.383

Narrated Abu Said Al-Khudri:

Allah's Apostle said, "Do not sell gold for gold unless equivalent in weight, and do not sell less amount for greater amount or vice versa; and do not sell silver for silver unless equivalent in weight, and do not sell less amount for greater amount or vice versa and do not sell gold or silver that is not present at the moment of exchange for gold or silver that is present.

Bukhari 34.385

Real estate agents will not love the following:

Narrated Abu Huraira:

The Prophet forbade two kinds of dressing; (one of them) is to sit with one's legs drawn up while wrapped in one garment. (The other) is to lift that garment on one's shoulders. And also forbade two kinds of sale: Al-Limas *("a sale in which the deal is completed if the buyer touches a thing, without seeing or checking it properly")* and An-Nibadh *("a sale in which the deal is completed if the seller throws a thing towards the buyer giving him no opportunity to see, touch or check it")*.

Bukhari 34.355

The advantage of being the nearest neighbour if you covet your neighbour's home and he puts it up for sale:

Narrated 'Amr bin Ash-Sharid:

While I was standing with Sad bin Abi Waqqas, Al-Miswar bin Makhrama came and put his hand on my shoulder. Meanwhile Abu Rafi', the freed slave of the Prophet came and asked Sad to buy from him the (two) dwellings which were in his house. Sad said, "By Allah I will not buy them."

Al-Miswar said, "By Allah, you shall buy them."

Sad replied, "By Allah, I will not pay more than four thousand (Dirhams) by installments."

Abu Rafi' said, "I have been offered five hundred Dinars (for it) and had I not heard the Prophet saying, 'The neighbor has more right than anyone else because of his nearness', I would not give them to you for four-thousand (Dirhams) while I am offered five-hundred Dinars (one Dinar equals ten Dirhams) for them."

So, he sold it to Sad.

Bukhari 35.459

Another advantage of being a neighbour and your neighbour is in a gift giving mood but does not have enough gifts to go around:

Narrated Aisha:

I said, "O Allah's Apostle! I have two neighbors and would like to know to which of them I should give presents."

He replied, "To the one whose door is nearer to you."

Bukhari 35.460

Mixing it up!

Narrated Abu Huraira:

Allah's Apostle forbade the selling of things by a town dweller on behalf of a desert dweller; and similarly Najsh (to offer a high price for something you do not care for simply to deprive someone else of it) was forbidden. And one should not urge somebody to return the goods to the seller so as to sell him his own goods; nor should one demand the hand of a girl who has already been engaged to someone else; and a woman should not try to cause some other woman to be divorced in order to take her place.

Bukhari 34.350

Arranged marriages can provide a novel way of settling dispute, including one about mineral rights after a sale.

Narrated Abu Huraira:

Allah's Apostle said, "A man bought a piece of and from another man, and the buyer found an earthenware jar filled with gold in the land. The buyer said to the seller. 'Take your gold, as I have bought only the land from you, but I have not bought the gold from you.'

The (former) owner of the land said, 'I have sold you the land with everything in it.' So both of them took their case before a man who asked, 'Do you have children?'

One of them said, 'I have a boy.'

The other said, 'I have a girl.'

The man said, 'Marry the girl to the boy and spend the money on both of them and give the rest of it in charity.'"

Bukhari 56.678

You can probably buy and sell gold jewelry but wearing your

purchase may be out of the question unless it is some kind of gold broach in the form of an insect (remember Job) .

Narrated Abu Huraira:

The Prophet forbade the wearing of a gold ring.

Bukhari 72.754

Narrated 'Abdullah:

Allah's Apostle wore a gold or silver ring and placed its stone towards the palm of his hand. The people also started wearing gold rings like it, but when the Prophet saw them wearing such rings, he threw away that golden ring and then wore a silver ring.

Bukhari 72.755

Narrated Abu Huraira:

The Prophet said, "While Job was naked, taking a bath, a swarm of gold locusts fell on him and he started collecting them in his garment. His Lord called him, 'O Job! Have I not made you rich enough to need what you see? He said, 'Yes, O Lord! But I cannot dispense with your Blessing.'"

Bukhari 55.604

Wearing gold bracelets may also be inadvisable because of what transpired in a dream of the Prophet.

Narrated Abu Huraira:

Allah's Apostle said, "We (Muslims) are the last (to come) but (will be) the foremost (on the Day of Resurrection)."

Allah's Apostle further said, "While sleeping, I was given the treasures of the world and two golden bangles were put in my hands, but I felt much annoyed, and those two bangles distressed me very much, but I was inspired that I should blow them off, so I blew them and they flew away. Then I interpreted that those two bangles were the liars between whom I was (i.e., the one of San'a' and the one of Yamama)."

Bukhari 87.160

More items for which there is limited trade among believers.

Narrated Hudhaifa:

The Prophet forbade us to drink out of gold and silver vessels, or eat in it, and also forbade the wearing of silk and Dibaj (silk cloth) or sitting on it.

Bukhari 72.728

Silk and Effeminates

In the first hadith a wearer of silk in the here-and-now will not be allowed to wear silk in the Hereafter. In the second, it would appear a wearer of silk in the here-and-now will be denied access to Paradise altogether. This is the type of stuff a religious scholar could probably sort out.

Narrated Anas bin Malik:

The Prophet said, "Whoever wears silk in this world shall not wear it in the Hereafter."

Bukhari B 72.723

Narrated 'Umar bin Al-Khattab:

Allah's Apostle said, "None wears silk in this world, but he who will have no share in the Hereafter."

Bukhari 72.726

I am sure a religious scholar somewhere has offered a definitive opinion as to how much silk a seamstress can use as decoration on a garment and remain within the Law, but I am sorry, I can't be bothered to look him up, and neither should you.

Narrated Aba 'Uthman An-Nahdi:

While we were with 'Utba bin Farqad at Adharbijan, there came 'Umar's letter indicating that Allah's Apostle had forbidden the use of silk except this much, then he pointed with his index and middle fingers. To our knowledge, by that he meant embroidery.

Bukhari 72.718

The Prophet made an exception for men with skin problems, and for that small mercy believing men with a skin irritant should be thankful.

Narrated Anas:

The Prophet allowed 'Abdur-Rahman bin 'Auf and Az-Zubair to wear silken shirts because they had a skin disease causing itching.

Bukhari 52.168

The Prophet did not seem to have any objections to women wearing silk, even in pieces. Of course, the following hadith begs the question as to why God's Messenger gave a silk suit to his son-in-law if he did not want him to wear it.

Narrated 'Ali:

> The Prophet gave me a silk suit and I wore it, but when I noticed anger on his face, I cut it and distributed it among my women-folk.

Bukhari 63.279

More fodder for religious scholars. In the following hadith it is not clear if it was silk-wearing, fornicating, boozing, music loving followers of the Prophet whom Allah buried in a landslide and transformed the survivors into monkeys and pigs

Narrated Abu 'Amir or Abu Malik Al-Ash'ari:

> That he heard the Prophet saying, "From among my followers there will be some people who will consider illegal sexual intercourse, the wearing of silk, the drinking of alcoholic drinks and the use of musical instruments, as lawful. And there will be some people who will stay near the side of a mountain and in the evening their shepherd will come to them with their sheep and ask them for something, but they will say to him, 'Return to us tomorrow.' Allah will destroy them during the night and will let the mountain fall on them, and He will transform the rest of them into monkeys and pigs and they will remain so till the Day of Resurrection."

Bukhari 69.494

The Prophet's newfound aversion to silk was very much another of those spur of the moment thing. There was not even a pause during his prayers to indicate, as often happened, that Allah was interrupting his Messenger's devotion with an urgent message from Paradise.

Narrated 'Uqba bin 'Amir:

> A silken Farruj was presented to Allah's Apostle and he put it on and offered the prayer in it. When he finished the prayer, he took it off violently as if he disliked it and said, "This (garment) does not befit those who fear Allah!"

Bukhari 72.693

The people hoped that the Prophet had changed his mind when someone else presented him with a silk garment; but not a chance, and I don't think it had anything do with the religion of the gift giver.

Narrated Anas:

A Jubba (i.e. cloak) made of thick silken cloth was presented to the Prophet. The Prophet used to forbid people to wear silk. So, the people were pleased to see it.

The Prophet said, "By Him in Whose Hands Muhammad's soul is, the handkerchiefs of Sad bin Mu'adh (*the mortally wounded Sad was asked by the Prophet to decide the fate of the Jews of Medina after the Battle of the Ditch*) in Paradise are better than this."

Anas added, "The present was sent to the Prophet by Ukaidir (a Christian) from Dauma."

Bukhari 47.785

Is it possible that the soft mellifluous texture of the garment made him uncomfortable, that it was the type of attire that effeminate men might wear?

Narrated Um Salama:

The Prophet came to me while there was an effeminate man sitting with me, and I heard him (i.e. the effeminate man) saying to 'Abdullah bin Abi Umaiya, "O 'Abdullah! See if Allah should make you conquer Ta'if tomorrow, then take the daughter of Ghailan (in marriage) as (she is so beautiful and fat that) she shows four folds of flesh when facing you, and eight when she turns her back."

The Prophet then said, "These (effeminate men) should never enter upon you (O women!)."

Ibn Juraij said, "That effeminate man was called Hit."

Bukhari 59.613

The Prophet's example, like everything God's Messenger said and did, was not lost on those who would lead the believers after his passing.

Narrated Ibn 'Abbas:

The Prophet cursed the effeminate men and those women who assume the similitude (manners) of men. He also said, "Turn them out of your houses."

He turned such-and-such person out, and 'Umar also turned out such-and-such person.

Bukhari 82.820

Silk invites touching!

Narrated Al-Bara:

The Prophet was given a silk garment as a gift and we started touching it with our hands and admiring it. On that the Prophet said, "Do you wonder at this?"

We said, "Yes."

He said, "The handkerchiefs of Sad bin Mu'adh in Paradise are better than this "

Bukhari 72.727

Anyone who has slept between silk sheets, or cuddled with a woman in a silk negligee will understand the senses that are often awakened, and maybe that is why the prudish Prophet that was God's Messenger made silk cushions for riders halal.

Narrated Al-Bara' bin 'Azib:

The Prophet ordered us to do seven (things) and forbade us from seven. He ordered us to visit the patients, to follow the funeral procession, to reply to the sneezer (i.e., say to him, 'Yarhamuka-l-lah (May Allah bestow His Mercy upon you), if he says 'Al-hamdulillah' (Praise be to Allah), to help others to fulfill their oaths, to help the oppressed, to greet (whomever one should meet), and to accept the invitation (to a wedding banquet).

He forbade us to wear golden rings, to use silver utensils, to use Mayathir (cushions of silk stuffed with cotton and placed under the rider on the saddle), the Qasiyya (linen clothes containing silk brought from an Egyptian town), the Istibraq (thick silk) and the Dibaj (another kind of silk).

Bukhari 62.104

You name the garment, or the cushion, if it's made of silk, it is forbidden; for men that is a certainty.

Narrated Al-Bara:

The Prophet ordered us to observe seven things: To visit the sick; follow funeral processions; say 'May Allah bestow His Mercy on you', to the sneezer if he says, 'Praise be to Allah!'; He forbade us to wear silk, Dibaj, Qassiy and Istibarq (various kinds of silken clothes); or to use red Mayathir (silk-cushions).

Bukhari 72.740

Slavery

The Prophet's pulpit was built by a slave.

Narrated Sahl:

Allah's Apostle sent someone to a woman telling her to "Order her slave, carpenter, to prepare a wooden pulpit for him to sit on."

Bukhari 8.439

Narrated Jabir:

A woman said, "O Allah's Apostle! Shall I get something constructed for you to sit on as I have a slave who is a carpenter?"

He replied, "Yes, if you like."

So she had that pulpit constructed.

Bukhari 8.440

The punishment for having intercourse while fasting is to free a slave if you can afford to do so.

Narrated Abu Huraira:

While we were sitting with the Prophet a man came and said, "O Allah's Apostle! I have been ruined."

Allah's Apostle asked what was the matter with him.

He replied "I had sexual intercourse with my wife while I was fasting."

Allah's Apostle asked him, "Can you afford to manumit a slave?"

He replied in the negative.

Allah's Apostle asked him, "Can you fast for two successive months?"

He replied in the negative.

The Prophet asked him, "Can you afford to feed sixty poor persons?"

He replied in the negative.

The Prophet kept silent and while we were in that state, a big basket full of dates was brought to the Prophet.

He asked, "Where is the questioner?"

He replied, "I (am here)."

The Prophet said (to him), "Take this (basket of dates) and give it in charity."

The man said, "Should I give it to a person poorer than I? By Allah; there is no family between its (i.e. Medina's) two mountains who are poorer than I."

The Prophet smiled till his pre-molar teeth became visible and then said, "Feed your family with it."

Bukhari 31.157

To whom belongs the son a now deceased has fathered with a slave-girl:

Narrated Aisha:

Abu bin Zam'a and Sad bin Abi Waqqas carried the case of their claim of the (ownership) of the son of a slave-girl of Zam'a before the Prophet.

Sad said, "O Allah's Apostle! My brother, before his death, told me that when I would return (to Mecca), I should search for the son of the slave-girl of Zam'a and take him into my custody as he was his son."

Abu bin Zam'a said, "the boy is my brother and the son of the slave-girl of my father, and was born on my father's bed."

The Prophet noticed a resemblance between Utba and the boy but he said, "O 'Abu bin Zam'a! You will get this boy, as the son goes to the owner of the bed. You, Sauda (one of the Prophet's wives), screen yourself from the boy."

Bukhari 41.603

A man once broke his slave's cupping cups and explained to his son that he had done so because of a list of what God's Messenger forbade, a list which did not include cupping, and rightly so, for the Prophet was very much into cupping as curative medicine.

Narrated 'Aun bin Abu Juhaifa:

My father bought a slave who practiced the profession of cupping. (My father broke the slave's instruments of cupping). I asked my father why he had done so.

He replied, "The Prophet forbade the acceptance of the price of a dog or blood, and also forbade the profession of tattooing, getting tattooed and receiving or giving Riba, (usury), and cursed the picture-makers."

Bukhari 34.299

You paid whoever "cupped" you as you would a physician.

Narrated Ibn 'Abbas:

Once the Prophet got his blood out (medically) and paid that person who had done it. If it had been illegal, the Prophet would not have paid him.

Bukhari 34.316

The cupping was often done by a slave, a slave who paid taxes.

Narrated Anas bin Malik:

Abu Taiba cupped Allah's Apostle so he ordered that he be paid one Sa of dates and ordered his masters to reduce his tax (as he was a slave and had to pay a tax to them).

Bukhari 34.315

As the Prophet's reputation for knowing about the right and the wrong way to do everything grew, many quit thinking for themselves altogether and asked God's Messenger to rule on what could be considered silly, trivial matters such as, "is a sheep killed by a slave-girl lawful to eat?"

Narrated Ibn Ka'b bin Malik from his father:

We had some sheep which used to graze at Sala. One of our slave-girls saw a sheep dying and she broke a stone and slaughtered the sheep with it. My father said to the people, "Don't eat it till I ask the Prophet about it (or till I send somebody to ask the Prophet)."

So, he asked or sent somebody to ask the Prophet, and the Prophet permitted him to eat it.

Ubaidullah (a sub-narrator) said, "I admire that girl, for though she was a slave-girl, she dared to slaughter the sheep."

Bukhari 38.500

Freeing the "it" of two owners who can afford it:

Narrated Ibn 'Umar:

The Prophet said, "Whoever manumits a slave owned by two masters, should manumit him completely (not partially) if he is rich after having its price evaluated."

Bukhari 46.697

If only one owner remits his share of a jointly owned slave, the slave remains a slave.

Narrated Nafi:

Ibn 'Umar said, "Allah's Apostle said, 'If one manumits his share of a jointly possessed slave, and can afford the price of the other shares according to the adequate price of the slave, the slave will be completely manumitted; otherwise he will be partially manumitted.'"

Bukhari 44.671

When you read a hadith like the following about pre-Islamic slave-owners freeing their human chattel without reservations or cost considerations as a tribute to their god, you have to wonder who are the ignorant ones.

Narrated 'Abdullah:

The Muslims did not free slaves as Sa'iba (set free in the names of their gods), but the People of the pre-lslamic Period of Ignorance used to do so.

Bukhari 80.745

An incentive to be a good and obedient indentured servant:

Narrated Ibn 'Umar:

Allah's Apostle said, "If a slave is honest and faithful to his master and worships his Lord (Allah) in a perfect manner, he will get a double reward."

Bukhari 46.722

A married woman, under Islamic law, had less freedom than an indentured servant e.g. permanent seclusion in the home of her husband, therefore, marrying your slave-girl was not necessarily doing her any favours.

Narrated Abu Burda's father:

Allah's Apostle said "Three persons will have a double reward:

1. A Person from the people of the scriptures who believed in his prophet (Jesus or Moses) and then believed in the

Prophet Muhammad (i .e. has embraced Islam).

2. A slave who discharges his duties to Allah and his master.

3. A master of a woman-slave who teaches her good manners and educates her in the best possible way (the religion) and manumits her and then marries her."

Bukhari 3.97

That persistent illegal intercourse bugaboo of Allah and His Messenger rears its ugly head again. The punishment for a slave-girl who committed illegal intercourse – the only type of intercourse she could engage in – was a severe whipping ending perhaps with her being put back on the auction block. You could consider this another advantage of being a slave-girl over a married woman who would have been stoned to death for the same offence.

Narrated Abu Huraira and Zaid bin Khalid:

The Prophet said, "If a slave-girl (Ama) commits illegal sexual intercourse, scourge her; if she does it again, scourge her again; if she repeats it, scourge her again."

The narrator added that on the third or the fourth offence, the Prophet said, "Sell her even for a hair rope."

Bukhari 46.731

Female slaves made handy, cheap wet nurses.

Narrated Uqba bin Al-Harith:

That he had married Um Yahya bint Abu Ihab. He said. "A black slave-lady came and said, 'I suckled you both.' I then mentioned that to the Prophet who turned his face aside."

Uqba further said, "I went to the other side and told the Prophet about it."

He said, "How can you (keep her as your wife) when the lady has said that she suckled both of you (i.e. you and your wife?)"

So, the Prophet ordered him to divorce her.

Bukhari 48.827

Eclipses were good omen for some slaves.

Narrated Asma' bint Abu Bakr:

The Prophet ordered us to free slaves at the time of solar eclipses.

Bukhari 46.695

Narrated Asma' bint Abu Bakr:

We were ordered to free slaves at the time of lunar eclipses.

Bukhari 46.696

For a slave, the chance of obtaining his or her freedom increased substantially if they were related to a dead Prophet, in this instance Ishmael, the son of Abraham and Hagar, the father of the Arabs.

Narrated Abu Huraira:

I have loved the people of the tribe of Bani Tamim ever since I heard, three things, Allah's Apostle said about them. I heard him saying, these people (of the tribe of Bani Tamim) would stand firm against Ad-Dajjal (*the false messiah*).

When the Sadaqat (gifts of charity) from that tribe came, Allah's Apostle said, "These are the Sadaqat (i.e. charitable gifts) of our folk."

Aisha had a slave-girl from that tribe, and the Prophet said to Aisha, "Manumit her as she is a descendant of Ishmael (the Prophet)."

Bukhari 46.719

A slave for a slave:

Narrated Ibn Abbas:

The law of Qisas (i.e. equality in punishment) was prescribed for the children of Israel, but the Diya (i.e. blood money was not ordained for them).

So Allah said to this Nation (i.e. Muslims): "O you who believe! The law of Al-Qisas (i.e. equality in punishment) is prescribed for you in cases of murder: The free for the free, the slave for the slave, and the female for the female. But if the relatives (or one of them) of the killed (person) forgive their brother (i.e. the killers something of Qisas (i.e. not to kill the killer by accepting blood money in the case of intentional murder) then the relatives (of the killed person) should demand blood-money in a reasonable manner and the killer must pay with handsome gratitude. This is an alleviation and a Mercy from your Lord, (in comparison to what was prescribed for the nations before you).

So after this, whoever transgresses the limits (i.e. to kill the killer after taking the blood-money) shall have a painful torment." (2:178)

Bukhari 60.25

Slaves as payment for causing a miscarriage:

Narrated Abu Huraira:

Two ladies (had a fight) and one of them hit the other with a stone on the abdomen and caused her to abort. The Prophet judged that the victim be given either a slave or a female slave (as blood-money).

Narrated Ibn Shihab: Said bin Al-Musayyab said, "Allah's Apostle judged that in case of child killed in the womb of its mother, the offender should give the mother a slave or a female slave in recompense. The offender said, 'How can I be fined for killing one who neither ate nor drank, neither spoke nor cried: a case like that should be denied' On that Allah's Apostle said 'He is one of the brothers of the foretellers.'"

Bukhari 71.655

Slaves belonging to a Muslim are tax-exempt.

Narrated Abu Huraira:

Allah's Apostle said, "There is no Zakat either on a horse or a slave belonging to a Muslim"

Bukhari 24.542

Foretellers (or soothsayers) often challenged the Prophet's predictions and his rulings. This did not endear them to God's Messenger. But I digress. A slave as precursor to Judgement Day (surely he is dead, so what happened?).

Narrated Anas:

A Bedouin came to the Prophet and said, "O Allah's Apostle! When will The Hour be established?"

The Prophet said, "Wailaka (Woe to you), What have you prepared for it?"

The Bedouin said, "I have not prepared anything for it, except that I love Allah and His Apostle."

The Prophet said, "You will be with those whom you love."

We (the companions of the Prophet) said, "And will we too be so?"

The Prophet said, "Yes."

So we became very glad on that day. In the meantime, a slave of Al-Mughira passed by, and he was of the same age as I was. The Prophet said. "If this (slave) should live long, he will not reach the geriatric old age, but the Hour will be established."

Bukhari 73.188

The following probably applies to both a free believer and a believing slave:

Narrated Anas bin Malik:

Allah's Apostle said, "Allah is more pleased with the repentance of His slave than anyone of you is pleased with finding his camel which he had lost in the desert."

Bukhari 75.321

The Prophet was very much in favour of emancipating slaves who had submitted to the Will of Allah i.e. become Muslims. One of the more persuasive incentives to do so:

Narrated Abu Huraira:

The Prophet said, "If somebody manumits a Muslim slave, Allah will save from the Fire every part of his body for freeing the corresponding parts of the slave's body, even his private parts will be saved from the Fire) because of freeing the slave's private parts."

Bukhari 79.706

What if a slave is your ruler (the ruling slave would have to be a Muslim) and his "head looks like a raisin"?

Narrated Anas bin Malik:

Allah's Apostle said, "You should listen to and obey, your ruler even if he was an Ethiopian (black) slave whose head looks like a raisin."

Bukhari 88.256

The Prophet rebuked one of his wives for freeing a slave-girl instead of giving her to an uncle.

Narrated Kurib:

The freed slave of Ibn 'Abbas, that Maimuna bint Al-Harith told him that she manumitted (freed) a slave-girl without taking the permission of the Prophet. On the day when it was her turn to be with the Prophet, she said, "Do you know, O Allah's Apostle, that I have manumitted my slave-girl?"

He said, "Have you really?"

She replied in the affirmative.

He said, "You would have got more reward if you had given her (i.e. the slave-girl) to one of your maternal uncles."

Bukhari 47.765

The Prophet helped a man in need of money by selling his slave for him.

Narrated Jabir bin Abdullah:

A man decided that a slave of his would be manumitted after his death and later on he was in need of money, so the Prophet took the slave and said, "Who will buy this slave from me?"

Nu'aim bin 'Abdullah bought him for such and such price and the Prophet gave him the slave.

Bukhari 34.351

The Prophet cancelled the freeing of a slave (perhaps the slave in the preceding hadith) and sold it for its former owner who had no other chattel.

Narrated Jabir:

A man manumitted a slave and he had no other property than that, so the Prophet cancelled the manumission (and sold the slave for him).

No'aim bin Al-Nahham bought the slave from him.

Bukhari 41.598

The Prophet cancelled a dying man's wish that six of his slaves be freed, manumitting only two and keeping the other four for himself or for someone else.

'Imran b. Husain reported that a person who had no other property emancipated six slaves of his at the time of his death. Allah's Messenger (may peace be upon him) called for them and divided them into three sections, cast lots amongst them, and set two free and kept four in slavery; and he (the Holy Prophet) spoke severely of him.

Imam Muslim 15.4112

Another hadith about the Prophet ignoring the wish of a dying man that his slave be freed after his passing.

Narrated Jabir bin 'Abdullah:

A man amongst us declared that his slave would be freed

after his death. The Prophet called for that slave and sold him. The slave died the same year.

Bukhari 46.711

The Prophet would not part with his slaves even to help out the daughter who gave him two grandsons.

Narrated 'Ali:

Fatima complained of what she suffered from the hand mill and from grinding, when she got the news that some slave girls of the booty had been brought to Allah's Apostle. She went to him to ask for a maid-servant, but she could not find him, and told 'Aisha of her need. When the Prophet came, Aisha informed him of that.

The Prophet came to our house when we had gone to our beds. (On seeing the Prophet) we were going to get up, but he said, 'Keep at your places,'

I felt the coolness of the Prophet's feet on my chest. Then he said, "Shall I tell you a thing which is better than what you asked me for? When you go to your beds, say: 'Allahu Akbar (i.e. Allah is Greater)' for 34 times, and 'Alhamdu Lillah (i.e. all the praises are for Allah)' for 33 times, and Subhan Allah (i.e. Glorified be Allah) for 33 times. This is better for you than what you have requested."

Bukhari 53.344

A next to last hadith about what the Prophet had to say about slavery, and it is somewhat of a confounding one:

Narrated Anas bin Malik:

The Prophet said, "The freed slave belongs to the people who have freed him."

Bukhari 80.753

The Prophet's son-in-law, Ali, may have the beginning of an explanation, that if a freed slave wants to return to his former status as a slave, he must return to his former masters. Read to the end of the following hadith for Ali's take on what his father-in-law said about a freed slave belonging the those who freed him.

Narrated Ibrahim At Tamii's father:

Ali addressed us while he was standing on a brick pulpit and carrying a sword from which was hanging a scroll He said "By Allah, we have no book to read except Allah's Book and whatever is on this scroll."

And then he unrolled it, and behold, in it was written what

sort of camels were to be given as blood money, and there was also written in it: "Medina is a sanctuary from 'Air (mountain) to such and such place so whoever innovates in it an heresy or commits a sin therein, he will incur the curse of Allah, the angles, and all the people and Allah will not accept his compulsory or optional good deeds."

There was also written in it: "The asylum (pledge of protection) granted by any Muslims is one and the same, (even a Muslim of the lowest status is to be secured and respected by all the other Muslims, and whoever betrays a Muslim in this respect (by violating the pledge) will incur the curse of Allah, the angels, and all the people, and Allah will not accept his compulsory or optional good deeds."

There was also written in it: "Whoever (freed slave) befriends (takes as masters) other than his real masters (manumitters sic) without their permission will incur the curse of Allah, the angels, and all the people, and Allah will not accept his compulsory or optional good deeds."

Bukhari 92.403

Stoning

Narrated 'Abdullah:

I or somebody, asked Allah's Apostle "Which is the biggest sin in the Sight of Allah?"

He said, "That you set up a rival (in worship) to Allah though He Alone created you."

I asked, "What is next?"

He said, "Then, that you kill your son, being afraid that he may share your meals with you."

I asked, "What is next?"

He said, "That you commit illegal sexual intercourse with the wife of your neighbor."

Then the following Verse was revealed to confirm the statement of Allah's Apostle: "Those who invoke not with Allah, any other god, nor kill life as Allah has forbidden except for just cause, nor commit illegal sexual intercourse." (25:68)

Bukhari 60.284

The Prophet said that having illegal intercourse is the third worst sin you can commit. From a woman's point of view it may be the first. As to the first two, you can ask forgiveness from Allah, and do it right and all is forgiven; but a woman cannot expect any mercy from the All Merciful, All Compassionate for having illegal sex.

Alice: Adultery is not a sin against Allah or His Messenger, so why is an adulteress not deserving of Allah's Mercy?

Imam: Because there is no way for a woman to make amends for having had sex with someone other than her husband. How would you undo that? How could she undo the dishonour that she has brought on herself, her family and her husband? It is not enough that the adulteress will roast in Hell for eternity, but steps must be taken in the here-and-now to eradicate the reminder of this dishonour and to discourage such destructive behavior.

Alice: Such as stoning the adulteress to death.

From the one act play *Alice visits a Mosque to learn about Judgement Day*, Boreal Books, 2013

It is definitely not a laughing matter:

> [The Prophet] said, "O community of Muhammad! By Allah, there is no-one more jealous than Allah of a male or female slave of his who commits adultery. O community of Muhammad! By Allah, if you knew what I knew, you would laugh little and weep much."
>
> *Malik's Muwatta 12.12.1.1*

God's Messenger acquired the unlikely moniker *Prophet of Mercy* after the fall of Mecca when he publically spared the lives of some of his opponents while quietly having those with no protectors assassinated e.g. poets and apostates. Other vulnerable human beings for whom the Prophet of Mercy had no compassion were women and girls who committed *illegal intercourse*, even when the less than self-evident crime resulted in a pregnancy. One of the more wretched decisions of the Prophet of Mercy:

> Malik related to me from Yaqub ibn Zayd ibn Talha from his father Zayd ibn Talha that Abdullah ibn Abi Mulayka informed him that a woman came to the Messenger of Allah, may Allah bless him and grant him peace, and informed him that she had committed adultery and was pregnant.
>
> The Messenger of Allah, may Allah bless him and grant him peace, said to her, "Go away until you give birth."
>
> When she had given birth, she came to him. The Messenger of Allah, may Allah bless him and grant him peace, said to her, "Go away until you have suckled and weaned the baby."
>
> When she had weaned the baby, she came to him. He said, "Go and entrust the baby to someone."
>
> She entrusted the baby to someone and then came to him. He gave the order and she was stoned.
>
> *Malik's Muwatta 41.41.1.5*

The preceding action of God's Messenger is also occasionally given as proof by Islamic scholars that the man believers consider the embodiment of the perfect human being, whose every action must be emulated as closely as possible, cared for the welfare of children because he did not have their mothers horribly put to death until they no longer needed her breast milk. In another hadith about a defenceless woman being put to death on orders from God's Messenger, the Prophet of Mercy simply sent a trusted assassin to enquire from a woman if she had committed adultery and if she answered in the affirmative, to stone her.

Narrated Zaid bin Khalid and Abu Huraira:

The Prophet said, "O Unais! Go to the wife of this (man) and if she confesses (that she has committed illegal sexual intercourse), then stone her to death."

Bukhari 38.508

A more complete account of why this unfortunate woman had to die.

Narrated Abu Huraira and Zaid bin Khalid Al-Juhani:

A bedouin came to Allah's Apostle and said, "O Allah's apostle! I ask you by Allah to judge my case according to Allah's Laws."

His opponent, who was more learned than he, said, "Yes, judge between us according to Allah's Laws, and allow me to speak."

Allah's Apostle said, "Speak."

He (i .e. the bedouin or the other man) said, "My son was working as a laborer for this (man) and he committed illegal sexual intercourse with his wife. The people told me that it was obligatory that my son should be stoned to death, so in lieu of that I ransomed my son by paying one hundred sheep and a slave girl. Then I asked the religious scholars about it, and they informed me that my son must be lashed one hundred lashes, and be exiled for one year, and the wife of this (man) must be stoned to death."

Allah's Apostle said, "By Him in Whose Hands my soul is, I will judge between you according to Allah's Laws. The slave-girl and the sheep are to be returned to you, your son is to receive a hundred lashes and be exiled for one year. You, Unais, go to the wife of this (man) and if she confesses her guilt, stone her to death."

Unais went to that woman next morning and she confessed. Allah's Apostle ordered that she be stoned to death.

Bukhari 50.885

I doubt very much if the person appearing before him had been a female, that God's Messenger would have encouraged her, as he does a man in the following hadith, to confess to a lesser crime.

Narrated Abu Huraira:

A man from Bani Aslam came to Allah's Apostle while he was in the mosque and called (the Prophet) saying, "O

Allah's Apostle! I have committed illegal sexual intercourse."

On that the Prophet turned his face from him to the other side, whereupon the man moved to the side towards which the Prophet had turned his face, and said, "O Allah's Apostle! I have committed illegal sexual intercourse."

The Prophet turned his face (from him) to the other side whereupon the man moved to the side towards which the Prophet had turned his face, and repeated his statement.

The Prophet turned his face (from him) to the other side again. The man moved again (and repeated his statement) for the fourth time.

So when the man had given witness four times against himself, the Prophet called him and said, "Are you insane?"

He replied, "No."

The Prophet then said (to his companions), "Go and stone him to death."

The man was a married one. Jabir bin 'Abdullah Al-Ansari said: I was one of those who stoned him. We stoned him at the Musalla (the praying area outside a mosque) in Medina. When the stones hit him with their sharp edges, he fled, but we caught him at Al-Harra and stoned him till he died.

Bukhari 63.196

In another account of the stoning of the man from Aslam, the adulterer confesses five, not four times, and the Prophet conducts a much more extensive, explicit interrogation in which again he tries to save the man from himself. The chagrin God's Messenger experiences in having to sentence a man to be stoned to death is very much evident in his demand that the people who said he had died like a dog eat from the decaying corpse of an ass. Also, stoning does not purify a woman who has committed adultery, but it does seem to have that effect on a man guilty of committing the same offence. She is going to Hell, he is going to Paradise.

Narrated AbuHurayrah:

A man of the tribe of Aslam came to the Prophet (peace be upon him) and testified four times against himself that he had had illicit intercourse with a woman, while all the time the Prophet (peace be upon him) was turning away from him. Then when he confessed a fifth time, he turned round and asked: Did you have intercourse with her?

He replied: Yes.

He asked: Have you done it so that your sexual organ penetrated hers?

He replied: Yes.

He asked: Have you done it like a collyrium stick when enclosed in its case and a rope in a well?

He replied: Yes.

He asked: Do you know what fornication is?

He replied: Yes. I have done with her unlawfully what a man may lawfully do with his wife.

He then asked: What do you want from what you have said?

He said: I want you to purify me.

So he gave orders regarding him and he was stoned to death. Then the Prophet (peace be upon him) heard one of his companions saying to another: Look at this man whose fault was concealed by Allah but who would not leave the matter alone, so that he was stoned like a dog.

He said nothing to them but walked on for a time till he came to the corpse of an ass with its legs in the air. He asked: Where are so and so?

They said: Here we are, Apostle of Allah (peace be upon him)!

He said: Go down and eat some of this ass's corpse.

They replied: Apostle of Allah! Who can eat any of this?

He said: The dishonour you have just shown to your brother is more serious than eating some of it. By Him in Whose hand my soul is, he is now among the rivers of Paradise and plunging into them.

Abu Dawud 38.4414

One last hadith about a man who would not take a hint, and thereby compelled the Prophet of Mercy to order that he be stoned to death.

Narrated Ibn 'Abbas:

When Ma'iz bin Malik came to the Prophet (in order to confess), the Prophet said to him, "Probably you have only kissed (the lady), or winked, or looked at her?"

He said, "No, O Allah's Apostle!"

The Prophet said, using no euphemism, "Did you have sexual intercourse with her?"

The narrator added: At that, (i.e. after his confession) the Prophet ordered that he be stoned (to death).

Bukhari 82.813

An unmarried slave girl who had sex was shown some mercy by the Prophet with the oxymoronic moniker for compassion, but not much.

Narrated Abu Huraira and Said bin Khalid:

The verdict of Allah's Apostle was sought about an unmarried slave girl guilty of illegal intercourse.

He replied, "If she commits illegal sexual intercourse, then flog her (fifty stripes), and if she commits illegal sexual intercourse (after that for the second time), then flog her (fifty stripes), and if she commits illegal sexual intercourse (for the third time), then flog her (fifty stripes) and sell her for even a hair rope."

Ibn Shihab said, "I am not sure whether the Prophet ordered that she be sold after the third or fourth time of committing illegal intercourse."

Bukhari 82.822

The Prophet's fondness for stoning those who committed illegal intercourse was undoubtedly influenced by the punishment specified in the Torah.

Narrated 'Abdullah bin 'Umar:

The Jews came to Allah's Apostle and told him that a man and a woman from amongst them had committed illegal sexual intercourse.

Allah's Apostle said to them, "What do you find in the Torah (old Testament) about the legal punishment of Ar-Rajm (stoning)?"

They replied, (But) we announce their crime and lash them."

Abdullah bin Salam said, "You are telling a lie; Torah contains the order of Rajm."

They brought and opened the Torah and one of them solaced his hand on the Verse of Rajm and read the verses preceding and following it.

Abdullah bin Salam said to him, "Lift your hand."

When he lifted his hand, the Verse of Rajm was written there. They said, "Muhammad has told the truth; the Torah has the Verse of Rajm."

The Prophet then gave the order that both of them should

be stoned to death.

('Abdullah bin 'Umar said, "I saw the man leaning over the woman to shelter her from the stones."

Bukhari 56.829

God's Messenger boasted, that through him Allah would eliminate adultery. This may also explain his pitiless rulings, especially where women accused of adultery were concerned.

Narrated Jubair bin Mutim:

Allah's Apostle said, "I have five names: I am Muhammad and Ahmad; I am Al-Mahi through whom Allah will eliminate infidelity; I am Al-Hashir who will be the first to be resurrected, the people being resurrected there after; and I am also Al-'Aqib (i.e. There will be no prophet after me)."

Bukhari 56.732

Today you never hear of a man getting stoned for illegal intercourse, it is always women and girls, and here's why, according to Syed Shahabuddin writing in the Milli Gazette, Indian Muslim's leading English newspaper:

Apart from the brutality of the 'Rajm' (stoning), repugnant to conscience, here is an element of gender injustice in the operation of the traditional law which allows the male partner to get off scot-free, even if he has coerced and raped the female. If the woman lodges a complaint, her complaint is taken as a testimony against herself and, therefore, amounts to admission and requires no further evidence while it is necessary to get 4 witnesses against the man. Also the woman may bear a child, as in Amina's case (Amina Lawal was sentenced to death by stoning by a Nigerian Islamic Sharia Court. Amina had an 8 month old daughter), which is admitted as evidence of zena (guilt) against the woman. Man suffers from no such disability.

If the slaves of Allah, women mostly, are stoned to death for illegal intercourse it is not their fault, really, it all has to do with Allah's self-respect.

Narrated 'Aisha:

In the life-time of Allah's Apostle (p.b.u.h) the sun eclipsed, so he led the people in prayer, and stood up and performed a long Qiyam, then bowed for a long while. He stood up again and performed a long Qiyam but this time the period of standing was shorter than the first.

He bowed again for a long time but shorter than the first one, then he prostrated and prolonged the prostration. He did the same in the second Raka as he did in the first and then finished the prayer; by then the sun (eclipse) had cleared.

He delivered the Khutba (sermon) and after praising and glorifying Allah he said, "The sun and the moon are two signs against the signs of Allah; they do not eclipse on the death or life of anyone. So when you see the eclipse, remember Allah and say Takbir, pray and give Sadaqa."

The Prophet then said, "O followers of Muhammad! By Allah! There is none who has more Ghira (self-respect) than Allah as He has forbidden that His slaves, male or female commit adultery (illegal sexual intercourse). O followers of Muhammad! By Allah! If you knew that which I know you would laugh little and weep much."

Bukhari 17.154

Male competition as to who has the greatest self-respect, a self-respect that comes closest to the Ghira of Allah may have a lot to do with so-called honour killings.

Narrated Al-Mughira:

Sa'd bin 'Ubada said, "If I saw a man with my wife, I would strike him (behead him) with the blade of my sword."

This news reached Allah's Apostle who then said, "You people are astonished at Sa'd's Ghira. By Allah, I have more Ghira than he, and Allah has more Ghira than I, and because of Allah's Ghira, He has made unlawful Shameful deeds and sins (illegal sexual intercourse etc.) done in open and in secret. And there is none who likes that the people should repent to Him and beg His pardon than Allah, and for this reason He sent the warners and the givers of good news. And there is none who likes to be praised more than Allah does, and for this reason, Allah promised to grant Paradise (to the doers of good)."

Abdul Malik said, "No person has more Ghira than Allah."

Bukhari 93.512

If only the Prophet had shown the same disgust at launching rocks at a woman's head until she died as he did at throwing stones at animals.

Narrated 'Abdullah bin Mughaffal Al-Muzani:

The Prophet forbade the throwing of stones (with the thumb and the index or middle finger), and said "It neither hunts a game nor kills (or hurts) an enemy, but it gouges out an eye or breaks a tooth."

Bukhari 73.239

The Stoning Ritual

Amina would have been placed in a cloth sack with her hands tied behind her back and buried in the ground up to her shoulders. She is not buried up to her neck allegedly to allow her to wriggle free and prove her innocence before a missile hits its mark, and not to make the whole thing more sporting for the men who will be hurling stones at her head while chanting "Allah hu Akbar" (God is great). On October 27, 2008 13-year-old Aisha Ibrahim Duhulow was killed in this manner in a stadium in the southern port of Kismayu, Somalia in front of an estimated 1,000 spectators.

Why you still have these atrocities committed to this day:

Narrated Ibn 'Abbas:

'Umar said, "I am afraid that after a long time has passed, people may say, "We do not find the Verses of the Rajam (stoning to death) in the Holy Book," and consequently they may go astray by leaving an obligation that Allah has revealed. Lo! I confirm that the penalty of Rajam be inflicted on him who commits illegal sexual intercourse, if he is already married and the crime is proved by witnesses or pregnancy or confession."

Sufyan added, "I have memorized this narration in this way."

'Umar added, "Surely Allah's Apostle carried out the penalty of Rajam, and so did we after him."

Bukhari 82.816.

One Gutsy Lucky Woman!

If a woman stuck to her story and repeated five times that she had not committed illegal intercourse, and her husband could not produce a witness to contradict her testimony, then, according to the Koran, she was not guilty and therefore could not be stoned to death. In the following hadith, the Prophet is somewhat disappointed at the outcome, but dares not overrule Allah.

Narrated Ibn Abbas:

Hilal bin Umaiya accused his wife of committing illegal sexual intercourse with Sharik bin Sahma' and filed the case before the Prophet.

The Prophet said (to Hilal), "Either you bring forth a proof (four witnesses) or you will receive the legal punishment (lashes) on your back."

Hilal said, "O Allah's Apostle! If anyone of us saw a man over his wife, would he go to seek after witnesses?"

The Prophet kept on saying, "Either you bring forth the witnesses or you will receive the legal punishment (lashes) on your back."

Hilal then said, "By Him Who sent you with the Truth, I am telling the truth and Allah will reveal to you what will save my back from legal punishment."

Then Gabriel came down and revealed to him: 'As for those who accuse their wives...' (24:6-9)

The Prophet recited it till he reached: '... (her accuser) is telling the truth.'

Then the Prophet left and sent for the woman, and Hilal went (and brought) her and then took the oaths (confirming the claim).

The Prophet was saying, "Allah knows that one of you is a liar, so will any of you repent?"

Then the woman got up and took the oaths and when she was going to take the fifth one, the people stopped her and said, "It (the fifth oath) will definitely bring Allah's curse on you (if you are guilty)."

So she hesitated and recoiled (from taking the oath) so much that we thought that she would withdraw her denial. But then she said, "I will not dishonor my family all through these days," and carried on (the process of taking oaths).

The Prophet then said, "Watch her; if she delivers a black-eyed child with big hips and fat shins then it is Sharik bin Sahma's child."

Later she delivered a child of that description. So the Prophet said, "If the case was not settled by Allah's Law, I would punish her severely."

Bukhari 60.271

The Prophet's obvious disappointment in the preceding hadith at not being able to severely punish the wife of Umaiya, by having her stoned to death it has to be assumed, and his predilection for stoning women guilty of the made-up crime of illegal intercourse would indicate that a verse prescribing the ghastly punishment did exist.

The Koran

The Koran was put together in a hurry from what could be considered mainly second-rate sources after those who remembered Allah's' revelations best were killed putting down a rebellion against Muslim rule known as the *War of the Apostates*. In the last phase of that war, 7,000 apostates were surrounded and shown no mercy.

The believers' opponents were not into extermination, therefore Muslim casualties tended to be less, but still, at the battle of Yamama 70 or so fanatics of the Koran, the professional reciters of Islam's Holy Book, were killed. The loss of the best "Koranic memories" meant that the young man tasked with putting together the first and only approved version of the Koran had to depend on less reliable sources to create a written record of what Allah first told the angel Gabriel, and which he, in turn, revealed to the Prophet Muhammad.

Narrated Zaid bin Thabit Al-Ansari who was one of those who used to write the Divine Revelation:

Abu Bakr sent for me after the (heavy) casualties among the warriors (of the battle) of Yamama (where a great number of Qurra' (reciters of the Koran) were killed). 'Umar was present with Abu Bakr who said, "'Umar has come to me and said, 'The people have suffered heavy casualties on the day of (the battle of) Yamama, and I am afraid that there will be more casualties among the Qurra' (those who know the Qur'an by heart) at other battle-fields, whereby a large part of the Qur'an may be lost, unless you collect it. And I am of the opinion that you should collect the Qur'an.'"

Abu Bakr added, "I said to 'Umar, 'How can I do something which Allah's Apostle has not done?'"

'Umar said (to me), "By Allah, it is (really) a good thing." So 'Umar kept on pressing, trying to persuade me to accept his proposal, till Allah opened my bosom for it and I had the same opinion as 'Umar.

(Zaid bin Thabit added:) Umar was sitting with him, Abu Bakr, and was not speaking to me).

"You are a wise young man and we do not suspect you (of telling lies or of forgetfulness): and you used to write the Divine Inspiration for Allah's Apostle. Therefore, look for the Qur'an and collect it (in one manuscript)."

By Allah, if he (Abu Bakr) had ordered me to shift one of the mountains (from its place) it would not have been harder for me than what he had ordered me concerning the collection of the Qur'an. I said to both of them, "How dare you do a thing which the Prophet has not done?"

Abu Bakr said, "By Allah, it is (really) a good thing." So I kept on arguing with him about it till Allah opened my bosom for that which He had opened the bosoms of Abu Bakr and Umar. So I started locating Quranic material and collecting it from parchments, scapula, leaf-stalks of date palms and from the memories of men (who knew it by heart).

I found with Khuzaima two Verses of Surat-at-Tauba which I had not found with anybody else, (and they were): "Verily there has come to you an Apostle (Muhammad) from amongst yourselves. It grieves him that you should receive any injury or difficulty He (Muhammad) is ardently anxious over you (to be rightly guided)" (9:128)

The manuscript on which the Quran was collected, remained with Abu Bakr till Allah took him unto Him, and then with 'Umar till Allah took him unto Him, and finally it remained with Hafsa, Umar's daughter.

Bukhari 60.201

The finished product appears to have been put together in a haphazard manner. There is no timeline. The only allowance given to any kind of order is the sequencing of most of the 114 chapters from longest to shortest. Because no attention seems to have been given to arranging the chapters and verses in some kind of chronological order, you often get answers to questions that have yet to be asked. And duplicates, triplicates, quadruplicates and even quintuplets abound. There is little scholarship evident in its production, although, some editing may have been done in producing copies for distribution from Thabit's original which the daughter of Caliph Umar kept under her bed. It was retrieved on order of Uthman who succeeded Umar as caliph.

Narrated Anas bin Malik:

Hudhaifa bin Al-Yaman came to Uthman at the time when the people of Sham and the people of Iraq were Waging war to conquer Arminya and Adharbijan. Hudhaifa was afraid of their (the people of Sham and Iraq) differences in the recitation of the Qur'an, so he said to 'Uthman, "O chief of the Believers! Save this nation before they differ about the Book (Quran) as Jews and the Christians did before."

So 'Uthman sent a message to Hafsa saying, "Send us the

manuscripts of the Qur'an so that we may compile the Qur'anic materials in perfect copies and return the manuscripts to you."

Hafsa sent it to 'Uthman. 'Uthman then ordered Zaid bin Thabit, 'Abdullah bin AzZubair, Said bin Al-As and 'Abdur Rahman bin Harith bin Hisham to rewrite the manuscripts in perfect copies.

'Uthman said to the three Quraishi men, "In case you disagree with Zaid bin Thabit on any point in the Qur'an, then write it in the dialect of Quraish, the Qur'an was revealed in their tongue."

They did so, and when they had written many copies, 'Uthman returned the original manuscripts to Hafsa.

'Uthman sent to every Muslim province one copy of what they had copied, and ordered that all the other Qur'anic materials, whether written in fragmentary manuscripts or whole copies, be burnt.

Said bin Thabit added, "A Verse from Surat Ahzab was missed by me when we copied the Qur'an and I used to hear Allah's Apostle reciting it. So we searched for it and found it with Khuzaima bin Thabit Al-Ansari. (That Verse was): 'Among the Believers are men who have been true in their covenant with Allah.'" (33:23)

Bukhari 61.510

The opinion of two eminent historians on the end product:

A confused, jumble, crude, incondite, endless iteration…

Thomas Carlyle [1795 - 1881]

As toilsome a reading a I ever undertook; a wearisome confused jumble.

Edward Gibbon [1737 - 1794]

One of the things which makes the Koran a tedious, repetitive read is Allah constantly praising himself. This has led some to speculate that the Koran is not so much a revelation from God but more of a multi-faceted prayer where the supplicant praises his would-be benefactor ad nauseum in the hope of currying His favour. Allah, the Prophet let it be known, is addicted to praise; he cannot get enough of it, which is why He praises himself.

Narrated Abdullah bin Mas'ud:

Allah's Apostle said, "None has more sense of ghaira (*self-respect, also spelled ghira*) than Allah, and for this He has forbidden shameful sins whether committed openly or secretly, and none loves to be praised more than Allah does, and this is why He Praises Himself."

Bukhari 60.161

The constant praise and repetitiveness others have speculated is simply a form of brainwashing. Perhaps, but it does make it easier to memorize the equivalent of three hundred page book which, as the Prophet reminded the believers, must be constantly recited (you may have a point about operant conditioning) to avoid Its verses escaping.

Narrated Abdullah:

The Prophet said, "It is a bad thing that some of you say, 'I have forgotten such-and-such verse of the Qur'an,' for indeed, he has been caused (by Allah) to forget it. So you must keep on reciting the Qur'an because it escapes from the hearts of men faster than camels do."

Bukhari 61.550

Narrated Ibn Umar:

Allah's Apostle said, "The example of the person who knows the Qur'an by heart is like the owner of tied camels. If he keeps them tied, he will control them, but if he releases them, they will run away."

Bukhari 61.549

Knowing the Koran by heart could bring unexpected benefits.

Narrated Sahl bin Sad:

A woman came to Allah's Apostle and said, "O Allah's Apostle! I want to give up myself to you." A man said, "Marry her to me." The Prophet said, "We agree to marry her to you with what you know of the Qur'an by heart."

Bukhari 38.505

The Koran must be recited out loud. Not only will it make it easier to remember what God revealed to His Messenger, it will help others who may have forgotten this or that verse, and will make you stand out as the best of examples for both believers and unbelievers.

Narrated Aisha:

Allah's Apostle heard a man reciting the Qur'an at night, and said, "May Allah bestow His Mercy on him, as he has reminded me of such-and-such Verses of such-and-such Suras, which I was caused to forget."

Bukhari 61.558

Narrated Abu Musa Al-Ash'ari:

The Prophet said, "The example of him (a believer) who recites the Qur'an is like that of a citron which tastes good and smells good. And he (a believer) who does not recite the Qur'an is like a date which is good in taste but has no smell. And the example of a dissolute wicked person who recites the Qur'an is like the Raihana (sweet basil) which smells good but tastes bitter. And the example of a dissolute wicked person who does not recite the Qur'an is like the colocynth which tastes bitter and has no smell."

Bukhari 61.538

An Account of the Physical Symptoms of Revelation

The second hadith in Bukhari's extensive collective is about some of the physical symptoms and manifestations that accompanied the delivery of Allah's Revelations by the angel Gabriel.

Narrated 'Aisha:

Al-Harith bin Hisham asked Allah's Apostle "O Allah's Apostle! How is the Divine Inspiration revealed to you?"

Allah's Apostle replied, "Sometimes it is (revealed) like the ringing of a bell, this form of Inspiration is the hardest of all and then this state passes off after I have grasped what is inspired. Sometimes the Angel comes in the form of a man and talks to me and I grasp whatever he says."

Aisha added: "Verily I saw the Prophet being inspired Divinely on a very cold day and noticed the sweat dropping from his forehead (as the Inspiration was over)."

Bukhari 1.2

Could the symptoms, which are described in even more detail in the Koran, have been the result of brain damage caused by a severe sunstroke? The structure that sheltered the stone of the Ka'ba had been extensively damaged by a fire and water. It was decided to build a new Ka'ba next to the old one. When it came time to move the stone of Paradise to its new location, every leader of the ten clans vied for the honour, some willing to fight to the death for the right to move the most sacred rock in the universe. A compromise was reached. The next person to enter the Sacred Mosque, the enclosure surrounding the Ka'ba, would decide who would move the stone. Guess who showed up?

Muhammad's solution: the rock would be rolled unto a large sheet, and each clan chief would grab a hold of the sheet and move the rock to its new enclosure. The clan leaders were very impressed with the thirthy-something Muhammad and he was highly praised by one and all. The enthralled future Prophet then stripped to the waist to help out, and shortly suffered what we might call a "heat or sun stroke" from which he nearly died.

Personal Vendettas

In an eternal Book that is meant to elevate and to guide humanity to God, it always comes as a surprise when you encounter revelations where Allah takes it upon Himself to make sure that a person who has even slightly slighted His Messenger will get a horrible personalized punishment. Allah's boasting about the physical, emotional and psychological pain He will inflict on a fellow by the name of Abu Lahab and his wife, once He gets His Hands on them, reveals a refined, attention-to-detail sadism that one might expect from the nemesis of the self-proclaimed essence of compassion and mercy.

THE FIBRE

111 Al-Masad

In the Name of Allah,
the Compassionate, the Merciful

1. Perish the hands of Abu Lahab, and may he perish too;

2. Neither his wealth nor what he has earned will avail him anything.

3. He will roast in a flaming fire,

4. And his wife will be a carrier of fire-wood,

5. She shall have a rope of fibre around her neck.

The hadith about the circumstances that provoked one of Allah's most savage sadistic rage against an individual in the entire Koran.

Narrated Ibn Abbas:

When the Verse: 'And warn your tribe of near-kindred' (26:214), was revealed, the Prophet ascended the Safa (mountain) and started calling, "O Bani Fihr! O Bani 'Adi!" addressing various tribes of Quraish till they were assembled. Those who could not come themselves, sent their messengers to see what was there.

Abu Lahab and other people from Quraish came and the Prophet then said, "Suppose I told you that there is an (enemy) cavalry in the valley intending to attack you, would you believe me?"

They said, "Yes, for we have not found you telling anything other than the truth."

He then said, "I am a warner to you in face of a terrific punishment."

Abu Lahab said (to the Prophet) "May your hands perish all this day. Is it for this purpose you have gathered us?"

Then it was revealed: "Perish the hands of Abu Lahab (one of the Prophet's uncles), and perish he! His wealth and his children will not profit him...." (111:1-5)

Bukhari 60.293

Khidr

The merchant Muhammad spent about a quarter of a century retracing the trade routes of the Middle East, the most travelled being between Mecca and Damascus. The future Prophet must have spent hundreds, if not thousands of evenings around a campfire trading stories and tall tales with people along his trade itinerary. It is unfortunate that because of the vaunted illiteracy of God's Messenger very little was written about what the Prophet heard; human memory being what it is, recollections, over time, often morph into confabulations i.e. fabricated, distorted or misinterpreted memories. An example, in the Koran the Good Samaritan of the Gospels becomes the Bad Samaritan of the Exodus.

For Zayd ibn Thabit, the compiler of the Koran, it must have been difficult at times to differentiate between an old anecdote heard and reprised by the Prophet and a revealed story to be included in the Koran. The reported trials of Khidr and Moses may have presented Thabit with that type of dilemma.

The following hadith is mess, as are the variations (you may want to skip directly to the edited version that made it into the Koran, it is slightly less confusing). It is a second-hand account of the Prophet's Khidr story, a rather confusing one with three people arguing among themselves (the mix of double and single parenthesis not helping) about what he said. It is a story which, I hope, will give you an appreciation of some of the difficulties Thabit must have faced with the Prophet no longer around to help decide what should be included in the Koran from the mountain of often contradictory hearsay evidence of which God's Messenger was the primary source.

The following is also presented as evidence that complex and confusing stories such as Khidr's, with different narrators arguing among themselves or presenting different account of what was said, must have been edited to make any sense at all before being included in the Koran.

Narrated Ibn Juraij:

Ya'la bin Muslim and 'Amr bin Dinar and some others narrated the narration of Said bin Jubair.

Narrated Said: While we were at the house of Ibn 'Abbas, Ibn 'Abbas said, "Ask me (any question)"

I said, "O Abu Abbas! May Allah let me be sacrificed for you! There is a man at Kufa who is a story-teller called Nauf; who claims that he (Al-Khadir's companion) is not Moses of Bani Israel."

As for 'Amr, he said to me, Ibn 'Abbas said, "(Nauf) the enemy of Allah told a lie."

But Ya'la said to me, "Ibn 'Abbas said, Ubai bin Ka'b said, Allah's Apostle said, 'Once Moses, Allah's Apostle, preached to the people till their eyes shed tears and their hearts became tender, whereupon he finished his sermon. Then a man came to Moses and asked, 'O Allah's Apostle! Is there anyone on the earth who is more learned than you?'

Moses replied, 'No.' So Allah admonished him (Moses), for he did not ascribe all knowledge to Allah. It was said, (on behalf of Allah), 'Yes, (there is a slave of ours who knows more than you).'

Moses said, 'O my Lord! Where is he?'

Allah said, 'At the junction of the two seas.'

Moses said, 'O my Lord! Tell me of a sign whereby I will recognize the place.'"

Amr said to me, Allah said, "That place will be where the fish will leave you."

Ya'la said to me, "Allah said (to Moses), 'Take a dead fish (and your goal will be) the place where it will become alive.'" So Moses took a fish and put it in a basket and said to his boy-servant "I don't want to trouble you, except that you should inform me as soon as this fish leaves you."

He said (to Moses), "You have not demanded too much." And that is as mentioned by Allah: 'And (remember) when Moses said to his attendant .... ' (18:60)

Yusha' bin Nun. (Said did not state that). The Prophet said, "While the attendant was in the shade of the rock at a wet place, the fish slipped out (alive) while Moses was sleeping. His attend[ant] said (to himself), 'I will not wake him', but when he woke up, he forgot to tell him the fish slipped out and entered the sea. Allah stopped the flow of the sea. where the fish was, so that its trace looked as if it was made on a rock."

Amr forming a hole with his two thumbs an index fingers, said to me, "Like this, as in its trace was made on a rock."

Moses said "We have suffered much fatigue on this journey of ours." (This was not narrate by Said). Then they returned back and found Al-Khadir. 'Uthman bin Abi Sulaiman said to me, (they found him) on a green carpet in the middle of the sea.

Al-Khadir was covered with his garment with one end under his feet and the other end under his head. When Moses greeted, he uncovered his face and said astonishingly, 'Is there such a greeting in my land? Who are you?'

Moses said, 'I am Moses.'

Al-Khadir said, 'Are you the Moses of Bani (tribe of) Israel?'

Moses said, 'Yes.'

Al-Khadir said, "What do you want?'

Moses said, ' I came to you so that you may teach me of the truth which you were taught.'

Al-Khadir said, 'Is it not sufficient for you that the Torah is in your hands and the Divine Inspiration comes to you, O Moses? Verily, I have a knowledge that you ought not learn, and you have a knowledge which I ought not learn.'

At that time a bird took with its beak (some water) from the sea: Al-Khadir then said, 'By Allah, my knowledge and your knowledge besides Allah's Knowledge is like what this bird has taken with its beak from the sea.' Until, when they went on board the boat (18:71). They found a small boat which used to carry the people from this sea-side to the other sea-side. The crew recognized Al-Khadir and said, 'The pious slave of Allah.'

(We said to Said "Was that Khadir?" He said, "Yes.")

The boat men said, 'We will not get him on board with fare.'

Al-Khadir scuttled the boat and then plugged the hole with a piece of wood.

Moses said, 'Have you scuttle it in order to drown these people surely, you have done a dreadful thing. (18:71) (Mujahid said. "Moses said so protestingly (sic).")

Al-Khadir said, didn't I say that you can have no patience with me?' (18:72) The first inquiry of Moses was done because of forget fullness, the second caused him to be bound with a stipulation, and the third was done intentionally.

Moses said, 'Call me not to account for what I forgot and be not hard upon me for my affair (with you).' (18:73)

(Then) they found a boy and Al-Khadir killed him. Ya'la-said: Said said 'They found boys playing and Al-Khadir got hold of a handsome infidel boy laid him down and then slew him with knife.

Moses said, 'Have you killed a innocent soul who has killed nobody' (18:74) Then they proceeded and found a wall which was on the point of falling down, and Al-Khadir set it up straight Said moved his hand thus and said 'Al-Khadir raised his hand and the wall became straight.

Ya'la said, 'I think Said said, 'Al-Khadir touched the wall with his hand and it became straight (Moses said to Al-Khadir), 'If you had wished, you could have taken wages for it.'

Said said, 'Wages that we might had eaten.' And there was a king in furor (ahead) of them" (18:79) And there was in front of them.

Ibn 'Abbas recited: 'In front of them (was) a king.' It is said on the authority of somebody other than Said that the king was Hudad bin Budad. They say that the boy was called Haisur. 'A king who seized every ship by force. (18:79) So I wished that if that boat passed by him, he would leave it because of its defect and when they have passed they would repair it and get benefit from it.

Some people said that they closed that hole with a bottle, and some said with tar. 'His parents were believers, and he (the boy) was a non-believer and we(Khadir) feared lest he would oppress them by obstinate rebellion and disbelief.' (18.80) (i.e. that their love for him would urge them to follow him in his religion, 'so we (Khadir) desired that their Lord should change him for them for one better in righteousness and near to mercy' (18:81).

This was in reply to Moses' saying: Have you killed an innocent soul.'? (18.74). 'Near to mercy" means they will be more merciful to him than they were to the former whom Khadir had killed. Other than Sa'id, said that they were compensated with a girl.

Dawud bin Abi 'Asim said on the authority of more than one that this next child was a girl.

Bukhari 60.250

The Veil

How the Veil Came To Be and Why

A women's hair, like beautiful flowers, makes the world a more attractive place and should not be covered by a symbol of backwardness. *Former Egyptian Minister of Culture Farouk Hosni*

In His Koran, Allah invites women, in revelation 24:33 to cover up their private parts and to "drape their bosom with their veil", not their face – it would seem: "And tell the believing women to cast down their eyes and guard their private parts and not show their finery, except the outward part of it. And let them drape their bosoms with their veils and not show their finery, except to their husbands, their fathers, their husbands' fathers, their sons, the sons of their husbands, their brothers, the sons of their brothers, the sons of their sisters, their women, their maid-servants, the men-followers who have no sexual desire, or infants who have no knowledge of women's sexual parts yet. Let them, also, not stamp their feet, so that what they have concealed of their finery might be known. Repent to Allah, all of you, O believers, that perchance you may prosper."

The revelation caught the Prophet's wives unprepared:

Narrated Safiya bint Shaiba:

'Aisha used to say: "When (the Verse): "They should draw their veils over their necks and bosoms," was revealed, (the ladies) cut their waist sheets at the edges and covered their faces with the cut pieces."

Bukhari 60.282

The veil, and Allah's interdiction against women dancing i.e. "not stamp their feet, so that what they have concealed of their finery might be known" is meant to conceal a woman's breasts and their tendency to jiggle when the owner is in motion and cause males, other than her husband, to be sexually aroused. Corsets, a 14th century invention, and the modern bra which 500 years later replaced that means of support for a woman's upper body's jiggly parts have, more or less, alleviated this danger. But then again, Allah might have had another use in mind for the veil – a totally appropriate use considering the time and place.

Revelation 24:31 is from An–Nûr (the Light). The 24th surah i.e. chapter, is recalled as Al-Hijab in one account of what caused Allah to send down the revelation about the veil.

Narrated 'Aisha:

The wives of the Prophet used to go to Al-Manasi, a vast open place (near Baqia at Medina) to answer the call of nature at night. 'Umar used to say to the Prophet "Let your wives be veiled," but Allah's Apostle did not do so.

One night Sauda bint Zam'a the wife of the Prophet went out at 'Isha' time and she was a tall lady. 'Umar addressed her and said, "I have recognized you, O Sauda."

He said so, as he desired eagerly that the verses of Al-Hijab may be revealed. So Allah revealed the verses of "Al-Hijab"

Bukhari 5.148

Narrated Umar:

I said, "O Allah's Apostle! Good and bad persons enter upon you, so I suggest that you order the mothers of the Believers (i.e. your wives) to observe veils." Then Allah revealed the Verses of Al-Hijab

Bukhari 60.313

If corsets and bras have eliminated the need for bosom-covering-veils, could the same not be said for the face-covering-veil, the niqab, with the widespread availability of women-only public "restrooms"? Perhaps, but men demanding that women be veiled may have little, or nothing to do with concealing jiggling breasts and the identity of women answering the call of nature, and everything to do with their own insecurities. The revelation about the veil is contained in the same surah where Allah is incensed that people would think His Messenger a cuckold after the Prophet's child bride Aisha got lost in the desert and was found by a young man, who brought her back the next day (see *The Necklace*). The Al-Hijab verse was another of Allah's spur-of-the-moment interventions, in this case while His Messenger was eating.

In any event, the veil ordained by the Koran would not have been sufficient to conceal Sauda's identity; and for the Prophet and his Mentor this was not that big a deal. The suggestion did not even come from Allah or His Messenger but from an impertinent friend of the Prophet, reducing its religious significance, if any, significantly. Therefore, it should not be a pressing concern for modern Muslim women who need or wish to temporally leave the home of their husbands or fathers for other than the call of nature.

Narrated Aisha:

Sauda (the wife of the Prophet) went out to answer the call of nature after it was made obligatory (for all the Muslims ladies) to observe the veil. She was a fat huge lady, and everybody who knew her before could recognize her. So

'Umar bin Al-Khattab saw her and said, "O Sauda! By Allah, you cannot hide yourself from us, so think of a way by which you should not be recognized on going out."

Sauda returned while Allah's Apostle was in my house taking his supper and a bone covered with meat was in his hand. She entered and said, "O Allah's Apostle! I went out to answer the call of nature and 'Umar said to me so-and-so."

Then Allah inspired him (the Prophet) and when the state of inspiration was over and the bone was still in his hand as he had not put in down, he said (to Sauda), "You (women) have been allowed to go out for your needs."

Bukhari 60.318

The *Verse of the Veil* is often confused with the *Verse of the Curtain*; even narrators confuse the two. The *Verse of the Curtain* was "revealed on the night of the wedding of the Prophet and Zaynab b. Jahsh" when uninvited guests kept showing up at the Prophet's home after the wedding feast, or overstayed their welcome. Revelation 33:53 is also famous for Allah making sure that the Prophet's widows stay celibate after His Messenger's passing by threatening any man who would marry them: "O believers, do not enter the houses of the Prophet, unless you are invited to a meal, without awaiting the hour; but if you are invited, then enter; but when you have eaten, disperse, without lingering for idle talk. That is vexing to the Prophet who might be wary of you, but Allah is not wary of the truth. If you ask them (the wives of the Prophet) for an object, ask them from behind a curtain. That is purer for your hearts and theirs. You should never hurt the Messenger of Allah, nor take his wives in marriage after him. That is truly abominable in the sight of Allah."

A hadith as to the when and why of the timely revelation:

Narrated Anas bin Malik:

I, of all the people, know best this verse of Al-Hijab. When Allah's Apostle married Zainab bint Jahsh she was with him in the house and he prepared a meal and invited the people (to it). They sat down (after finishing their meal) and started chatting. So the Prophet went out and then returned several times while they were still sitting and talking.

So Allah revealed the Verse: "O you who believe! Enter not the Prophet's houses until leave is given to you for a meal, (and then) not (so early as) to wait for its preparation .....ask them from behind a screen." (33:53)

So the screen was set up and the people went away.

Bukhari 60.315

Three Precocious Babies

Jesus, the Prophet informs us in the following hadith was one of only three babies to speak almost from the moment of birth. The story of the other two is somewhat convoluted, as such tales tend to be, therefore take your time.

Narrated Abu Huraira:

The Prophet said, "None spoke in cradle but three: (The first was) Jesus, (the second was), there a man from Bani (Children of) Israel called Juraij. While he was offering his prayers, his mother came and called him.

He said (to himself), 'Shall I answer her or keep on praying?'

(He went on praying) and did not answer her, his mother said, 'O Allah! Do not let him die till he sees the faces of prostitutes.' So while he was in his hermitage, a lady came and sought to seduce him, but he refused. So she went to a shepherd and presented herself to him to commit illegal sexual intercourse with her and then later she gave birth to a child and claimed that it belonged to Juraij.

The people, therefore, came to him and dismantled his hermitage and expelled him out of it and abused him.

Juraij performed the ablution and offered prayer, and then came to the child and said, 'O child! Who is your father?'

The child replied, 'The shepherd.'

(After hearing this) the people said, 'We shall rebuild your hermitage of gold,' but he said, 'No, of nothing but mud.'

(The third was the hero of the following story) A lady from Bani Israel was nursing her child at her breast when a handsome rider passed by her. She said, 'O Allah! Make my child like him.'

On that the child left her breast, and facing the rider said, 'O Allah! Do not make me like him.' The child then started to suck her breast again.

(Abu Huraira further said, 'As if I were now looking at the Prophet sucking his finger (in way of demonstration.')

After a while the people passed by, with a lady slave and she (i.e. the child's mother) said, 'O Allah! Do not make my child like this (slave girl)!' On that the child left her breast and said, 'O Allah! Make me like her.'

When she asked why, the child replied, 'The rider is one of the tyrants while this slave girl is falsely accused of theft and illegal sexual intercourse.'"

Bukhari 55.645

An abridged version with Jesus left out, among other telling differences:

Narrated Abu Huraira:

That he heard Allah's Apostle saying, "While a lady was nursing her child, a rider passed by and she said, 'O Allah! Don't let my child die till he becomes like this (rider).'

The child said, 'O Allah! Don't make me like him,' and then returned to her breast (sucking it).

(After a while) they passed by a lady who was being pulled and teased (by the people).

The child's mother said, 'O Allah! Do not make my child like her.' The child said, 'O Allah! Make me like her.'

Then he said, 'As for the rider, he is an infidel, while the lady is accused of illegal sexual intercourse (falsely) and she says: Allah is sufficient for me (He knows the truth).'"

Bukhari 56.672

Wigs, Tattoos and Hair Everywhere

What can you say about a religion which forbids a woman from removing facial hair because she is disfiguring God's creation, but encourages her to shave her pubic hair so as to give her pubes that pre-pubescent look as a way of making herself more attractive to her husband?

Narrated 'Abdullah:

Allah has cursed those women who practice tattooing and those who get themselves tattooed, and those who remove their face hairs, and those who create a space between their teeth artificially to look beautiful, and such women as change the features created by Allah.

Why then should I not curse those whom the Prophet has cursed? And that is in Allah's Book. i.e. His Saying: 'And what the Apostle gives you take it and what he forbids you abstain (from it).' (59:7)

Bukhari 72.815

Narrated Jabir bin Abdullah:

While we were returning from a Ghazwa (Holy Battle) with the Prophet, I started driving my camel fast, as it was a lazy camel A rider came behind me and pricked my camel with a spear he had with him, and then my camel started running as fast as the best camel you may see. Behold! The rider was the Prophet himself.

He said, "What makes you in such a hurry?"

I replied, "I am newly married."

He said, "Did you marry a virgin or a matron?"

I replied, "A matron."

He said, "Why didn't you marry a young girl so that you may play with her and she with you?"

When we were about to enter (Medina), the Prophet said, "Wait so that you may enter (Medina) at night so that the lady of unkempt hair may comb her hair and the one whose husband has been absent may shave her pubic region."

Bukhari 62.16

Until such a time as Allah instructed him otherwise, the Prophet followed the scriptures of the Jews, although nowhere in the Koran does Allah explicitly (or implicitly to my knowledge) mention the parting of one's hair.

Narrated 'Abdullah bin Abbas:

The Prophet used to keep his hair falling loose while the pagans used to part their hair, and the People of the Scriptures used to keep their hair falling loose, and the Prophet liked to follow the People of the Scriptures in matters about which he had not been instructed differently, but later on the Prophet started parting his hair.

Bukhari 58.280

After the falling out with the Jews of Medina, in part because they would not acknowledge that a Prophet of God could emerge from the Arab people, God's latest Messenger looked for ways to differentiate Muslim rituals and practices from those of the Jews. The earliest significant change was Allah ordering Muslims to no longer prostrate themselves in the direction of Jerusalem during the prayers, but Mecca. This innovation was followed by His Messenger deliberately making Friday the Muslim Holy Day, ahead of the holy day of the Jews and Christians as benefited the superior religion.

In things big and small, such as grooming, Allah and His Messenger attempted to differentiate the Muslims from Jews, and on occasion, the pagans.

Narrated Abu Huraira:

The Prophet said, "Jews and Christians do not dye their hair so you should do the opposite of what they do.

Bukhari 72.786

Narrated Nafi':

Ibn Umar said, The Prophet said, 'Do the opposite of what the pagans do. Keep the beards (as it is) and cut the moustaches short.'

Bukhari 72.780

The Prophet's newfound disagreement with the Jews may also have been the reason why he banned wigs and hair extensions for women.

Narrated Sa'id bin Al-Musaiyab:

Mu'awiya came to Medina for the last time and delivered a sermon. He took out a tuft of hair and said, "I thought that none used to do this (i.e. use false hair) except Jews. The Prophet labelled such practice, (i.e. the use of false hair), as cheating."

Bukhari 72.821

The Prophet cursed a woman who would improve her appearance after a sickness caused her hair to fall out.

Narrated Asma (the daughter of Abu' Bakr):

A woman came to Allah's Apostle and said, "I married my daughter to someone, but she became sick and all her hair fell out, and (because of that) her husband does not like her. May I let her use false hair?"

On that the Prophet cursed such a lady as artificially lengthening (her or someone else's) hair or got her hair lengthened artificially.

Bukhari 72.818

Allah took it even further, cursing any women who would artificially lengthening whatever curls she had left.

Narrated 'Aisha:

An Ansari woman gave her daughter in marriage and the hair of the latter started falling out. The Ansari women came to the Prophet and mentioned that to him and said, "Her (my daughter's) husband suggested that I should let her wear false hair."

The Prophet said, "No, (don't do that) for Allah sends His curses upon such ladies who lengthen their hair artificially."

Bukhari 62.133

Not only that, but Allah will curse the one who assists in lengthening someone else's hair. Don't do it, it's not worth it!

Narrated 'Aisha:

An Ansari girl was married and she became sick and all her hair fell out intending to provide her with false hair. They asked the Prophet who said, "Allah has cursed the lady who artificially lengthens (her or someone else's) hair and also the one who gets her hair lengthened."

Bukhari 72.817

The Prophet, on more than one occasion, banned both wigs and tattoos in the same breath, although there is no mention of the Jews decorating their bodies that way.

Narrated Ibn Umar:

Allah's Apostle said, "Allah has cursed such a lady as lengthens (her or someone else's) hair artificially or gets it lengthened, and also a lady who tattoos (herself or someone else) or gets herself tattooed."

Bukhari 72.820

Men, like women, are expected to shave their pubic hair. It's all part of the five physical manifestation of Fitra i.e. what it is to be a Muslim.

Narrated Abu Huraira:

I heard the Prophet saying. "Five practices are characteristics of the Fitra: circumcision, shaving the pubic hair, cutting the moustaches short, clipping the nails, and depilating the hair of the armpits."

Bukhari 72.779

Women

Chapter should be read in conjunction with *Women and the Koran, Boreal Books (2012)* or *Pain, Pleasure and Prejudice – Women and the Koran, Boreal Books (2012)*.

A Western reader of the Koran and the sayings of the Prophet Muhammad is struck by the male-centric universe about which Allah and His Messenger expound and praise, and the low esteem in which both hold females. Women must have an even lower opinion of themselves, for how can you explain why, not only do they remain committed to Islam to the point of joining the ranks of suicide bombers, but, particularly in the West, become believers of their own freewill? Of course, this is assuming God and His Messenger are wrong in their assessment of their character and intellectual capabilities.

Narrated Abu Said Al-Khudri:

Once Allah's Apostle went out to the Musalla (to offer the prayer) o 'Id-al-Adha or Al-Fitr prayer. Then he passed by the women and said, "O women! Give alms, as I have seen that the majority of the dwellers of Hell-fire were you (women)."

They asked, "Why is it so, O Allah's Apostle?"

He replied, "You curse frequently and are ungrateful to your husbands. I have not seen anyone more deficient in intelligence and religion than you. A cautious sensible man could be led astray by some of you."

The women asked, "O Allah's Apostle! What is deficient in our intelligence and religion?"

He said, "Is not the evidence of two women equal to the witness of one man?"

They replied in the affirmative.

He said, "This is the deficiency in her intelligence. Isn't it true that a woman can neither pray nor fast during her menses?"

The women replied in the affirmative.

He said, "This is the deficiency in her religion."

Bukhari 6.301

A few more hadiths where women are compared to domestic animals:

Masruq reported:

It was mentioned before 'A'isha that prayer is invalidated (in case of passing) of a dog, an ass and a woman (before the worshipper, when he is not screened). Upon this 'A'isha said: You likened us to the asses and the dogs.

Sahih Muslim 4.1038

A'isha said [to Muhammad]: "You have made us equal to the dogs and the asses."

Sahih Muslim 4:1039

Ikrimah reported on the authority of Ibn Abbas, saying:

I think the Apostle of Allah said: "When one of you prays without a sutrah (a barrier), a dog, an ass, a pig, a Jew, a Magian, and a woman cut off his prayer, but it will suffice if they pass in front of him at a distance of over a stone's throw."

Abu Dawud 2.0704

Is it because her husband has compared her to a donkey or because she does not want to annul his prayer, that Aisha, in the following hadith, does not care to face her husband?

Narrated 'Aisha:

The things which annul the prayers were mentioned before me. They said, "Prayer is annulled by a dog, a donkey and a woman (if they pass in front of the praying people)."

I said, "You have made us (i.e. women) dogs. I saw the Prophet praying while I used to lie in my bed between him and the Qibla. Whenever I was in need of something, I would slip away for I disliked to face him."

Bukhari 9.490

As if being intellectually challenged was not enough, the Prophet further characterized women as being petty, selfish liars; the vast majority of which will burn in Hell for an eternity for being ungrateful to the men who tightly control every facet of their often miserable existence. And still women flock to his banner.

Narrated 'Abdullah bin Abbas:

The sun eclipsed in the life-time of the Prophet (p.b.u.h). Allah's Apostle offered the eclipse prayer and stood for a long period equal to the period in which one could recite Surat-al-Baqara. Then he bowed for a long time and then stood up for a long period which was shorter than that of the first standing, then bowed again for a long time but for a shorter period than the first; then he prostrated twice and then stood up for a long period which was shorter than that of the first standing; then he bowed for a long time which was shorter than the previous one, and then he raised his head and stood up for a long period which was shorter than the first standing, then he bowed for a long time which was shorter than the first bowing, and then prostrated (twice) and finished the prayer. By then, the sun (eclipse) had cleared.

The Prophet then said, "The sun and the moon are two of the signs of Allah. They eclipse neither because of the death of somebody nor because of his life (i.e. birth). So when you see them, remember Allah."

The people say, "O Allah's Apostle! We saw you taking something from your place and then we saw you retreating."

The Prophet replied, "I saw Paradise and stretched my hands towards a bunch (of its fruits) and had I taken it, you would have eaten from it as long as the world remains. I also saw the Hell-fire and I had never seen such a horrible sight. I saw that most of the inhabitants were women."

The people asked, "O Allah's Apostle! Why is it so?"

The Prophet replied, "Because of their ungratefulness."

It was asked whether they are ungrateful to Allah. The Prophet said, "They are ungrateful to their companions of life (husbands) and ungrateful to good deeds. If you are benevolent to one of them throughout the life and if she sees anything (undesirable) in you, she will say, 'I have never had any good from you.' "

Bukhari 18.161

Why should such people, who left to their own device could only survive through deceit and seduction be allowed an equal share of an inheritance. Better to give it to a brother so he may look after his mentally and morally deficient sisters until he finds a wife, somebody else's sister for whom he will render the same service. And still women flock to his banner.

Narrated Ibn Abbas:

(In the Pre-Islamic Period) the children used to inherit all the property but the parents used to inherit only through a will. So Allah cancelled that which He liked to cancel and put decreed that the share of a son was to be twice the share of a daughter, and for the parents one-sixth for each one of them, or one third, and for the wife one-eighth or one-fourth, and for the husband one-half, or one-fourth.

Bukhari 60.102

He changed the rules so that it is the father and his father's relative who inherits from a son leaving nothing for the mother. And still they flock to his banner.

Narrated Abu Huraira:

The Prophet said, "I am closer to the believers than their selves in this world and in the Hereafter, and if you like, you can read Allah's Statement: "The Prophet is closer to the believers than their own selves." (33.6) So, if a true believer dies and leaves behind some property, it will be for his inheritors (from the father's side), and if he leaves behind some debt to be paid or needy offspring, then they should come to me as I am the guardian of the deceased."

Bukhari 41.584

Towards the end of his life, the Prophet's young wives had fun at the old man's expense. This may explain the following remarks concerning his legacy, but it is also evidence of how ingrained was his misogyny.

Narrated Usama bin Zaid:

The Prophet said, "After me I have not left any affliction more harmful to men than women."

Bukhari 62.33

These evil, affliction-ridden, ungrateful simpletons will not find the equally misogynist epitome of Compassion and Mercy receptive to their plea for mercy on Judgement Day.

Narrated Ibn 'Abbas:

The Prophet said: "I was shown the Hell-fire and that the majority of its dwellers were women who were ungrateful."

It was asked, "Do they disbelieve in Allah?" (or are they ungrateful to Allah?)

He replied, "They are ungrateful to their husbands and are ungrateful for the favors and the good (charitable deeds) done to them. "

Bukhari 2.28

Women as evil omens?

Narrated Abdullah bin 'Umar:

Allah's Apostle said, "Evil omen is in the women, the house and the horse. "

Bukhari 62.30

Your wives may be harmful to your wellbeing in ways only God's Messenger could appreciate, but that is no reason to flog them the way you do a slave or a camel, if you plan on having sex with them that night.

Narrated 'Abdullah bin Zam'a:

The Prophet said, "None of you should flog his wife as he flogs a slave and then have sexual intercourse with her in the last part of the day."

Bukhari 62.132

Narrated 'Abdullah bin Zam'a:

The Prophet forbade laughing at a person who passes wind, and said, "How does anyone of you beat his wife as he beats the stallion camel and then he may embrace (sleep with) her?"

Bukhari 73.68

The type of woman the Prophet recommends believing men marry.

Narrated Abu Huraira:

The Prophet said, "A woman is married for four things, i.e., her wealth, her family status, her beauty and her religion. So you should marry the religious woman (otherwise) you will be losers.

Bukhari 62.27

Men did not wear underwear under their Izars, a type of skirt made of "a long, light weight cloth that can be easily wrapped around the waist by tying two ends of the garment into a large knot". During prayer, we are told, men tied their Izars around their necks, probably to avoid soiling it during the prostrations, and risked exposing, if only briefly, their private parts to the women in the back. This would not have been a problem if God's Messenger had said "women in the front, men in the back" during worship, as opposed to the other way around. The Prophet's solution:

Narrated Sahl:

The men used to pray with the Prophet with their Izars tied around their necks as boys used to do; therefore the Prophet told the women not to raise their heads till the men sat down straight (while praying).

Bukhari 8.358

God's Messenger would not make an exception even for an old woman who made him supper.

Narrated Ishaq:

Anas bin Malik said, "My grand-mother Mulaika invited Allah's Apostle for a meal which she herself had prepared. He ate from it and said, 'Get up! I will lead you in the prayer.'"

Anas added, "I took my Hasir, washed it with water as it had become dark because of long use and Allah's Apostle stood on it. The orphan (Damira or Ruh) and I aligned behind him and the old lady (Mulaika) stood behind us. Allah's Apostle led us in the prayer and offered two Rak'at and then left."

Bukhari 8.377

For Islamists, women and girls are men's salvation when it comes to sex. Only a female can stop a male's private parts from committing an indictable offence i.e. having or desiring to have sex outside of marriage, by marrying the owner of the private parts before *the parts* developed an irresistible urge to copulate. This valuable service did not, and still does not earn them any respect in many parts of the word.

Narrated 'Alqama:

While I was walking with 'Abdullah he said, "We were in the company of the Prophet and he said, 'He who can afford to marry should marry, because it will help him refrain from looking at other women, and save his private parts from looking at other women, and save his private parts from committing illegal sexual relation; and he who cannot afford to marry is advised to fast, as fasting will diminish his sexual power.'"

Bukhari 31.129

In praise of some women ...

Narrated Abu Huraira:

The Prophet said, "Avoid the seven great destructive sins."

The people enquired, "O Allah's Apostle! What are they?"

He said, "To join others in worship along with Allah, to practice sorcery, to kill the life which Allah has forbidden except for a just cause, (according to Islamic law), to eat up Riba (usury), to eat up an orphan's wealth, to give back to the enemy and fleeing from the battlefield at the time of fighting, and to accuse, chaste women, who never even think of anything touching chastity and are good believers.

Bukhari 51.28

One women for which the Prophet showed unequivocal admiration and respect, and which he got the old fashion way i.e. an arranged marriage, was his first wife Khadijah (also spelled Khadija).

Narrated 'Aisha:

I did not feel jealous of any of the wives of the Prophet as much as I did of Khadija though I did not see her, but the Prophet used to mention her very often, and whenever he slaughtered a sheep, he would cut its parts and send them to the women friends of Khadija.

When I sometimes said to him, "(You treat Khadija in such a way) as if there is no woman on earth except Khadija", he would say, "Khadija was such-and-such, and from her I had children."

Bukhari 58.166

God's Messenger could only identify two women who reached perfection since Adam and Eve; something that many men achieved as a matter of course. Aisha, in the following hadith is, of course the Prophet's child bride. Her husband's admiration may have very much been the admiration of a pedophile or someone who wishes to assure a child who is upset at being told she is not as beautiful as someone else. Aisha may or may not have been superior to Asia and Mary (it is not clear in the hadith), but her superiority above every other women is uncontested in one of the many compliments paid to her by her husband, comparing her to Tharid ("traditional Arabic dish made of pieces of bread in vegetable or meat broth"), will attest.

Narrated Abu Musa:

Allah's Apostle said, "Many amongst men reached (the level of) perfection but none amongst the women reached this level except Asia, Pharaoh's wife, and Mary, the daughter of 'Imran. And no doubt, the superiority of 'Aisha to other women is like the superiority of Tharid (i.e. a meat and bread dish) to other meals."

Bukhari 55.623

The Prophet trusted women to look after their husband's properties, having none of their own, and to ride camels. That has to be more difficult than driving a car.

Narrated Abu Huraira:

I heard Allah's Apostle saying, "Amongst all those women who ride camels (i.e. Arabs), the ladies of Quraish (the Prophet's tribe) are the best. They are merciful and kind to their off-spring and the best guardians of their husbands' properties."

Bukhari 55.643

The women in the Prophet's household defied their husband by talking among themselves about their husband *en commun*. God's Messenger quashed this rebellion of sorts by threatening them with ignominy and poverty i.e. divorce in a revelation using the exact warning given to them by the narrator (the future caliph Umar) of the following hadith.

Narrated 'Umar (bin Al-Khattab):

My Lord agreed with me in three things:

1. I said, "O Allah's Apostle, I wish we took the station of Abraham as our praying place (for some of our prayers). So came the Divine Inspiration: 'And take you (people) the station of Abraham as a place of prayer' (for some of your prayers e.g. two Rakat of Tawaf of Ka'ba)". (2:125)

2. And as regards the (verse of) the veiling of the women, I said, "O Allah's Apostle! I wish you ordered your wives to cover themselves from the men because good and bad ones talk to them." So the verse of the veiling of the women was revealed.

3. Once the wives of the Prophet made a united front against the Prophet and I said to them, "It may be if he (the Prophet) divorced you, (all) that his Lord (Allah) will give him instead of you wives better than you." So this verse (the same as I had said) was revealed. (66:5).

Bukhari 8.395

Clapping is what women do.

Narrated Sahl bin Sa'd As-Sa'idi:

Allah's Apostle went to establish peace among Bani 'Amr bin

'Auf. In the meantime the time of prayer was due and the Mu'adh-dhin went to Abu Bakr and said, "Will you lead the prayer, so that I may pronounce the Iqama?"

Abu Bakr replied in the affirmative and led the prayer. Allah's Apostle came while the people were still praying and he entered the rows of the praying people till he stood in the (first row).

The people clapped their hands. Abu Bakr never glanced sideways in his prayer but when the people continued clapping, Abu Bakr looked and saw Allah's Apostle. Allah's Apostle beckoned him to stay at his place. Abu Bakr raised his hands and thanked Allah for that order of Allah's Apostle and then he retreated till he reached the first row. Allah's Apostle went forward and led the prayer.

When Allah's Apostle finished the prayer, he said, "O Abu Bakr! What prevented you from staying when I ordered you to do so?"

Abu Bakr replied, "How can Ibn Abi Quhafa (Abu Bakr) dare to lead the prayer in the presence of Allah's Apostle?"

Then Allah's Apostle said, "Why did you clap so much? If something happens to anyone during his prayer he should say Subhan Allah (Glorious is God). If he says so he will be attended to, for clapping is for women."

Bukhari 11.652

For some women clapping was out of the question.

Narrated 'Urwa bin Az-Zubair:

A woman committed theft in the Ghazwa (battle) of the Conquest (of Mecca) and she was taken to the Prophet who ordered her hand to be cut off.

'Aisha said, "Her repentance was perfect and she was married (later) and used to come to me (after that) and I would present her needs to Allah's Apostle."

Bukhari 48.816

One of the ways the Prophet established harmony among the fair sex.

Narrated Abu Huraira:

The Prophet said, "O Muslim women! None of you should look down upon the gift sent by her she-neighbour even if it were the trotters of the sheep (fleshless part of legs)."

Bukhari 47.740

It is not always the woman's fault if she does not bear healthy sons who will grow up eager to fight in Allah's Cause.

Narrated Abu Huraira:

Allah's Apostle said, "Once Solomon, son of David said, '(By Allah) Tonight I will have sexual intercourse with one hundred (or ninety-nine) women each of whom will give birth to a knight who will fight in Allah's Cause.' On that a (i.e. if Allah wills) but he did not say, 'Allah willing.' Therefore only one of those women conceived and gave birth to a half-man. By Him in Whose Hands Muhammad's life is, if he had said, 'Allah willing', (he would have begotten sons) all of whom would have been knights striving in Allah's Cause."

Bukhari 52.74

Prostitution by any other name.

Narrated Abdullah:

We used to participate in the holy wars carried on by the Prophet and we had no women (wives) with us. So we said (to the Prophet). "Shall we castrate ourselves?"

But the Prophet forbade us to do that and thenceforth he allowed us to marry a woman (temporarily) by giving her even a garment, and then he recited: "O you who believe! Do not make unlawful the good things which Allah has made lawful for you."

Bukhari 60.139

During the war to established Islam's dominance on the Arabian Peninsula, women who crossed into Muslim held territory were not trusted, and were required to pledge their allegiance to God's Messenger personally.

Narrated Urwa:

Aisha the wife of the Prophet, said, "Allah's Apostle used to examine the believing women who migrated to him in accordance with this Verse: 'O Prophet! When believing women come to you to take the oath of allegiance to you... Verily! Allah is Oft-Forgiving Most Merciful.' (60:12)"

'Aisha said, "And if any of the believing women accepted the condition (assigned in the above-mentioned Verse), Allah's Apostle would say to her. 'I have accepted your pledge of allegiance.'"

He would only say that, for, by Allah, his hand never touched, any lady during that pledge of allegiance. He did not receive their pledge except by saying, "I have accepted your pledge of allegiance for that."

Bukhari 60.414

What is it with women's fascination with bad boys?

Narrated Sahl bin Sad:

A lady came to the Prophet and declared that she had decided to offer herself to Allah and His Apostle.

The Prophet said, "I am not in need of women."

A man said (to the Prophet) "Please marry her to me."

The Prophet said (to him), "Give her a garment."

The man said, "I cannot afford it."

The Prophet said, "Give her anything, even if it were an iron ring." The man apologized again.

The Prophet then asked him, "What do you know by heart of the Qur'an?"

He replied, "I know such-and-such portion of the Qur'an (by heart)."

The Prophet said, "Then I marry her to you for that much of the Qur'an which you know by heart."

Bukhari 61.547

The most important clause in a marriage contract.

Narrated 'Uqba:

The Prophet said: "The stipulations most entitled to be abided by are those with which you are given the right to enjoy the (women's) private parts (i.e. the stipulations of the marriage contract)."

Bukhari 62.81

Something a bride should not ask for on her wedding day.

Narrated Abu Huraira:

The Prophet said, "It is not lawful for a woman (at the time of wedding) to ask for the divorce of her sister (i.e. the other wife of her would-be husband) in order to have everything for herself, for she will take only what has been written for her."

Bukhari 62.82

A wife should not touch another woman, even at the request of her husband.

Narrated 'Abdullah bin Mas'ud:

The Prophet said, "A woman should not look at or touch another woman to describe her to her husband in such a way as if he was actually looking at her."

Bukhari 62.167

Pity the poor believing woman who marries an impotent man.

Narrated 'Ikrima:

Rifa'a divorced his wife whereupon 'Abdur-Rahman bin Az-Zubair Al-Qurazi married her.

'Aisha said that the lady (came), wearing a green veil (and complained to her (Aisha) of her husband and showed her a green spot on her skin caused by beating).

It was the habit of ladies to support each other, so when Allah's Apostle came, 'Aisha said, "I have not seen any woman suffering as much as the believing women. Look! Her skin is greener than her clothes!"

When 'Abdur-Rahman heard that his wife had gone to the Prophet, he came with his two sons from another wife.

She said, "By Allah! I have done no wrong to him but he is impotent and is as useless to me as this," holding and showing the fringe of her garment.

'Abdur-Rahman said, "By Allah, O Allah's Apostle! She has told a lie! I am very strong and can satisfy her but she is disobedient and wants to go back to Rifa'a."

Allah's Apostle said, to her, "If that is your intention, then know that it is unlawful for you to remarry Rifa'a unless Abdur-Rahman has had sexual intercourse with you." Then the Prophet saw two boys with 'Abdur-Rahman and asked (him), "Are these your sons?"

On that 'Abdu-Rahman said, "Yes."

The Prophet said, "You claim what you claim (i.e.. that he is impotent)? But by Allah, these boys resemble him as a crow resembles a crow,"

Bukhari 72.715

Thinking of losing weight? Better get your husband's permission.

Narrated Abu Huraira:

The Prophet said, "A woman should not fast (optional fasts) except with her husband's permission if he is at home (staying with her)."

Bukhari 62.120

On mourning for a husband:

Narrated Um-'Atiya:

We were forbidden to mourn for a dead person for more than three days except in the case of a husband for whom mourning was allowed for four months and ten days.

(During that time) we were not allowed to put kohl (eye power) in our eyes or to use perfumes or to put on colored clothes except a dress made of 'Asb (a kind of Yemen cloth, very coarse and rough).

We were allowed very light perfumes at the time of taking a bath after menses and also we were forbidden to go with the funeral procession.

Bukhari 6.310

Women sully men simply by being intimate with them, which is why the Prophet said a man needs to take a bath after sexual intercourse with the defiler, to return to a state of purity whereby Allah will accept his prayers and supplications. If anyone is sullied by the sex act it is the woman who is often forcibly penetrated and unceremoniously spewed with the man's discharge.

Narrated Abu Huraira:

The Prophet said, "When a man sits in between the four parts of a woman and did the sexual intercourse with her, bath becomes compulsory."

Bukhari 5:290

In the hadiths the Prophet refers to a man's sexual organs by name e.g. penis, but when it comes to a woman's sexual organs, it's all about parts, her private parts mostly, as if he was describing an object. And still women flock to this misogynous man's banner!

Misogyny

Misogyny (hatred of or hostility towards women) is perhaps too strong a term, yet a prejudicial view of women is perhaps not strong enough when describing Allah's attitude towards women, an attitude largely shared by His Messenger.

Prudish men are known to be both attracted and repelled by the sex act, a trait often shared with misogynous males. For both stereotypes, a woman is both an object of desire and of contempt. The kind of contempt clearly evident in the hadiths where the Prophet compares women to dogs and asses in fixing the distance a woman can pass in front of a man without annulling his prayer.

Could this prudish middle-aged man's struggle between contempt and desire for the dozens of mostly young females he secluded within his household be responsible for the double standard in Islamic law. Did contempt win out, which is why women are in a class by themselves, the lowest class, a class whose members will make up the vast majority of Hell's unfortunates?

Ibn Abbas reported that Allah's Messenger said:

I had a chance to look into paradise and I found that [the] majority of the people was poor and I looked into the Fire and there I found the majority constituted by women.

Bukhari 62.126

Usama b. Zaid reported that Allah's Messenger (may peace be upon him) said: "I stood at the door of Paradise and I found that the overwhelming majority of those who entered therein was that of poor persons and the wealthy persons were detained to get into that. The denizens of Hell were commanded to get into Hell, and I stood upon the door of Fire and the majority amongst them who entered there was that of women."

Sahih Muslim 36.6596

Ibn Abbas reported that Allah's Messenger (may peace be upon him) said: "I had a chance to look into the Paradise and I found that majority of the people was poor and I looked into the Fire and there I found the majority constituted by women."

Sahih Muslim 36.6597

If prejudicial hadiths about women were the exceptions then women venerating a man who compared them to dogs and asses and who would see them in Hell might be understandable. The Bukhari collection alone contains at least seventeen hadiths where the Companions of the Prophet remember God's Messenger preaching that women, mothers mostly, will vastly outnumber men in Hell. What do these disparaging, despicable, outrageous observations about women have to do with Islamic law?

EVERYTHING, and those who see no harm in establishing Sharia tribunals to deal with financial and family matters please take note: there is the concept in Western law that, not only are men and women equal before the Law, but also that the presiding judge not be biased as to whom to believe in disputes involving members of the opposite sex e.g. a husband and wife.

Allah's revelations and His Messenger equally depreciating observations about women are part and parcel of Islamic law and can only prejudice the men who sit in judgment to rule in favour of the men who appear before them.

Islam considers females unfit to so sit on Sharia tribunals. Considering the Prophet's abysmal portrayal of their sex, it is only right.

Zaid

Allah, it is clear, was extremely concerned that His Messenger be sexually fulfilled, and in so doing broke two taboos from what the hadiths and the Koran refer to as the period of ignorance i.e. the time before Islam. Allah's casual dismissal of two abiding moral imperatives would prove particularly detrimental to both the physical and emotional wellbeing of children, to this day.

The first God-sanctioned travesty of the Prophet, which you should already have read about in the hadiths concerning the union of the child Aisha to a man old enough to be her grandfather, significantly lowered the age of implied consent, thereby making female children as young as nine legal prey for pedophiles. The second breaking of a moral imperative from the time of ignorance would deny many an orphan boy a home and someone to call father. Again, it all had to do with God's Messenger lusting after a female who would ordinarily have been morally out reach.

The Prophet was already married to six women, not counting concubines and slave-girls, who could, depending on the circumstances satisfy any his sexual needs, when he walked in on his daughter-in-law Zaynab when she was almost naked and just had to have her. During the time of ignorance, to encourage the adoptions of sons who had lost their fathers, men adopted orphaned boys who then became part of the adopted father's lineage and his de facto progeny e.g. his heir. Because laws and traditions from the time of ignorance did not distinguish between an adopted and a natural born son, the taboo against marrying your natural born son's wife extended to an adopted descendant.

Until Allah changed the rules so that His Messenger could add his cousin and former daughter-in-law to his collection of wives, concubines and slave-girls, orphan boys were a rarity in the Middle East. Allah not only demoted adopted sons, thereby denying them an inheritance, but also made it a crime that would see the perpetrator in Hell, to call your adopted father, father, even when you did not know who your real father was. To avoid His Messenger being embarrassed by having a young man whose wife he had taken in marriage after him call him father, Allah created the greatest disincentive for men to take in orphan boys and raise them as their own. To make matters even worse, Allah's actions have been interpreted to mean that He is against Western style adoption, resulting in an untold number of children in the Islamic world who have no one to call father.

After Allah made what was taboo during the time ignorance at thing of the pass, and after Zaid prudently divorced Zaynab, God's Messenger was free to marry the object of his lust having relegated her former husband to no more than an acquaintance for whom he provided room and board. Allah had again redefine morality to satisfy His Messenger's baser instincts and in the process made life more complicated and at lot worse for others. This was not as significant as making taking the life and property of an unbeliever morally acceptable, but significant nonetheless.

Some of the hadiths pertaining to Allah's watershed changes concerning adopted sons.

Narrated 'Aisha:

Abu Hudhaifa, one of those who fought the battle of Badr with Allah's Apostle, adopted Salim as his son and married his niece Hind bint Al-Wahd bin 'Utba to him and Salim was a freed slave of an Ansari woman. Allah's Apostle also adopted Zaid as his son.

In the Pre-Islamic period of ignorance the custom was that, if one adopted a son, the people would call him by the name of the adopted-father [from] whom he would inherit as well, till Allah revealed: "Call them (adopted sons) By (the names of) their fathers." (33:5)

Bukhari 59.335

Narrated Abdullah bin Umar:

We used not to call Zaid bin Haritha the freed slave of Allah's Apostle except Zaid bin Muhammad till the Qu'anic Verse was revealed: "Call them (adopted sons) by (the names of) their fathers. That is more than just in the Sight of Allah." (33:5)

Bukhari 60.305

Narrated Anas bin Malik:

The Verse: "But you did hide in your mind that which Allah was about to make manifest." (33:37) was revealed concerning Zainab bint Jahsh and Zaid bin Haritha.

Bukhari 60.310

The Prophet's adopted son would die in one of the innumerable bloody pitiless battles to convert the people of the Peninsula and beyond. God's Messenger ordered that the woman who were mourning Zaid's passing a little too loudly be silenced, but that proved impossible.

Narrated Aisha:

When the news of the martyrdom of Zaid bin Haritha, Ja'far and 'Abdullah bin Rawaha came, the Prophet sat down looking sad, and I was looking through the chink of the door. A man came and said, "O Allah's Apostle! The women of Ja'far," and then he mentioned their crying.

The Prophet (p.b.u.h) ordered him to stop them from crying. The man went and came back and said, "I tried to stop them but they disobeyed."

The Prophet (p.b.u.h) ordered him for the second time to forbid them. He went again and came back and said, "They did not listen to me, (or "us": the sub-narrator Muhammad bin Haushab is in doubt as to which is right)."

'Aisha added: The Prophet said, "Put dust in their mouths."

I said (to that man), "May Allah stick your nose in the dust (i.e. humiliate you). By Allah, you could not (stop the women from crying) to fulfill the order, besides you did not relieve Allah's Apostle from fatigue."

Bukhari 23.392

Zakat

The merchant in the Prophet is very much in evidence in the hundreds of hadiths where God's Messenger sets down, in writing, what exactly is God's share of what He has given you. One of his last acts was to write a letter to the governors of conquered territories explaining their obligations regarding Zakat owed on camels and goats, with the amount to be paid in camels and goats. He died before it was ever sent.

Narrated Abdullah ibn Umar:

The Apostle of Allah (peace be upon him) wrote a letter about sadaqah (zakat) but he died before he could send it to his governors. He had kept it with his sword. So Abu Bakr acted upon it till he died, and then Umar acted upon it till he died.

It contained: "For five camels one goat is to be given; for ten camels two goats are to be given; for fifteen camels three goats are to be given; for twenty camels four goats are to be given; for twenty-five to thirty-five camels a she-camel in her second year is to be given.

If the number exceeds by one up to seventy camels, a she-camel in her fourth year is to be given; if they exceed by one up to seventy-five camels, a she-camel in her fifth year is to be given; if they exceed by one up to ninety camels, two she-camels in their third year are to be given; if they exceed by one up to one hundred and twenty, two she-camels in their fourth year are to be given.

If the camels are more than this, a she-camel in her fourth year is to be given for every fifty camels, and a she-camel in her third year is to be given for every forty camels.

For forty to one hundred and twenty goats one goat is to be given; if they exceed by one up to two hundred, two goats are to be given. If they exceed by one up to three hundred, three goats are to be given; if the goats are more than this, one goat for every hundred goats is to be given. Nothing is payable until they reach one hundred. Those which are in one flock are not to be separated, and those which are in separate flocks are not be brought together from fear of sadaqah (zakat).

Regarding that which belongs to two partners, they can make claims for restitution from each other with equity. An old goat and a defective one are not to be accepted as sadaqah (zakat)."

Az-Zuhri said: When the collector comes, the goats will be apportioned into three flocks: one containing bad, the second good, and the third moderate. The collector will take zakat from the moderate.

Az-Zuhri did not mention the cows (to be apportioned in three flocks).

Abu Dawud 9.1563

The Zakat is, in essence, God's fee for purifying your property.

Narrated Abdullah ibn Abbas:

When this verse was revealed: "[9:34 O believers, many of the rabbis and monks devour the property of the people unjustly and bar others from the Path of Allah.] And those who hoard gold and silver [and do not spend them in Allah's Path, announce to them a very painful punishment.]" the Muslims were grieved about it.

Umar said: I shall dispel your care.

He, therefore, went and said: Prophet of Allah, your Companions were grieved by this verse.

The Apostle of Allah (peace be upon him) said: Allah has made zakat obligatory simply to purify your remaining property, and He made inheritances obligatory that they might come to those who survive you.

Umar then said: Allah is most great.

He (the Prophet) then said to him: Let me inform you about the best a man hoards; it is a virtuous woman who pleases him when he looks at her, obeys him when he gives her a command, and guards his interests when he is away from her.

Abu Dawud 9.1660

Allah instructed His Messenger on the calculation of the Zakat, at least where payment in camel was concerned.

Narrated Anas:

Abu Bakr wrote to me what Allah had instructed His Apostle to do regarding the one who had to pay one Bint Makhad (i.e. one year-old she-camel) as Zakat, and he did not have it but had got Bint Labun (two year old she-camel).

(He wrote that) it could be accepted from him as Zakat, and the collector of Zakat would return him 20 Dirhams or two sheep; and if the Zakat payer had not a Bint Makhad, but he had Ibn Labun (a two year old he-camel) then it could be accepted as his Zakat, but he would not be paid anything.

Bukhari 24.528

Still, some had doubts.

Narrated Imran ibn Husayn:

Habib al-Maliki said: A man said to Imran ibn Husayn: AbuNujayd, you narrate to us traditions whose basis we do not find in the Qur'an.

Thereupon, Imran got angry and said to the man: Do you find in the Qur'an that one dirham is due on forty dirhams (as zakat), and one goat is due on such-and-such number of goats, and one camel will be due on such-and-such number of camels?

He replied: No.

He said: From whom did you take it? You took it from us, from the Apostle of Allah (peace be upon him).

He mentioned many similar things.

Abu Dawud 9.1556

The obligations that define a believer are known as the Pillars of Faith of which there are five.

1. Shahadah, declaring allegiance to God.

2. Salat, daily prayers.

3. Zakat, annual charity.

4. Saum, month-long fasting.

5. Hajj, the pilgrimage to Mecca.

All religions have their rituals and demands from God, or His spokesperson at the time, which encompasses the Faith. Islam, however, is the only mainstream religion where not observing what makes you a believer in the prescribed manner, or indicating your intention not to do so e.g. the compulsory pilgrimage to Mecca, is a death defying act of rebellion against God.

The Koran may say there is no compulsion in religion, but in Islam, coercion is everything, with the promise of death being the main incentive to do exactly as you have been told, or have been shown by the ultimate flesh-and-blood stickler, the Prophet Muhammad. A pathetic hadith and example, with which you may already be familiar if you have read my chapter on hadiths relating to prayer:

Narrated 'Abdullah bin Masud:

The Prophet recited Suratan-Najm at Mecca and prostrated while reciting it and those who were with him did the same except an old man who took a handful of small stones or earth and lifted it to his forehead and said, "This is sufficient for me."

Later on, I saw him killed as a non-believer.

Bukhari 19.173

Not paying the Zakat, unlike not mimicking the Prophet perfectly during prayers, was not always a death defying act of rebellion against God.

Narrated Abu Huraira

Allah's Apostle ordered (a person) to collect Zakat, and that person returned and told him that Ibn Jamil, Khalid bin Al-Walid, and Abbas bin 'Abdul Muttalib had refused to give Zakat."

The Prophet said, "What made Ibn Jamll refuse to give Zakat though he was a poor man, and was made wealthy by Allah and His Apostle? But you are unfair in asking Zakat from Khalid as he is keeping his armor for Allah's Cause (for Jihad). As for Abbas bin 'Abdul Muttalib, he is the uncle of Allah's Apostle and Zakat is compulsory on him and he should pay it double."

Bukhari 24.547

All Zakat collected was taken directly to the Prophet, who counted it and branded what had been paid in livestock, the most common currency in which the obligatory charity was paid.

Narrated Abu Humaid Al-Sa'idi:

Allah's Apostle (p.b.u.h) appointed a man called Ibn Al-Lutbiya, from the tribe of Al-Asd to collect Zakat from Bani Sulaim. When he returned, (after collecting the Zakat) the Prophet checked the account with him.

Bukhari 24.576

Narrated Anas:

Bin Malik took 'Abdullah bin Abu Talha to Allah's Apostle to perform Tahnik for him. (Tahnik was a custom among the Muslims that whenever a child was born they used to take it to the Prophet who would chew a piece of date and put a part of its juice in the child's mouth). I saw the Prophet and he had an instrument for branding in his hands and was branding the camels of zakat.

Bukhari 24.578

While some, if not the lion's share of the Zakat was used to fund the Prophet's military expeditions, it was the Khumus, which in a hadith is equivalent to a principle of Islam, that was earmarked for military conquests.

Narrated Abu Jamra:

I used to sit with Ibn 'Abbas and he made me sit on his sitting place. He requested me to stay with him in order that he might give me a share from his property. So I stayed with him for two months. Once he told (me) that when the delegation of the tribe of 'Abdul Qais came to the Prophet, the Prophet asked them, "Who are the people (i.e. you)? (Or) who are the delegate?"

They replied, "We are from the tribe of Rabi'a."

Then the Prophet said to them, "Welcome! O people (or O delegation of 'Abdul Qais)! Neither will you have disgrace nor will you regret."

They said, "O Allah's Apostle! We cannot come to you except in the sacred month and there is the infidel tribe of Mudar intervening between you and us. So please order us to do something good (religious deeds) so that we may inform our people whom we have left behind (at home), and that we may enter Paradise (by acting on them)."

Then they asked about drinks (what is legal and what is illegal).

The Prophet ordered them to do four things and forbade them from four things. He ordered them to believe in Allah Alone and asked them, "Do you know what is meant by believing in Allah Alone?"

They replied, "Allah and His Apostle know better."

Thereupon the Prophet said, "It means:

1. To testify that none has the right to be worshipped but Allah and Muhammad is Allah's Apostle.

2. To offer prayers perfectly

3. To pay the zakat (obligatory charity)

4. To observe fast during the month of Ramadan.

5. And to pay Al-Khumus (one fifth of the booty to be given in Allah's Cause).

Then he forbade them four things, namely, Hantam, Dubba,' Naqir Ann Muzaffat or Muqaiyar; (These were the names of pots in which Alcoholic drinks were prepared) (The Prophet mentioned the container of wine and he meant the wine itself).

The Prophet further said (to them): "Memorize them (these instructions) and convey them to the people whom you have left behind."

Bukhari 2.50

The payment of Khumus, a tax in the furtherance of Islamic conquest may have been one of the five principals of Islam before being replaced by the Hajj, the pilgrimage to Mecca. Islam was imposed by the force of arms and the threat of death almost from the outset beginning with the murder of Amr-ben-al Hadra'mi, therefore, mentioning the payment of a war tax as a religions obligation early on, later to be replaced by a mandatory pilgrimage, makes sense. In any event, it quickly became superfluous when the pillage of unbelievers properties, of which twenty percent was dedicated to pursuing hostilities, became more than adequate to fund the everlasting war in Allah's Cause. Of course, as unlikely as it seems, a senior moment cannot be ruled out, as may have been the case when the Prophet informed a would-be Muslims of the three duties of a believer.

Narrated Talha bin 'Ubaidullah:

A man from Najd with unkempt hair came to Allah's Apostle and we heard his loud voice but could not understand what he was saying, till he came near and then we came to know that he was asking about Islam.

Allah's Apostle said, "You have to offer prayers perfectly five times in a day and night (24 hours)."

The man asked, "Is there any more (praying)?"

Allah's Apostle replied, "No, but if you want to offer the Nawafil prayers (you can)."

Allah's Apostle further said to him: "You have to observe fasts during the month of Ramadan."

The man asked, "Is there any more fasting?"

Allah's Apostle replied, "No, but if you want to observe the Nawafil fasts (you can.)"

Then Allah's Apostle further said to him, "You have to pay the zakat (obligatory charity)."

The man asked, "Is there anything other than the zakat for me to pay?"

Allah's Apostle replied, "No, unless you want to give alms of your own."

And then that man retreated saying, "By Allah! I will neither do less nor more than this."

Allah's Apostle said, "If what he said is true, then he will be successful (i.e. he will be granted Paradise)."

Bukhari 2.44

Yes, the narrator may not have heard the first part of the conversation where the first obligation of a Muslim, worshipping the one and only Allah may have been mentioned. However, that still does not explain the omission of the Pilgrimage to Mecca which would have been declared last.

Getting back to the Khumus for a moment, for reasons unknown, the *war tax* was also applicable to anything buried, everything from raw minerals to relics you unearthed, "Rikaz" in the following hadith:

Narrated Abu Huraira:

Allah's Apostle said, "There is no compensation for one killed or wounded by an animal or by falling in a well, or because of working in mines; but Khumus is compulsory on Rikaz."

Bukhari 24.575

After the death of God's Messenger, some believers thought they could avoid paying the Zakat, but they thought wrong.

Narrated Abu Huraira:

When Allah's Apostle died and Abu Bakr became the caliph some Arabs renegade (reverted to disbelief) (Abu Bakr decided to declare war against them), 'Umar, said to Abu Bakr, "How can you fight with these people although Allah's Apostle said, 'I have been ordered (by Allah) to fight the people till they say: "None has the right to be worshipped but Allah, and whoever said it then he will save his life and property from me except on trespassing the law (rights and conditions for which he will be punished justly), and his accounts will be with Allah.' "

Abu Bakr said, "By Allah! I will fight those who differentiate between the prayer and the Zakat as Zakat is the compulsory right to be taken from the property (according to Allah's orders) By Allah! If they refuse to pay me even a she-kid which they used to pay at the time of Allah's Apostle. I would fight with them for withholding it"

Then 'Umar said, "By Allah, it was nothing, but Allah opened Abu Bakr's chest towards the decision (to fight) and I came to know that his decision was right."

Bukhari 23.483

Paying Zakat with sick or silky animals was a dangerous thing to do, for it was demonstrating an imperfect faith, often requiring a ruthless application of Islamic eugenics.

Narrated Abdullah ibn Mu'awiyah al-Ghadiri:

Abu Dawud said: I read in a document possessed by Abdullah ibn Salim at Hims: Abdullah ibn Mu'awiyah al-Ghadiri reported the Prophet (peace be upon him) as saying: He who performs three things will have the taste of the faith. (They are:) One who worships Allah alone and one believes that there is no god but Allah; and one who pays the zakat on his property agreeably every year. One should not give an aged animal, nor one suffering from itch or ailing, and one most condemned, but one should give animals of medium quality, for Allah did not demand from you the best of your animals, nor did He command you to give the animals of worst quality.

Abu Dawud 9.1577

Allah, also did not especially care to get a male goat as His share either.

Narrated Anas:

Abu Bakr wrote to me what Allah had ordered His Apostle (about zakat) which goes: Neither an old nor a defected animal, nor a male-goat may be taken as zakat except if the zakat collector wishes (to take it).

Bukhari 24.535

Like the modern income tax, which the Zakat may have anticipated, there are no obligatory charitable donations due if your wealth in livestock, fruits and vegetables and valuable metals does not exceed a God-inspired amount.

Narrated Abu Said Al-Khudri:

The Prophet said, "There is no Zakat on less than five Awsuq (of dates), or on less than five camels, or on less than five Awaq of silver." (22 Yameni Riyals Faransa).

Bukhari 24.561

If the Prophet's revealed truths got the respect they deserved, Zakat would still be collected the old-fashion way today. Forget the mail, let alone electronic transfers.

Narrated Abdullah ibn Amr ibn al-'As:

The Prophet (peace be upon him) said: There is to be no collecting of sadaqah (zakat) from a distance, nor must people who own property remove it far away, and their sadaqahs are to be received in their dwelling.

Abu Dawud 9.1587

As honest collector of Zakat is equivalent to someone who kills in Allah's Cause. Wow!

Narrated Rafi' ibn Khadij:

I heard the Apostle of Allah (peace be upon him) say: The official who collects sadaqah (zakat) in a just manner is like him who fights in Allah's path till he returns home.

Abu Dawud 19.2930

The Prophet also elevated the humble shepherd who does all the other things, including paying the Zakat, to the rank of holy warrior.

It has been narrated on the authority of Abu Huraira that the Messenger of Allah (may peace be upon him) said: Of the men he lives the best life who holds the reins of his horse (ever ready to march) in the way of Allah, flies on its back whenever he hears a fearful shriek, or a call for help, flies to it seeking death at places where it can be expected. (Next to him) is a man who lives with his sheep at a hill-top or in a valley, says his prayers regularly, gives zakat and worships his Lord until death comes to him. There is no better person among men except these two.

Sahih Muslim 20.4655

A sales or value-added-tax of sorts:

Narrated Samurah ibn Jundub:

The Apostle of Allah (peace be upon him) used to order us to pay the sadaqah (zakat) on what we prepared for trade.

Abu Dawud 9.1557

The Prophet even made allowances for property in common in assessing Zakat owing.

Narrated Anas:

Abu Bakr wrote to me what Allah's Apostle has made compulsory (regarding Zakat) and this was mentioned in it: If a property is equally owned by two partners, they should pay the combined Zakat and it will be considered that both of them have paid their Zakat equally.

Bukhari 24.531

The Prophet also made a distinction between the Zakat owned on what you grew, depending on where the water to irrigate your crop came from.

Narrated Salim bin 'Abdullah from his father:

The Prophet said, "On a land irrigated by rain water or by natural water channels or if the land is wet due to a nearby water channel Ushr (i.e. one-tenth) is compulsory (as Zakat); and on the land irrigated by the well, half of an Ushr (i.e. one-twentieth) is compulsory (as Zakat on the yield of the land)."

Bukhari 24.560

The Prophet never missed an opportunity to collect Zakat.

Narrated Abdullah ibn Amr ibn al-'As:

A woman came to the Apostle of Allah (peace be upon him) and she was accompanied by her daughter who wore two heavy gold bangles in her hands.

He said to her: Do you pay zakat on them?

She said: No.

He then said: Are you pleased that Allah may put two bangles of fire on your hands?

Thereupon she took them off and placed them before the Prophet (peace be upon him) saying: They are for Allah and His Apostle.

Abu Dawud 9.1558

In the preceding hadith, if she had not paid Zakat on her bangles, the Prophet should have known that the penalty was half the property (he wrote the rules from instructions from Allah, after all) on which the obligatory charity was not paid. Therefore, he should not have accepted both bangles as payment, unless he accepted one as a gift.

Narrated Mu'awiyah ibn Haydah:

The Apostle of Allah (peace be upon him) said: For forty pasturing camels, one she-camel in her third year is to be given. The camels are not to be separated from reckoning. He who pays zakat with the intention of getting reward will be rewarded. If anyone evades zakat, we shall take half the property from him as a due from the dues of our Lord, the Exalted. There is no share in it (zakat) of the descendants of Muhammad (peace be upon him).

Abu Dawud 9.1570

The Prophet's rules governing charity, whether it was obligatory charity like Zakat or the giving freely of something you owned to someone in need, were often flexible where he was concerned.

Narrated Um 'Atiyya Al-Ansariya:

The Prophet went to 'Aisha and asked her whether she had something (to eat). She replied that she had nothing except the mutton (piece) which Nusaiba (Um 'Atiyya) had sent to us (Buraira) in charity."

The Prophet said, "It has reached its place and now it is not a thing of charity but a gift for us."

Bukhari 24.571

No Muslim escaped paying some form of Zakat.

Ibn Umar said that Allah's Messenger (peace be upon him) prescribed the payment of zakat-ul-Fitr (on breaking the fast) of Ramadan for people, for every freeman, or slave, male and female among the Muslims-one sa' of dried dates, or one sa' of barley.

Sahih Muslim 5.2149

Narrated Ibn 'Umar:

Allah's Apostle made it incumbent on all the slave or free Muslims, male or female, to pay one Sa' of dates or barley as zakat-ul-Fitr.

Bukhari 25.580

Zakat as a tax on income:

Narrated Ali ibn Abu Talib:

The Prophet (peace be upon him) said: "When you possess two hundred dirhams and one year passes on them, five dirhams are payable. Nothing is incumbent on you, that is, on gold, till it reaches twenty dinars. When you possess twenty dinars and one year passes on them, half a dinar is payable. Whatever exceeds, that will be reckoned properly."

Abu Dawud 9.1568

Zakat was also used by the Prophet to keep some believers believing.

Narrated Sad (bin Abi Waqqas):

Allah's Apostle distributed something (from the resources of Zakat) amongst a group of people while I was sitting amongst them, but he left a man whom I considered the best of the lot. So, I went up to Allah's Apostle and asked him secretly, "Why have you left that person? By Allah! I consider him a believer."

The Prophet said, "Or merely a Muslim."

I remained quiet for a while but could not help repeating my question because of what I knew about him. I said, "O Allah's Apostle! Why have you left that person? By Allah! I consider him a believer."

The Prophet said, "Or merely a Muslim."

I remained quiet for a while but could not help repeating my question because of what I knew about him. I said, "O Allah's Apostle! Why have you left that person? By Allah! I consider him a believer."

The Prophet said, "Or merely a Muslim." Then Allah's Apostle said, "I give to a person while another is dearer to me, for fear that he may be thrown in the Hell-fire on his face (by renegating from Islam)."

Bukhari 24.556

Some of the tribes with whom the Prophet made alliances in preparation for the taking of Mecca did not care to pay the Zakat. The Prophet was a patient man; he knew it was only a matter of time before he would make them see the error of their ways

Narrated Uthman ibn Abul'As:

When the deputation of Thaqif came to the Apostle of Allah (peace be upon him), he made them stay in the mosque, so that it might soften their hearts. They stipulated to him that they would not be called to participate in Jihad, to pay zakat and to offer prayer. The Apostle of Allah (peace be upon him) said: You may have the concession that you will not be called to participate in jihad and pay zakat, but there is no good in a religion which has no bowing (i.e. prayer).

Abu Dawud 19.3020

Narrated Jabir ibn Abdullah:

Wahb said: I asked Jabir about the condition of Thaqif when they took the oath of allegiance. He said: They stipulated to the Prophet (peace be upon him) that there would be no sadaqah (i.e. zakat) on them nor Jihad (striving in the way of Allah). He then heard the Prophet (peace be upon him) say: Later on they will give sadaqah (zakat) and will strive in the way of Allah when they embrace Islam.

Abu Dawud 19.3019

With all the wealth that flowed to God's Messenger from all corners of the Arabian Peninsula, you could have expected the needy to descend on the Prophet's abode in Medina in droves looking for the promised charity. God's Messenger obviously anticipated this, and issued dissuading hadiths, such as the following where in the first he warns those who would ask for financial help, and in the second praises the benefits of working for a living and not asking for charity.

Narrated Hakim bin Hizam:

The Prophet said, "The upper hand is better than the lower hand (i.e. he who gives in charity is better than him who takes it). One should start giving first to his dependents. And the best object of charity is that which is given by a wealthy person (from the money which is left after his expenses). And whoever abstains from asking others for some financial help, Allah will give him and save him from asking others, Allah will make him self-sufficient."

Bukhari 24.508

Narrated Abu Huraira:

Allah's Apostle said, "By Him in Whose Hand my life is, it is better for anyone of you to take a rope and cut the wood (from the forest) and carry it over his back and sell it (as a means of earning his living) rather than to ask a person for something and that person may give him or not."

Bukhari 24.549

The poor just had to hope that the person with the money became aware of their needs and gave to them without their asking. Good luck with that.

Narrated Abu Huraira:

Allah's Apostle said, "The poor person is not the one who goes round the people and ask them for a mouthful or two (of meals) or a date or two but the poor is that who has not enough (money) to satisfy his needs and whose condition is not known to others, that others may give him something in charity, and who does not beg of people."

Bukhari 24.557

Why a slave is like a horse when it comes to Zakat?

Narrated Abu Huraira:

Allah's Apostle said, "There is no zakat either on a horse or a slave belonging to a Muslim."

Bukhari 24.542

No Zakat was due on the property of a slave who was sold. This comes from an extrapolation of the respected hadith collector and preeminent Islamic jurist Imam Malik of what Umar ibn al-Khattab decreed. Umar was a close friend and confidant of the Prophet and the second of the four Rightly Guided Caliphs who succeeded the Prophet as Leader of the Believers (the meaning of Caliph).

Yahya related to me from Malik from Nafi from Abdullah ibn Umar that Umar ibn al-Khattab said, "If a slave who has wealth is sold, that wealth belongs to the seller unless the buyer stipulates its inclusion."

Malik said, "The generally agreed upon way of doing things among us is that if the buyer stipulates the inclusion of the slave's property whether it be cash, debts, or goods of known or unknown value, then they belong to the buyer, even if the slave possesses more than that for which he was purchased, whether he was bought for cash, as payment for a debt, or in exchange for goods. This is possible because a master is not asked to pay zakat on his slave's property. If a slave has a slave-girl, it is halal for him to have intercourse with her by his right of possession. If a slave is freed or put under contract (kitaba) to purchase his freedom, then his property goes with him. If he becomes bankrupt, his creditors take his property and his master is not liable for any of his debts."

Malik 31.31.2.2

Epilogue

The Last Brick

The Prophet, we are told, was a handsome man.

Narrated Al-Bara:

The Prophet was of moderate height having broad shoulders (long) hair reaching his ear-lobes. Once I saw him in a red cloak and I had never seen a more handsome [man] than him."

Bukhari 56.751

God's Messenger was a potent man, almost to the very end. Eleven was the number of surviving spouses when he died. Three of his fourteen official wives – Khadijah, Zaynab b. Khuzayma and Rayhanah (also spelled Rayhana) – did not live long enough to witness his passing.

Narrated Qatada:

Anas bin Malik said, "The Prophet used to visit all his wives in a round, during the day and night and they were eleven in number."

I asked Anas, "Had the Prophet the strength for it?"

Anas replied, "We used to say that the Prophet was given the strength of thirty (men)."

And Sa'id said on the authority of Qatada that Anas had told him about nine wives only (not eleven).

Bukhari 5.268

The Prophet may have had more body hair then most men.

Narrated Abu Ja'far:

Jabir bin Abdullah said to me, "Your cousin (Hasan bin Muhammad bin Al-Hanafiya) came to me and asked about the bath of Janaba.

I replied, 'The Prophet use to take three handfuls of water, pour them on his head and then pour more water over his body.'

Al-Hasan said to me, 'I am a hairy man.'

I replied, 'The Prophet had more hair than you'."

Bukhari 5.256

God's Messenger probably still parted his hair at the time of his death.

Narrated Ibn 'Abbas:

Allah's Apostle used to let his hair hang down while the infidels used to part their hair. The people of the Scriptures were used to letting their hair hang down and Allah's Apostle liked to follow the people of the Scriptures in the matters about which he was not instructed otherwise. Then Allah's Apostle parted his hair.

Bukhari 56.758

The Prophet undoubtedly did not needlessly expose his face to harmful UV rays.

Narrated Abu Ishaq:

Al-Bara' was asked, "Was the face of the Prophet (as bright) as a sword?"

He said, "No, but (as bright) as a moon."

Bukhari 56.752

A dark beard sparingly peppered with white bristles did not obscure the Prophet's resemblance to his grandson Al-Hasan bin 'Ali.

Narrated Isma'il bin Abi Khalid:

I heard Abii Juhaifa saying, "I saw the Prophet, and Al-Hasan bin 'Ali resembled him."

I said to Abu- Juhaifa, "Describe him for me."

He said, "He was white and his beard was black with some white hair. He promised to give us 13 young she-camels, but he expired before we could get them."

Bukhari 56.744

A bit of fuzz between the lower lip and the chin is normal for an old man.

Narrated Hariz bin 'Uthman:

That he asked 'Abdullah bin Busr (i.e. the companion of the Prophet), "Did you see the Prophet when he was old?"

He said, "He had a few white hairs between the lower lip and the chin."

Bukhari 56.746

The scent in the following hadith is probably henna which God's Messenger used to dye strands of his beard an orangey-red.

Narrated Rabia bin Abi Abdur-Rahman:

I heard Anas bin Malik describing the Prophet saying, "He was of medium height amongst the people, neither tall nor short; he had a rosy color, neither absolutely white nor deep brown; his hair was neither completely curly nor quite lank. Divine Inspiration was revealed to him when he was forty years old. He stayed ten years in Mecca receiving the Divine Inspiration, and stayed in Medina for ten more years. When he expired, he had scarcely twenty white hairs in his head and beard."

Rabi'a said, "I saw some of his hairs and it was red. When I asked about that, I was told that it turned red because of scent."

Bukhari 56.747

The Prophet dyed his beard, but not his hair.

Narrated Qatada:

I asked Anas, "Did the Prophet use to dye (his) hair?"

He said, "No, for there were only a few white hairs on his temples."

Bukhari 56.750

The Prophet was a creature of habit with many of his routines, especially those relating to prayers e.g. ablution, becoming the rituals of Islam.

Narrated Maimuna:

I placed water for the bath of the Prophet. He washed his hands twice or thrice and then poured water on his left hand and washed his private parts. He rubbed his hands over the earth (and cleaned them), rinsed his mouth, washed his nose by putting water in it and blowing it out, washed his face and both forearms and then poured water over his body. Then he withdrew from that place and washed his feet.

Bukhari 5.257

The Prophet's habits included starting everything from the right. Only people intent on doing bad things started from the left.

Narrated 'Aisha:

The Prophet used to start everything from the right (for good things) whenever it was possible in all his affairs; for example: in washing, combing or wearing shoes.

Bukhari 8.418

The Prophet's preference for bland clothing would become a fashion standard for believers to this day.

Narrated Aisha:

Allah's Apostle offered prayer while he was wearing a Khamisa of his that had printed marks. He looked at its marks and when he finished prayer, he said, "Take this Khamisa of mine to Abu Jahm, for it has just now diverted my attention from my prayer, and bring to me the Anbijania (a plain thick sheet) of Abu Jahm bin Hudhaifa bin Ghanim who belonged to Bani Adi bin Ka'b."

Bukhari 72.708

The Prophet's affinity for the less flamboyant did not extend to extravagances such as rings, as long as they were not gold rings. On one finger, God's Messenger slipped an all silver ring with a very unique engraving.

Narrated Anas:

The ring of the Prophet was of silver, and its stone was of silver too.

Bukhari 72.759

Narrated Anas bin Malik:

Allah's Apostle wanted to write a letter to a group of people or some non-Arabs. It was said to him, "They do not accept any letter unless it is stamped."

So the Prophet had a silver ring made for himself, and on it was engraved: 'Muhammad, the Apostle of Allah'. [It is] as if I am now looking at the glitter of the ring on the finger (or in the palm) of the Prophet.

Bukhari 72.761

The Prophet smiled but seldom laughed, and clouds made him wary, in part, because winds bring clouds and a famous pre-Islamic town in the Koran by the name of 'Ad was destroyed by hot hurricane force westerly winds.

Narrated 'Aisha:

I never saw Allah's Apostle laughing loudly enough to enable me to see his uvula, but he used to smile only. And whenever he saw clouds or winds, signs of deep concern would appear on his face.

I said, "O Allah's Apostle! When people see clouds they usually feel happy, hoping that it would rain, while I see that when you see clouds, one could notice signs of dissatisfaction on your face."

He said, "O 'Aisha! What is the guarantee for me that there will be no punishment in it, since some people were punished with a wind? Verily, some people saw (received) the punishment, but (while seeing the cloud) they said, 'This cloud will give us rain.' "

Bukhari 60.353

The Prophet would change the names of things on the spur of the moment, which his followers took as a revelation from Allah.

Narrated 'Abdur Rahman bin Abi Bakra's father:

Once the Prophet was riding his camel and a man was holding its rein. The Prophet asked, "What is the day today?"

We kept quiet, thinking that he might give that day another name.

He said, "Isn't it the day of Nahr (slaughtering of the animals of sacrifice)"

We replied, "Yes."

He further asked, "Which month is this?"

We again kept quiet, thinking that he might give it another name.

Then he said, "Isn't it the month of Dhul-Hijja?"

We replied, "Yes."

He said, "Verily! Your blood, property and honor are sacred to one another (i.e. Muslims) like the sanctity of this day of yours, in this month of yours and in this city of yours. It is incumbent upon those who are present to inform those who are absent because those who are absent might comprehend (what I have said) better than the present audience."

Bukhari 3.67

God's Messenger would even change the name of people.

Narrated Al-Musaiyab:

That his father (Hazn bin Wahb) went to the Prophet and the Prophet asked (him), "What is your name?"

He replied, "My name is Hazn."

The Prophet said, "You are Sahl."

Hazn said, "I will not change the name with which my father has named me."

Ibn Al-Musaiyab added: We have had roughness (in character) ever since.

Bukhari 73.209

Many of the sayings of the Prophet read like something you might find in the Koran and exhibit the same lack of a consistent timeframe. For example, whom did Allah show Mercy to in the following hadith, since He created his Throne before He created Adam whose descendants would be the recipient His anger.

Narrated Abu Huraira:

The Prophet said, "When Allah had finished His creation, He wrote over his Throne: 'My Mercy preceded My Anger.'"

Bukhari 93.518

The Prophet disliked people who disagreed with him and so did Allah.

Narrated 'Aisha:

The Prophet said, "The most hated person in the sight of Allah is the most quarrelsome person."

Bukhari 43.637

The Prophet's dislike for dogs extended to making illegal the proceeds from the sale of man's best friend.

Narrated Abu Masud Al-Ansari:

Allah's Apostle regarded illegal the price of a dog, the earnings of a prostitute, and the charges taken by a soothsayer.

Bukhari 36.482

Keeping a dog as a pet, God's Messenger warned, increased your odds of going to Hell.

Narrated Sufyan bin Abi Zuhair Ash-Shani:

That he heard Allah's Apostle saying, "If somebody keeps a dog that is neither used for farm work nor for guarding the livestock, he will lose one Qirat (of the reward) of his good deeds every day."

Bukhari 54.542

The Prophet was very much into deprecating generalizations. As an example, following is a sweeping statement about people in debt.

Narrated 'Aisha:

Allah's Apostle used to invoke Allah in the prayer saying, "O Allah, I seek refuge with you from all sins, and from being in debt." Someone said, O Allah's Apostle! (I see you) very often you seek refuge with Allah from being in debt. He replied, "If a person is in debt, he tells lies when he speaks, and breaks his promises when he promises."

Bukhari 41.582

A debtor could, however, still use a mortgaged animal as if it was his.

Narrated Abu Huraira:

The Prophet said, "One can ride the mortgaged animal because of what one spends on it, and one can drink the milk of a milch animal as long as it is mortgaged."

Bukhari 45.688

God's Messenger was not shy about offering binding advice on anything that had to do with sex, including how many days a newly married man should spend with a bride who is a virgin, and one who is not.

Narrated Anas:

The tradition, (of the Prophet) is that if someone marries a virgin and he has already a matron wife (with him), then he should stay with the virgin for seven days; and if someone marries a matron (and he has already a virgin wife with him) then he should stay with her for three days.

Bukhari 62.140

The Prophet had an opinion on just about everything; from eye cleansers, to picking your teeth with a toothpick to the correct way to relieve and wipe yourself. It is not often, however, that he was not categorical about how something should be done.

Narrated Abu Hurayrah:

The Prophet (peace be upon him) said: If anyone applies collyrium, he should do it an odd number of times. If he does so, he has done well; but if not, there is no harm.

If anyone cleanses himself with pebbles, he should use an odd number. If he does so, he has done well; but if not, there is no harm.

If anyone eats, he should throw away what he removes with a toothpick and swallow what sticks to his tongue. If he does so, he has done well; if not, there is no harm.

If anyone goes to relieve himself, he should conceal himself, and if all he can do is to collect a heap of sand, he should sit with his back to it, for the devil makes sport with the posteriors of the children of Adam. If he does so, he has done well; but if not, there is no harm.

Abu Dawud 1.35

The Prophet never overstayed his welcome, whether he had been invited or not.

Narrated Abu Talha:

Whenever the Prophet conquered some people, he would stay in their town for three days.

Bukhari 52.300

God's Messenger had a practical side.

Narrated 'Abdullah bin 'Abbas:

Once Allah's Apostle passed by a dead sheep and said to the people, "Wouldn't you benefit by its skin?"

The people replied that it was dead.

The Prophet said, "But its eating only is illegal."

Bukhari 34.424

More often it was the impractical side, some would say nonsensical dogmatic side which most often showed up. Consider the man who would pay to get a horse back he gave in charity because it was not well looked after.

Narrated 'Umar bin Al-Khattab:

I gave a horse in Allah's Cause. The person to whom it was given, did not look after it. I intended to buy it from him, thinking that he would sell it cheap. When I asked the Prophet he said, "Don't buy it, even if he gives it to you for one Dirham, as the person who takes back what he has given in charity, is like a dog that swallows back its vomit."

Bukhari 47.792

On the surface, many of the Prophet's verdicts and oversimplifications seem to make sense. Consider his ruling about lost and found things and animals. If it's a thing you look for the owner, if it's a sheep you can eat it, and if it's a camel you do nothing.

Narrated Zaid bin Khalid Al-Juhani:

A man asked the Prophet about the picking up of a "Luqata" (fallen lost thing). The Prophet replied, "Recognize and remember its tying material and its container, and make public announcement (about it) for one year, then utilize it but give it to its owner if he comes."

Then the person asked about the lost camel.

On that, the Prophet got angry and his cheeks or his face became red and he said, "You have no concern with it as it has its water container, and its feet and it will reach water, and eat (the leaves) of trees till its owner finds it."

The man then asked about the lost sheep.

The Prophet replied, "It is either for you, for your brother (another person) or for the wolf."

Bukhari 3.91

The Prophet believed that an animal hearing a recitation of the Koran experienced a change of behavior which he equated with a state of tranquility, even when the outward behavior, for the uninformed, would indicate the animal was spooked by what it heard.

Narrated Al-Bara:

While a man from the companions of the Prophet was reciting (Quran) and his horse was tied in the house, the horse got startled and started jumping. The man came out, looked around but could not find anything, yet the horse went on jumping. The next morning he mentioned that to the Prophet. The Prophet said, "That was the tranquility (calmness) which descended because of the recitation of the Quran."

Bukhari 60.363

The Prophet being a believer in, and a transmitter of revealed truths, had little faith that real knowledge would progress beyond what he knew to be true at the time.

Narrated Ibn 'Umar:

Allah's Apostle (p.b.u.h) said, "Keys of the unseen knowledge are five which nobody knows but Allah . . .

nobody knows what will happen tomorrow; nobody knows what is in the womb; nobody knows what he will gain tomorrow; nobody knows at what place he will die; and nobody knows when it will rain."

Bukhari 17.149

For the Prophet, experts in revealed truths, the imams, had all the answers.

Narrated 'Abdullah bin 'Amr bin Al' As:

I heard Allah's Apostle saying, "Allah does not take away the knowledge, by taking it away from (the hearts of) the people, but takes it away by the death of the religious learned men till when none of the (religious learned men) remains, people will take as their leaders ignorant persons who when consulted will give their verdict without knowledge. So they will go astray and will lead the people astray."

Bukhari 3.99

The Prophet, in what he asked his followers to do and believe, borrowed heavenly from the Torah and from rituals of the pagan Arabs which he Islamisized. But imitation had its limits!

Narrated 'Abaya bin Rafa'a bin Raft' bin Khadij:

My grandfather said, "We were in the company of the Prophet at Dhul-Hulaifa. The people felt hungry and captured some camels and sheep (as booty). The Prophet was behind the people. They hurried and slaughtered the animals and put their meat in pots and started cooking it.

(When the Prophet came) he ordered the pots to be upset and then he distributed the animals (of the booty), regarding ten sheep as equal to one camel.

One of the camels fled and the people ran after it till they were exhausted. At that time there were few horses. A man threw an arrow at the camel, and Allah stopped the camel with it.

The Prophet said, "Some of these animals are like wild animals, so if you lose control over one of these animals, treat it in this way (i.e. shoot it with an arrow)."

Before distributing them among the soldiers my grandfather said, "We may meet the enemies in the future and have no knives; can we slaughter the animals with reeds?"

The Prophet said, "Use whatever causes blood to flow, and eat the animals if the name of Allah has been mentioned on slaughtering them. Do not slaughter with teeth or fingernails and I will tell you why: It is because teeth are bones (i.e. cannot cut properly) and fingernails are the tools used by the Ethiopians (whom we should not imitate for they are infidels)."

Bukhari 43.668

The attitude of the Prophet towards women in the hadiths is very much a reflection of the attitude of the god for Whom he delivered the Koran.

You could argue, I guess, that considering that a believer's wife owns basically nothing except her dowry, not even a share of the family home, and that she must differ to her husband for whatever goes on in *his* home, including fasting, it is only logical that the reward of the charity she performs with her husband's money, he should get get half the rewards (brownie points for doing good that will nullify bad deeds on Judgement Day).

Narrated Abu Huraira:

Allah's Apostle said, "It is not lawful for a lady to fast (Nawafil) without the permission of her husband when he is at home; and she should not allow anyone to enter his house except with his permission; and if she spends of his wealth (on charitable purposes) without being ordered by him, he will get half of the reward."

Bukhari 62.123

The Prophet formulated what could be considered the golden rule of Islam: Do only what you know is legal, and you will avoid that which is illegal.

Narrated An-Nu'man bin Bashir:

The Prophet said "Both legal and illegal things are obvious, and in between them are (suspicious) doubtful matters. So who-ever forsakes those doubtful things lest he may commit a sin, will definitely avoid what is clearly illegal; and who-ever indulges in these (suspicious) doubtful things bravely, is likely to commit what is clearly illegal. Sins are Allah's Hima (i.e. private pasture) and whoever pastures (his sheep) near it, is likely to get in it at any moment."

Bukhari 34.267

With 6,000+ revelations of the Koran and tens of thousands of sayings and examples of the Prophet to inform a believer's every waking moment, Islam is fortunate to have so many scholars who devote their lives to acquainting themselves with this plethora of legal rulings and precedents so that a believer who is unsure about doing the right thing has a religious expert to turn to.

The self-proclaimed ultimate Messenger of God, before he discovered his true calling at forty-something, was for more than twenty years a merchant and a trader. The merchant mentality is very much evident in hundreds, if not thousands of hadiths: the merchant's calculating mind, the merchant's attention to every detail of a transaction whether it be a transaction involving animals, durable goods or human chattel such as women and slaves, the merchant's appreciation of the value of things he trades for and accumulates.

It may be the merchant in the man, which elevated to the equivalent of a martyr dying in Allah's Cause, a person who is killed protecting his worldly goods.

Narrated 'Abdullah bin 'Amr bin Al-'As:

I heard the Prophet saying, "Whoever is killed while protecting his property then he is a martyr."

Bukhari 43.660

The Prophet is said to have anticipated an event which the Koran verses 54:1-2 says will part of the Judgement Day spectacle, the splitting of the moon. It is the one miracle, the man who boasted he was not capable of such, is alleged to have agreed to perform.

Narrated Abu Huraira:

The Prophet said, "Every Prophet was given miracles because of which people believed, but what I have been given, is Divine Inspiration which Allah has revealed to me. So I hope that my followers will outnumber the followers of the other Prophets on the Day of Resurrection."

Bukhari 61.504

The splitting of the moon should have been viewable by people living thousands of miles from where God's Messenger stood when he did this, but we only have the hadiths, revealed truths, as evidence that it actually happened. Believe what you will!

Narrated Anas:

That the Meccan people requested Allah's Apostle to show them a miracle, and so he showed them the splitting of the moon.

Bukhari 56.831

The last brick!

Narrated Abu Huraira:

Allah's Apostle said, "My similitude in comparison with the other prophets before me, is that of a man who has built a house nicely and beautifully, except for a place of one brick in a corner. The people go about it and wonder at its beauty, but say: 'Would that this brick be put in its place!' So I am that brick, and I am the last of the Prophets."

Bukhari 56.735

The correct way to invoke Allah's blessing on His ultimate Messenger; remembering to repeat your request that He bless the Prophet's offsprings as He did those of Abraham (i.e. the Jews):

Narrated Abu Humaid As-Sa'idi:

The people asked, "O Allah's Apostle! How shall we (ask Allah to) send blessings on you?"

Allah's Apostle replied, "Say: O Allah! Send Your Mercy on Muhammad and on his wives and on his offspring, as You sent Your Mercy on Abraham's family; and send Your Blessings on Muhammad and on his offspring, as You sent Your Blessings on Abraham's family, for You are the Most Praise-worthy, the Most Glorious."

Bukhari 55.588

Afterword

Faith, someone once said, is believing in something you know to be untrue. Faith, by this definition is irrational. If after reading 1,001 sayings and deeds of the Prophet you are overwhelmed by misgivings and a sense that this is crazy talk, welcome to the rational world. For the believers, that other world is just as valid, and all you have to do to embrace it, is to love the one who dreamt that world into existence unconditionally above all others.

Narrated Anas:

The Prophet said "None of you will have faith till he loves me more than his father, his children and all mankind."

Bukhari 2.14

To love the Messenger is to believe in the Messenger and everything he said and did, even if what you have read about Abū al-Qāsim Muhammad ibn Abd Allāh ibn Abd al-Mutalib ibn Hāshim is largely the recollections of illiterates about the life and times of one of their own.

Narrated Ibn 'Umar:

The Prophet said, "We are an illiterate nation; we neither write, nor know accounts. The month is like this and this, i.e. sometimes of 29 days and sometimes of thirty days."

Bukhari 31.137

Narrated Ata bin Yasar:

I met Abdullah bin 'Amr bin Al-'As and asked him, "Tell me about the description of Allah's Apostle which is mentioned in Torah (i.e. Old Testament.")

He replied, "Yes. By Allah, he is described in Torah with some of the qualities attributed to him in the Quran as follows: 'O Prophet! We have sent you as a witness (for Allah's True religion) and a giver of glad tidings (to the faithful believers), and a warner (to the unbelievers) and guardian of the illiterates. You are My slave and My messenger (i.e. Apostle). I have named you Al-Mutawakkil (who depends upon Allah). You are neither discourteous, harsh nor a noise-maker in the markets and you do not do evil to those who do evil to you, but you deal with them with forgiveness and kindness.' Allah will not let him (the

Prophet) die till he makes straight the crooked people by making them say: 'None has the right to be worshipped but Allah', with which will ~~be opened~~ [open] blind and deaf ears and envelop~~ed~~ hearts."

Bukhari 34.335

The world fashioned by and for illiterates living during the Dark Ages is today at war with the modern world, a world born out of reason. Paradise is guaranteed for those who listen to the voice who knew only revealed truths – knowledge obtained through communication with a deity and reason's nemesis.

Narrated Abu Huraira:

Allah's Apostle said, "All my followers will enter Paradise except those who refuse."

They said, "O Allah's Apostle! Who will refuse?"

He said, "Whoever obeys me will enter Paradise, and whoever disobeys me is the one who refuses (to enter it)."

Bukhari 92.384

Time is on the side of those who obey without letting compassion or reason interfere with what is demanded of them, including killing those who refuse Paradise. Therefore, you should show some respect for what you now know about what the "guardian of the illiterates" said and did.